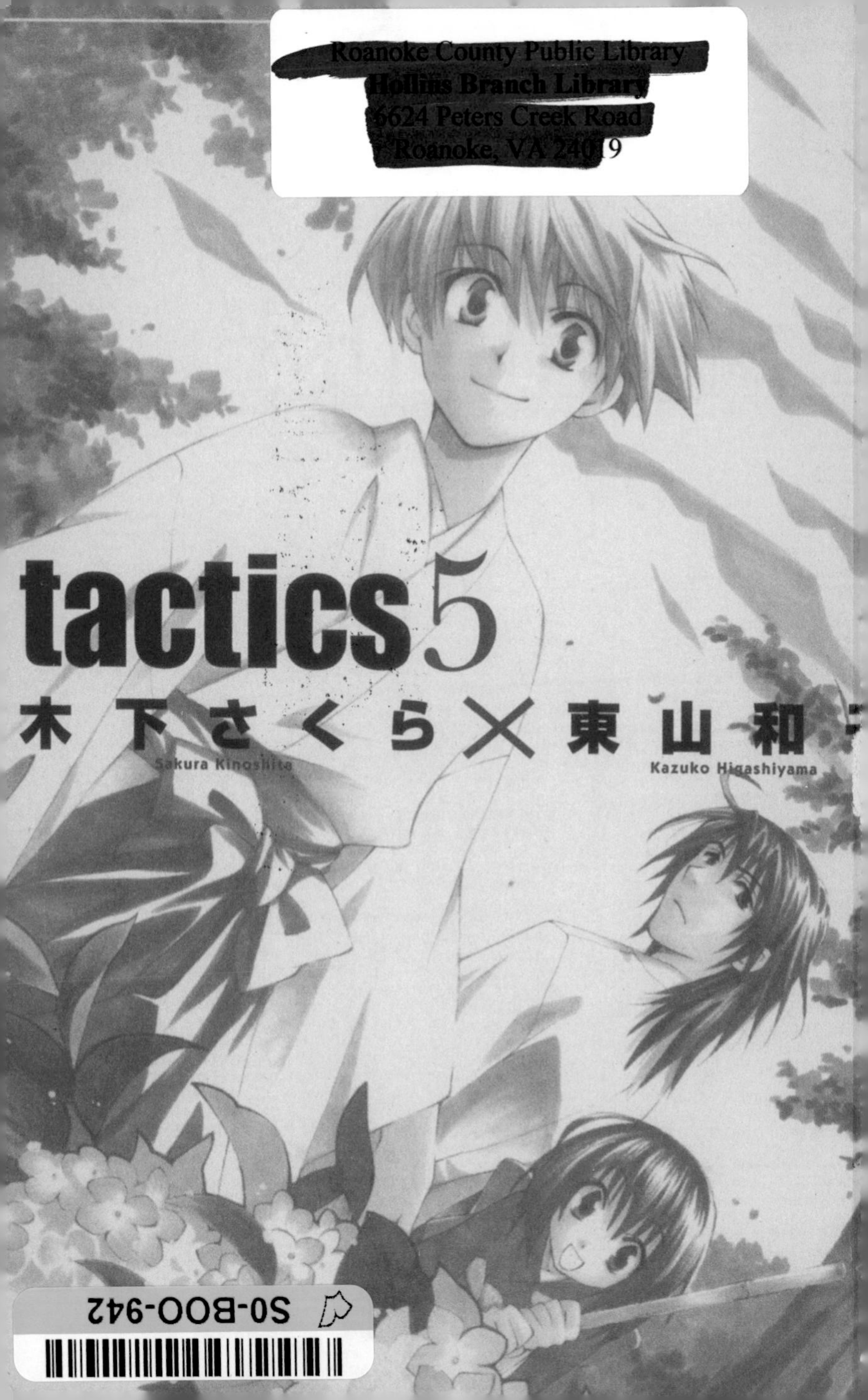
tactics 5
木下さくら×東山和
Sakura Kinoshita
Kazuko Higashiyama

tactics

Sakura Kinoshita × *Kazuko Higashiyama*

5

tactics

Volume 5
by Sakura Kinoshita and
Kazuko Higashiyama

TOKYOPOP®

HAMBURG // LONDON // LOS ANGELES // TOKYO

tactics Volume 5
ART & STORY BY: Sakura Kinoshita × Kazuko Higashiyama

Translation - Christine Schilling
English Adaptation - Lianne Sentar
Copy Editor - Shannon Watters
Retouch and Lettering - Star Print Brokers
Production Artist - Keila N. Ramos
Graphic Designer - James Lee

Editor - Stephanie Duchin
Digital Imaging Manager - Chris Buford
Pre-Production Supervisor - Lucas Rivera
Production Manager - Elisabeth Brizzi
Managing Editor - Vy Nguyen
Creative Director - Anne Marie Horne
Editor-in-Chief - Rob Tokar
Publisher - Mike Kiley
President and C.O.O. - John Parker
C.E.O. and Chief Creative Officer - Stu Levy

A  Manga

TOKYOPOP and  are trademarks or registered trademarks of TOKYOPOP Inc.

TOKYOPOP Inc.
5900 Wilshire Blvd. Suite 2000
Los Angeles, CA 90036

E-mail: info@TOKYOPOP.com
Come visit us online at www.TOKYOPOP.com

ISBN: 978-1-59816-964-5

First TOKYOPOP printing: June 2008
10 9 8 7 6 5 4 3 2 1
Printed in the USA

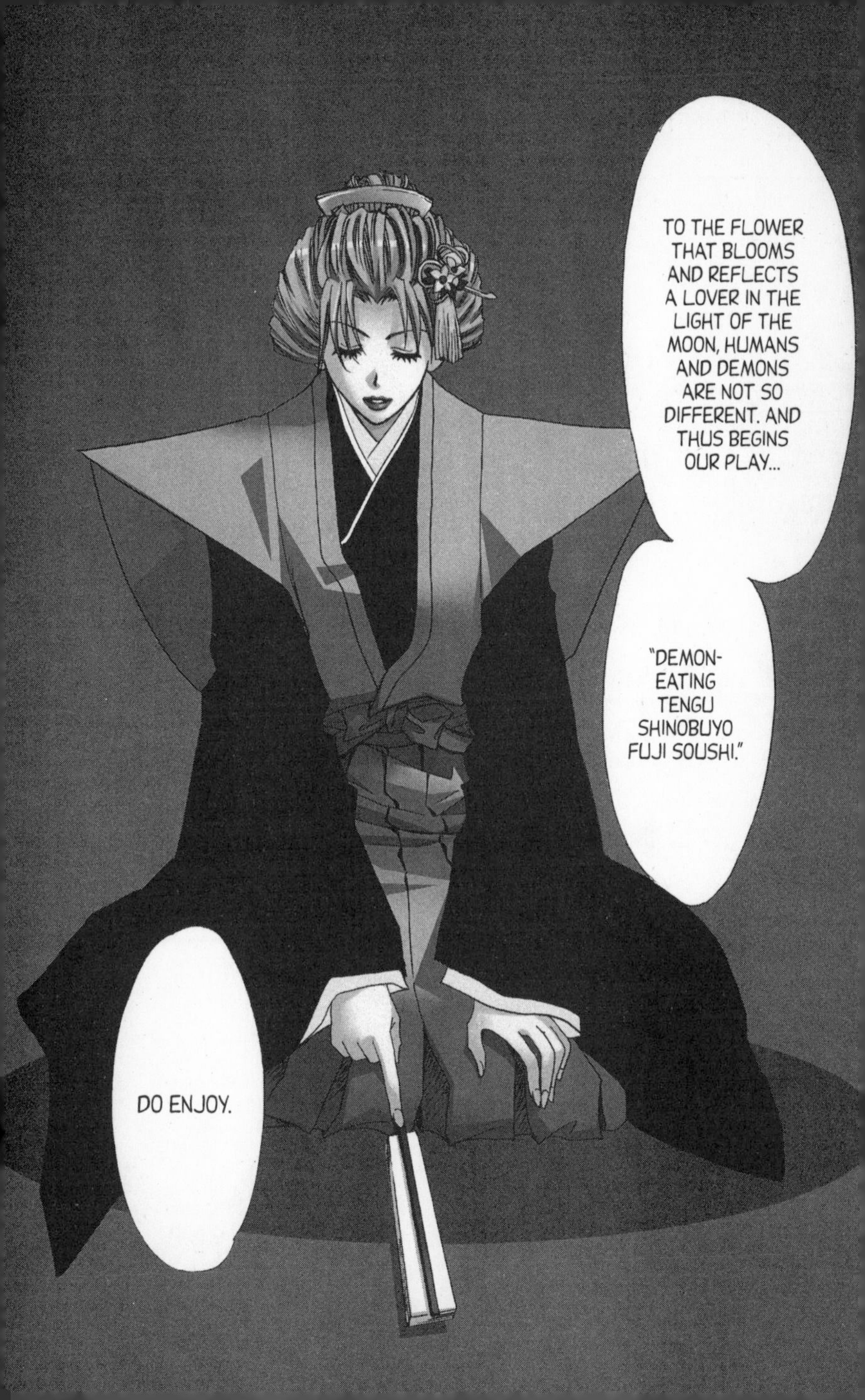
TO THE FLOWER THAT BLOOMS AND REFLECTS A LOVER IN THE LIGHT OF THE MOON, HUMANS AND DEMONS ARE NOT SO DIFFERENT. AND THUS BEGINS OUR PLAY...
"DEMON-EATING TENGU SHINOBUYO FUJI SOUSHI."
DO ENJOY.

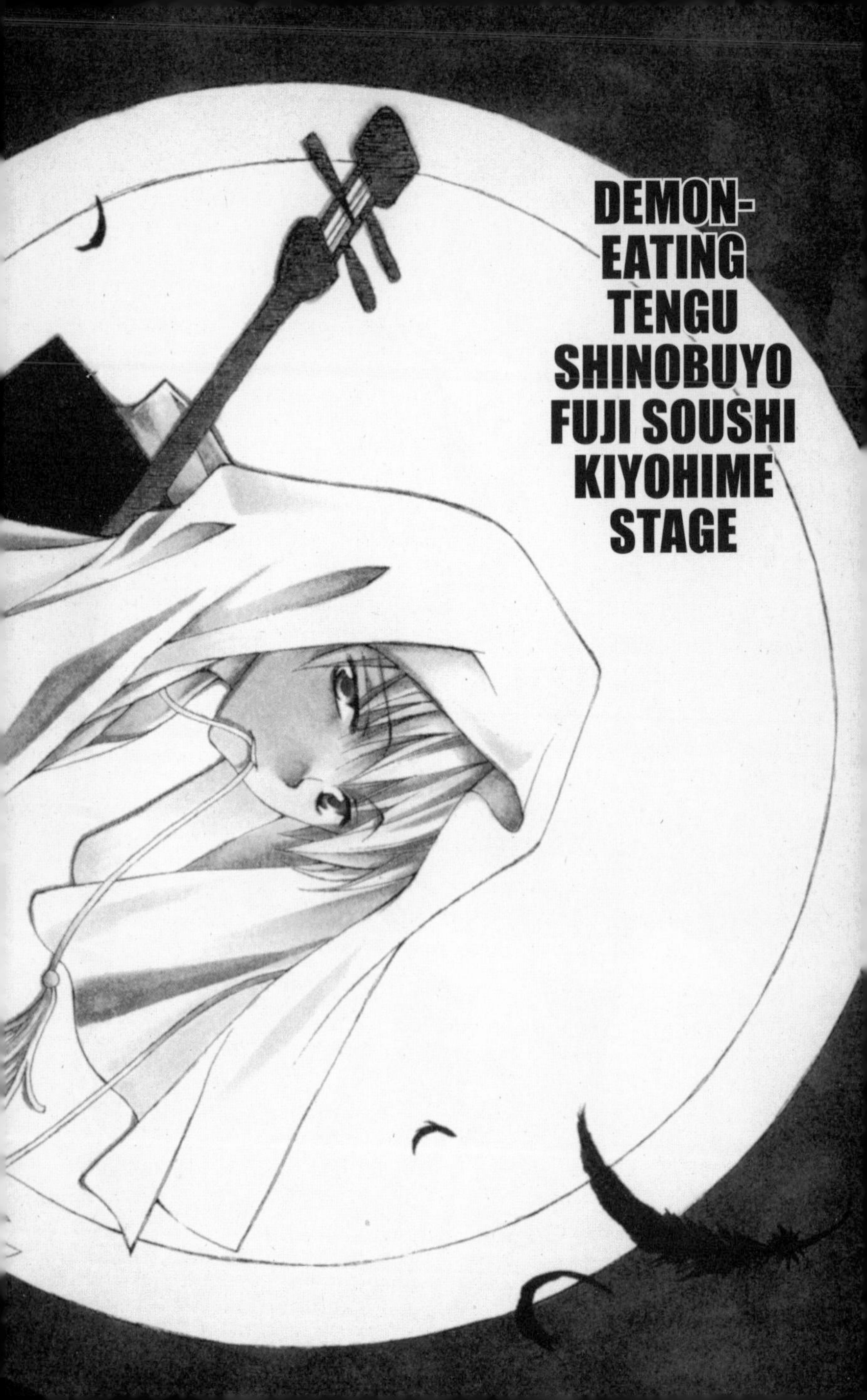
DEMON-
EATING
TENGU
SHINOBUYO
FUJI SOUSHI
KIYOHIME
STAGE

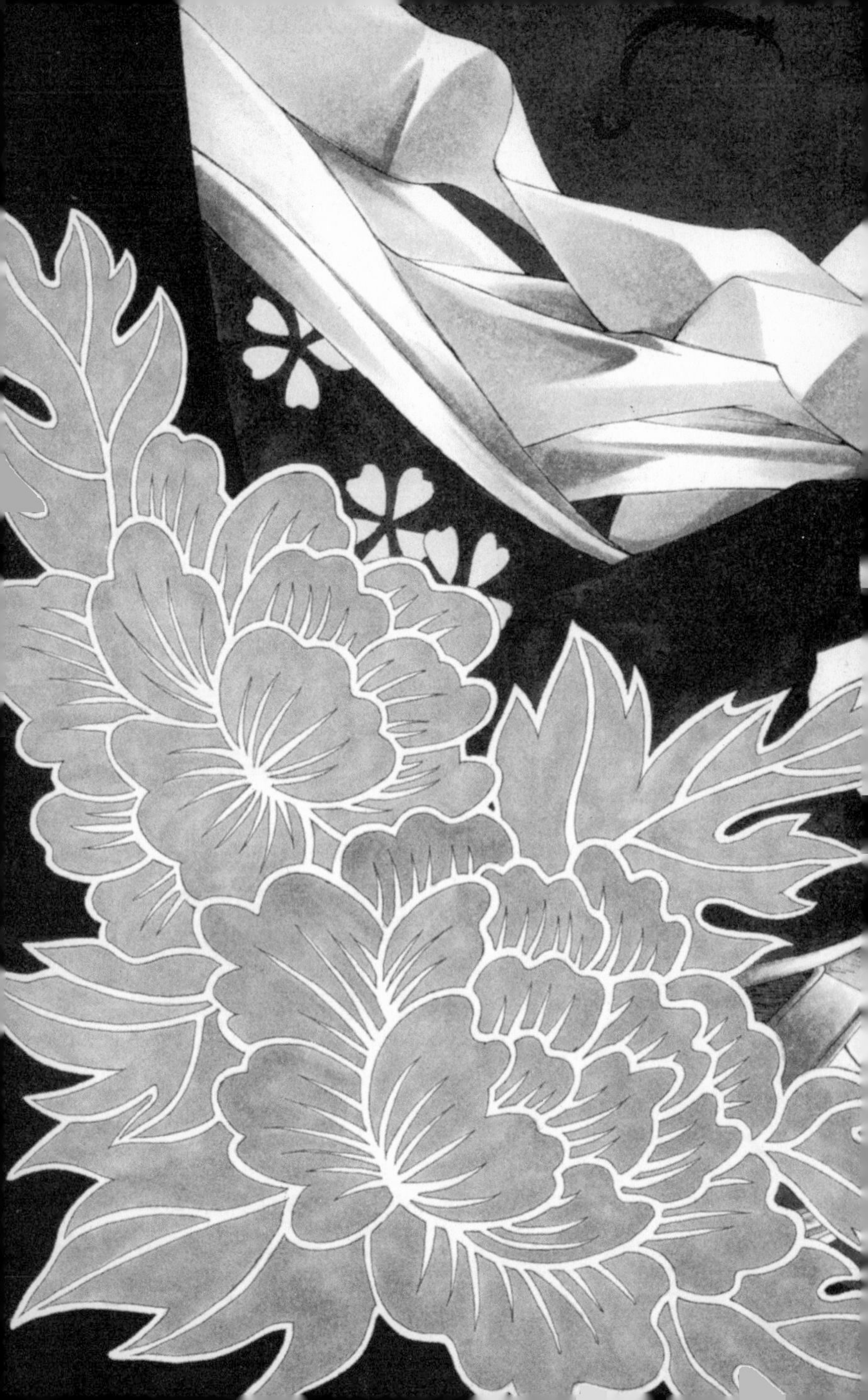

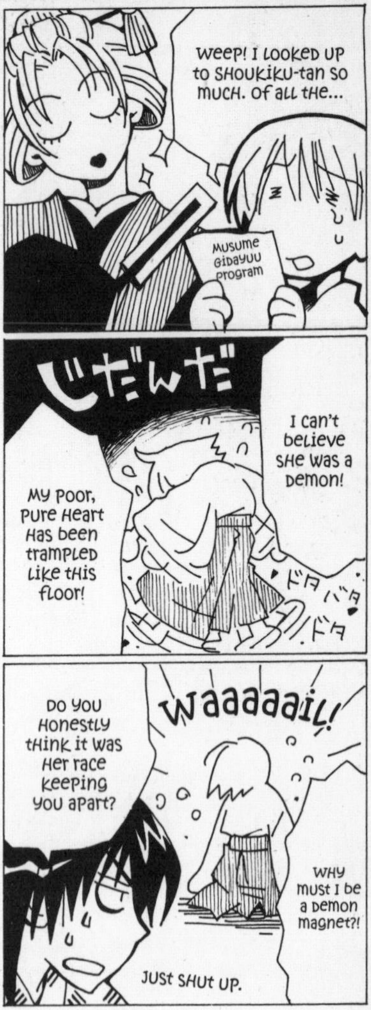
Weep! I looked up to Shoukiku-tan so much. Of all the...
Musume Gidayuu Program
I can't believe she was a demon!
じだんだ
My poor, pure heart has been trampled like this floor!
ドタバタドタ
Waaaaail!
Do you honestly think it was her race keeping you apart?
Why must I be a demon magnet?!
Just shut up.

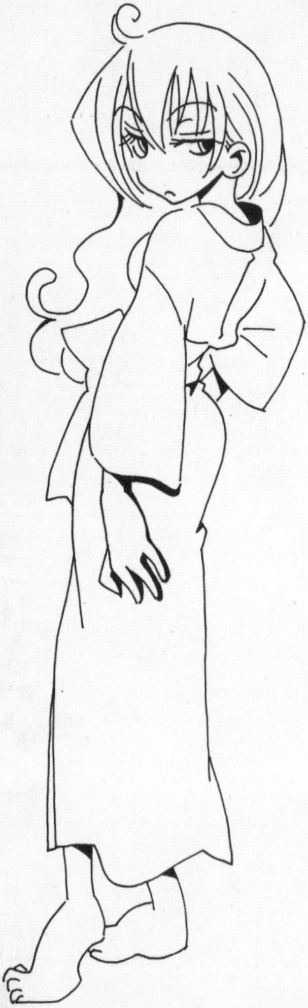

tactics

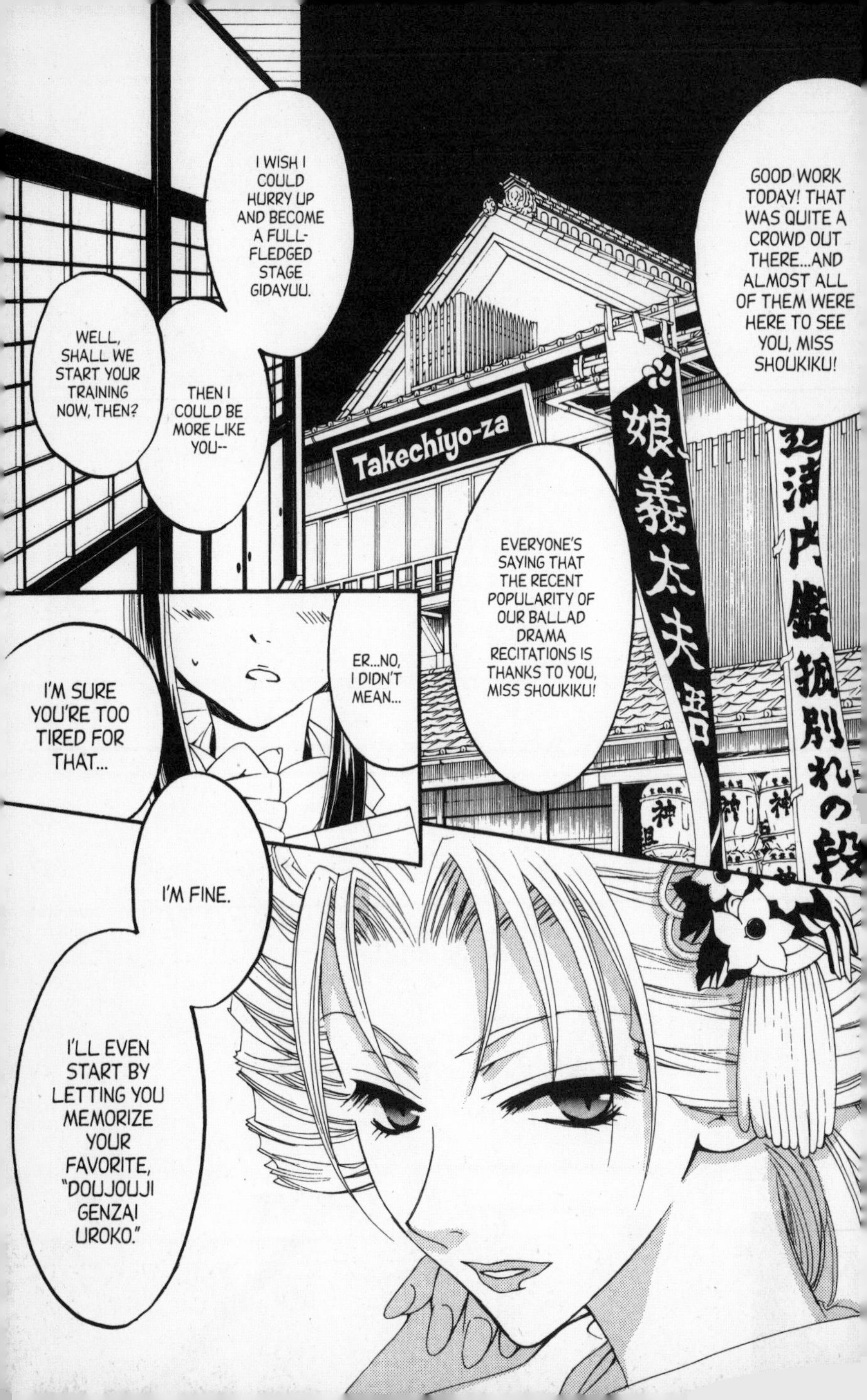
GOOD WORK TODAY! THAT WAS QUITE A CROWD OUT THERE...AND ALMOST ALL OF THEM WERE HERE TO SEE YOU, MISS SHOUKIKU!
Takechiyo-za
娘義太夫語
EVERYONE'S SAYING THAT THE RECENT POPULARITY OF OUR BALLAD DRAMA RECITATIONS IS THANKS TO YOU, MISS SHOUKIKU!
I WISH I COULD HURRY UP AND BECOME A FULL-FLEDGED STAGE GIDAYUU.
THEN I COULD BE MORE LIKE YOU--
WELL, SHALL WE START YOUR TRAINING NOW, THEN?
ER...NO, I DIDN'T MEAN...
I'M SURE YOU'RE TOO TIRED FOR THAT...
I'M FINE.
I'LL EVEN START BY LETTING YOU MEMORIZE YOUR FAVORITE, "DOUJOUJI GENZAI UROKO."

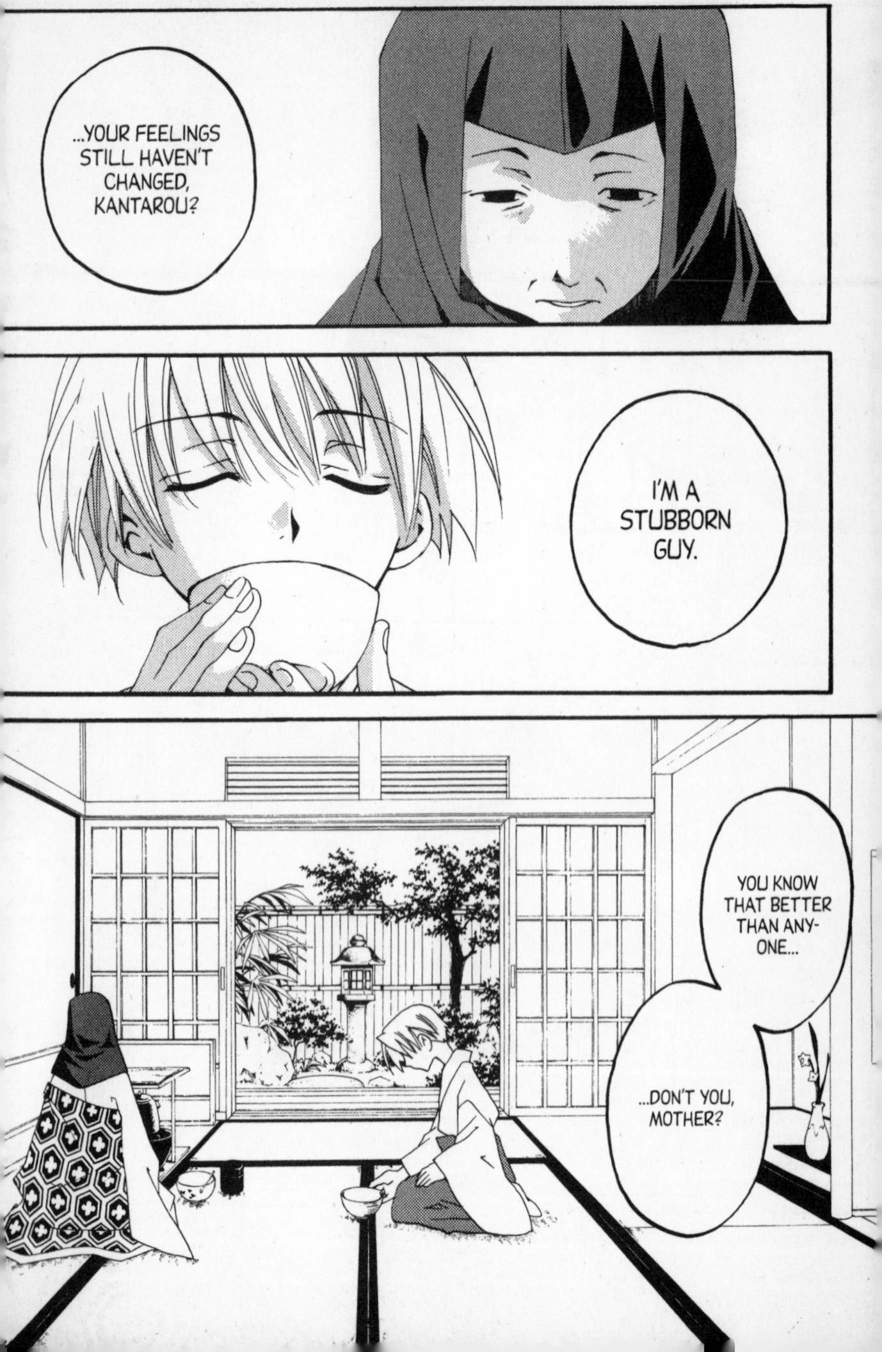
...YOUR FEELINGS STILL HAVEN'T CHANGED, KANTAROU?
I'M A STUBBORN GUY.
YOU KNOW THAT BETTER THAN ANY-ONE...
...DON'T YOU, MOTHER?

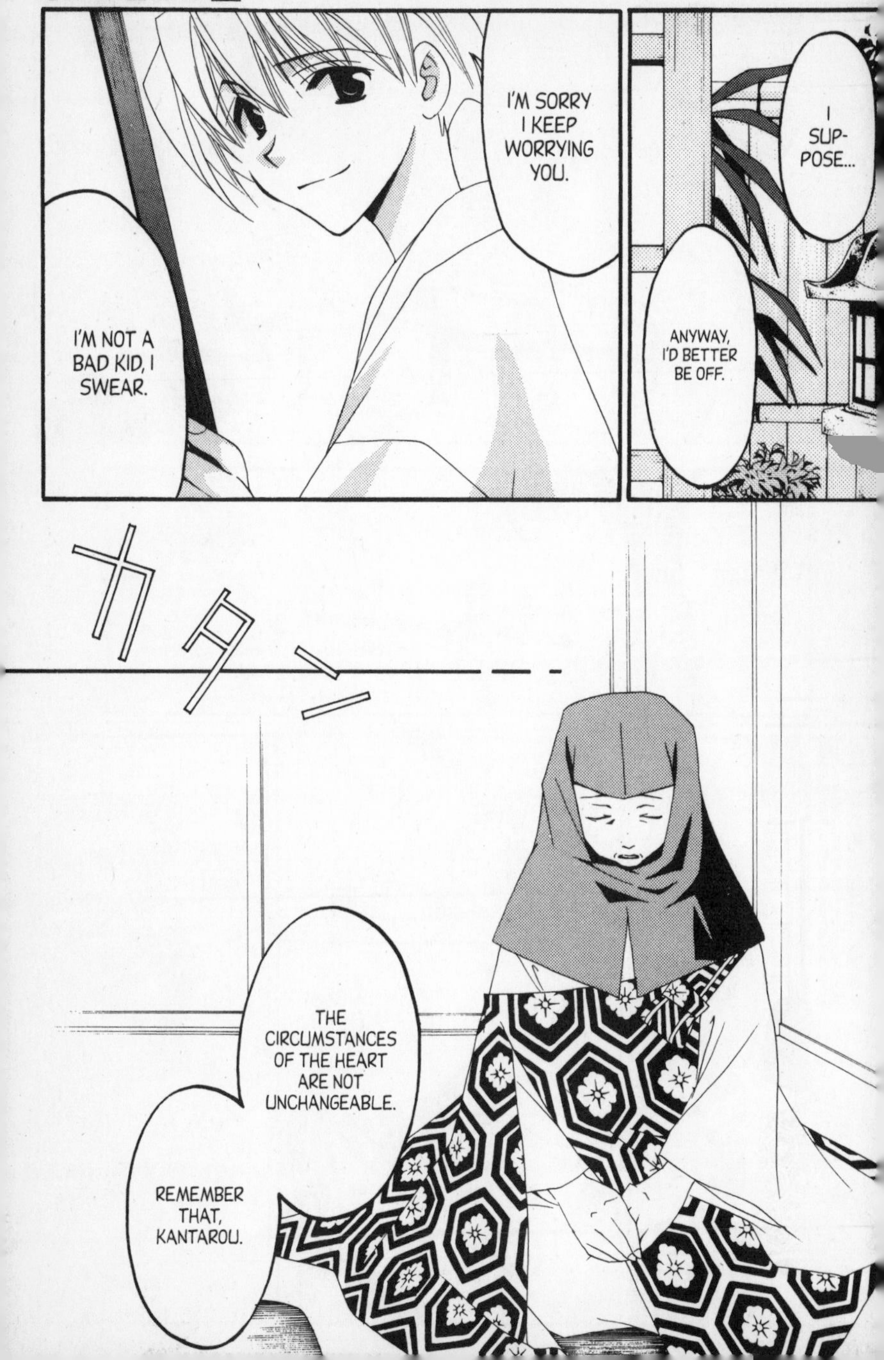
I SUP-POSE...
ANYWAY, I'D BETTER BE OFF.
I'M SORRY I KEEP WORRYING YOU.
I'M NOT A BAD KID, I SWEAR.
カターン
THE CIRCUMSTANCES OF THE HEART ARE NOT UNCHANGEABLE.
REMEMBER THAT, KANTAROU.

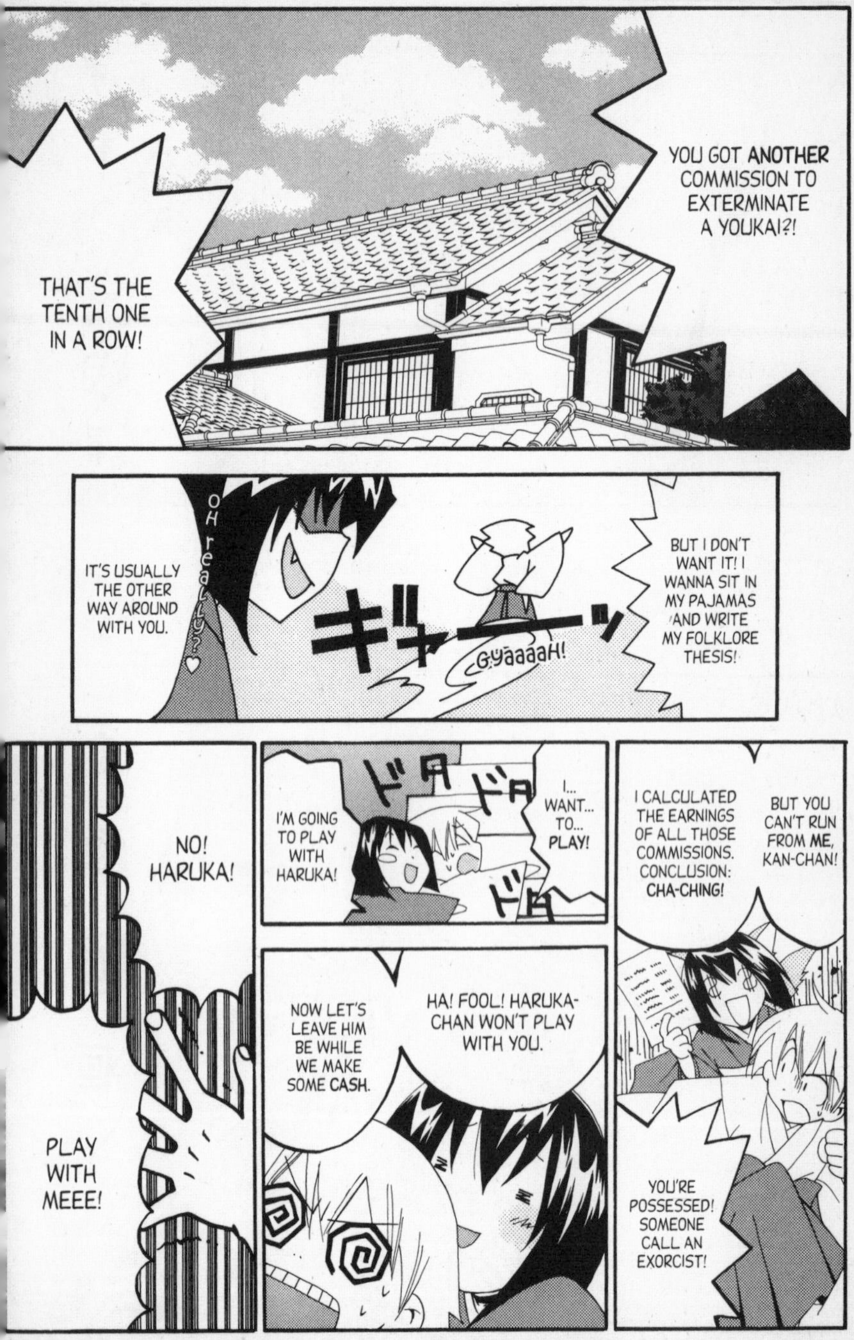
YOU GOT ANOTHER COMMISSION TO EXTERMINATE A YOUKAI?!
THAT'S THE TENTH ONE IN A ROW!
BUT I DON'T WANT IT! I WANNA SIT IN MY PAJAMAS AND WRITE MY FOLKLORE THESIS!
GYaaaaH!
OH really?♥
IT'S USUALLY THE OTHER WAY AROUND WITH YOU.
BUT YOU CAN'T RUN FROM ME, KAN-CHAN!
I CALCULATED THE EARNINGS OF ALL THOSE COMMISSIONS. CONCLUSION: CHA-CHING!
YOU'RE POSSESSED! SOMEONE CALL AN EXORCIST!
I... WANT... TO... PLAY!
I'M GOING TO PLAY WITH HARUKA!
HA! FOOL! HARUKA-CHAN WON'T PLAY WITH YOU.
NOW LET'S LEAVE HIM BE WHILE WE MAKE SOME CASH.
NO! HARUKA!
PLAY WITH MEEE!

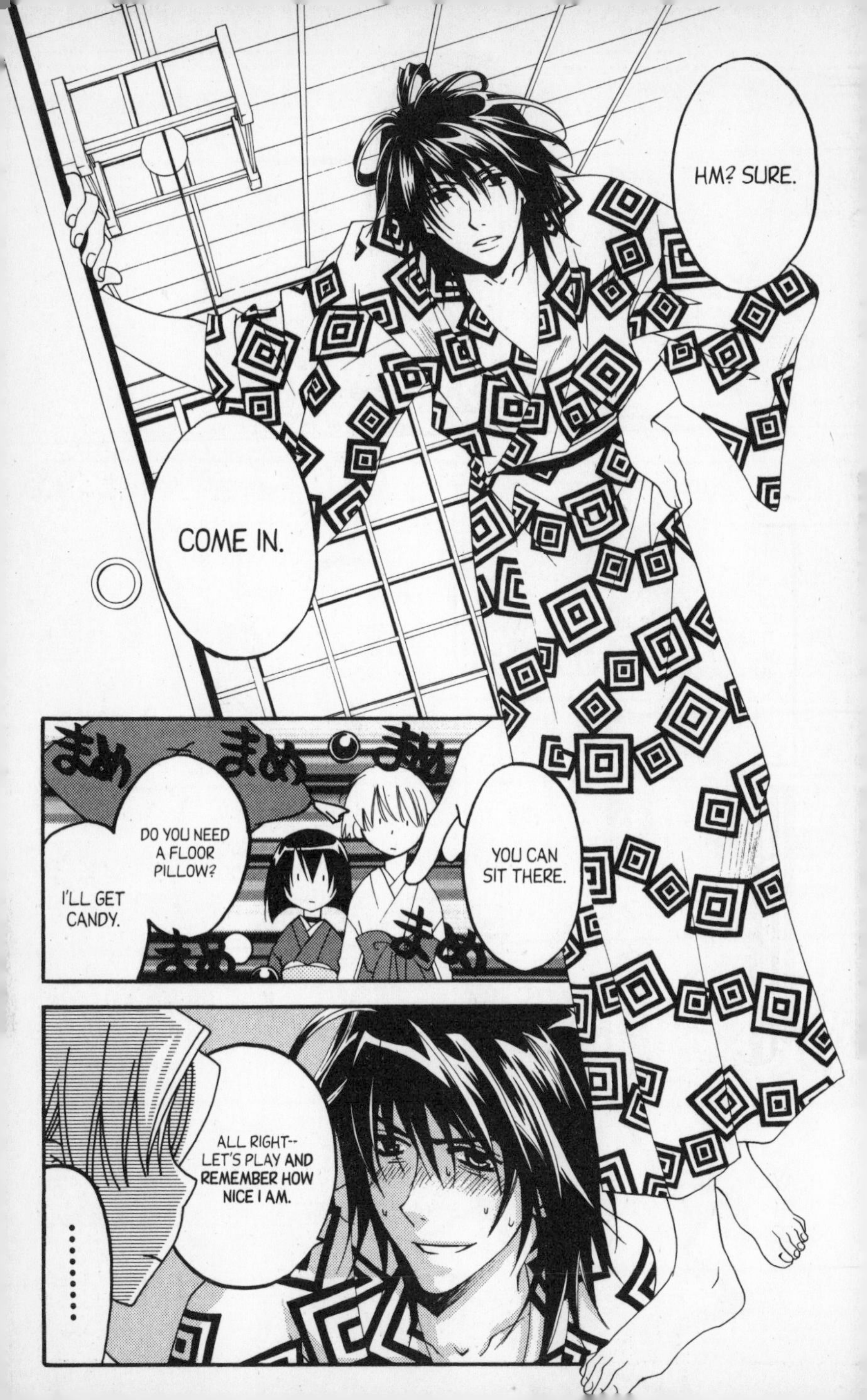
HM? SURE.
COME IN.
YOU CAN SIT THERE.
まめ まめ まめ
DO YOU NEED A FLOOR PILLOW?
I'LL GET CANDY.
まめ まめ
ALL RIGHT-- LET'S PLAY AND REMEMBER HOW NICE I AM.
....

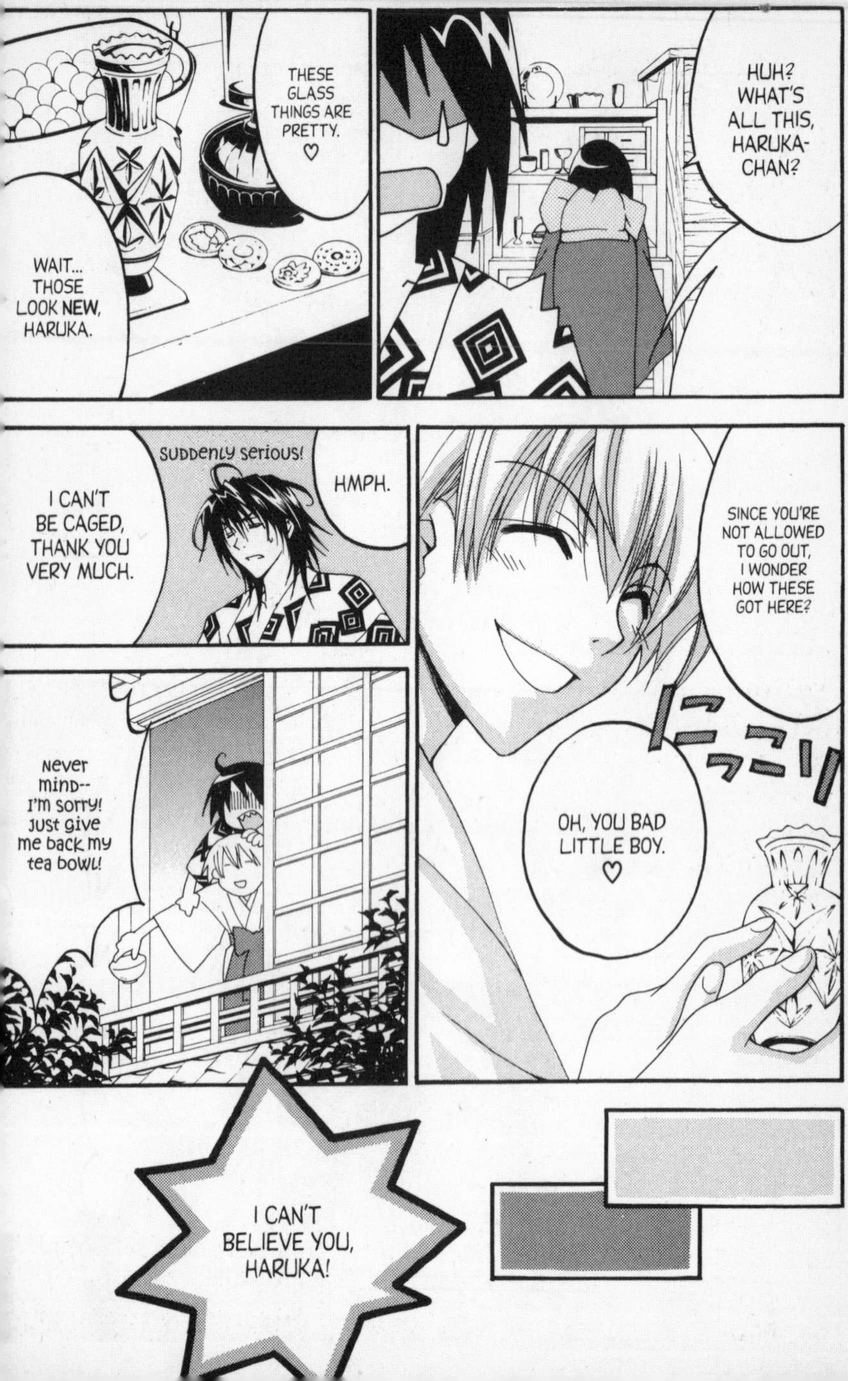
HUH? WHAT'S ALL THIS, HARUKA-CHAN?
THESE GLASS THINGS ARE PRETTY. ♡
WAIT... THOSE LOOK NEW, HARUKA.
SINCE YOU'RE NOT ALLOWED TO GO OUT, I WONDER HOW THESE GOT HERE?
OH, YOU BAD LITTLE BOY. ♡
HMPH.
SUDDENLY SERIOUS!
I CAN'T BE CAGED, THANK YOU VERY MUCH.
NEVER MIND-- I'M SORRY! JUST GIVE ME BACK MY TEA BOWL!
I CAN'T BELIEVE YOU, HARUKA!

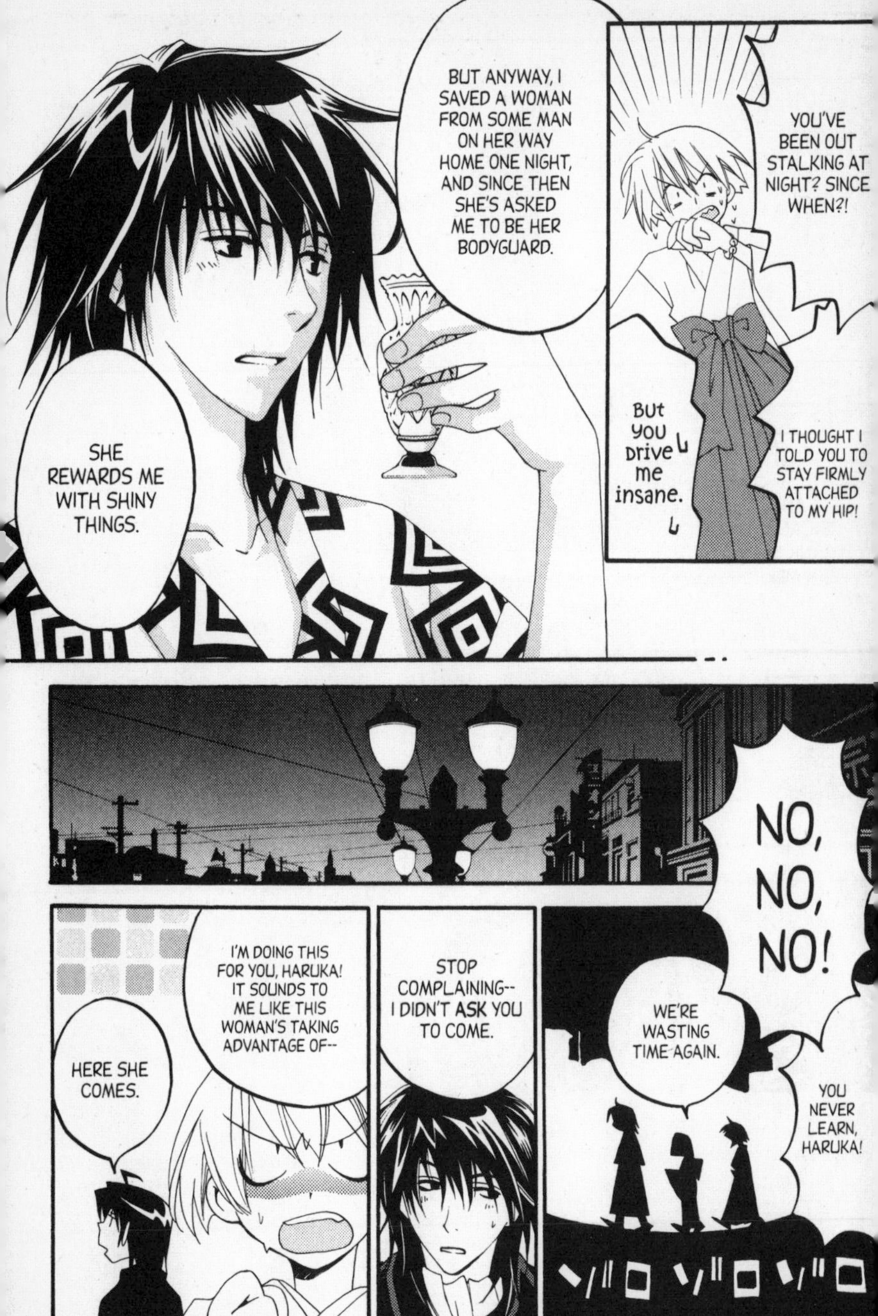
YOU'VE BEEN OUT STALKING AT NIGHT? SINCE WHEN?!
I THOUGHT I TOLD YOU TO STAY FIRMLY ATTACHED TO MY HIP!
But you drive me insane.
BUT ANYWAY, I SAVED A WOMAN FROM SOME MAN ON HER WAY HOME ONE NIGHT, AND SINCE THEN SHE'S ASKED ME TO BE HER BODYGUARD.
SHE REWARDS ME WITH SHINY THINGS.
NO, NO, NO!
YOU NEVER LEARN, HARUKA!
WE'RE WASTING TIME AGAIN.
STOP COMPLAINING-- I DIDN'T ASK YOU TO COME.
I'M DOING THIS FOR YOU, HARUKA! IT SOUNDS TO ME LIKE THIS WOMAN'S TAKING ADVANTAGE OF--
HERE SHE COMES.

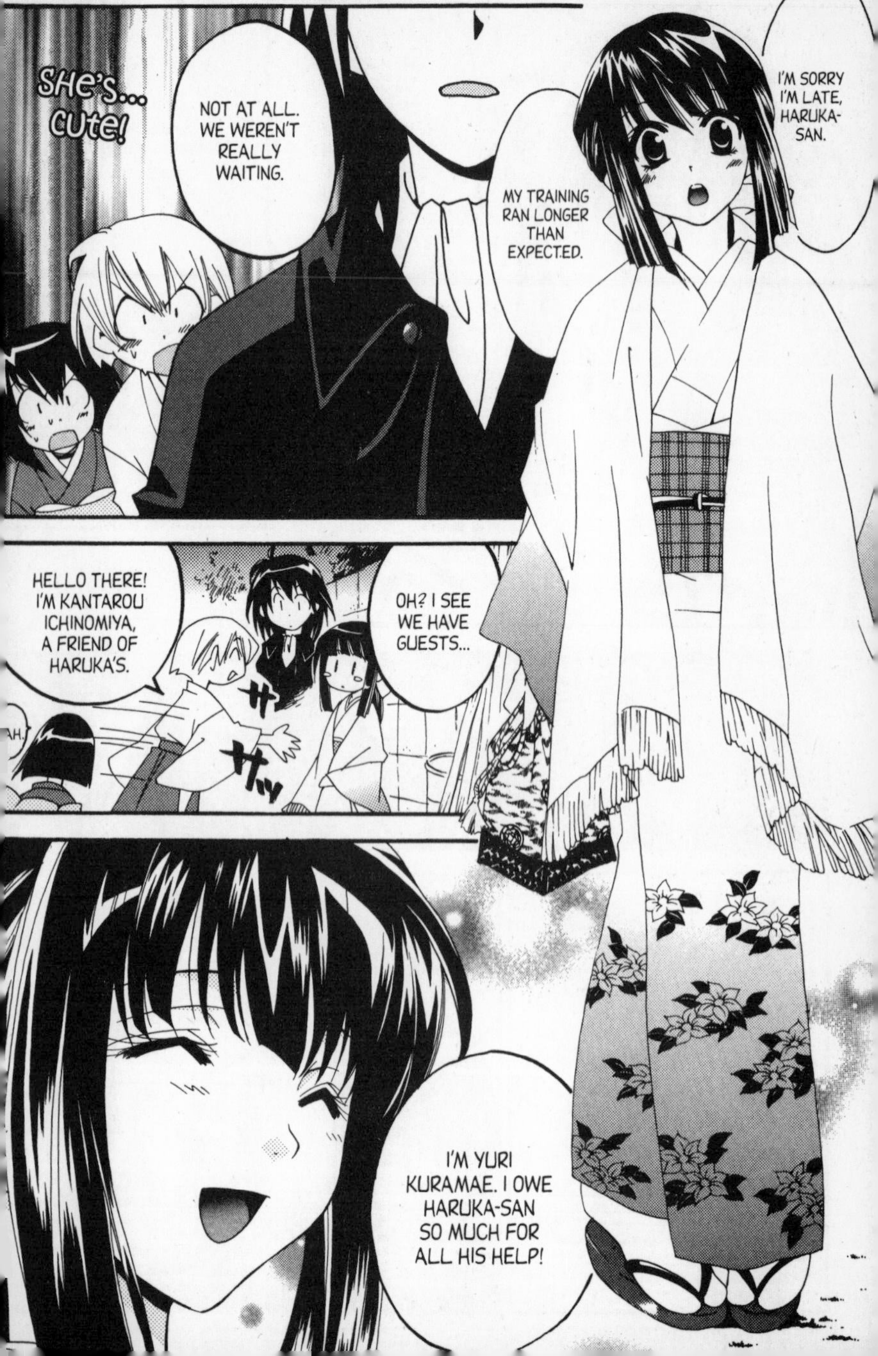
I'M SORRY I'M LATE, HARUKA-SAN.
MY TRAINING RAN LONGER THAN EXPECTED.
NOT AT ALL. WE WEREN'T REALLY WAITING.
SHE'S... CUTE!
OH? I SEE WE HAVE GUESTS...
HELLO THERE! I'M KANTAROU ICHINOMIYA, A FRIEND OF HARUKA'S.
サ
サッ
AH.
I'M YURI KURAMAE. I OWE HARUKA-SAN SO MUCH FOR ALL HIS HELP!

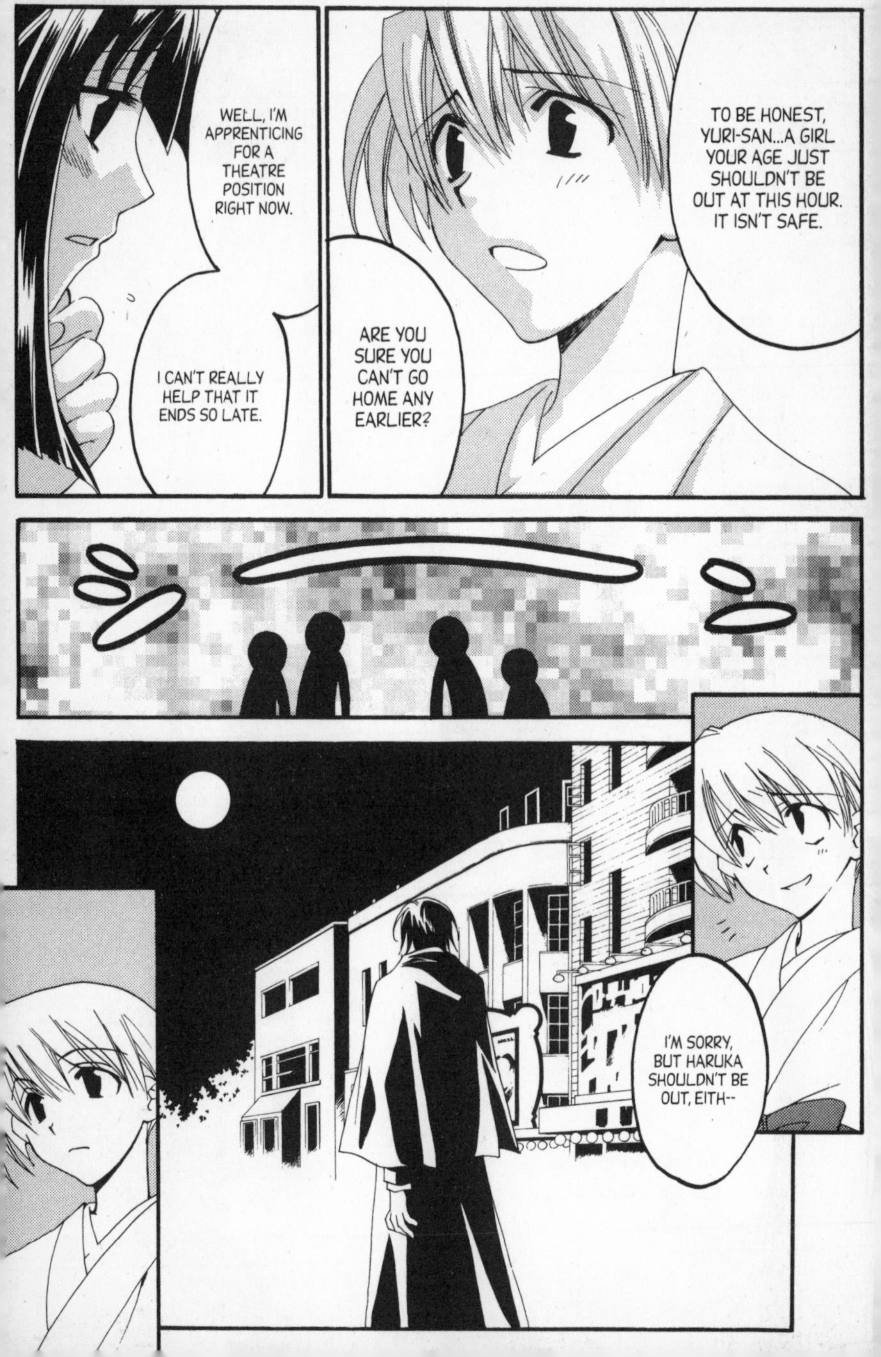
TO BE HONEST, YURI-SAN...A GIRL YOUR AGE JUST SHOULDN'T BE OUT AT THIS HOUR. IT ISN'T SAFE.
ARE YOU SURE YOU CAN'T GO HOME ANY EARLIER?
WELL, I'M APPRENTICING FOR A THEATRE POSITION RIGHT NOW.
I CAN'T REALLY HELP THAT IT ENDS SO LATE.
I'M SORRY, BUT HARUKA SHOULDN'T BE OUT, EITH--

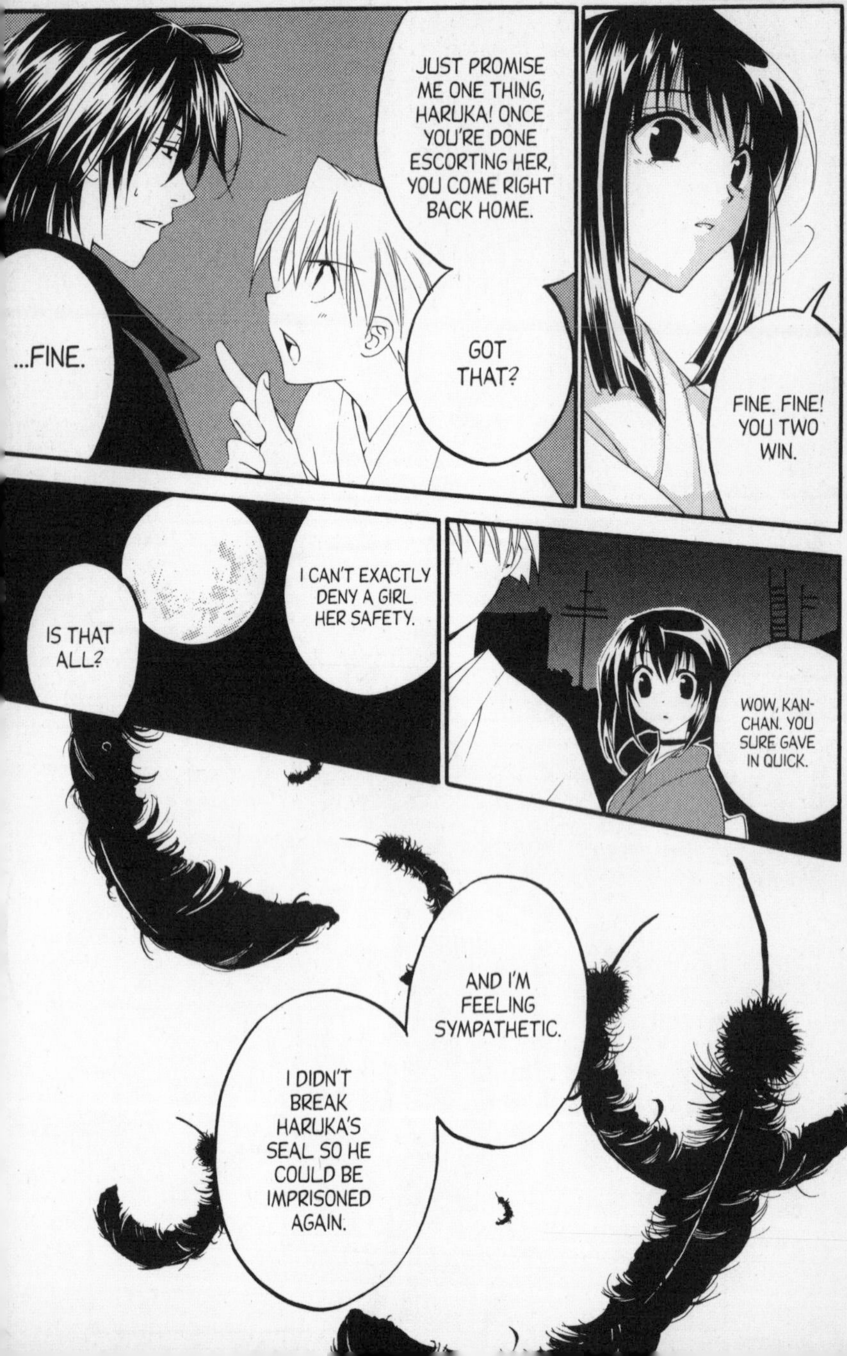
FINE. FINE! YOU TWO WIN.
JUST PROMISE ME ONE THING, HARUKA! ONCE YOU'RE DONE ESCORTING HER, YOU COME RIGHT BACK HOME.
GOT THAT?
...FINE.
WOW, KAN-CHAN. YOU SURE GAVE IN QUICK.
I CAN'T EXACTLY DENY A GIRL HER SAFETY.
IS THAT ALL?
AND I'M FEELING SYMPATHETIC.
I DIDN'T BREAK HARUKA'S SEAL SO HE COULD BE IMPRISONED AGAIN.

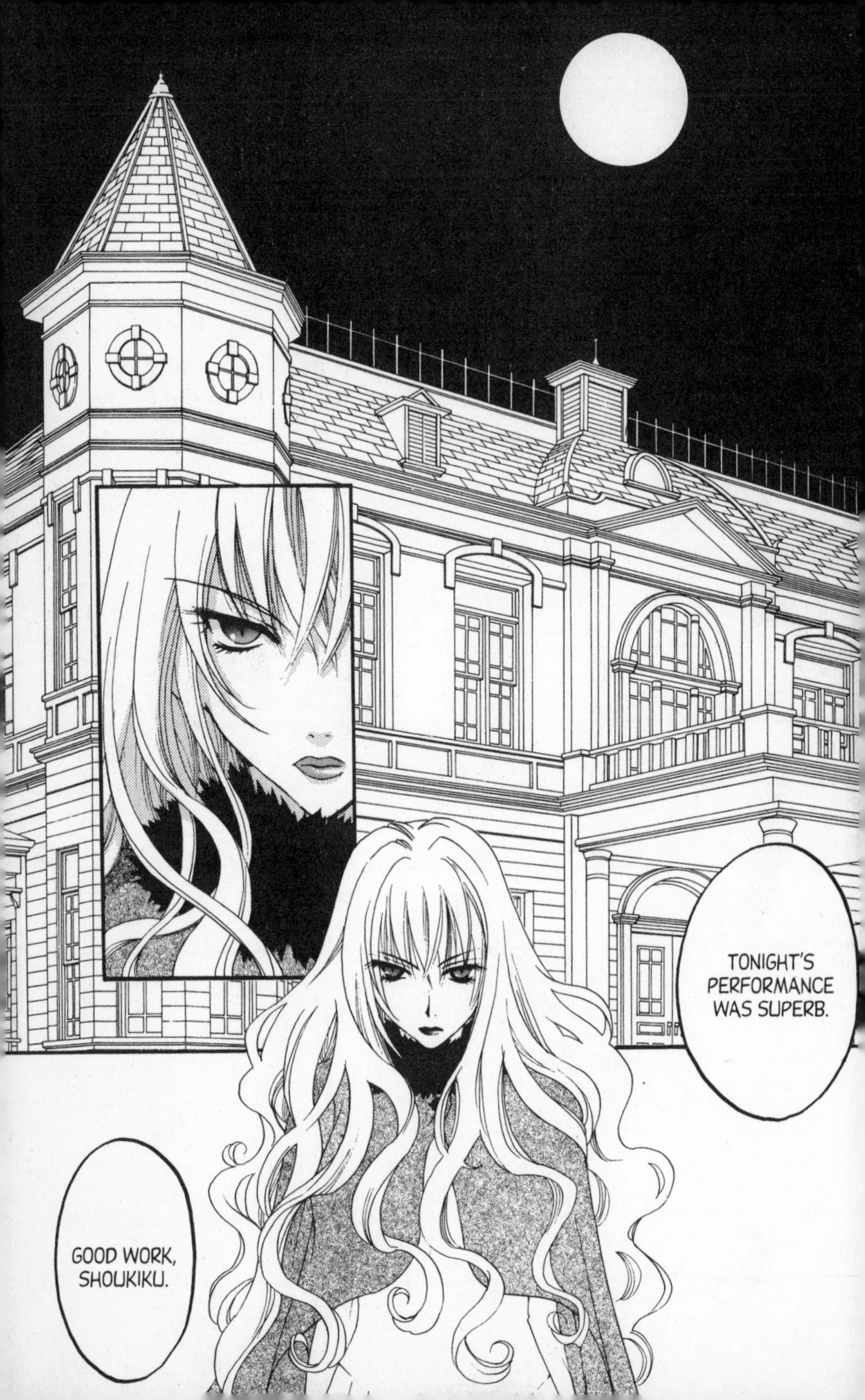
TONIGHT'S PERFORMANCE WAS SUPERB.
GOOD WORK, SHOUKIKU.

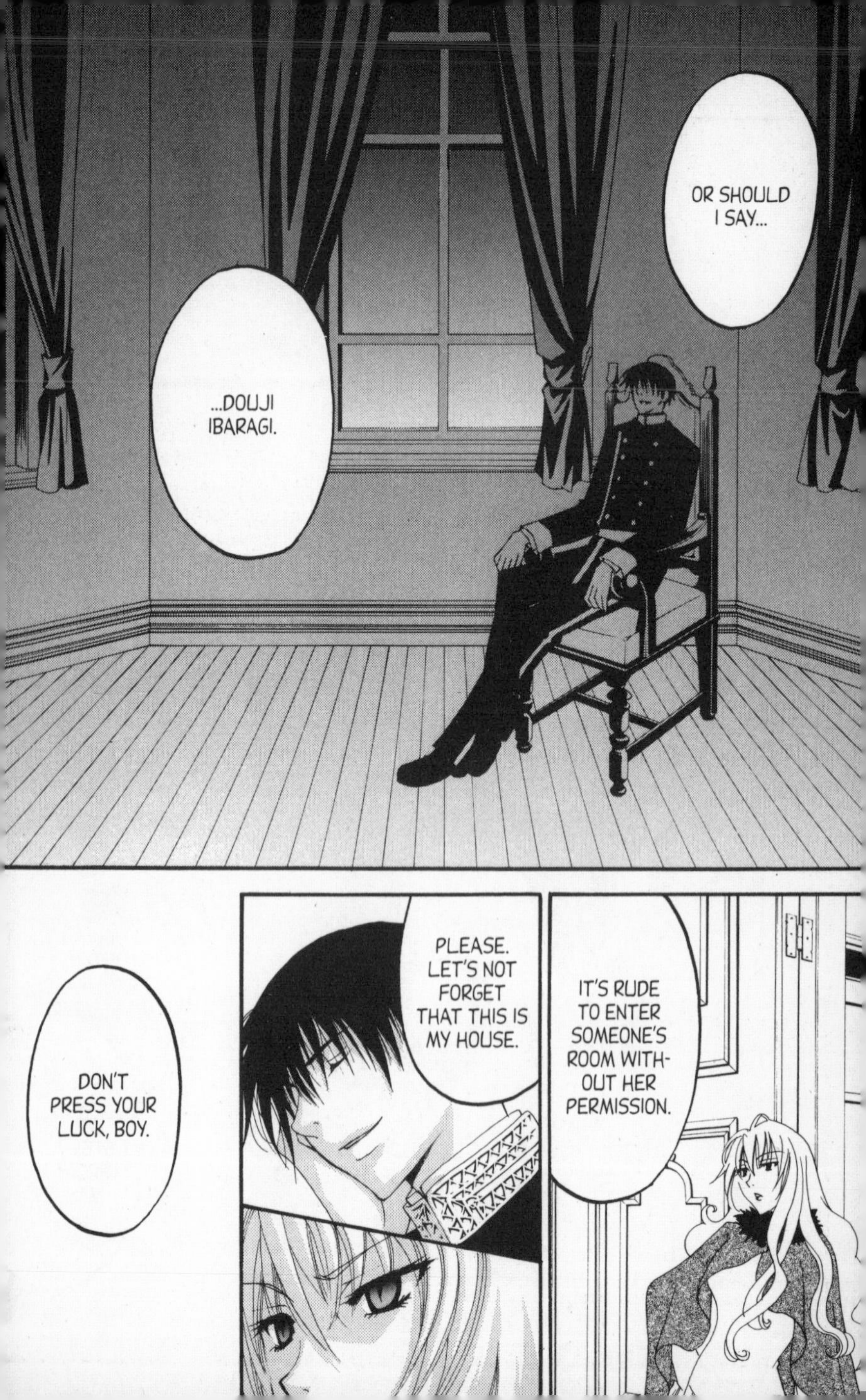
OR SHOULD I SAY...
...DOUJI IBARAGI.
IT'S RUDE TO ENTER SOMEONE'S ROOM WITH-OUT HER PERMISSION.
PLEASE. LET'S NOT FORGET THAT THIS IS MY HOUSE.
DON'T PRESS YOUR LUCK, BOY.

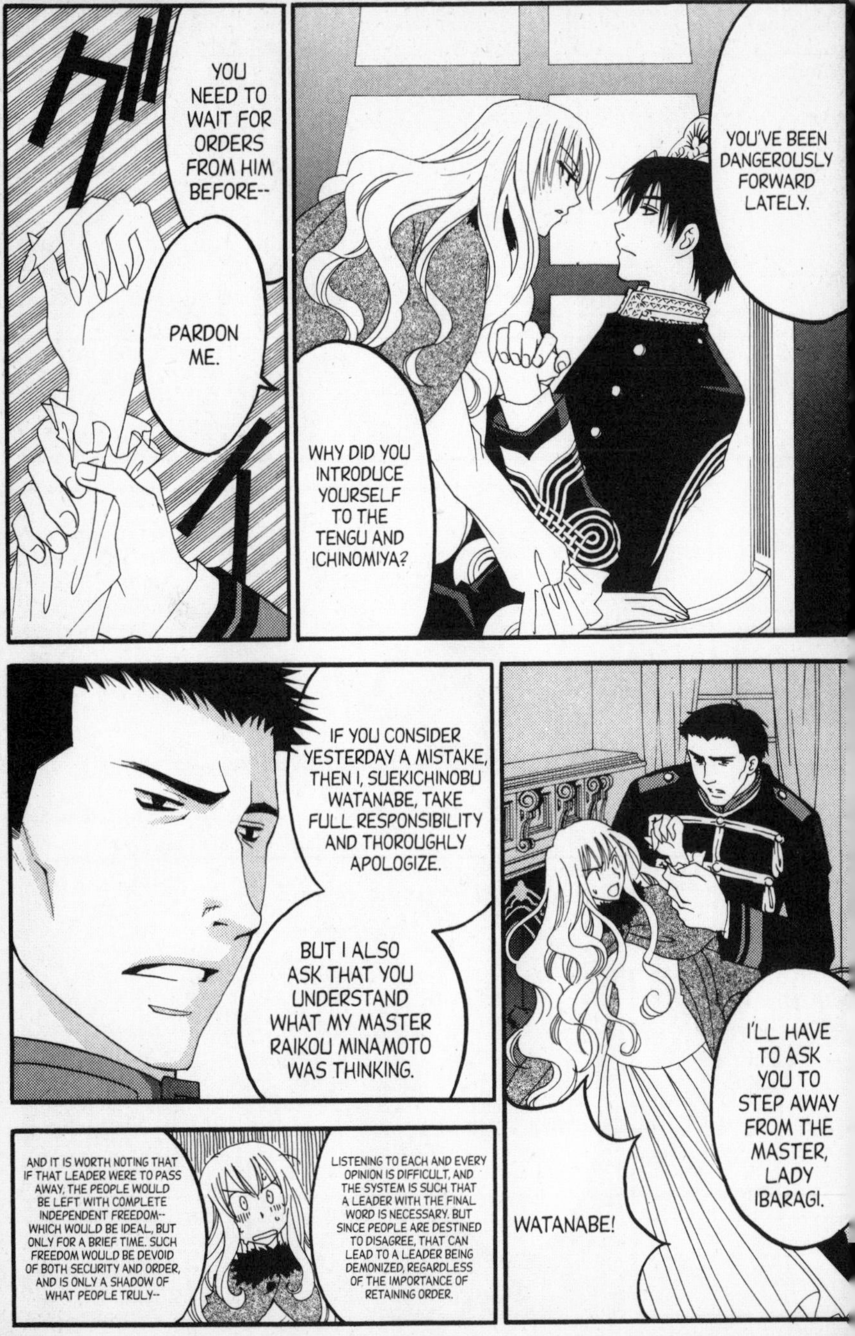
YOU'VE BEEN DANGEROUSLY FORWARD LATELY.
WHY DID YOU INTRODUCE YOURSELF TO THE TENGU AND ICHINOMIYA?
YOU NEED TO WAIT FOR ORDERS FROM HIM BEFORE--
PARDON ME.
I'LL HAVE TO ASK YOU TO STEP AWAY FROM THE MASTER, LADY IBARAGI.
WATANABE!
IF YOU CONSIDER YESTERDAY A MISTAKE, THEN I, SUEKICHINOBU WATANABE, TAKE FULL RESPONSIBILITY AND THOROUGHLY APOLOGIZE.
BUT I ALSO ASK THAT YOU UNDERSTAND WHAT MY MASTER RAIKOU MINAMOTO WAS THINKING.
LISTENING TO EACH AND EVERY OPINION IS DIFFICULT, AND THE SYSTEM IS SUCH THAT A LEADER WITH THE FINAL WORD IS NECESSARY. BUT SINCE PEOPLE ARE DESTINED TO DISAGREE, THAT CAN LEAD TO A LEADER BEING DEMONIZED, REGARDLESS OF THE IMPORTANCE OF RETAINING ORDER.
AND IT IS WORTH NOTING THAT IF THAT LEADER WERE TO PASS AWAY, THE PEOPLE WOULD BE LEFT WITH COMPLETE INDEPENDENT FREEDOM--WHICH WOULD BE IDEAL, BUT ONLY FOR A BRIEF TIME. SUCH FREEDOM WOULD BE DEVOID OF BOTH SECURITY AND ORDER, AND IS ONLY A SHADOW OF WHAT PEOPLE TRULY--

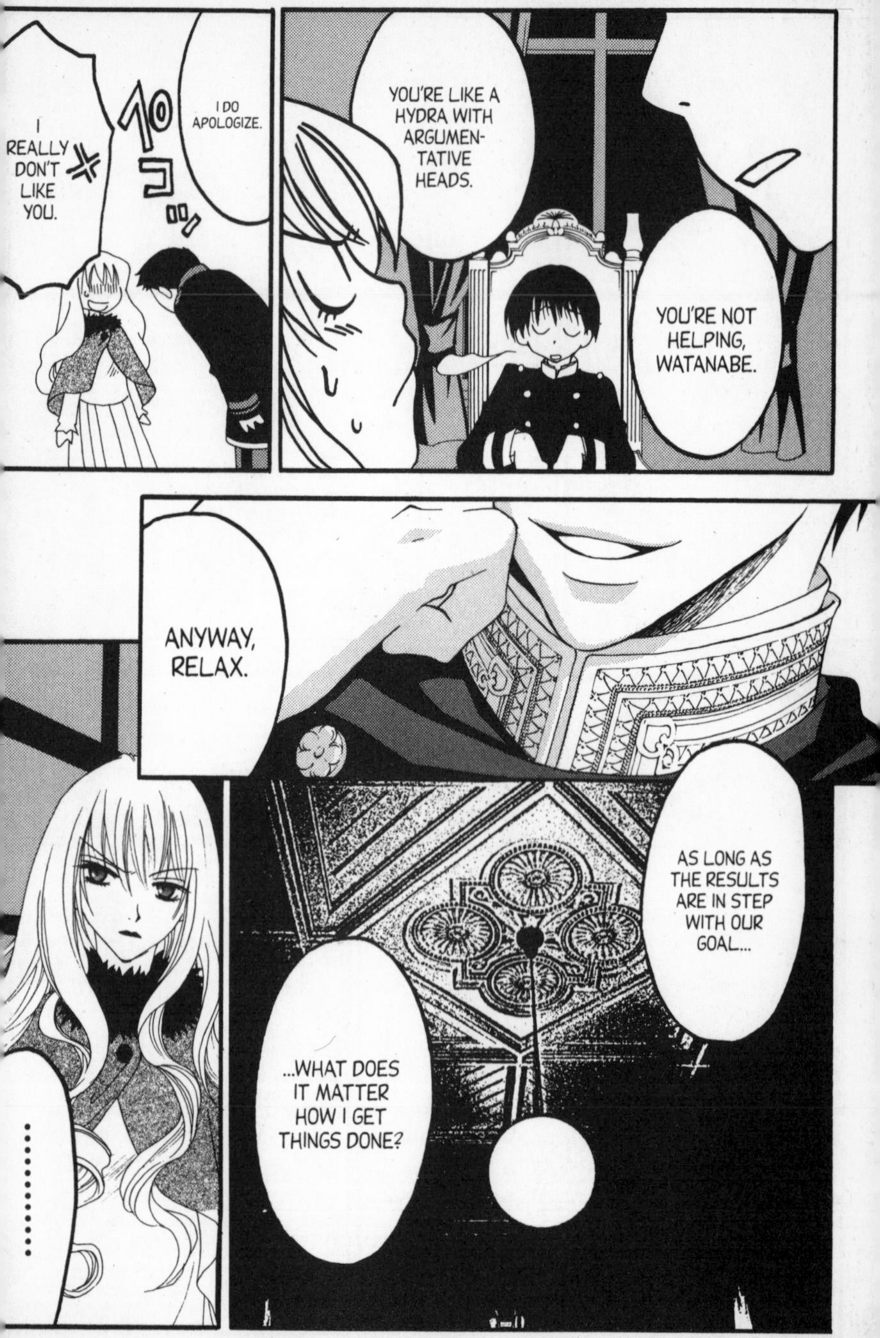
YOU'RE LIKE A HYDRA WITH ARGUMENTATIVE HEADS.
YOU'RE NOT HELPING, WATANABE.
I DO APOLOGIZE.
I REALLY DON'T LIKE YOU.
ANYWAY, RELAX.
AS LONG AS THE RESULTS ARE IN STEP WITH OUR GOAL...
...WHAT DOES IT MATTER HOW I GET THINGS DONE?
....

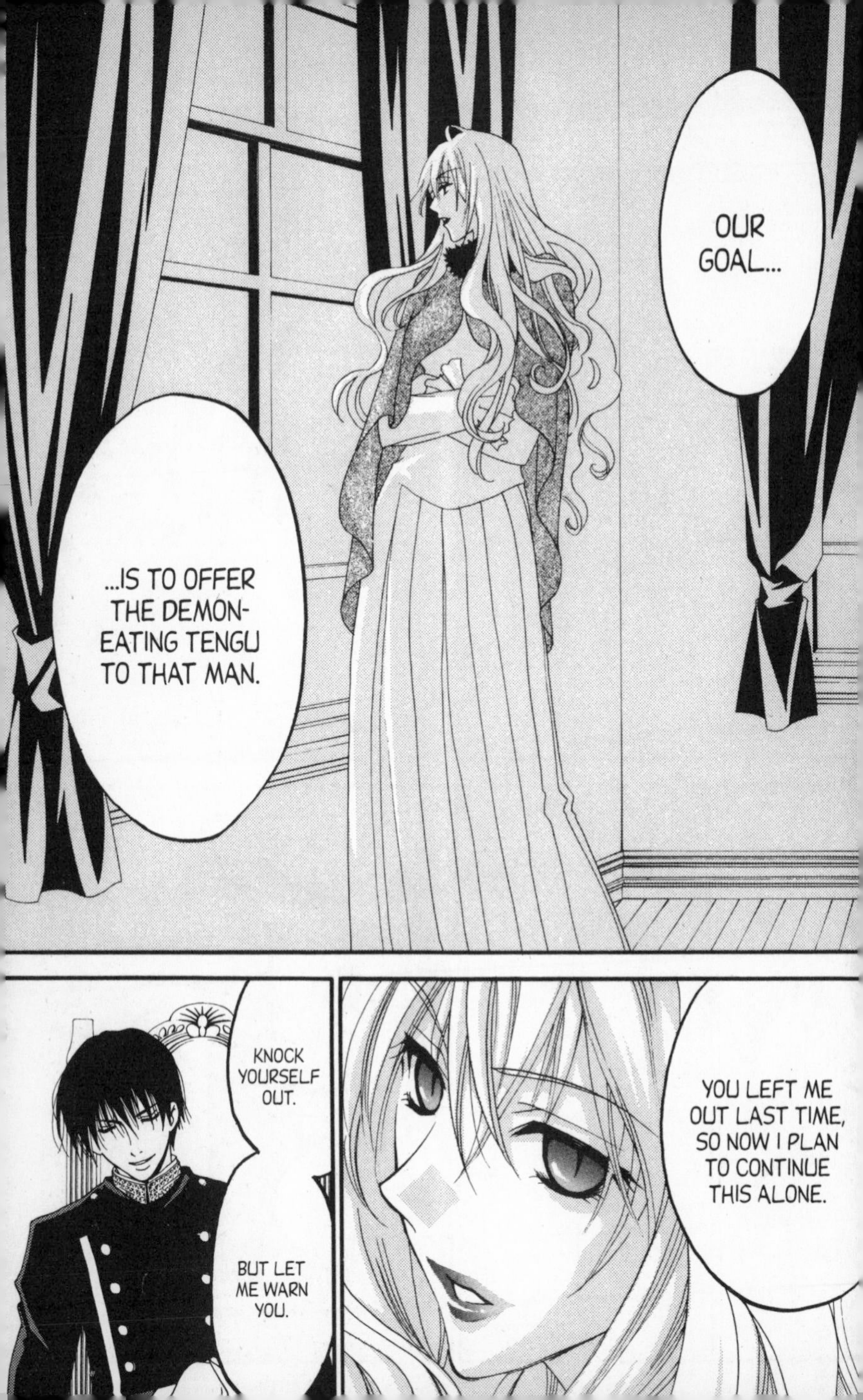
OUR GOAL...
...IS TO OFFER THE DEMON-EATING TENGU TO THAT MAN.
YOU LEFT ME OUT LAST TIME, SO NOW I PLAN TO CONTINUE THIS ALONE.
KNOCK YOURSELF OUT.
BUT LET ME WARN YOU.

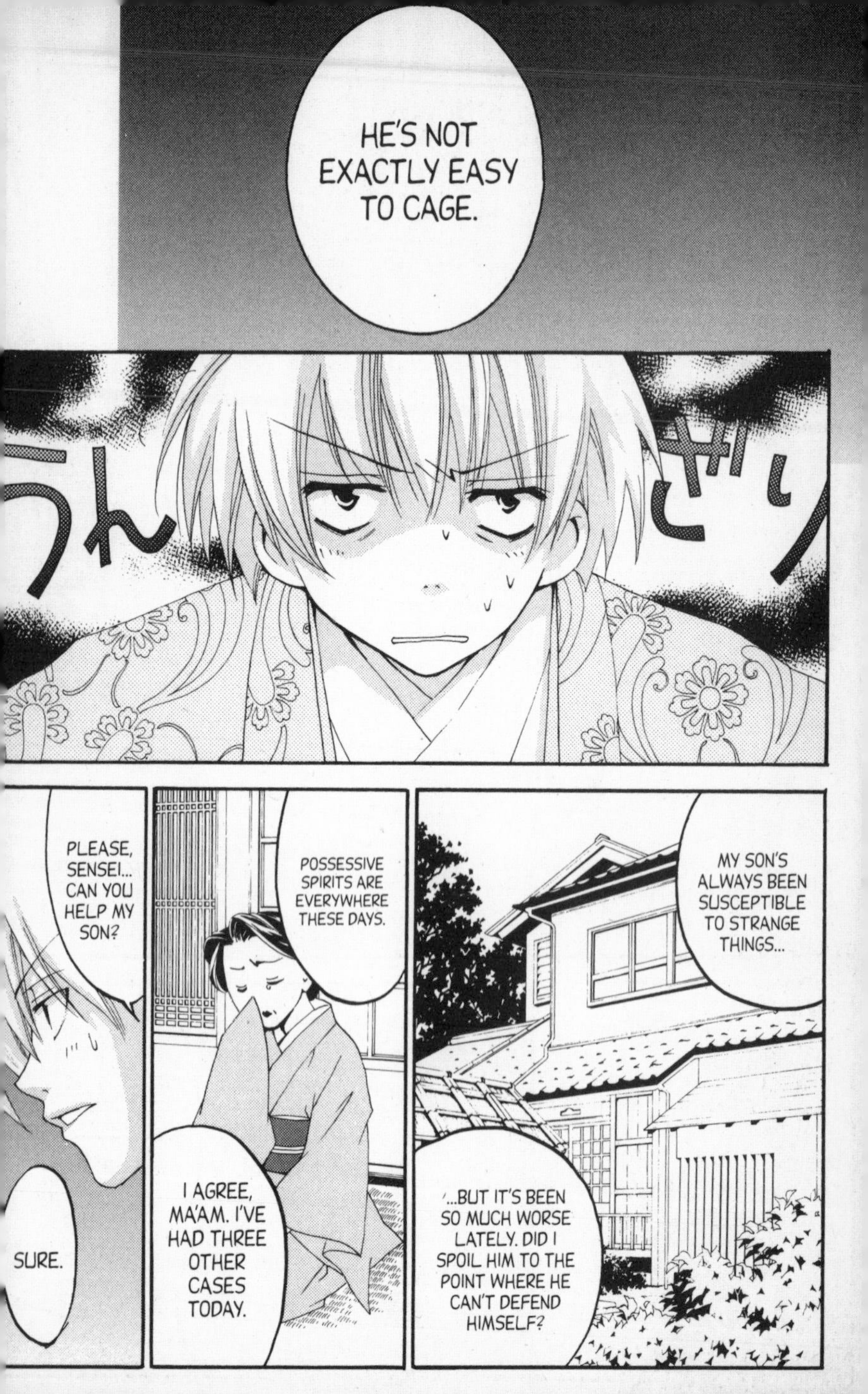
HE'S NOT EXACTLY EASY TO CAGE.
うんざり
MY SON'S ALWAYS BEEN SUSCEPTIBLE TO STRANGE THINGS...
...BUT IT'S BEEN SO MUCH WORSE LATELY. DID I SPOIL HIM TO THE POINT WHERE HE CAN'T DEFEND HIMSELF?
POSSESSIVE SPIRITS ARE EVERYWHERE THESE DAYS.
I AGREE, MA'AM. I'VE HAD THREE OTHER CASES TODAY.
PLEASE, SENSEI... CAN YOU HELP MY SON?
SURE.

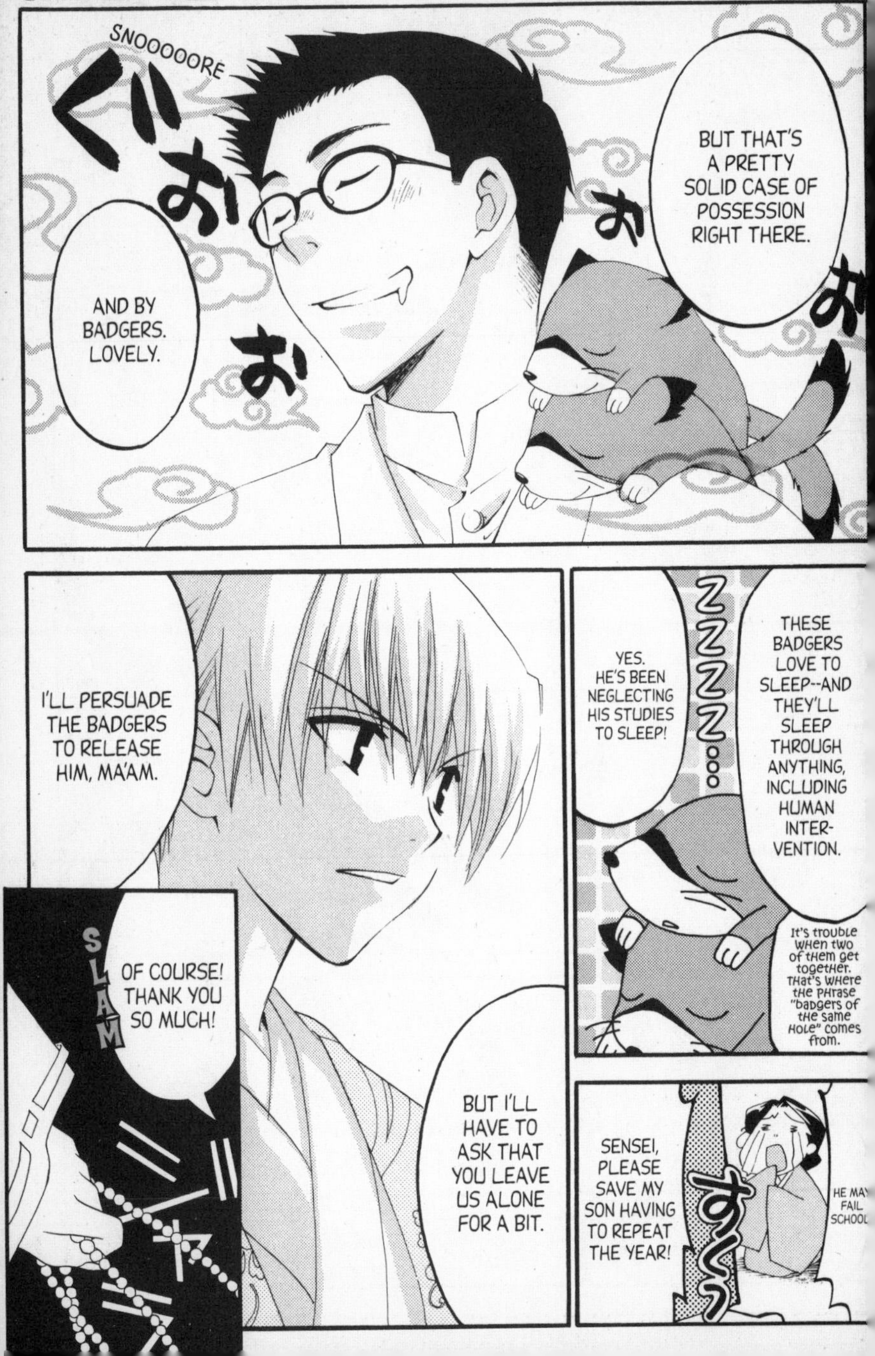
BUT THAT'S A PRETTY SOLID CASE OF POSSESSION RIGHT THERE.
SNOOOOORE
AND BY BADGERS. LOVELY.
THESE BADGERS LOVE TO SLEEP--AND THEY'LL SLEEP THROUGH ANYTHING, INCLUDING HUMAN INTER-VENTION.
ZZZZ...
YES. HE'S BEEN NEGLECTING HIS STUDIES TO SLEEP!
It's trouble when two of them get together. That's where the phrase "badgers of the same hole" comes from.
HE MAY FAIL SCHOOL
SENSEI, PLEASE SAVE MY SON HAVING TO REPEAT THE YEAR!
I'LL PERSUADE THE BADGERS TO RELEASE HIM, MA'AM.
BUT I'LL HAVE TO ASK THAT YOU LEAVE US ALONE FOR A BIT.
OF COURSE! THANK YOU SO MUCH!
SLAM

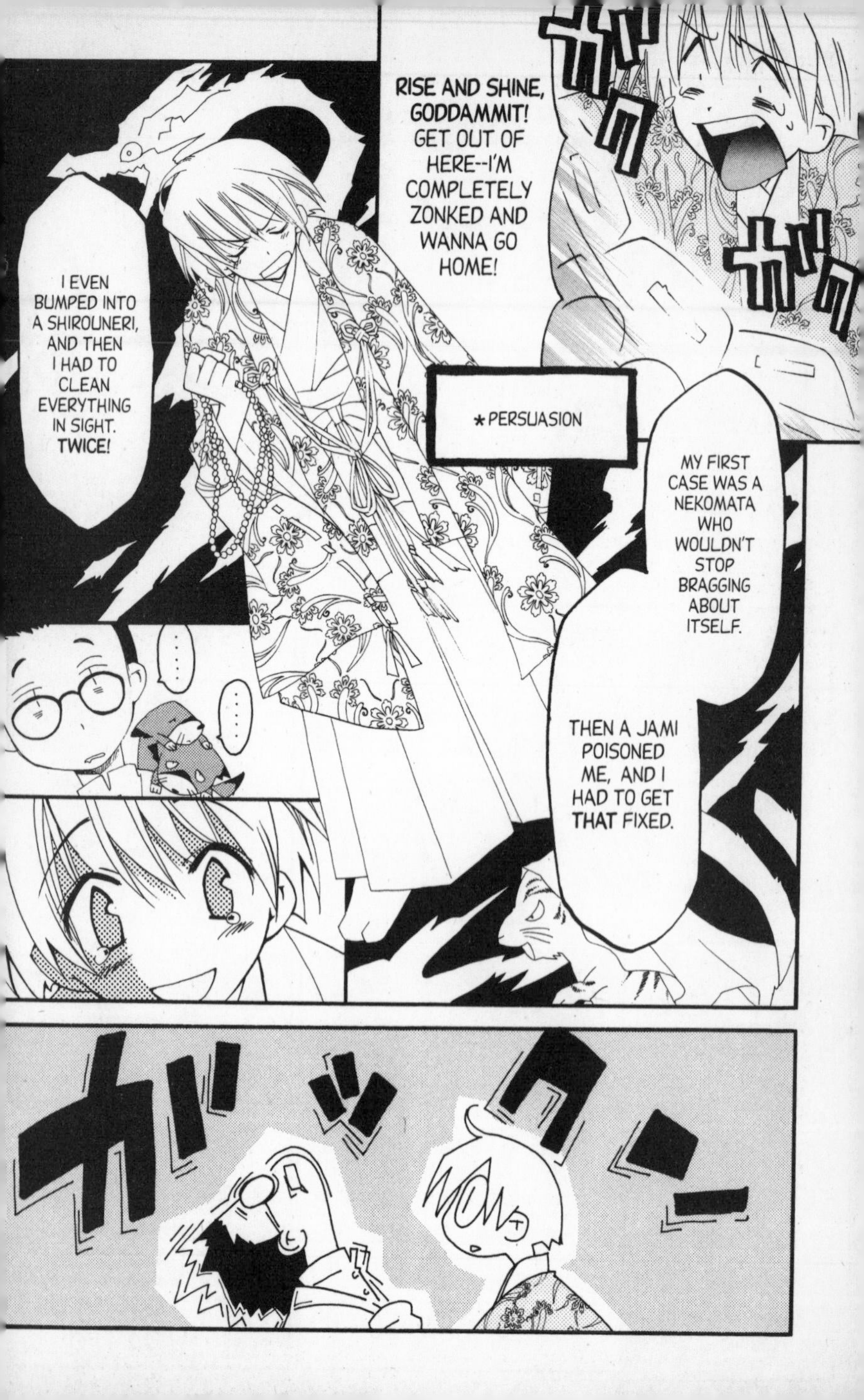

RISE AND SHINE, GODDAMMIT! GET OUT OF HERE--I'M COMPLETELY ZONKED AND WANNA GO HOME!
*PERSUASION
MY FIRST CASE WAS A NEKOMATA WHO WOULDN'T STOP BRAGGING ABOUT ITSELF.
THEN A JAMI POISONED ME, AND I HAD TO GET THAT FIXED.
I EVEN BUMPED INTO A SHIROUNERI, AND THEN I HAD TO CLEAN EVERYTHING IN SIGHT. TWICE!
......
......

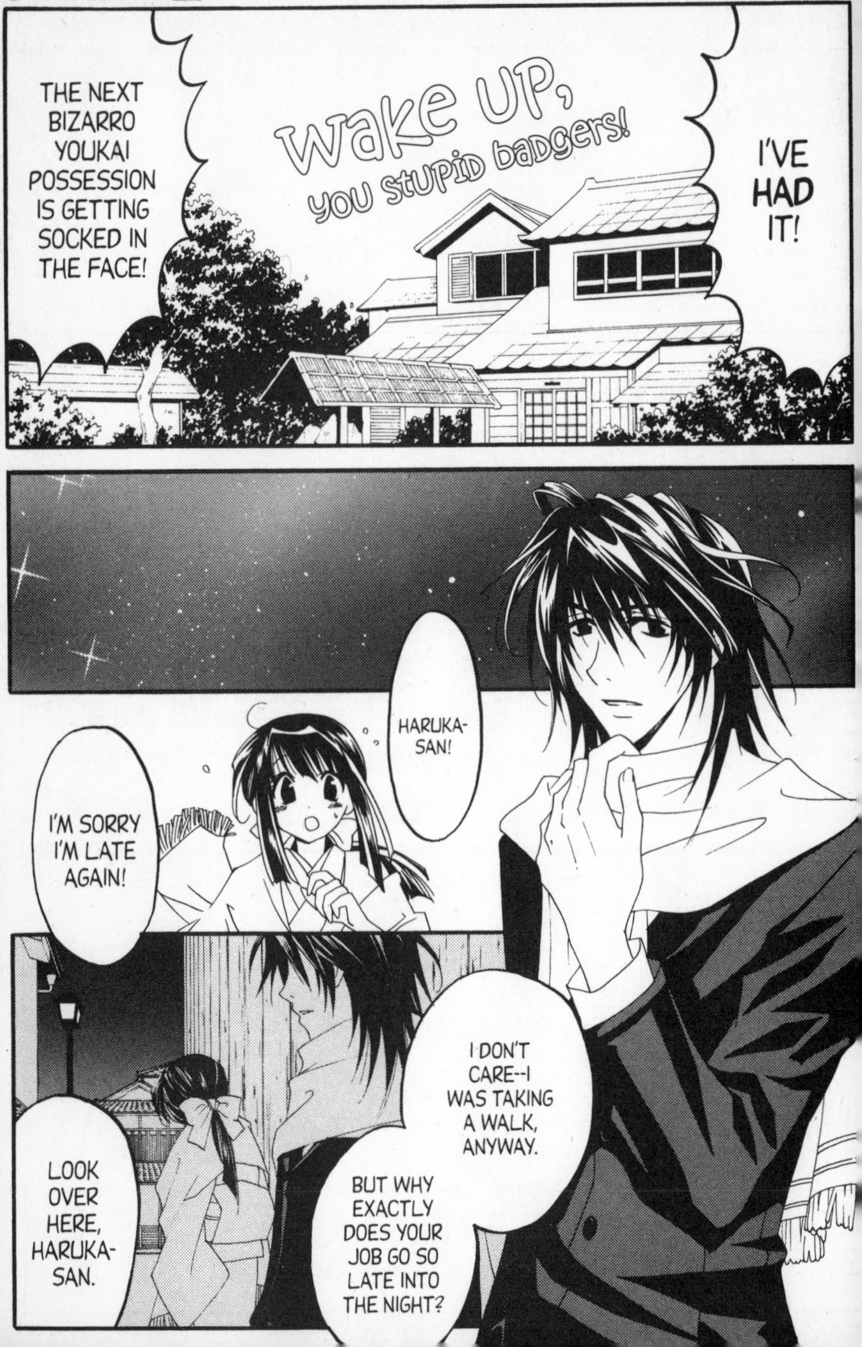
I'VE HAD IT!
Wake up, you stupid badgers!
THE NEXT BIZARRO YOUKAI POSSESSION IS GETTING SOCKED IN THE FACE!
HARUKA-SAN!
I'M SORRY I'M LATE AGAIN!
I DON'T CARE--I WAS TAKING A WALK, ANYWAY.
BUT WHY EXACTLY DOES YOUR JOB GO SO LATE INTO THE NIGHT?
LOOK OVER HERE, HARUKA-SAN.

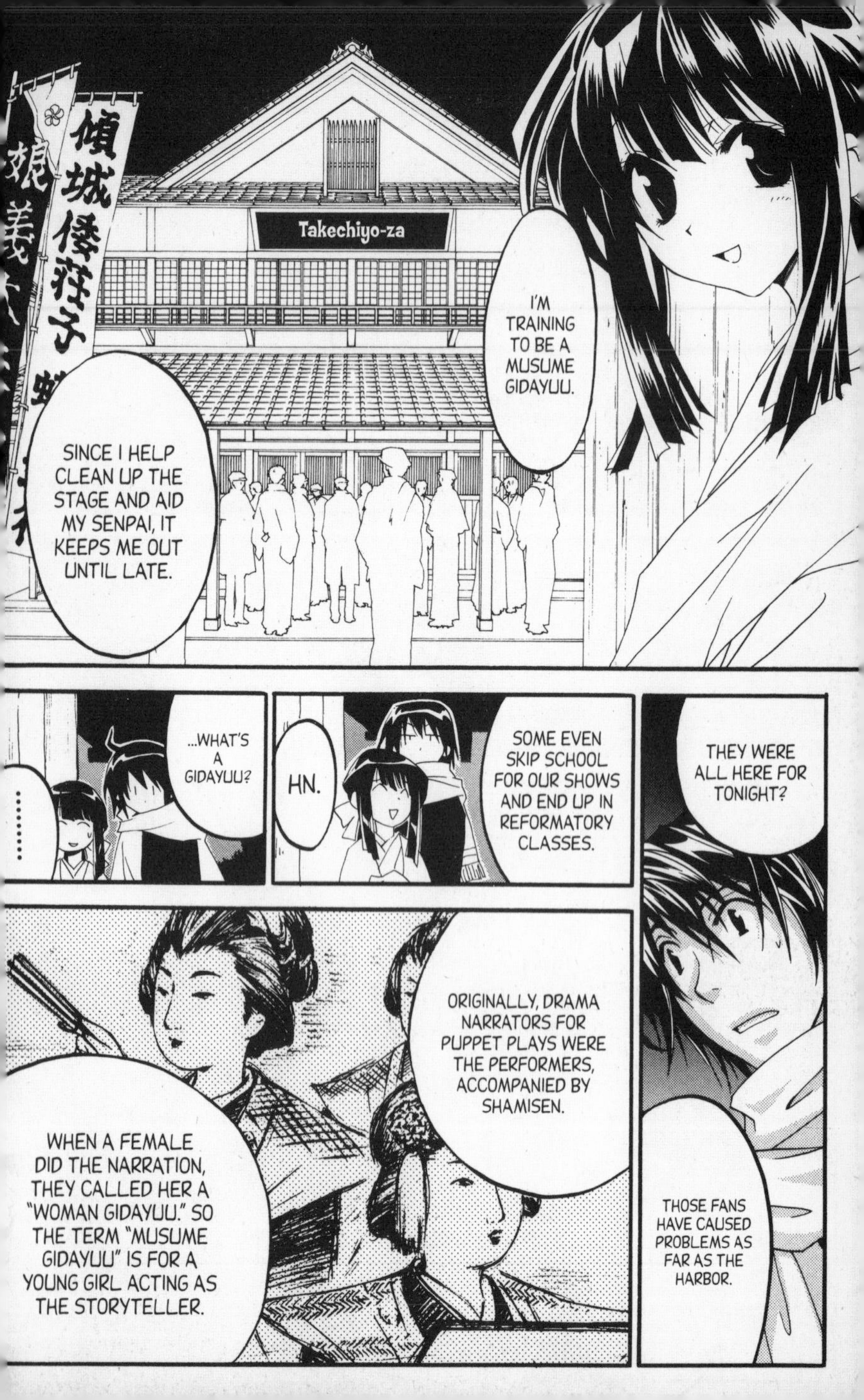
傾城倭荘子
Takechiyo-za
I'M TRAINING TO BE A MUSUME GIDAYUU.
SINCE I HELP CLEAN UP THE STAGE AND AID MY SENPAI, IT KEEPS ME OUT UNTIL LATE.
THEY WERE ALL HERE FOR TONIGHT?
THOSE FANS HAVE CAUSED PROBLEMS AS FAR AS THE HARBOR.
SOME EVEN SKIP SCHOOL FOR OUR SHOWS AND END UP IN REFORMATORY CLASSES.
HN.
...WHAT'S A GIDAYUU?
....
ORIGINALLY, DRAMA NARRATORS FOR PUPPET PLAYS WERE THE PERFORMERS, ACCOMPANIED BY SHAMISEN.
WHEN A FEMALE DID THE NARRATION, THEY CALLED HER A "WOMAN GIDAYUU." SO THE TERM "MUSUME GIDAYUU" IS FOR A YOUNG GIRL ACTING AS THE STORYTELLER.

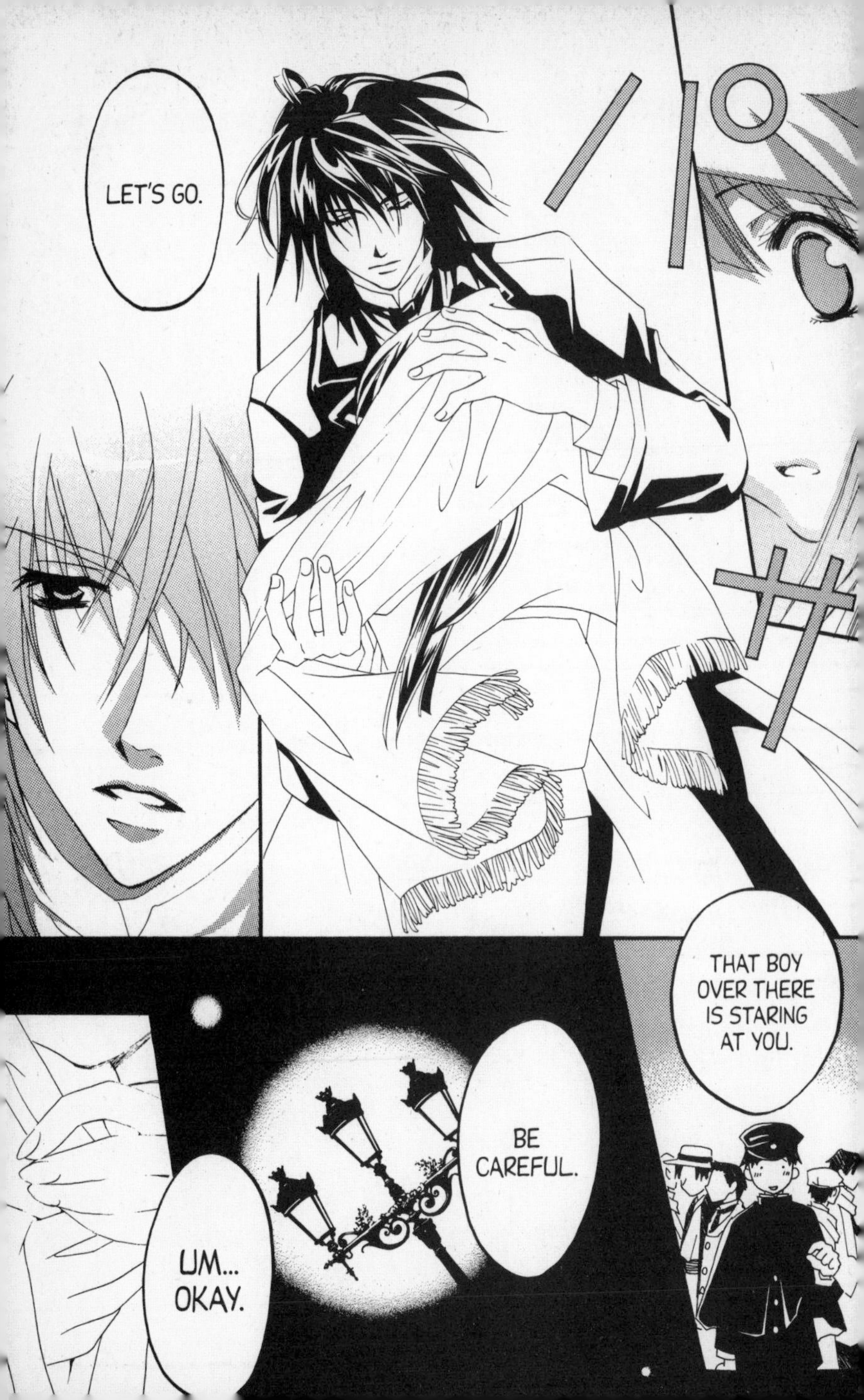
パサ
LET'S GO.
THAT BOY OVER THERE IS STARING AT YOU.
BE CAREFUL.
UM... OKAY.

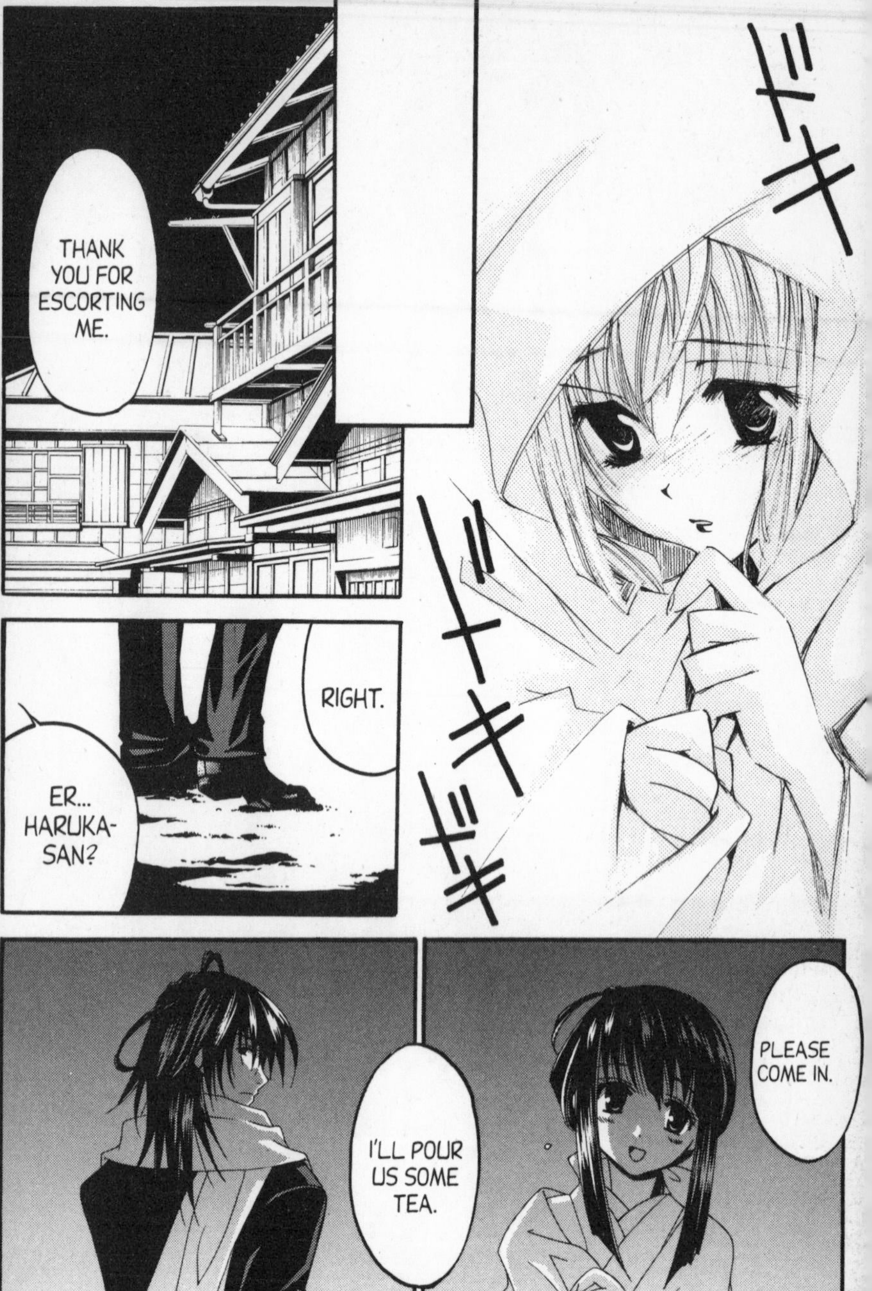
ドキ
ドキドキ
THANK YOU FOR ESCORTING ME.
RIGHT.
ER... HARUKA-SAN?
PLEASE COME IN.
I'LL POUR US SOME TEA.

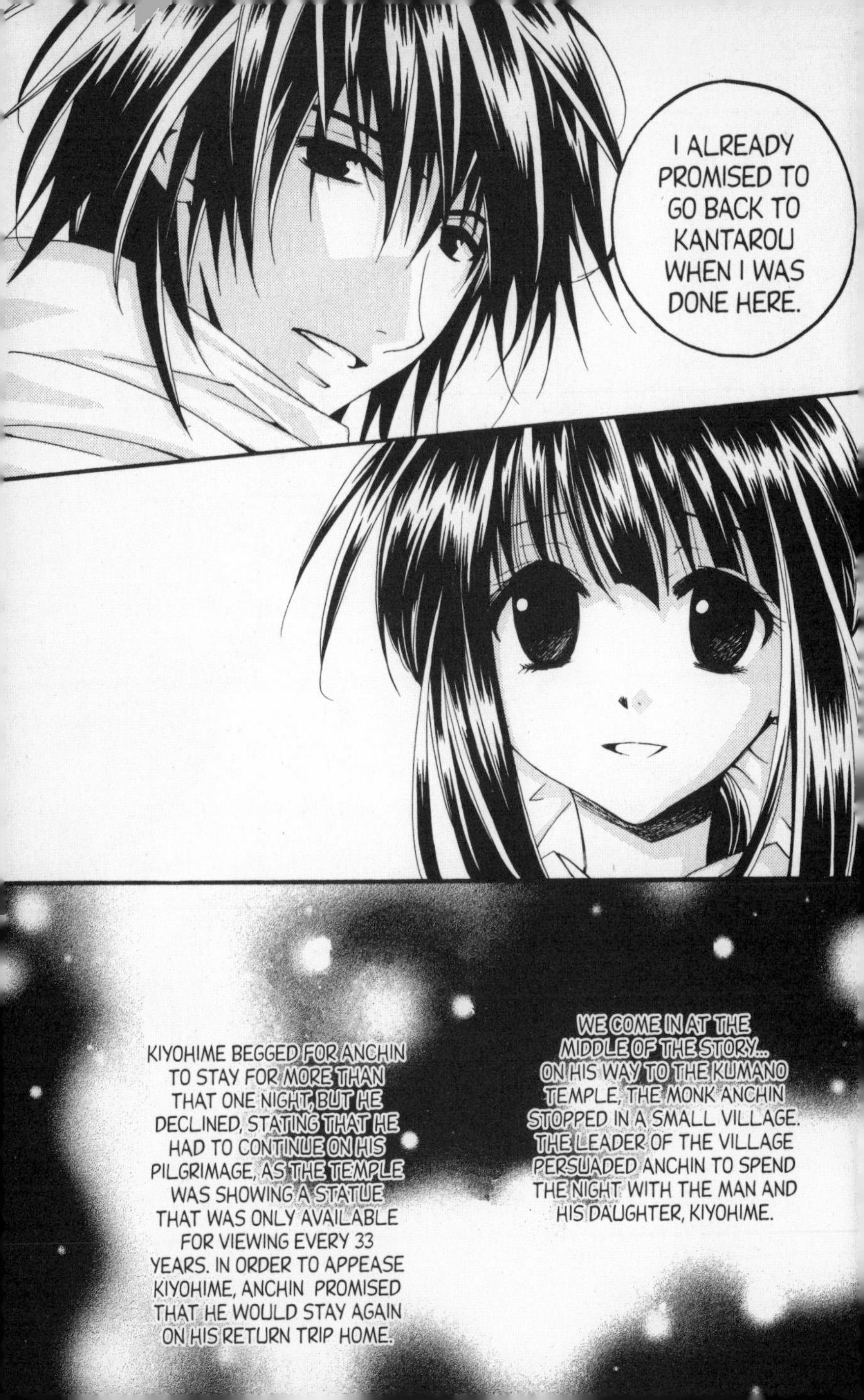
I ALREADY PROMISED TO GO BACK TO KANTAROU WHEN I WAS DONE HERE.
WE COME IN AT THE MIDDLE OF THE STORY... ON HIS WAY TO THE KUMANO TEMPLE, THE MONK ANCHIN STOPPED IN A SMALL VILLAGE. THE LEADER OF THE VILLAGE PERSUADED ANCHIN TO SPEND THE NIGHT WITH THE MAN AND HIS DAUGHTER, KIYOHIME.
KIYOHIME BEGGED FOR ANCHIN TO STAY FOR MORE THAN THAT ONE NIGHT, BUT HE DECLINED, STATING THAT HE HAD TO CONTINUE ON HIS PILGRIMAGE, AS THE TEMPLE WAS SHOWING A STATUE THAT WAS ONLY AVAILABLE FOR VIEWING EVERY 33 YEARS. IN ORDER TO APPEASE KIYOHIME, ANCHIN PROMISED THAT HE WOULD STAY AGAIN ON HIS RETURN TRIP HOME.

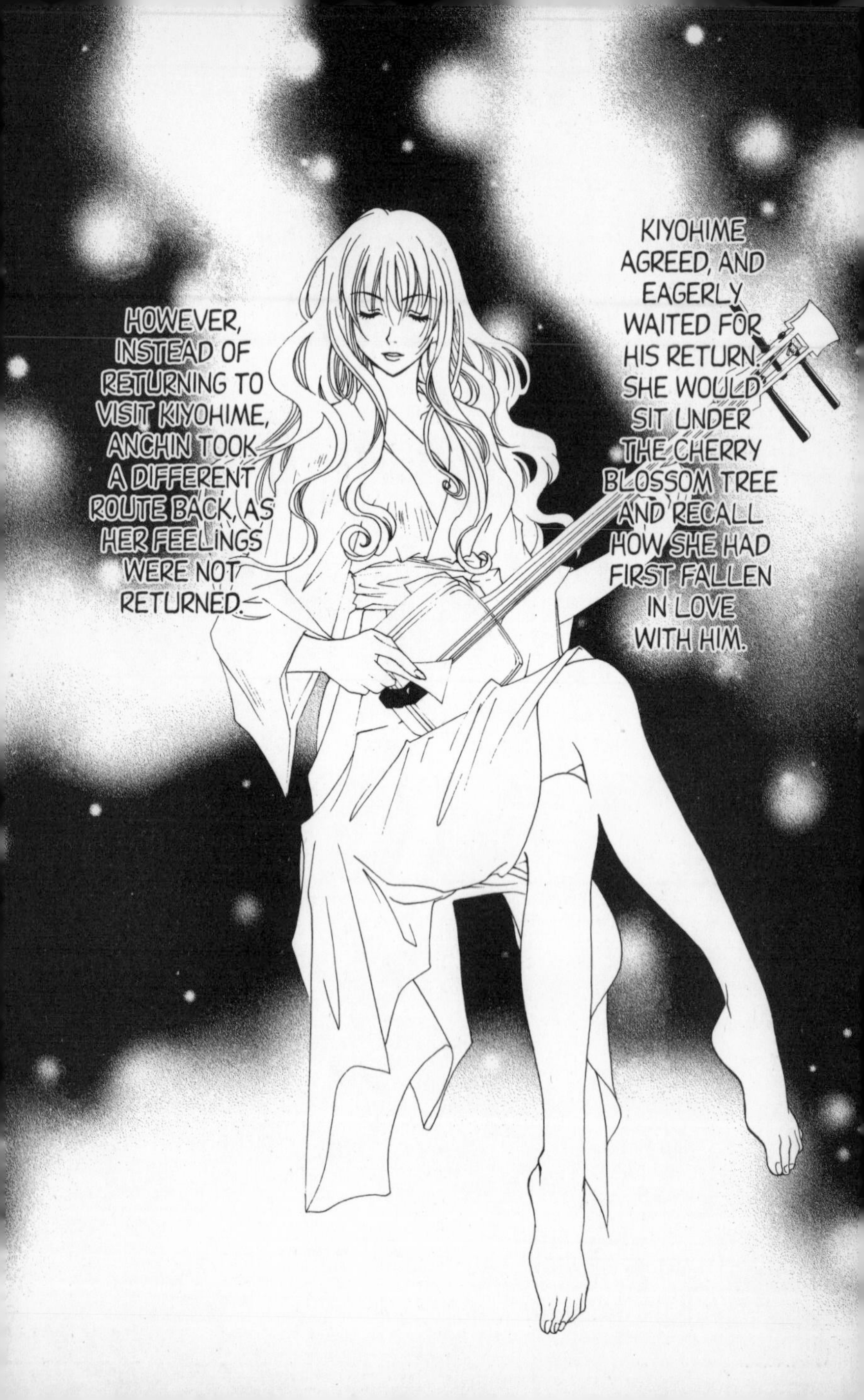
KIYOHIME AGREED, AND EAGERLY WAITED FOR HIS RETURN. SHE WOULD SIT UNDER THE CHERRY BLOSSOM TREE AND RECALL HOW SHE HAD FIRST FALLEN IN LOVE WITH HIM.
HOWEVER, INSTEAD OF RETURNING TO VISIT KIYOHIME, ANCHIN TOOK A DIFFERENT ROUTE BACK, AS HER FEELINGS WERE NOT RETURNED.

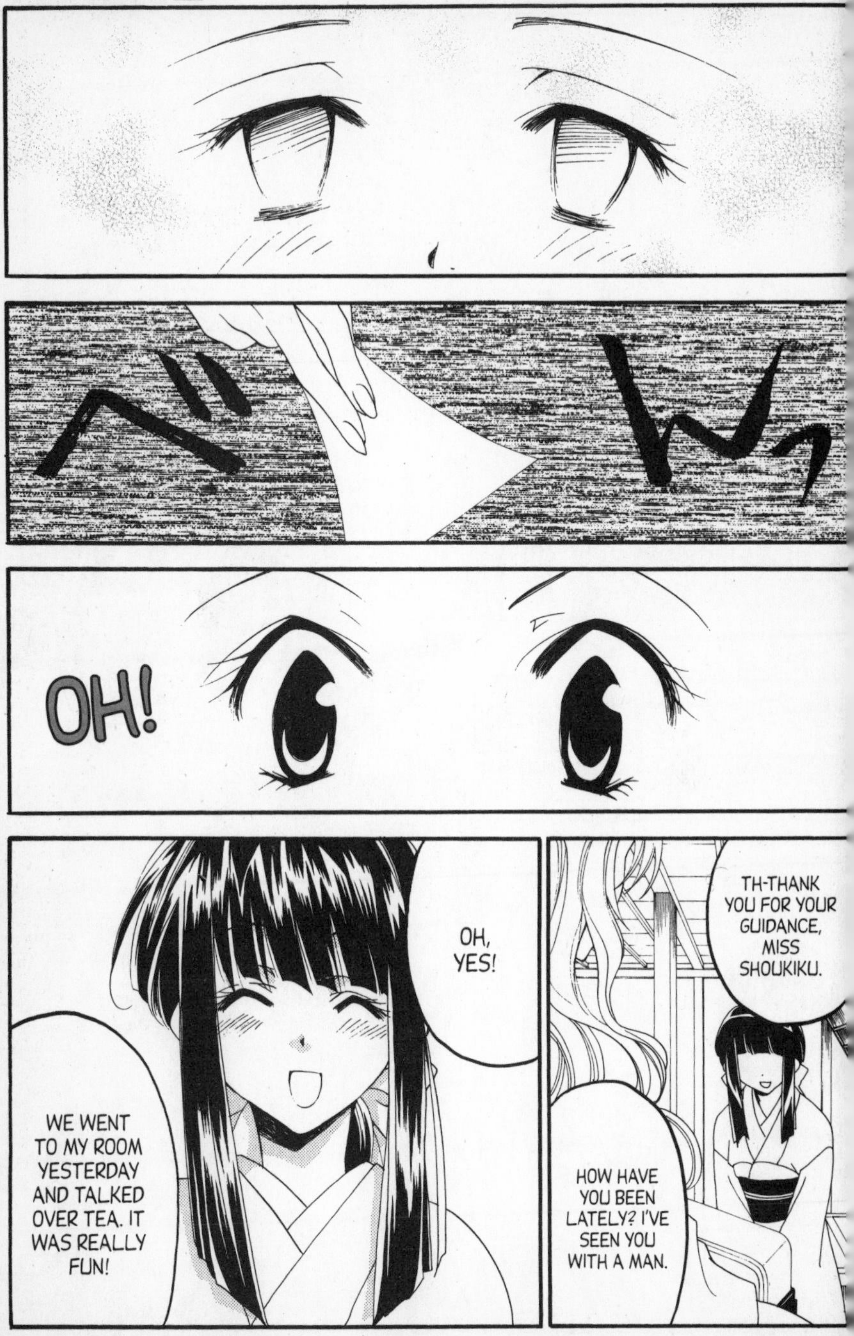
OH!
TH-THANK YOU FOR YOUR GUIDANCE, MISS SHOUKIKU.
HOW HAVE YOU BEEN LATELY? I'VE SEEN YOU WITH A MAN.
OH, YES!
WE WENT TO MY ROOM YESTERDAY AND TALKED OVER TEA. IT WAS REALLY FUN!

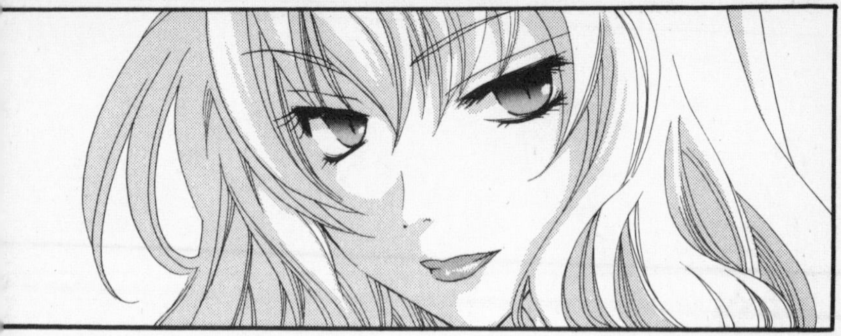

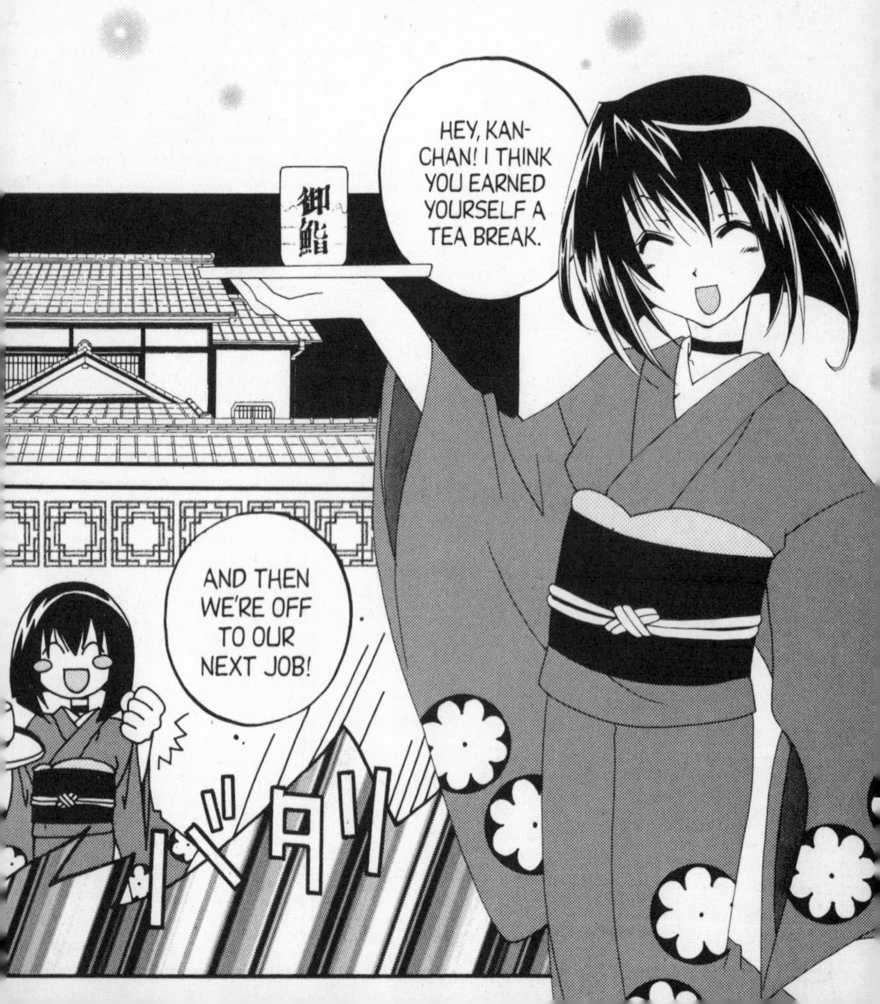
HEY, KAN-CHAN! I THINK YOU EARNED YOURSELF A TEA BREAK.
AND THEN WE'RE OFF TO OUR NEXT JOB!

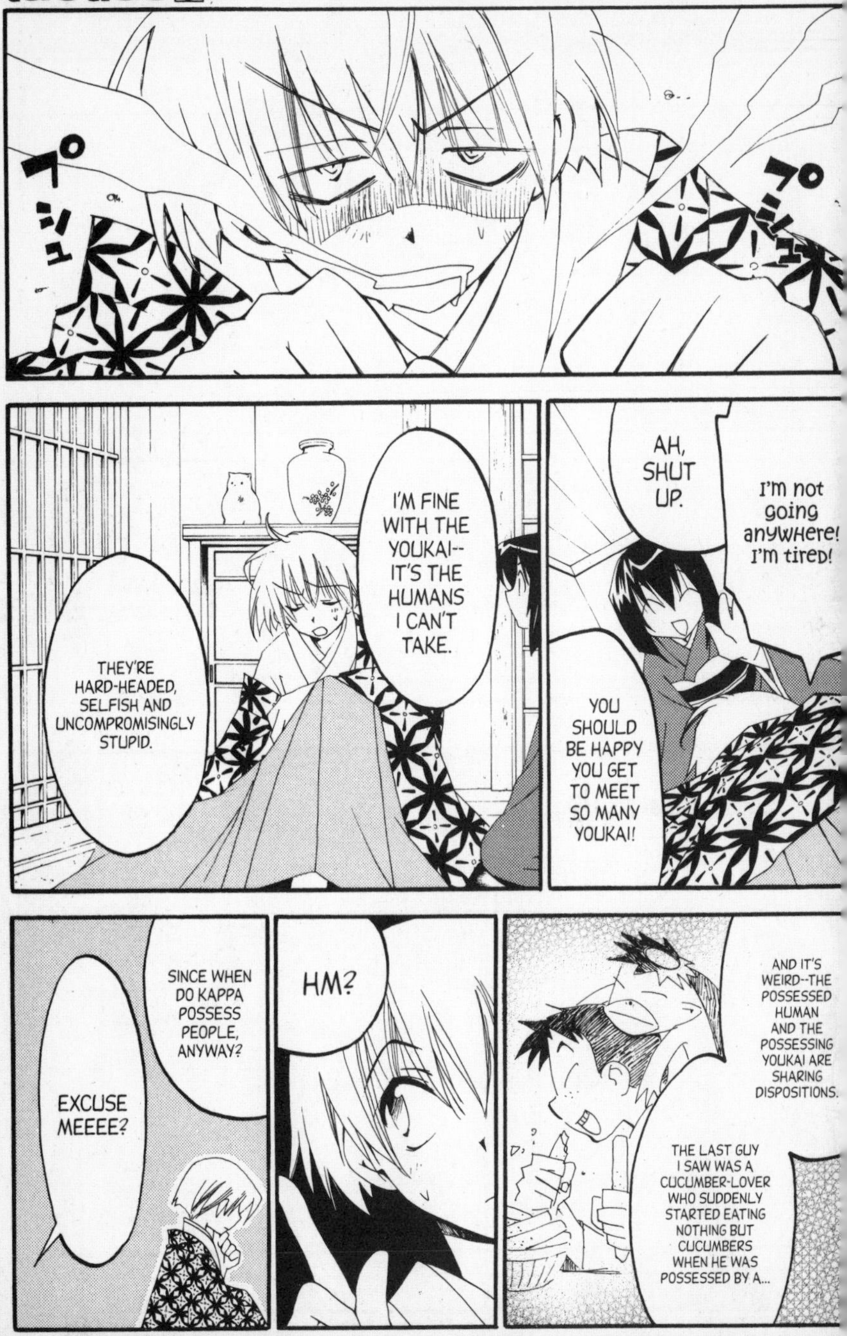
プシュ
プシュ
I'm not going anywhere! I'm tired!
AH, SHUT UP.
YOU SHOULD BE HAPPY YOU GET TO MEET SO MANY YOUKAI!
I'M FINE WITH THE YOUKAI-- IT'S THE HUMANS I CAN'T TAKE.
THEY'RE HARD-HEADED, SELFISH AND UNCOMPROMISINGLY STUPID.
AND IT'S WEIRD--THE POSSESSED HUMAN AND THE POSSESSING YOUKAI ARE SHARING DISPOSITIONS.
THE LAST GUY I SAW WAS A CUCUMBER-LOVER WHO SUDDENLY STARTED EATING NOTHING BUT CUCUMBERS WHEN HE WAS POSSESSED BY A...
HM?
SINCE WHEN DO KAPPA POSSESS PEOPLE, ANYWAY?
EXCUSE MEEEE?

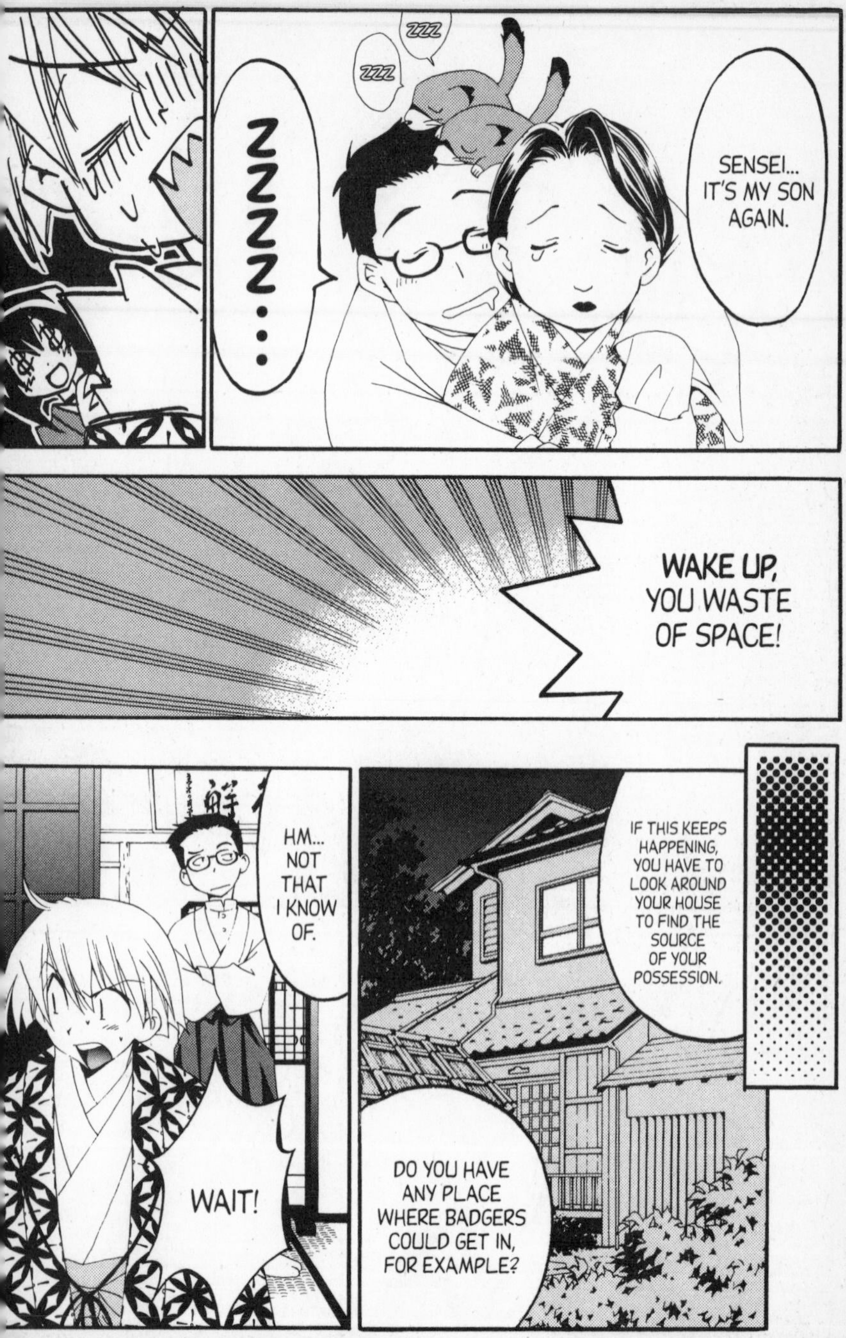
SENSEI... IT'S MY SON AGAIN.
ZZZ
ZZZ
ZZZZ...
WAKE UP, YOU WASTE OF SPACE!
IF THIS KEEPS HAPPENING, YOU HAVE TO LOOK AROUND YOUR HOUSE TO FIND THE SOURCE OF YOUR POSSESSION.
DO YOU HAVE ANY PLACE WHERE BADGERS COULD GET IN, FOR EXAMPLE?
HM... NOT THAT I KNOW OF.
WAIT!

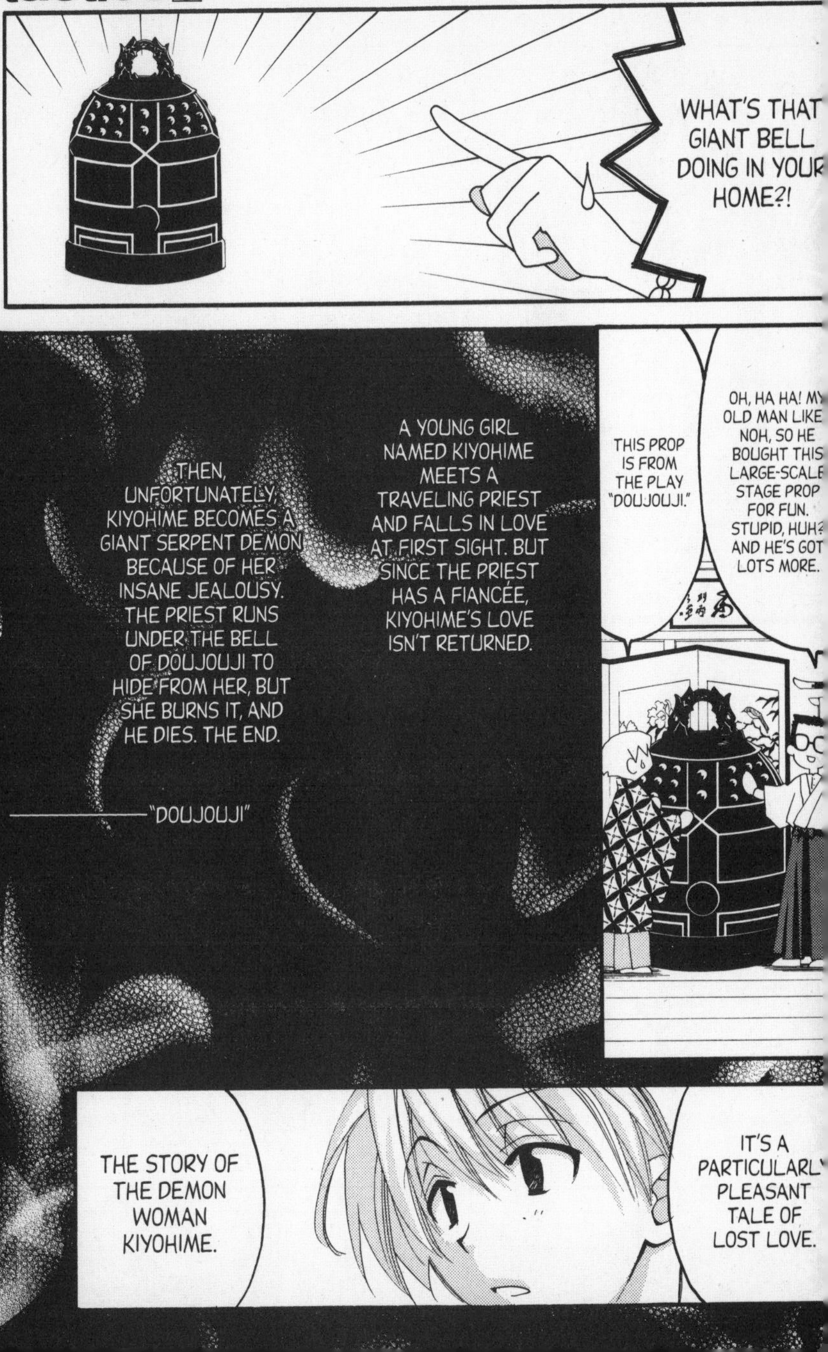
WHAT'S THAT GIANT BELL DOING IN YOUR HOME?!
OH, HA HA! MY OLD MAN LIKE NOH, SO HE BOUGHT THIS LARGE-SCALE STAGE PROP FOR FUN. STUPID, HUH? AND HE'S GOT LOTS MORE.
THIS PROP IS FROM THE PLAY "DOUJOUJI."
A YOUNG GIRL NAMED KIYOHIME MEETS A TRAVELING PRIEST AND FALLS IN LOVE AT FIRST SIGHT. BUT SINCE THE PRIEST HAS A FIANCÉE, KIYOHIME'S LOVE ISN'T RETURNED.
THEN, UNFORTUNATELY, KIYOHIME BECOMES A GIANT SERPENT DEMON BECAUSE OF HER INSANE JEALOUSY. THE PRIEST RUNS UNDER THE BELL OF DOUJOUJI TO HIDE FROM HER, BUT SHE BURNS IT, AND HE DIES. THE END.
——"DOUJOUJI"
IT'S A PARTICULARLY PLEASANT TALE OF LOST LOVE.
THE STORY OF THE DEMON WOMAN KIYOHIME.

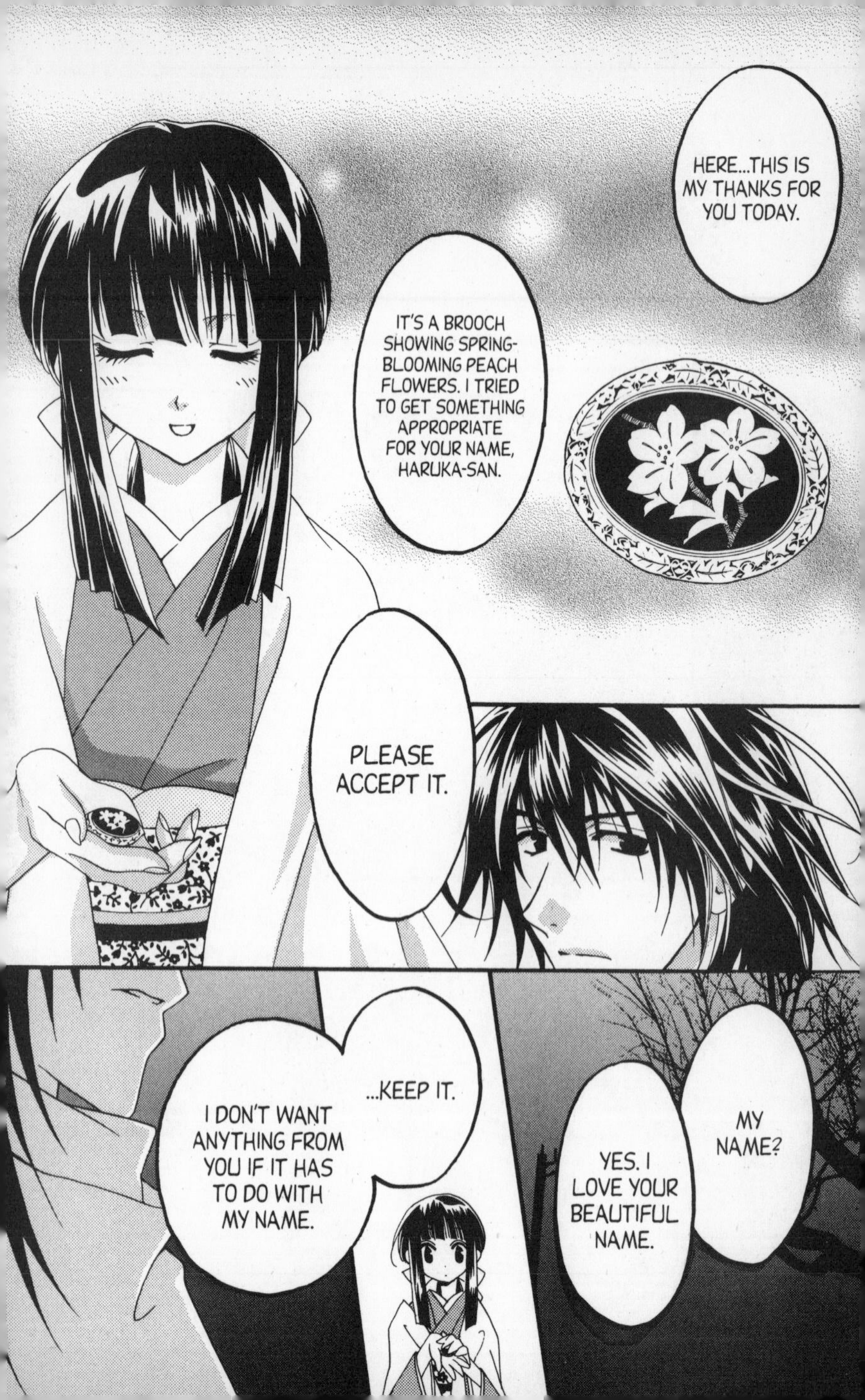
HERE...THIS IS MY THANKS FOR YOU TODAY.
IT'S A BROOCH SHOWING SPRING-BLOOMING PEACH FLOWERS. I TRIED TO GET SOMETHING APPROPRIATE FOR YOUR NAME, HARUKA-SAN.
PLEASE ACCEPT IT.
MY NAME?
YES. I LOVE YOUR BEAUTIFUL NAME.
...KEEP IT.
I DON'T WANT ANYTHING FROM YOU IF IT HAS TO DO WITH MY NAME.

MY NAME ISN'T SOMETHING TO BE TREATED SO CASUALLY.

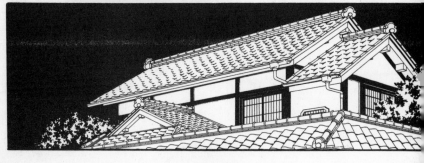

HARUKA.

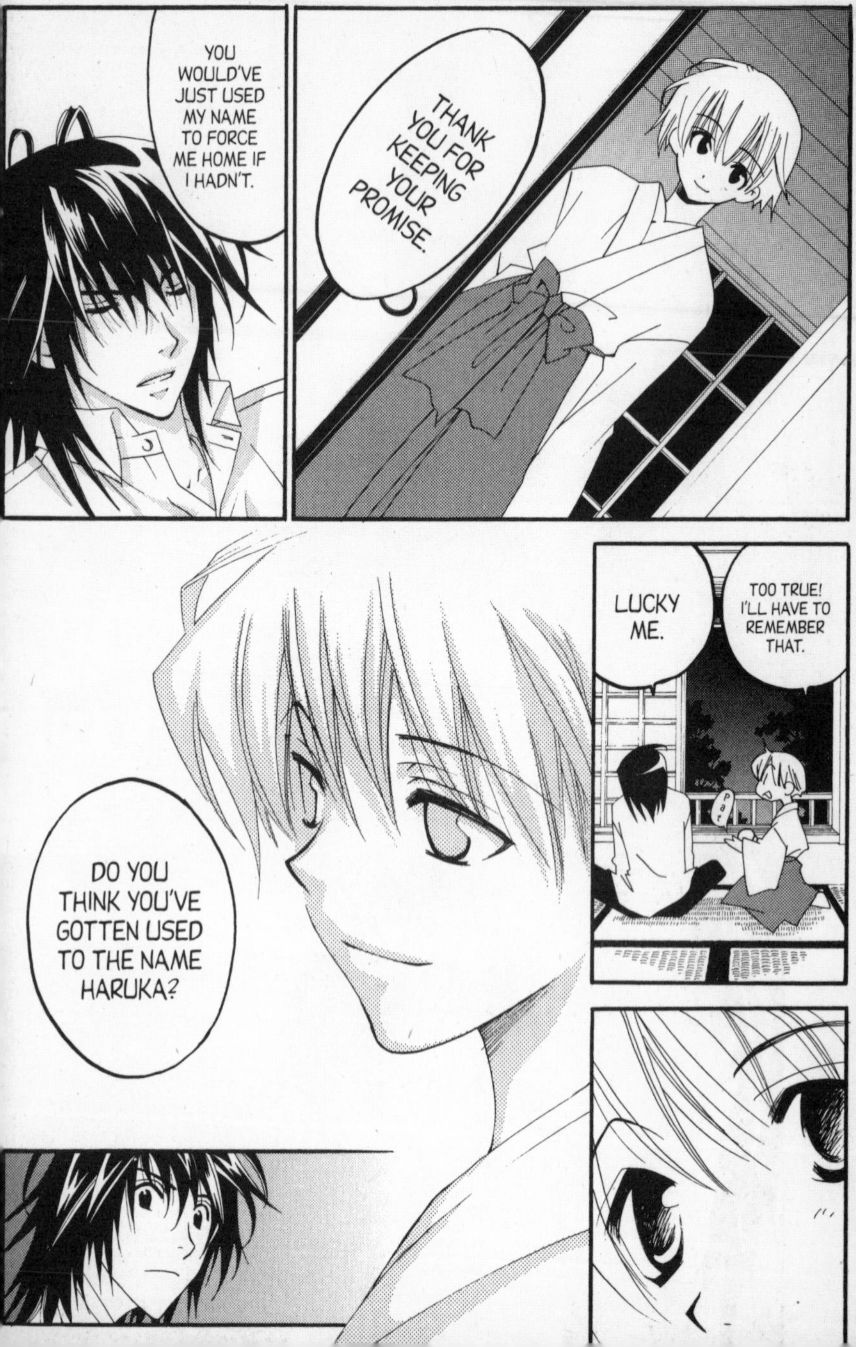
THANK YOU FOR KEEPING YOUR PROMISE.
YOU WOULD'VE JUST USED MY NAME TO FORCE ME HOME IF I HADN'T.
TOO TRUE! I'LL HAVE TO REMEMBER THAT.
LUCKY ME.
Pat
DO YOU THINK YOU'VE GOTTEN USED TO THE NAME HARUKA?

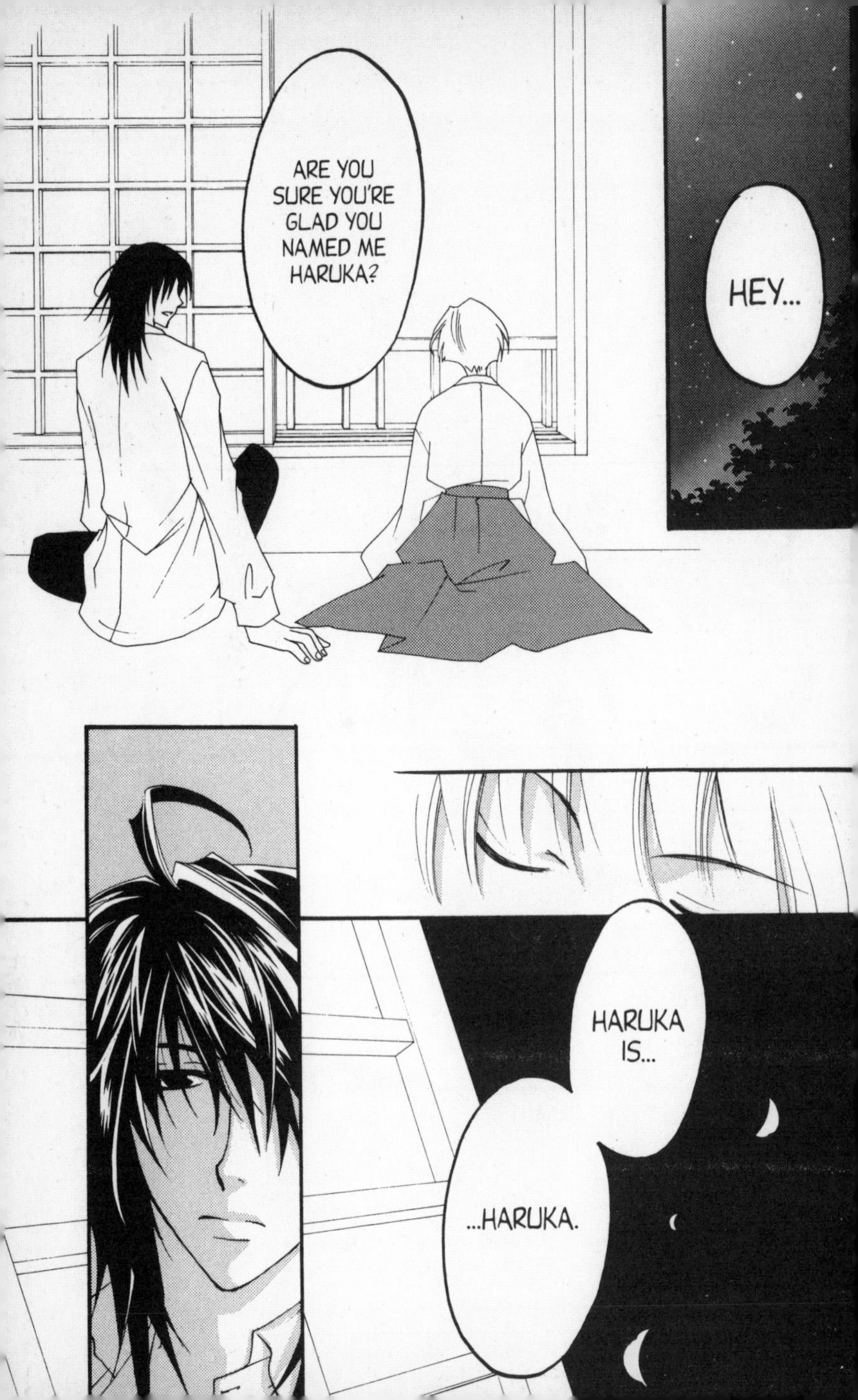
HEY...
ARE YOU SURE YOU'RE GLAD YOU NAMED ME HARUKA?
HARUKA IS...
...HARUKA.

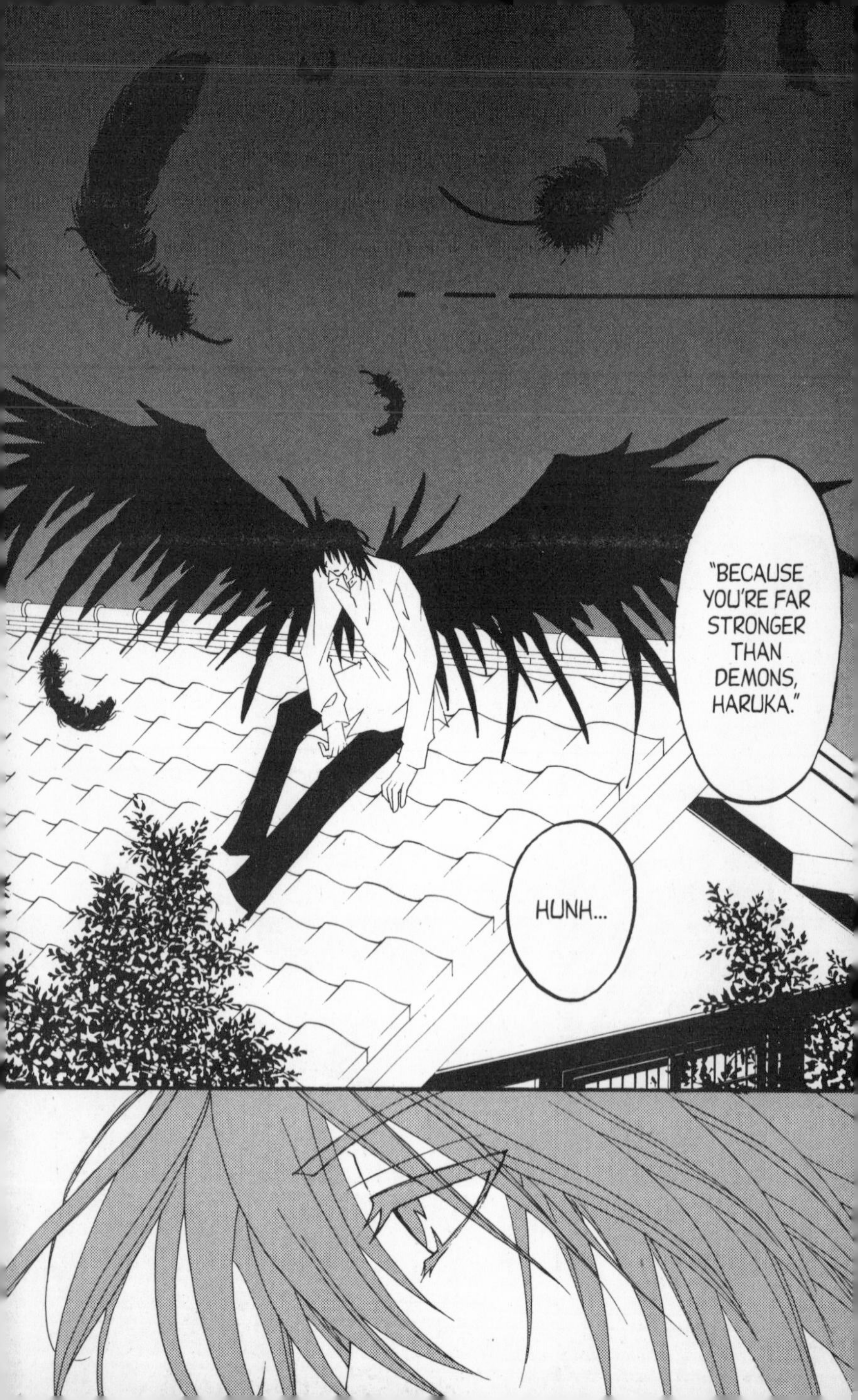
"BECAUSE YOU'RE FAR STRONGER THAN DEMONS, HARUKA."
HUNH...

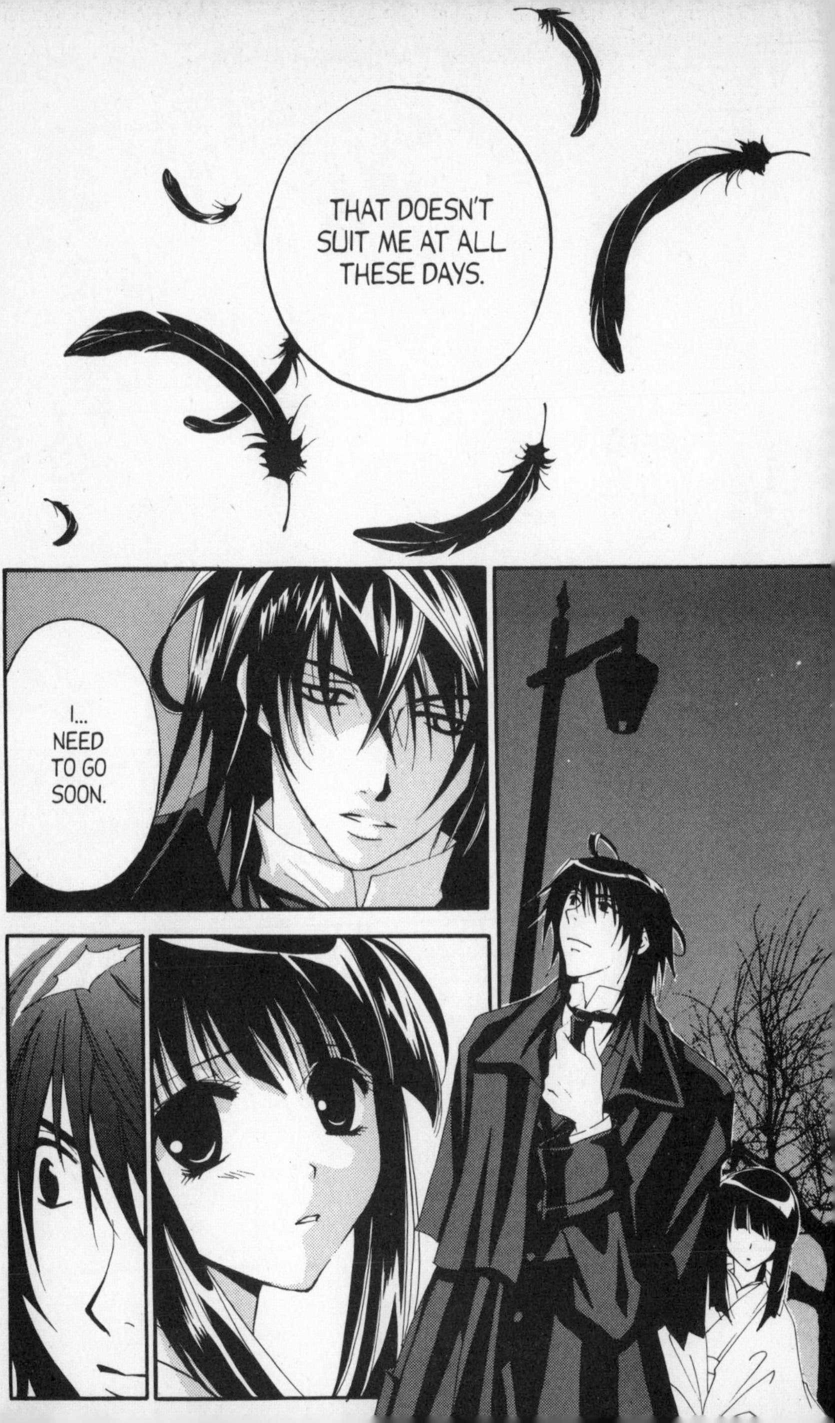
THAT DOESN'T SUIT ME AT ALL THESE DAYS.
I... NEED TO GO SOON.

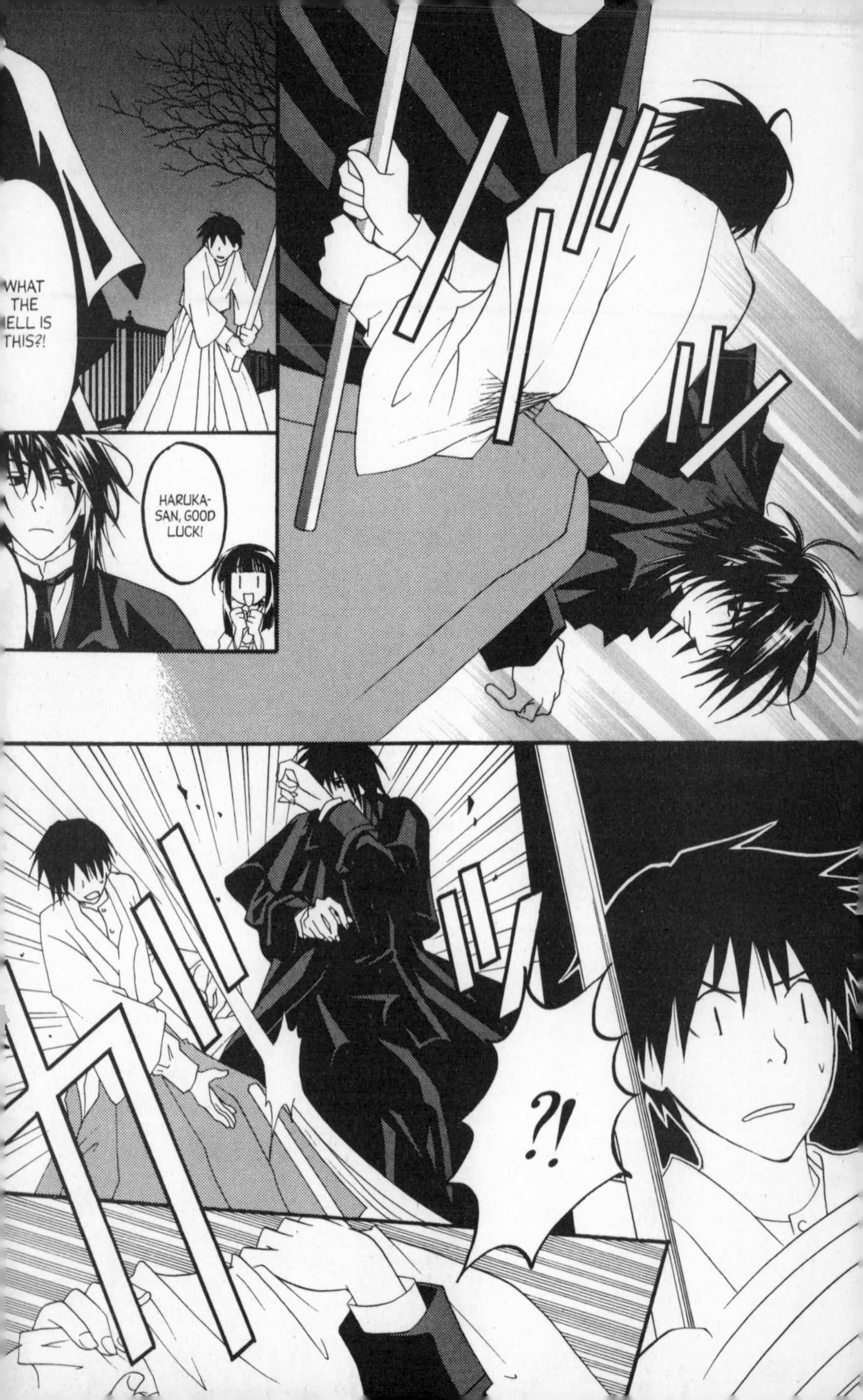
WHAT THE HELL IS THIS?!
HARUKA-SAN, GOOD LUCK!
?!

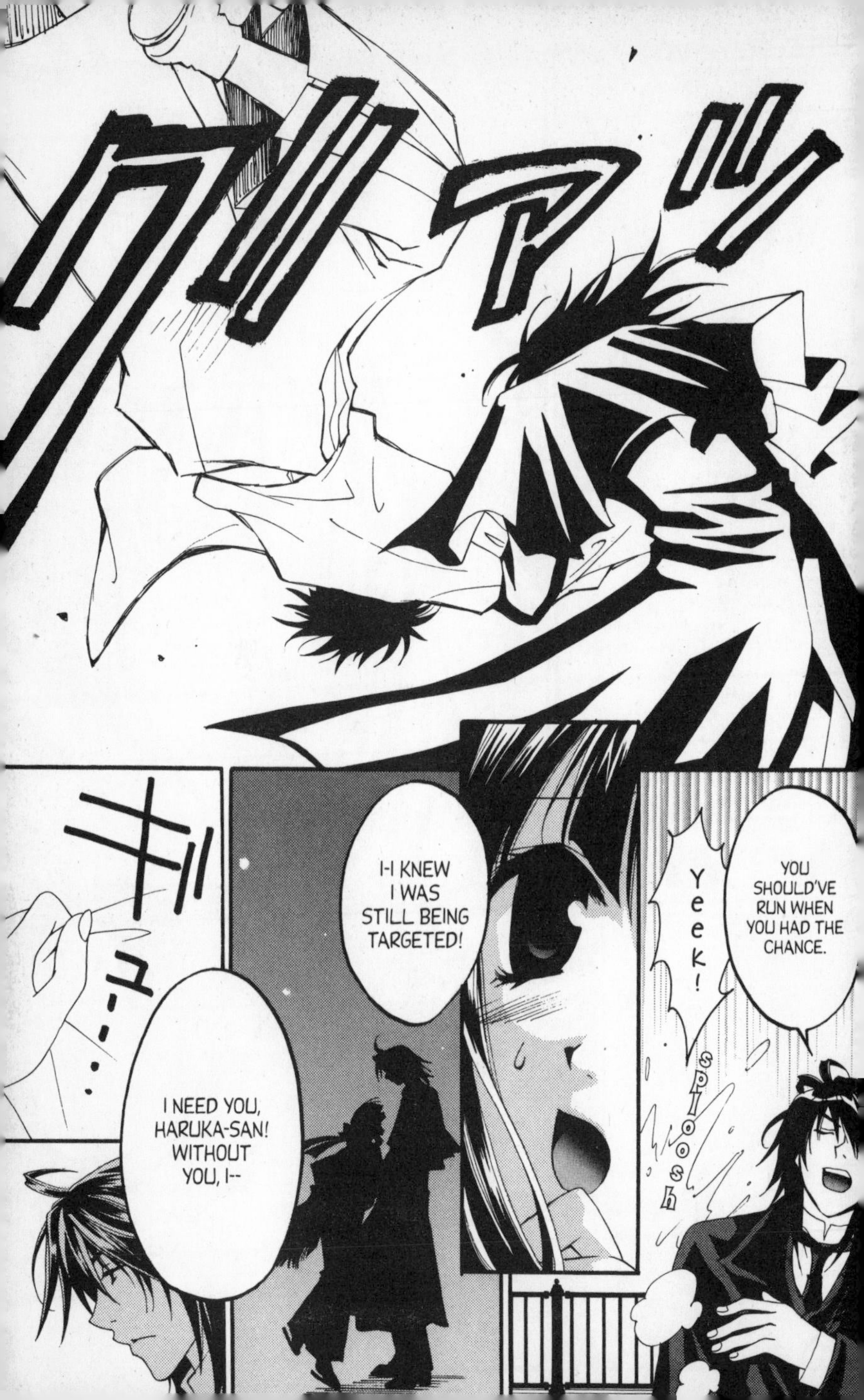

クリアッ
YOU SHOULD'VE RUN WHEN YOU HAD THE CHANCE.
Yeek!
sploosh
I-I KNEW I WAS STILL BEING TARGETED!
I NEED YOU, HARUKA-SAN! WITHOUT YOU, I--
ギュ…

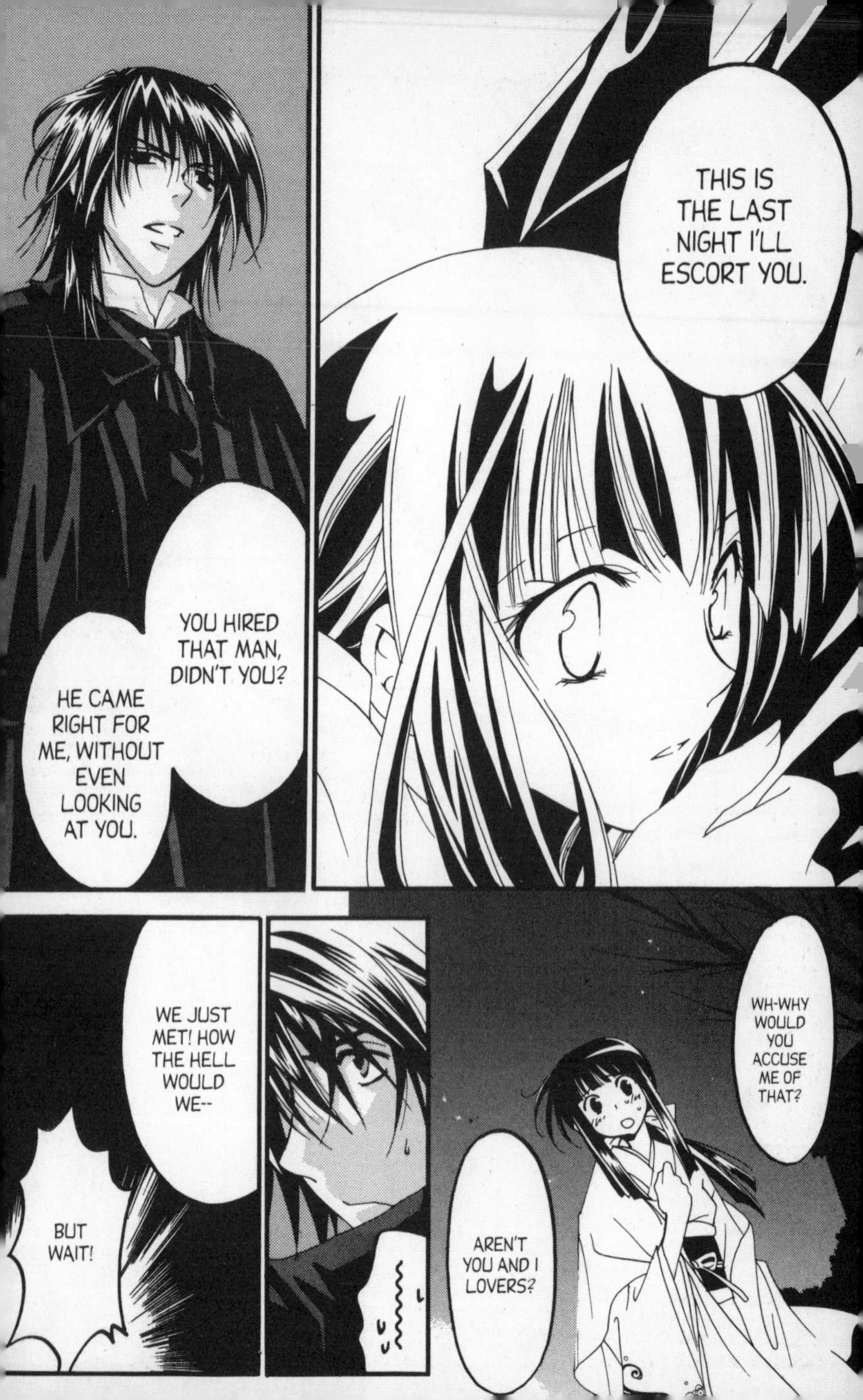
THIS IS THE LAST NIGHT I'LL ESCORT YOU.
YOU HIRED THAT MAN, DIDN'T YOU?
HE CAME RIGHT FOR ME, WITHOUT EVEN LOOKING AT YOU.
WH-WHY WOULD YOU ACCUSE ME OF THAT?
AREN'T YOU AND I LOVERS?
WE JUST MET! HOW THE HELL WOULD WE--
BUT WAIT!

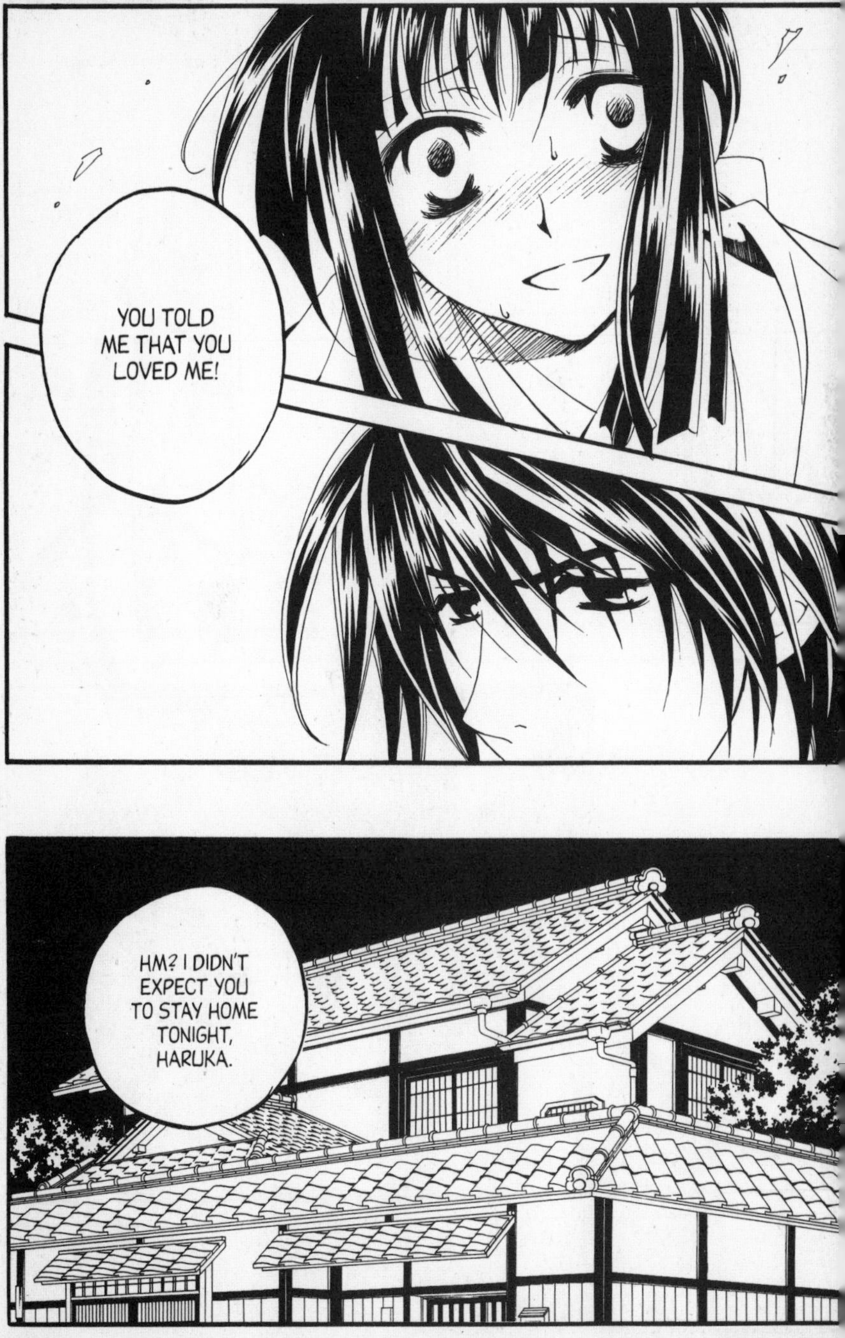
YOU TOLD ME THAT YOU LOVED ME!
HM? I DIDN'T EXPECT YOU TO STAY HOME TONIGHT, HARUKA.

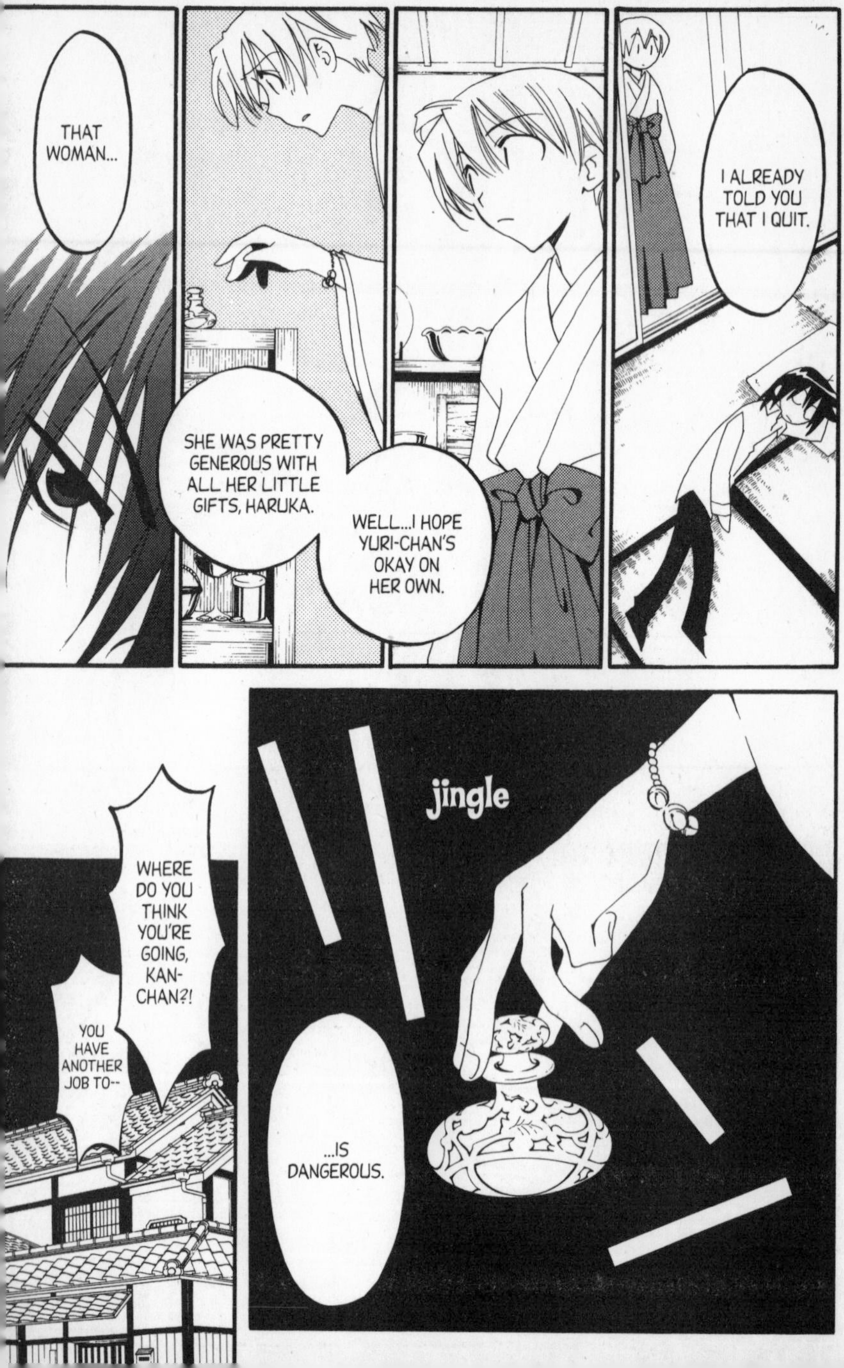

I ALREADY TOLD YOU THAT I QUIT.
SHE WAS PRETTY GENEROUS WITH ALL HER LITTLE GIFTS, HARUKA.
WELL...I HOPE YURI-CHAN'S OKAY ON HER OWN.
THAT WOMAN...
jingle
...IS DANGEROUS.
WHERE DO YOU THINK YOU'RE GOING, KAN-CHAN?!
YOU HAVE ANOTHER JOB TO--

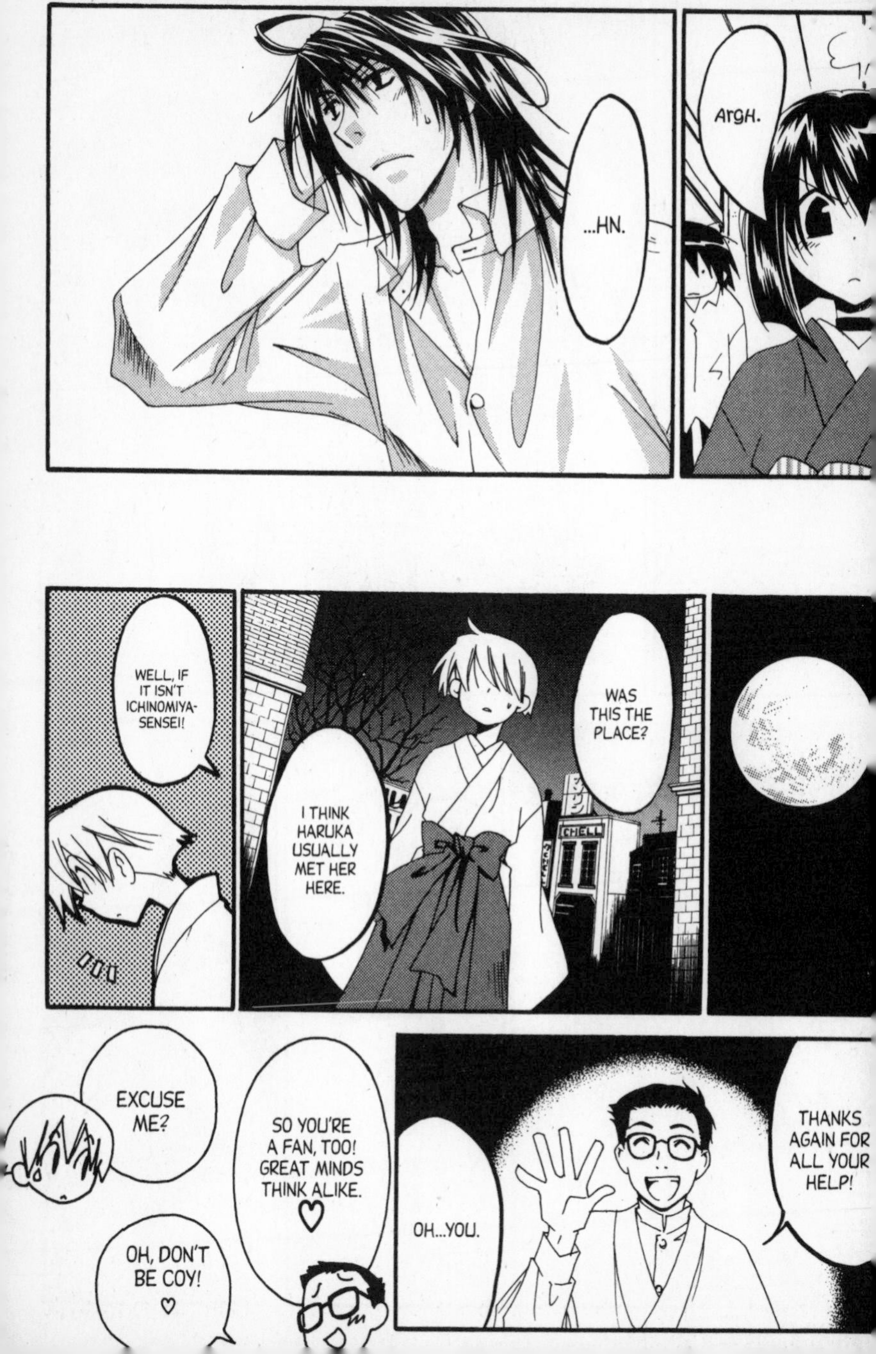
Argh.
...HN.
WAS THIS THE PLACE?
I THINK HARUKA USUALLY MET HER HERE.
WELL, IF IT ISN'T ICHINOMIYA-SENSEI!
THANKS AGAIN FOR ALL YOUR HELP!
OH...YOU.
SO YOU'RE A FAN, TOO! GREAT MINDS THINK ALIKE. ♡
EXCUSE ME?
OH, DON'T BE COY! ♡

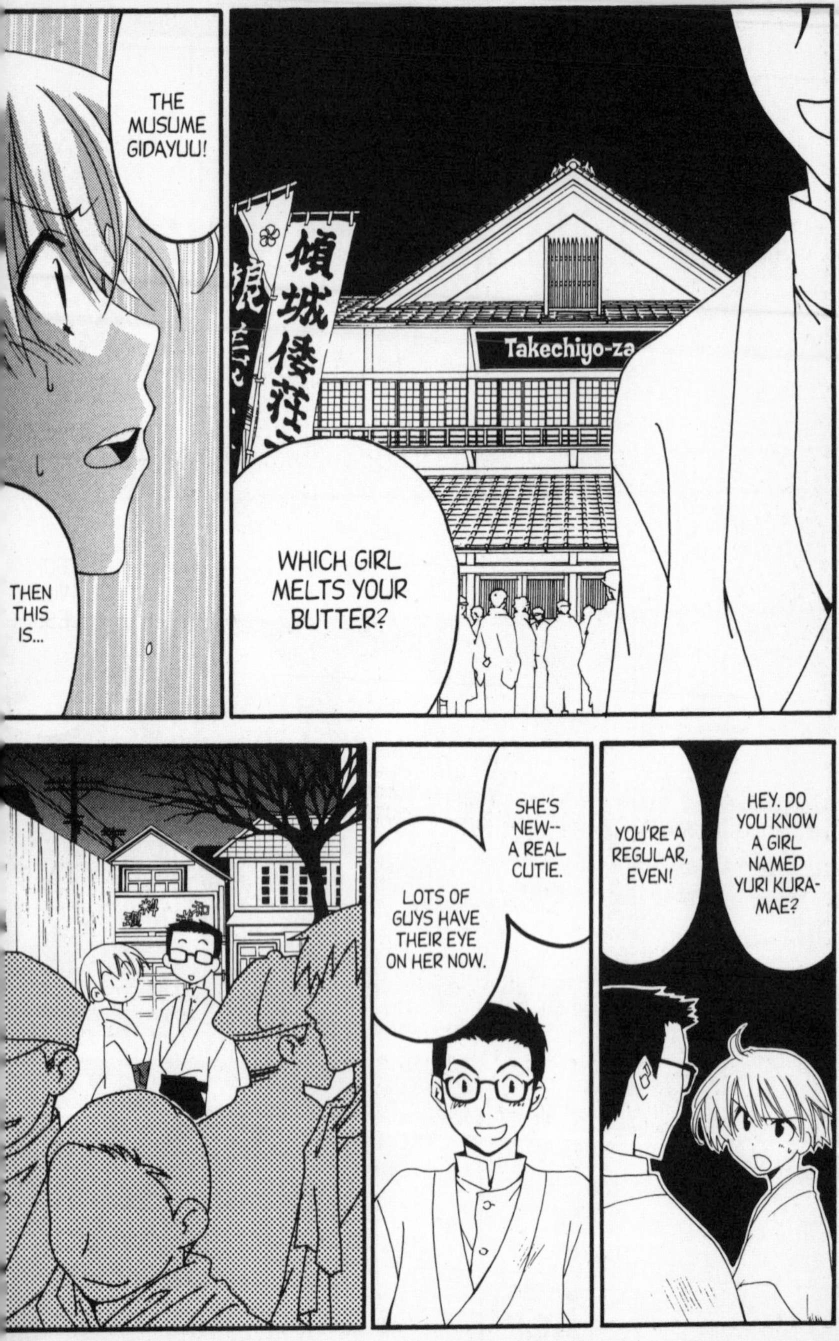
Takechiyo-za
WHICH GIRL MELTS YOUR BUTTER?
THE MUSUME GIDAYUU!
THEN THIS IS...
HEY. DO YOU KNOW A GIRL NAMED YURI KURA-MAE?
YOU'RE A REGULAR, EVEN!
SHE'S NEW-- A REAL CUTIE.
LOTS OF GUYS HAVE THEIR EYE ON HER NOW.

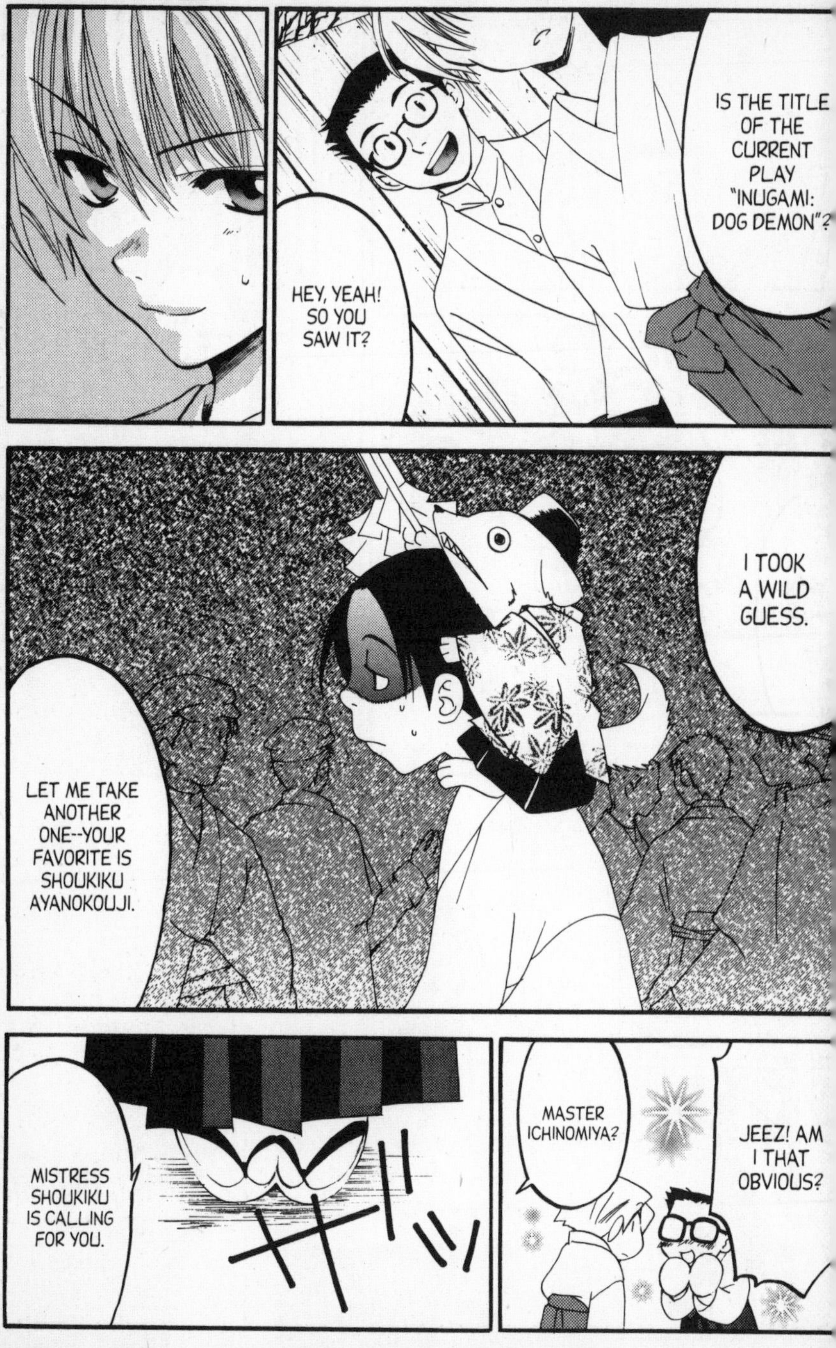
IS THE TITLE OF THE CURRENT PLAY "INUGAMI: DOG DEMON"?
HEY, YEAH! SO YOU SAW IT?
I TOOK A WILD GUESS.
LET ME TAKE ANOTHER ONE--YOUR FAVORITE IS SHOUKIKU AYANOKOUJI.
JEEZ! AM I THAT OBVIOUS?
MASTER ICHINOMIYA?
MISTRESS SHOUKIKU IS CALLING FOR YOU.

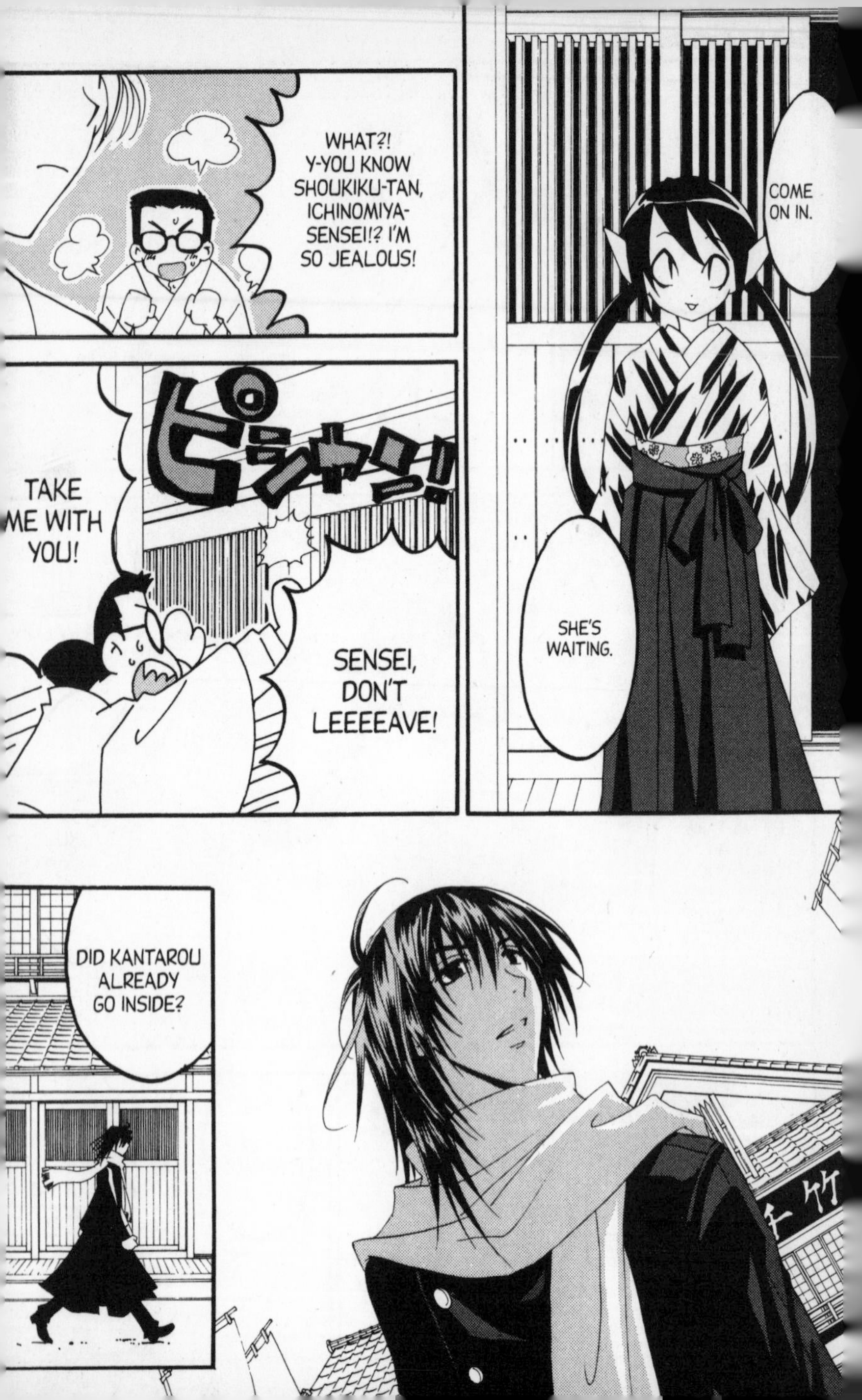
COME ON IN.
SHE'S WAITING.
WHAT?! Y-YOU KNOW SHOUKIKU-TAN, ICHINOMIYA-SENSEI!? I'M SO JEALOUS!
ピシャン!!
SENSEI, DON'T LEEEEAVE!
TAKE ME WITH YOU!
DID KANTAROU ALREADY GO INSIDE?

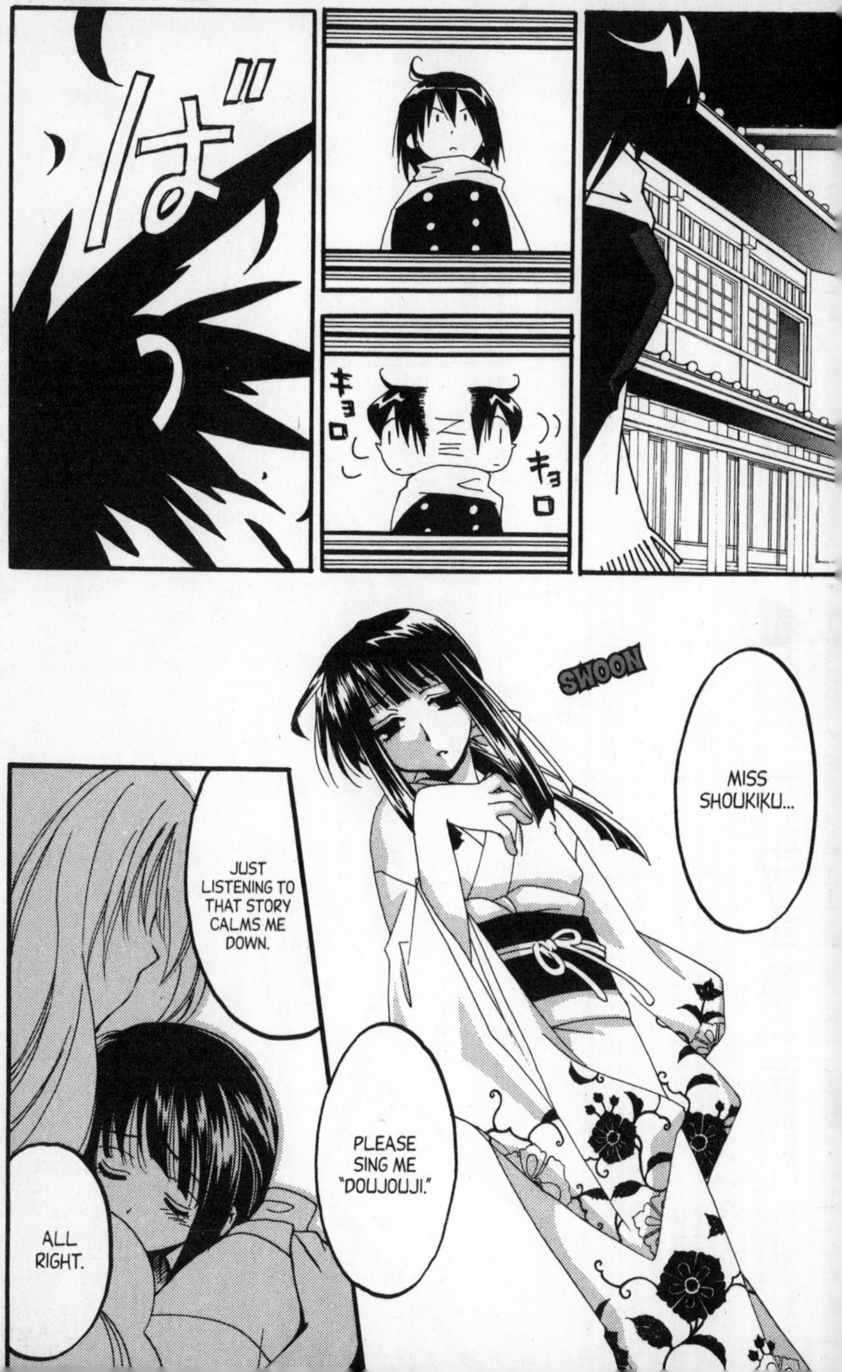
キョロ
キョロ
ばっ
SWOON
MISS SHOUKIKU...
JUST LISTENING TO THAT STORY CALMS ME DOWN.
PLEASE SING ME "DOUJOUJI."
ALL RIGHT.

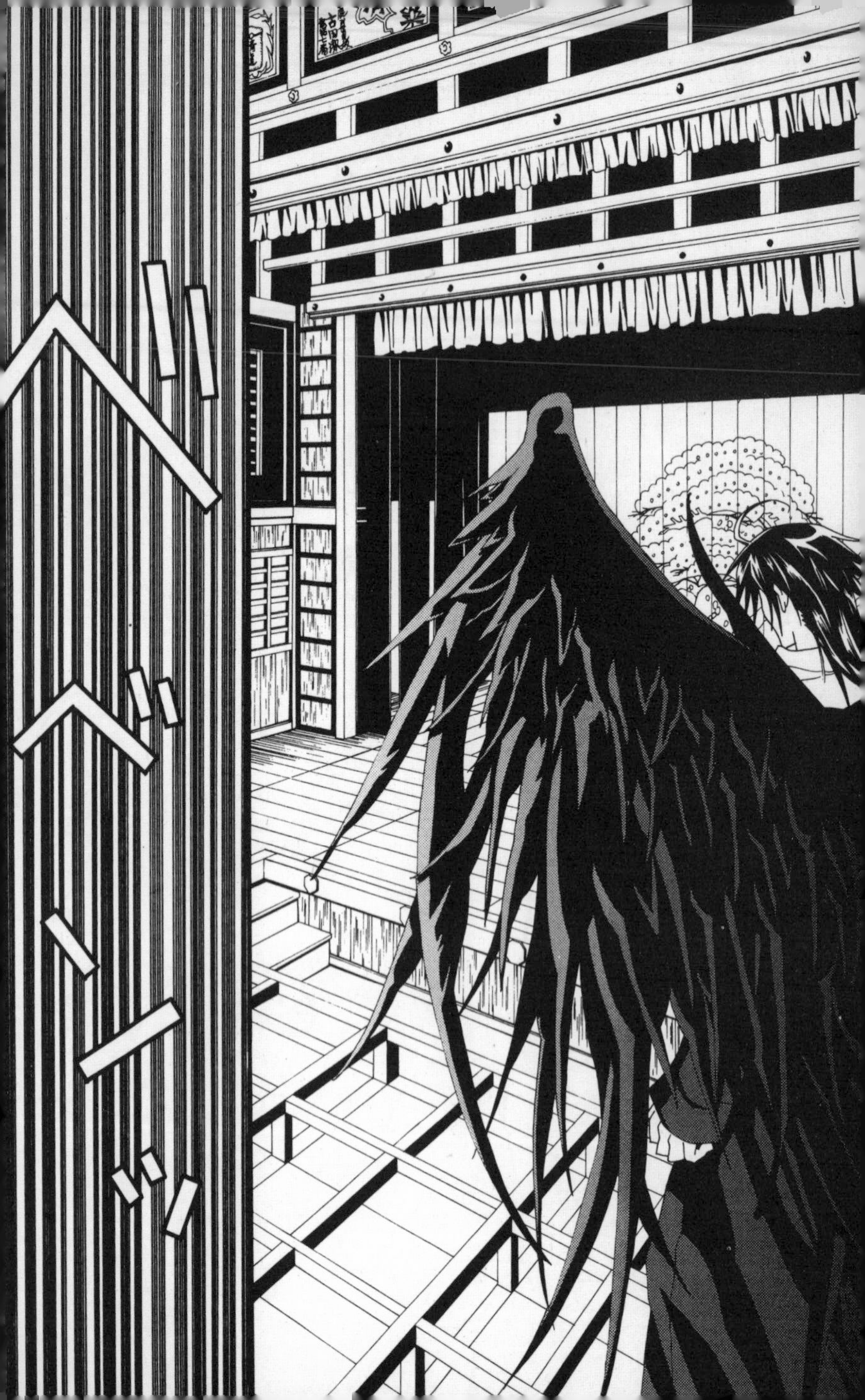

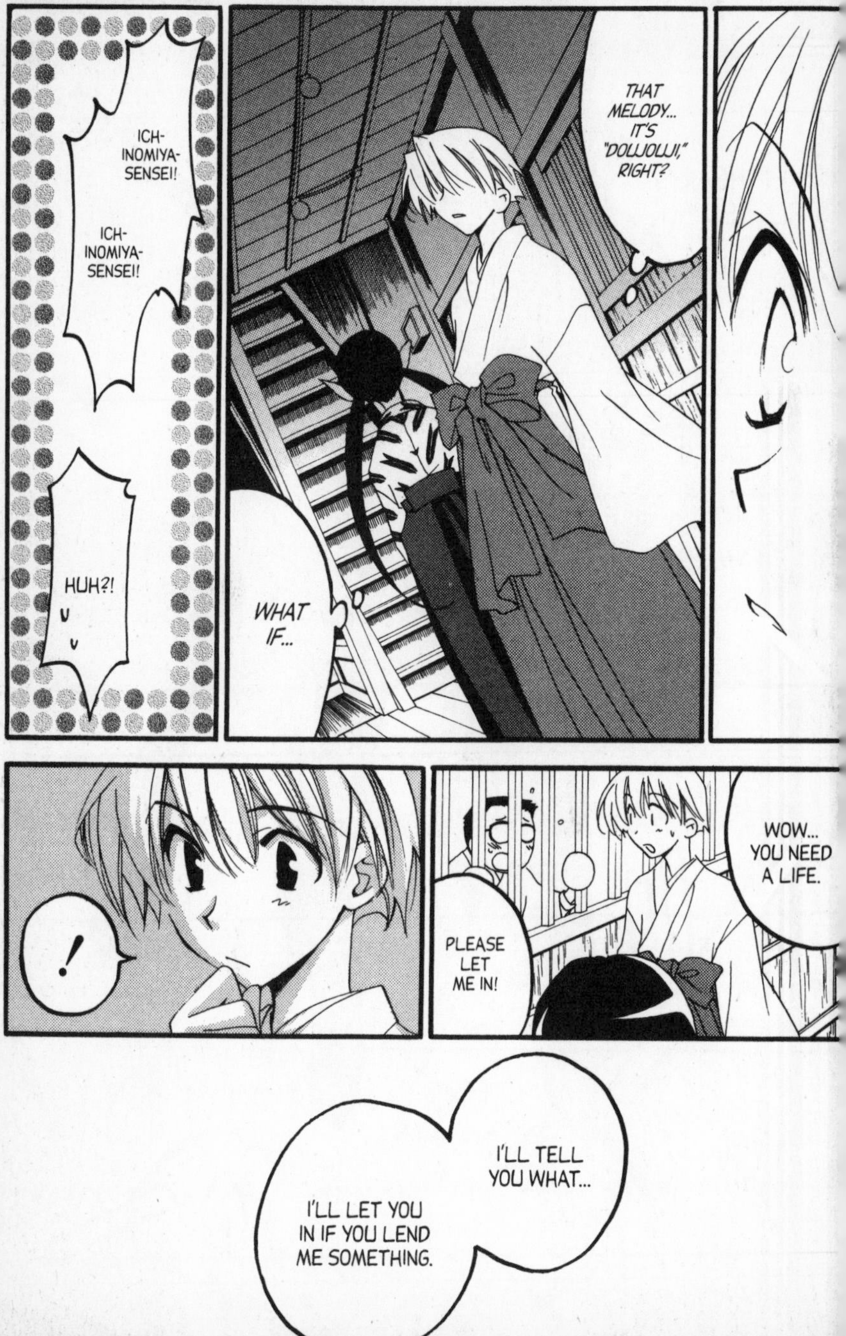
THAT MELODY... IT'S "DOUJOUJI," RIGHT?
WHAT IF...
ICH-INOMIYA-SENSEI!
ICH-INOMIYA-SENSEI!
HUH?!
WOW... YOU NEED A LIFE.
PLEASE LET ME IN!
!
I'LL TELL YOU WHAT...
I'LL LET YOU IN IF YOU LEND ME SOMETHING.

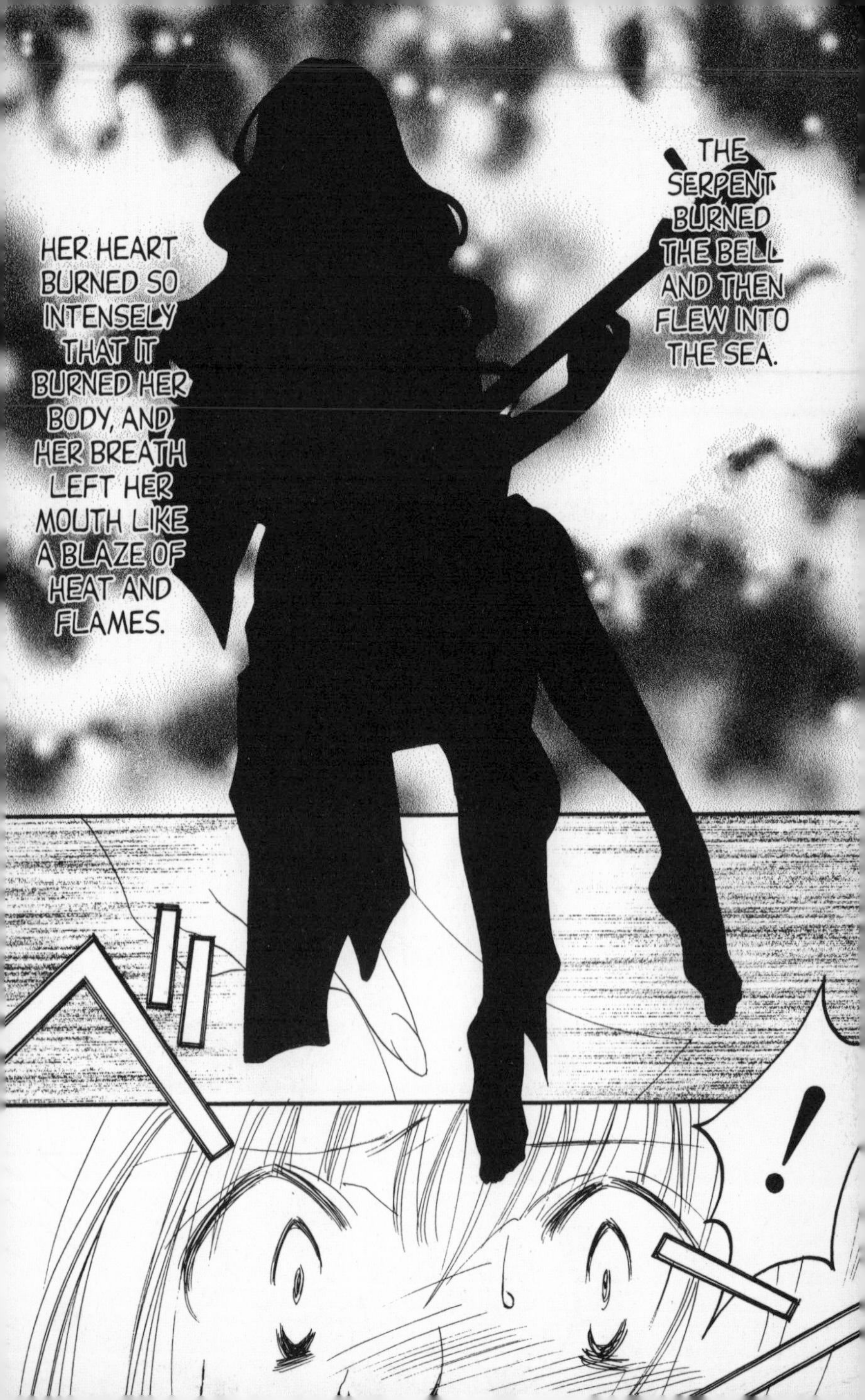
THE SERPENT BURNED THE BELL AND THEN FLEW INTO THE SEA.
HER HEART BURNED SO INTENSELY THAT IT BURNED HER BODY, AND HER BREATH LEFT HER MOUTH LIKE A BLAZE OF HEAT AND FLAMES.
!

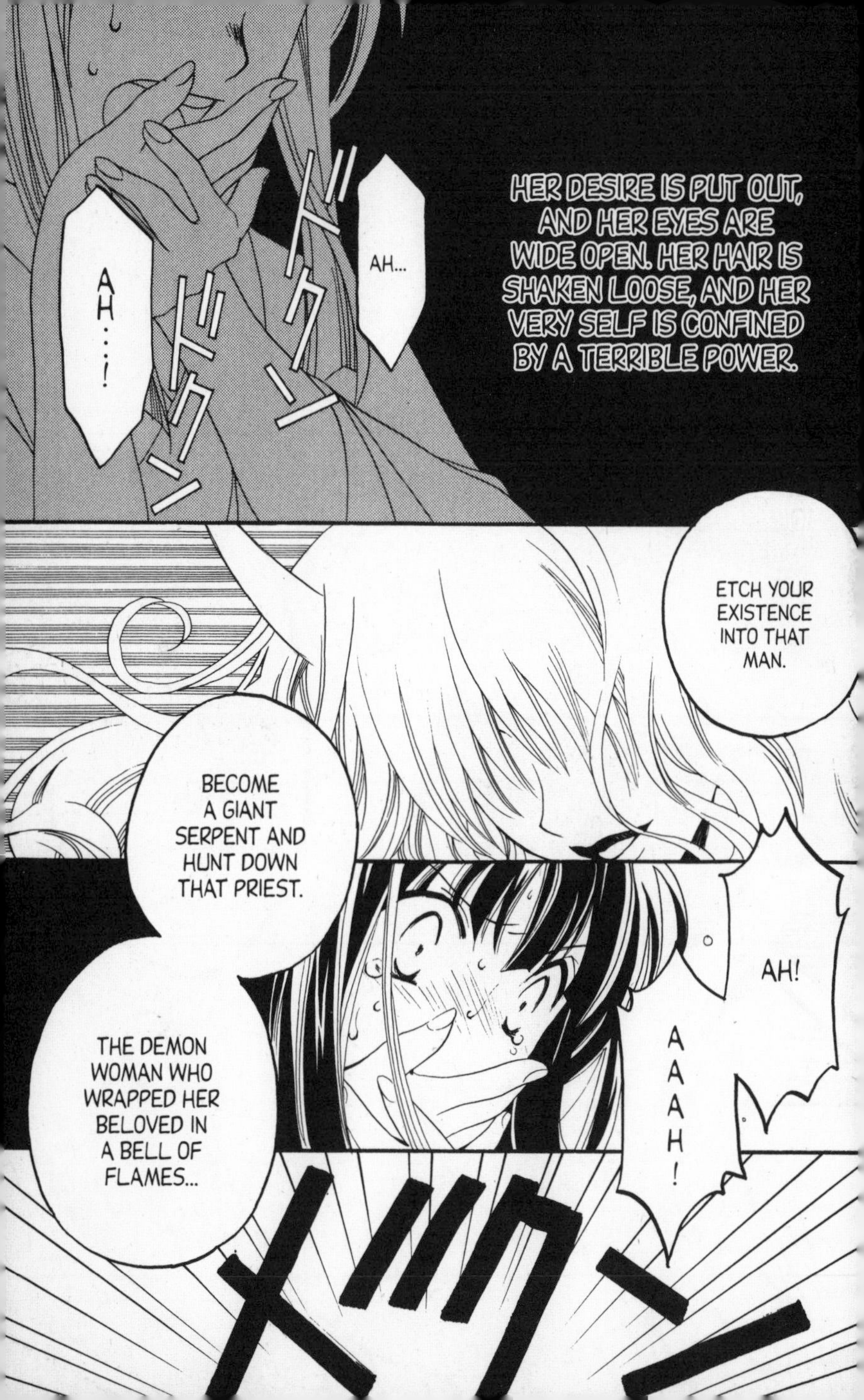
HER DESIRE IS PUT OUT, AND HER EYES ARE WIDE OPEN. HER HAIR IS SHAKEN LOOSE, AND HER VERY SELF IS CONFINED BY A TERRIBLE POWER.
AH...
AH...!
ETCH YOUR EXISTENCE INTO THAT MAN.
BECOME A GIANT SERPENT AND HUNT DOWN THAT PRIEST.
AH! AAAH!
THE DEMON WOMAN WHO WRAPPED HER BELOVED IN A BELL OF FLAMES...

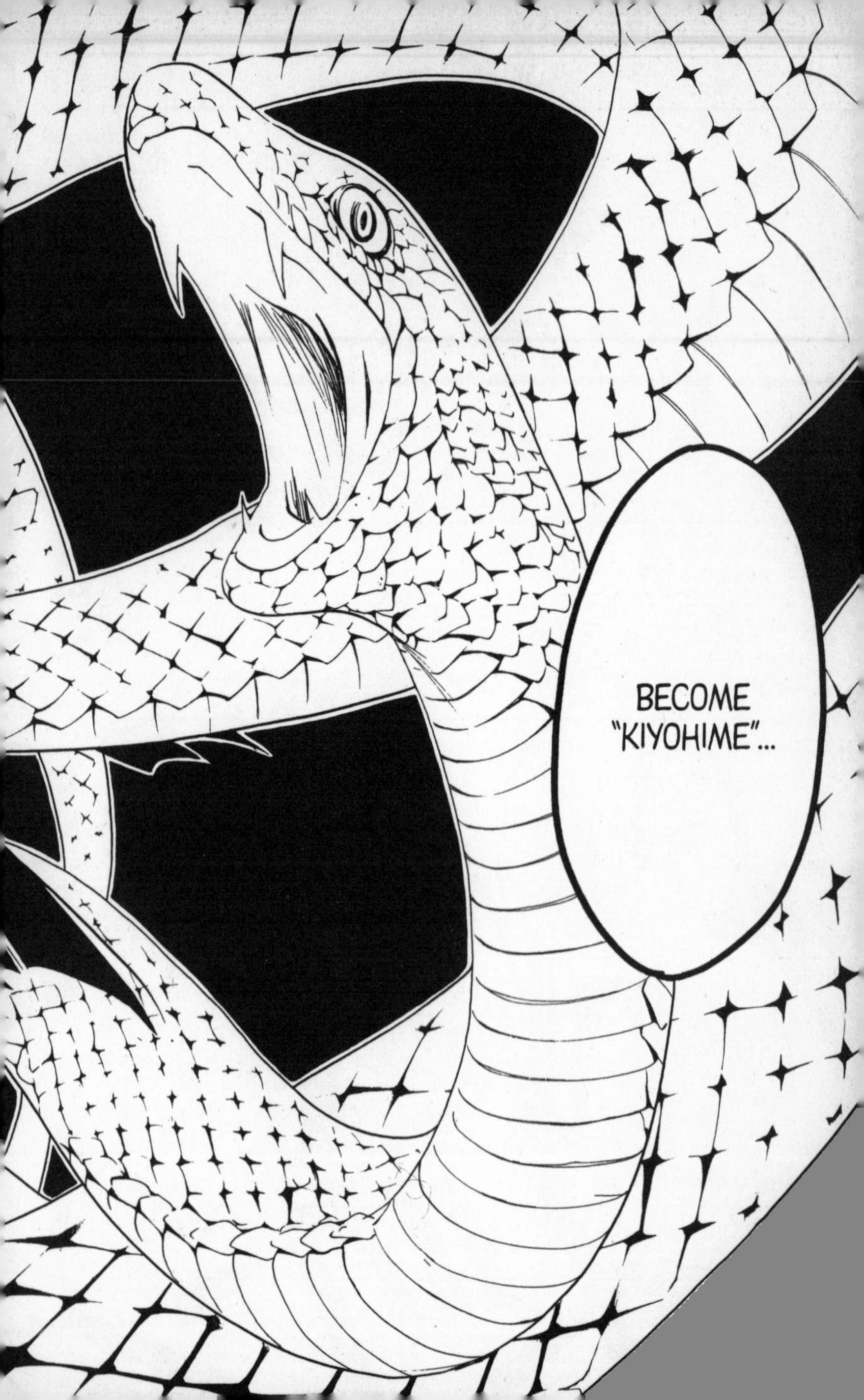
BECOME "KIYOHIME"...

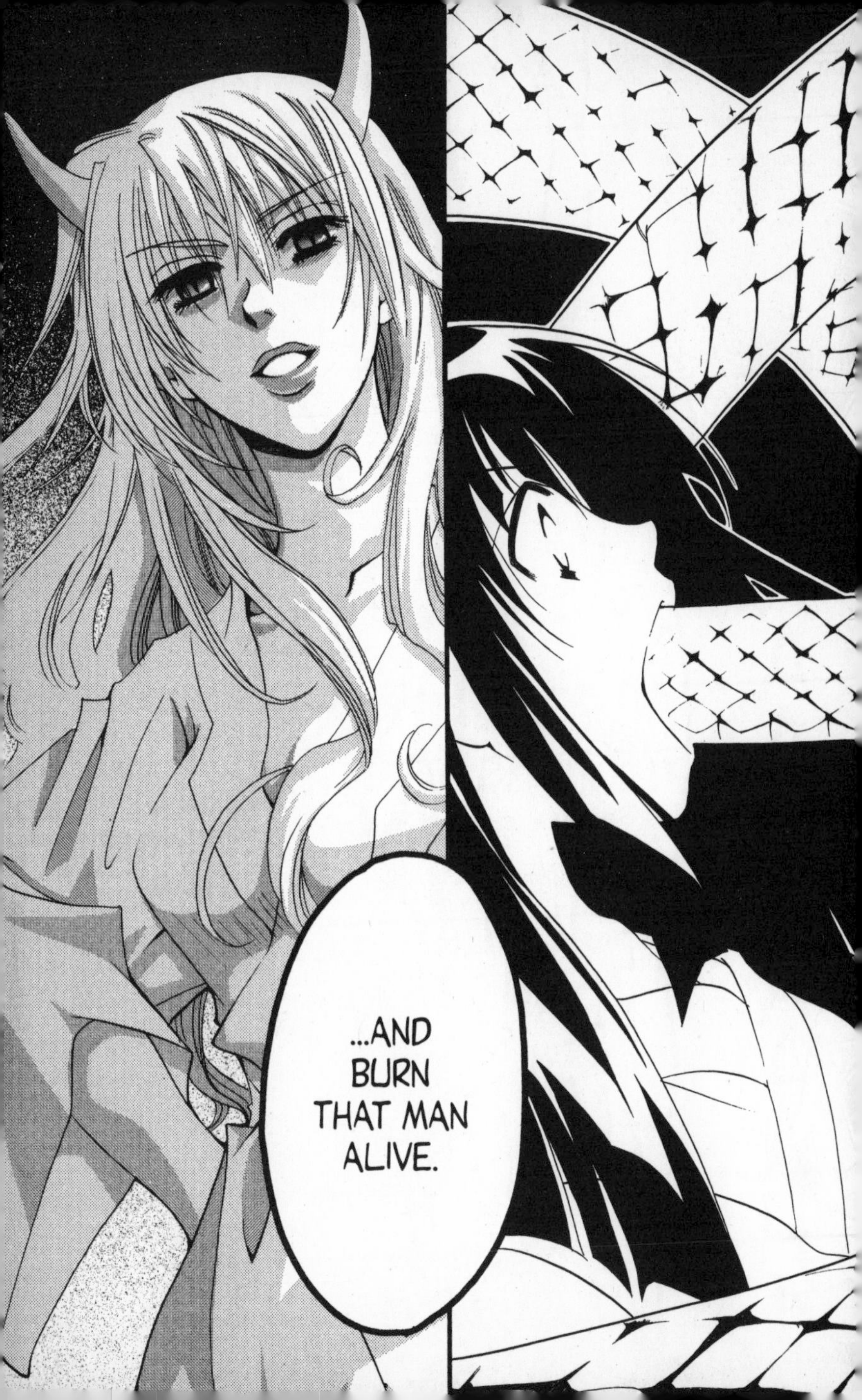
...AND BURN THAT MAN ALIVE.

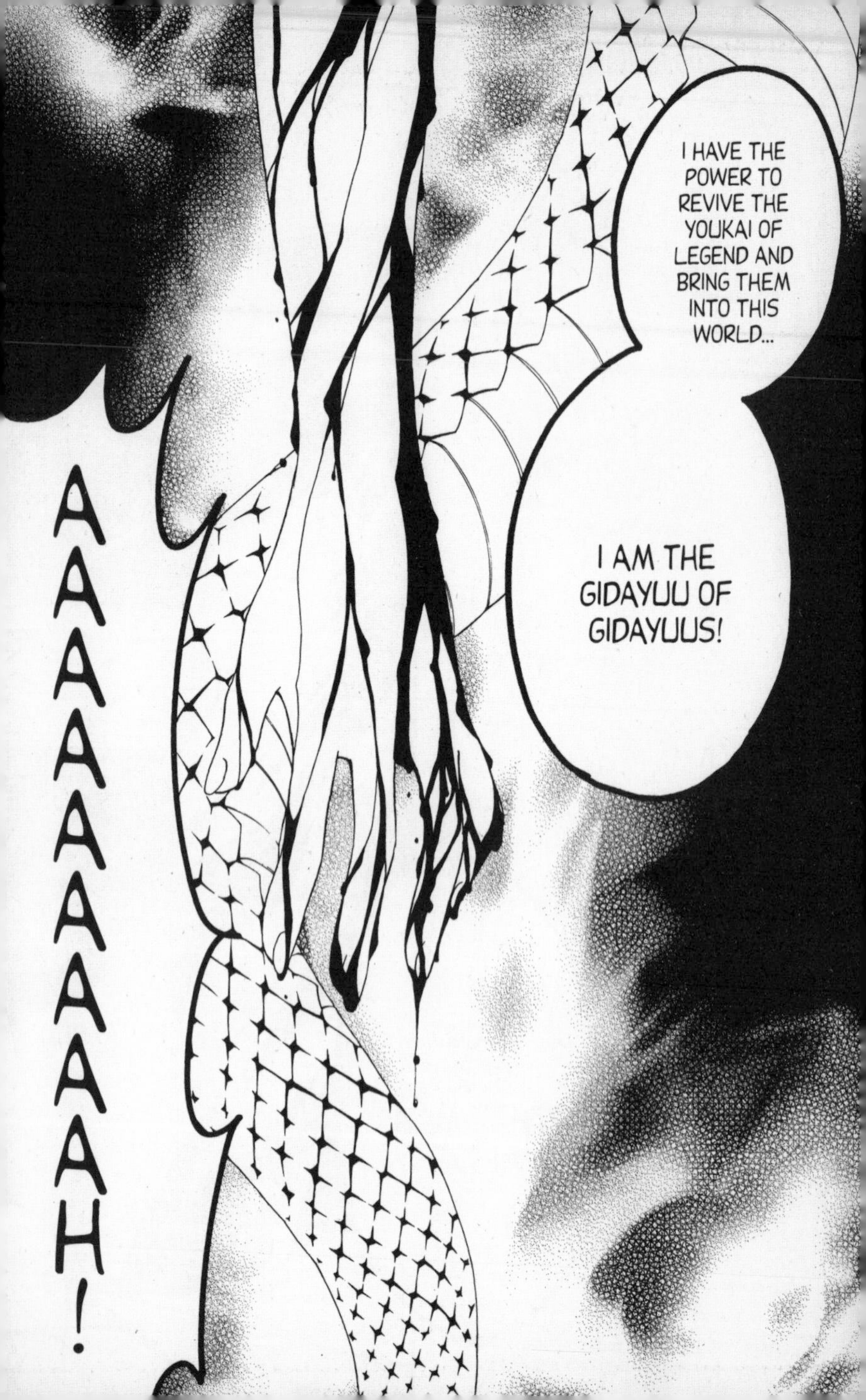
I HAVE THE POWER TO REVIVE THE YOUKAI OF LEGEND AND BRING THEM INTO THIS WORLD...
I AM THE GIDAYUU OF GIDAYUUS!
AAAAAAAAAH!

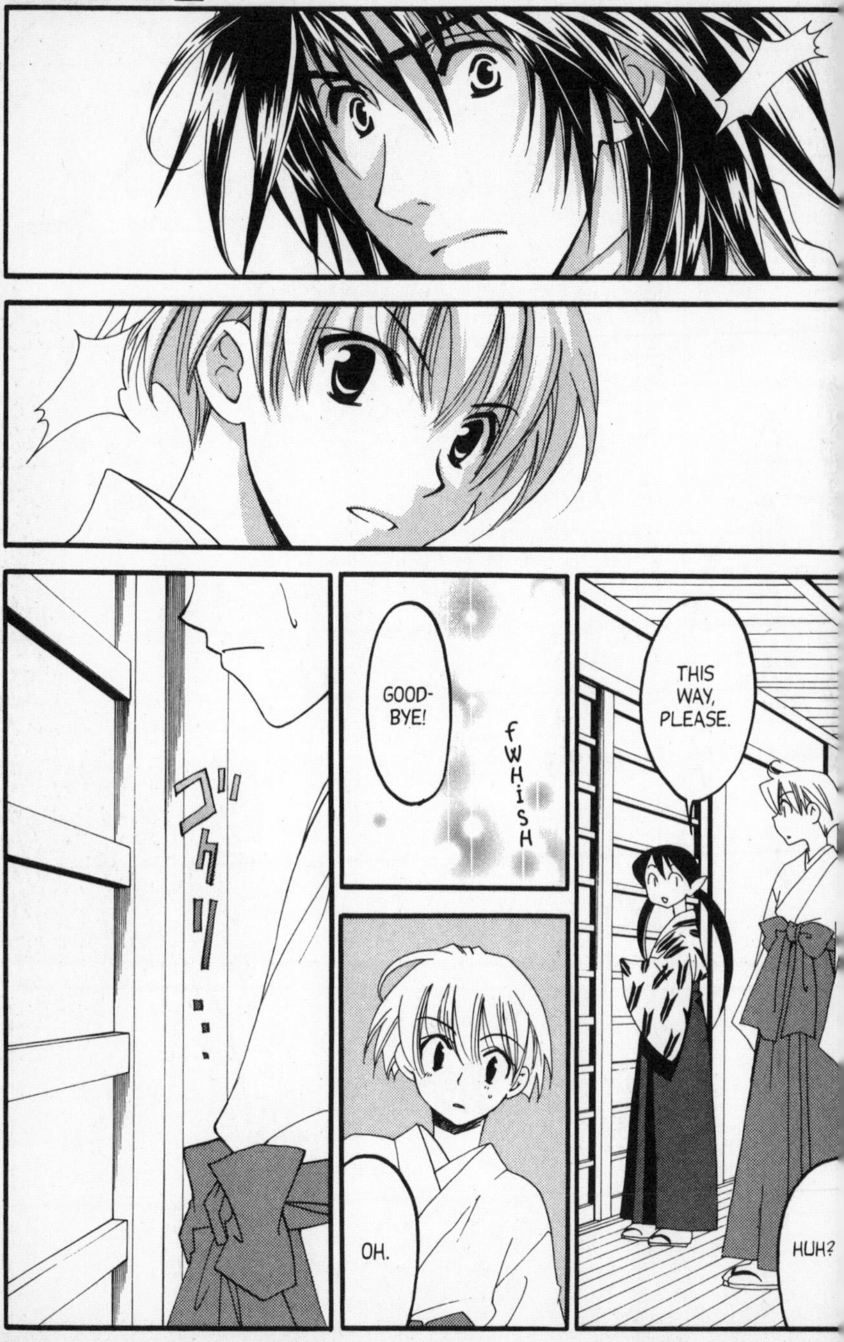
THIS WAY, PLEASE.
HUH?
GOOD-BYE!
FWHISH
OH.
ゴクリ...

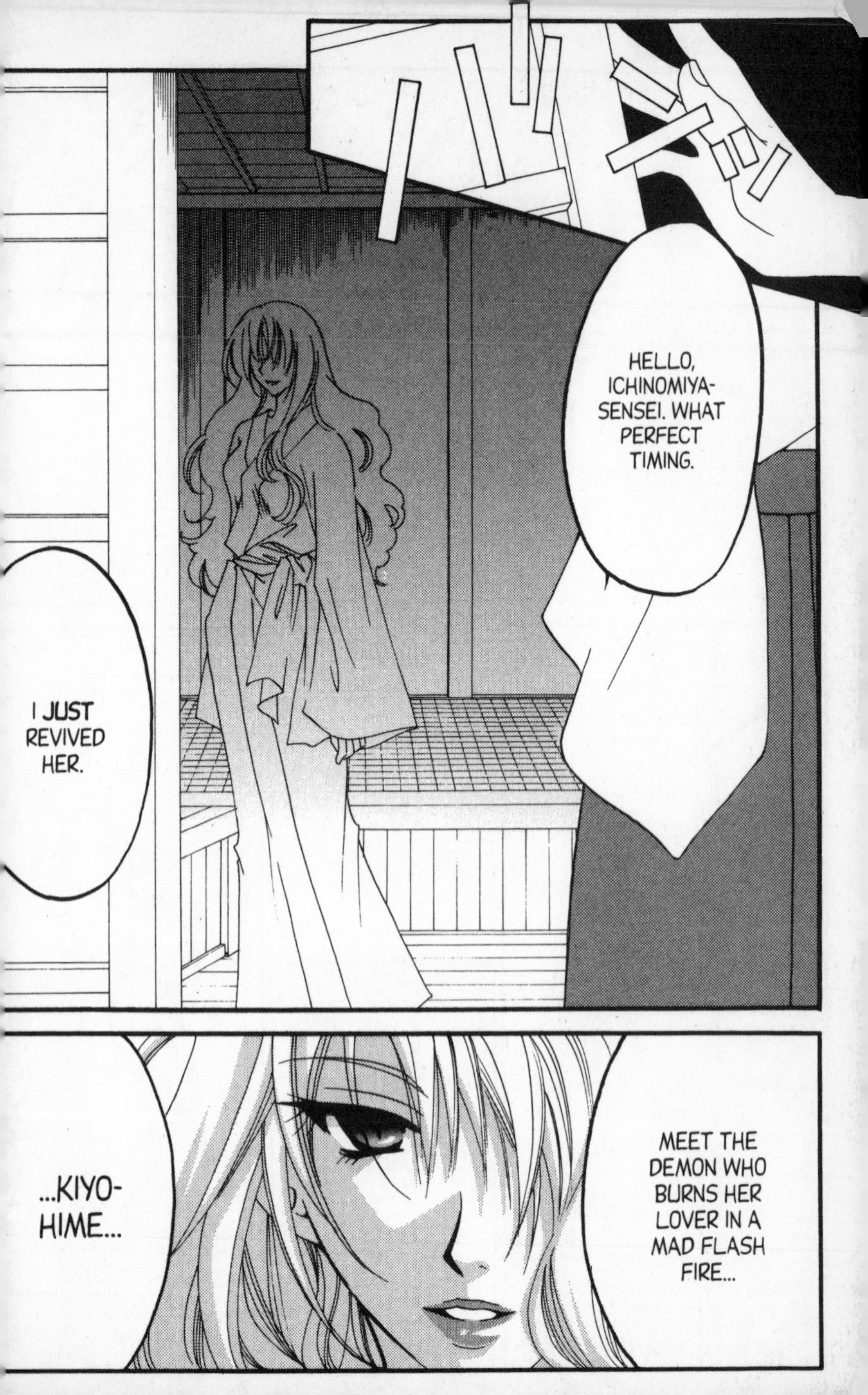
HELLO, ICHINOMIYA-SENSEI. WHAT PERFECT TIMING.
I JUST REVIVED HER.
MEET THE DEMON WHO BURNS HER LOVER IN A MAD FLASH FIRE...
...KIYO-HIME...

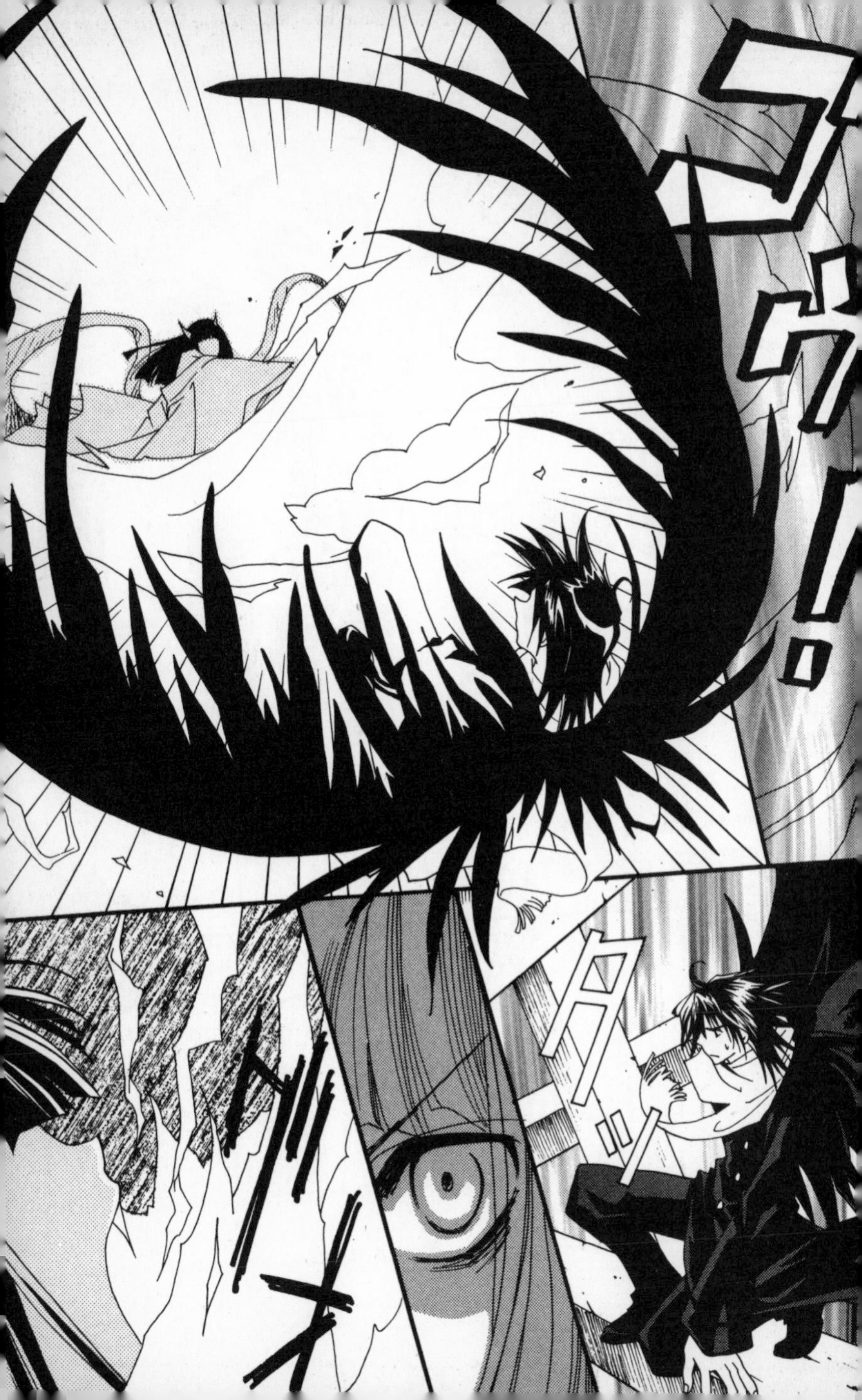
タッ

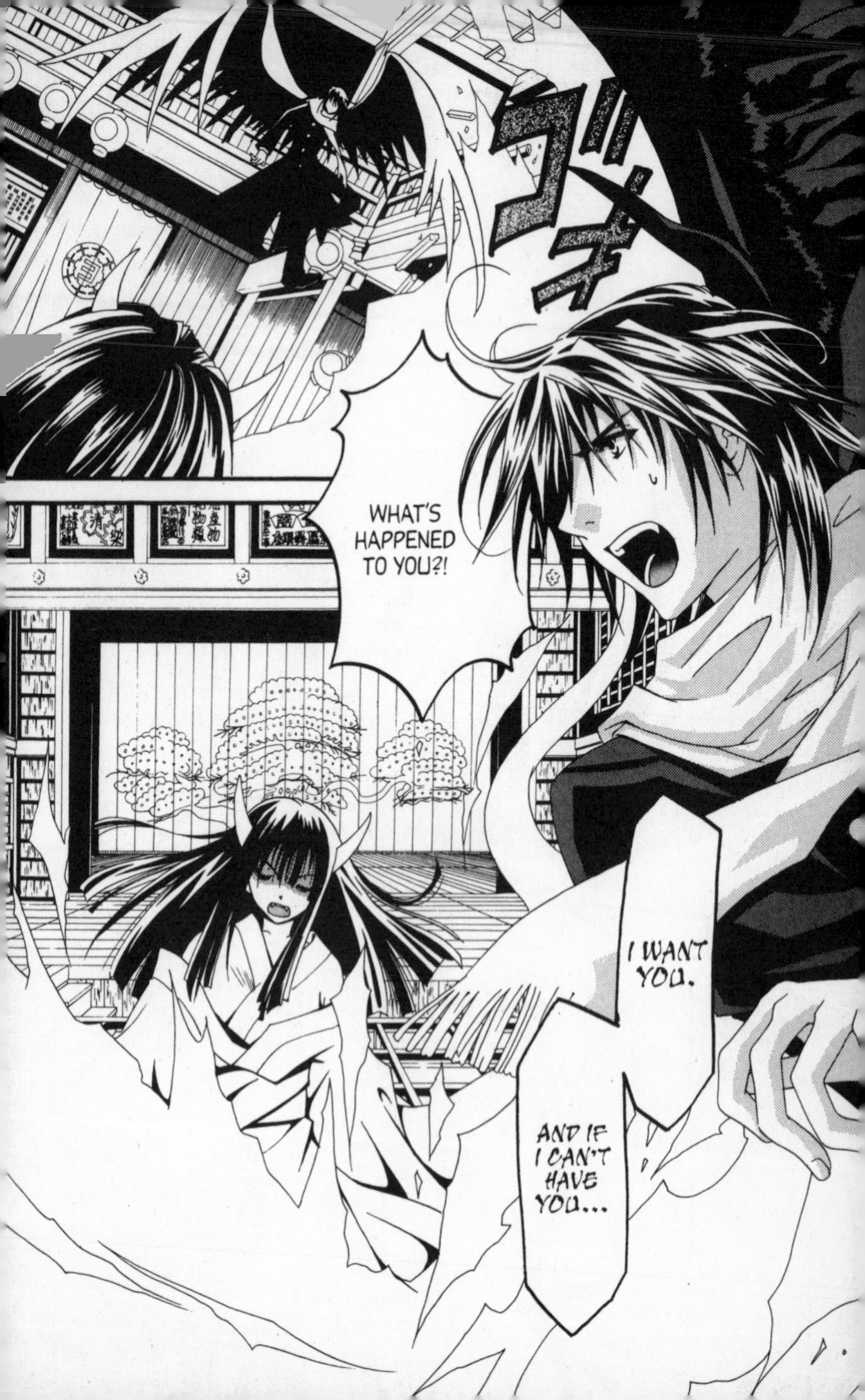
WHAT'S HAPPENED TO YOU?!
I WANT YOU.
AND IF I CAN'T HAVE YOU...

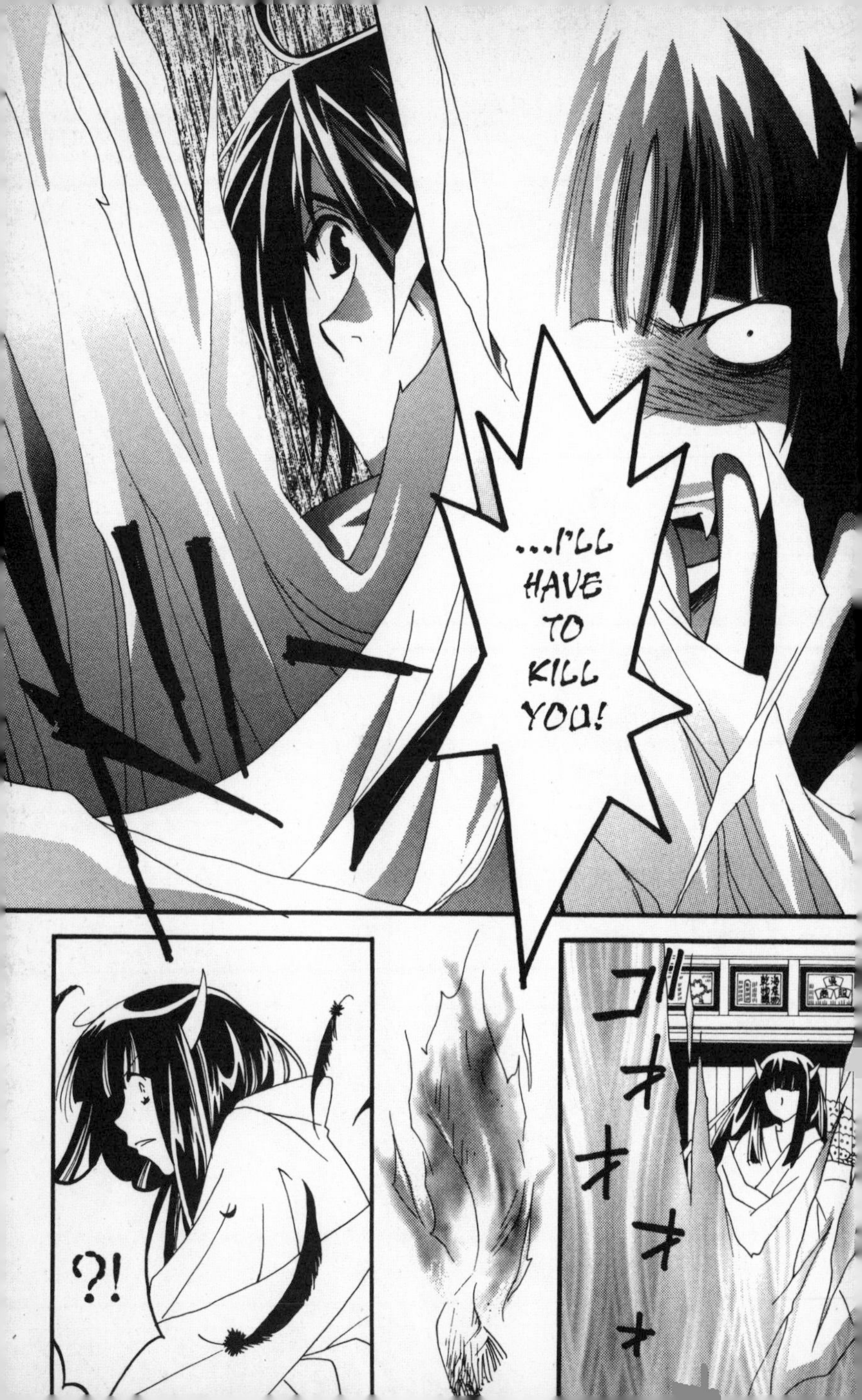
...I'LL HAVE TO KILL YOU!
?!

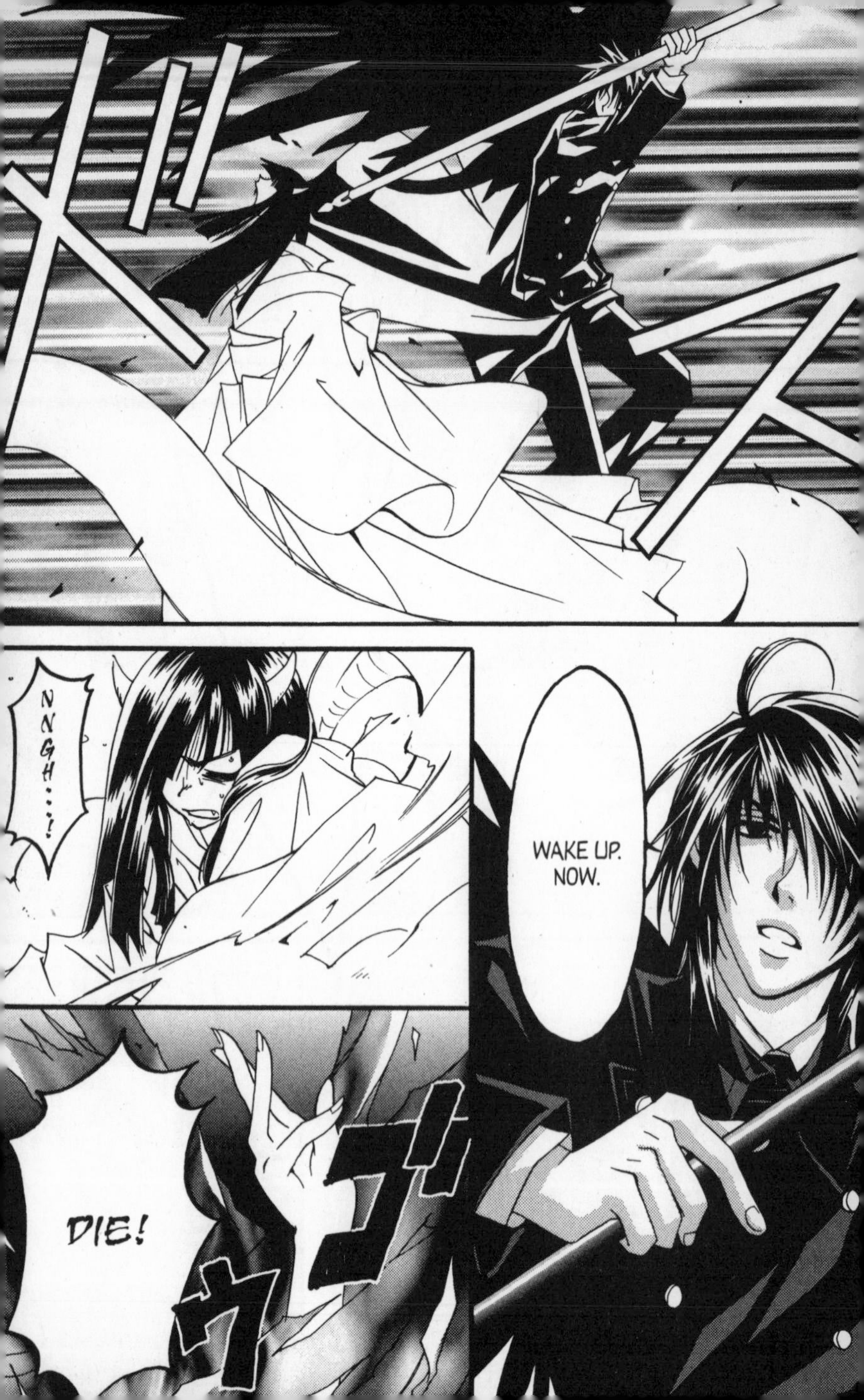
WAKE UP. NOW.
NNGH...!
DIE!

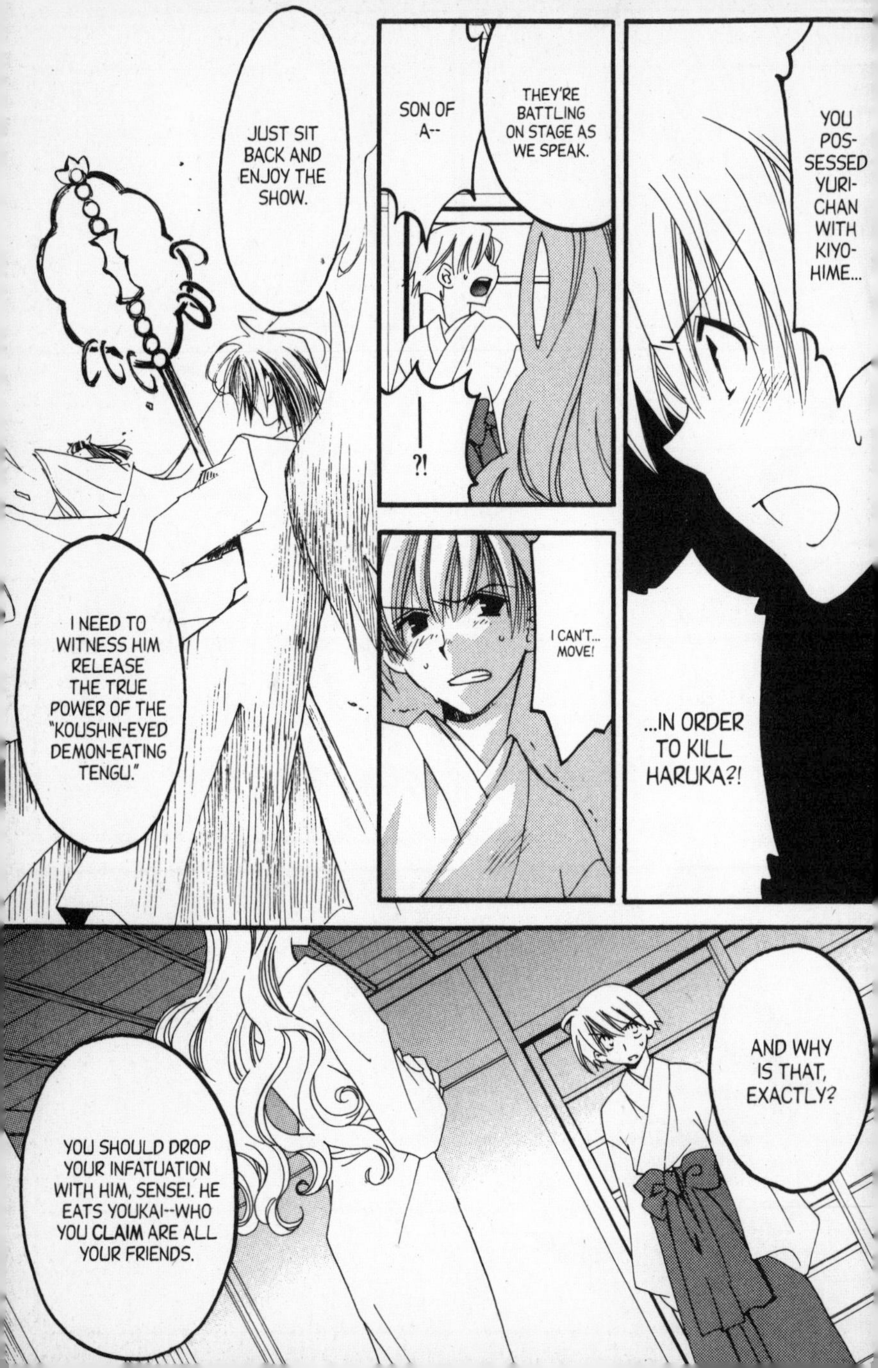
YOU POSSESSED YURI-CHAN WITH KIYO-HIME...
...IN ORDER TO KILL HARUKA?!
THEY'RE BATTLING ON STAGE AS WE SPEAK.
SON OF A--
--?!
I CAN'T... MOVE!
JUST SIT BACK AND ENJOY THE SHOW.
I NEED TO WITNESS HIM RELEASE THE TRUE POWER OF THE "KOUSHIN-EYED DEMON-EATING TENGU."
AND WHY IS THAT, EXACTLY?
YOU SHOULD DROP YOUR INFATUATION WITH HIM, SENSEI. HE EATS YOUKAI--WHO YOU CLAIM ARE ALL YOUR FRIENDS.

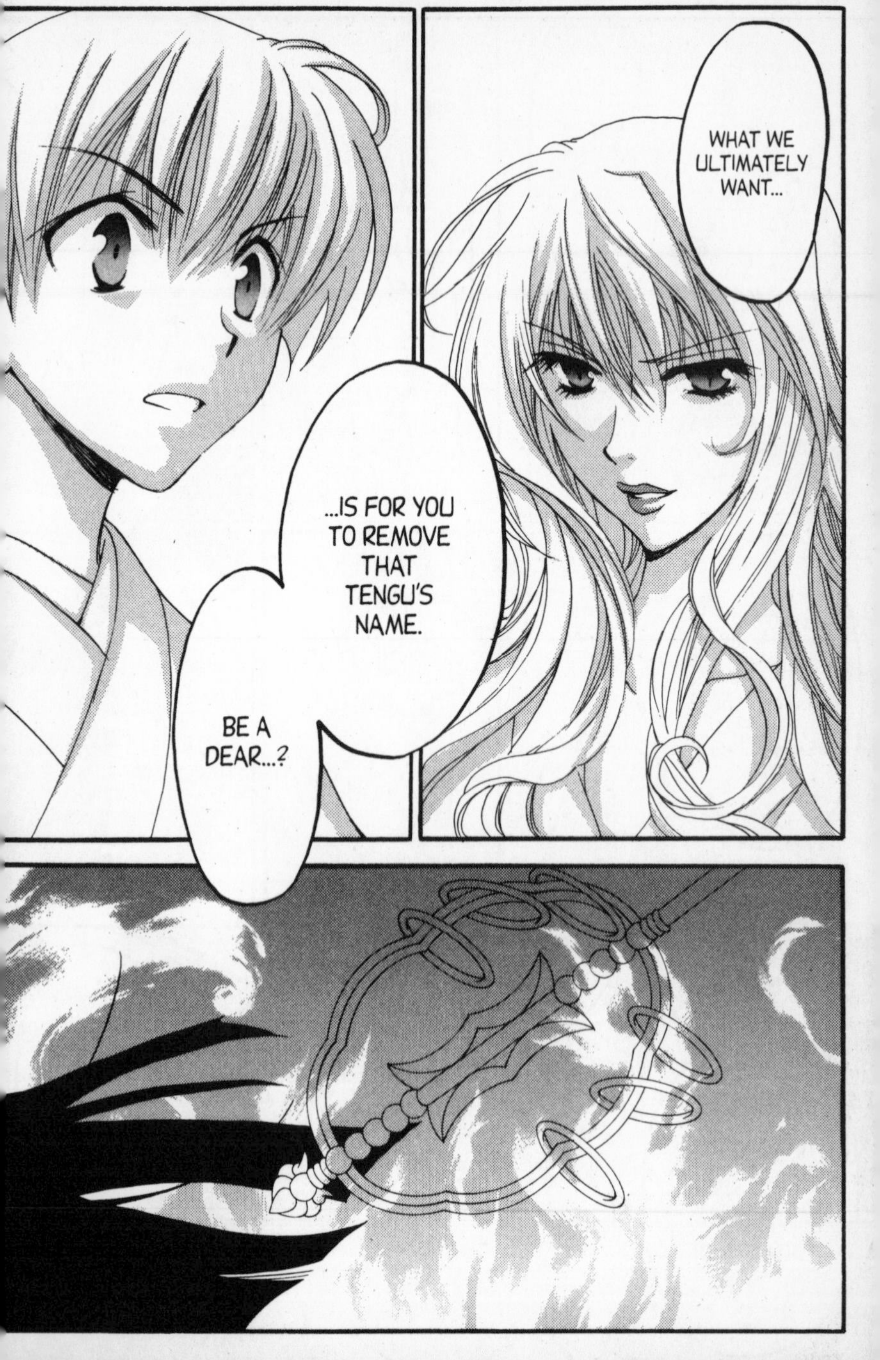
WHAT WE ULTIMATELY WANT...
...IS FOR YOU TO REMOVE THAT TENGU'S NAME.
BE A DEAR...?

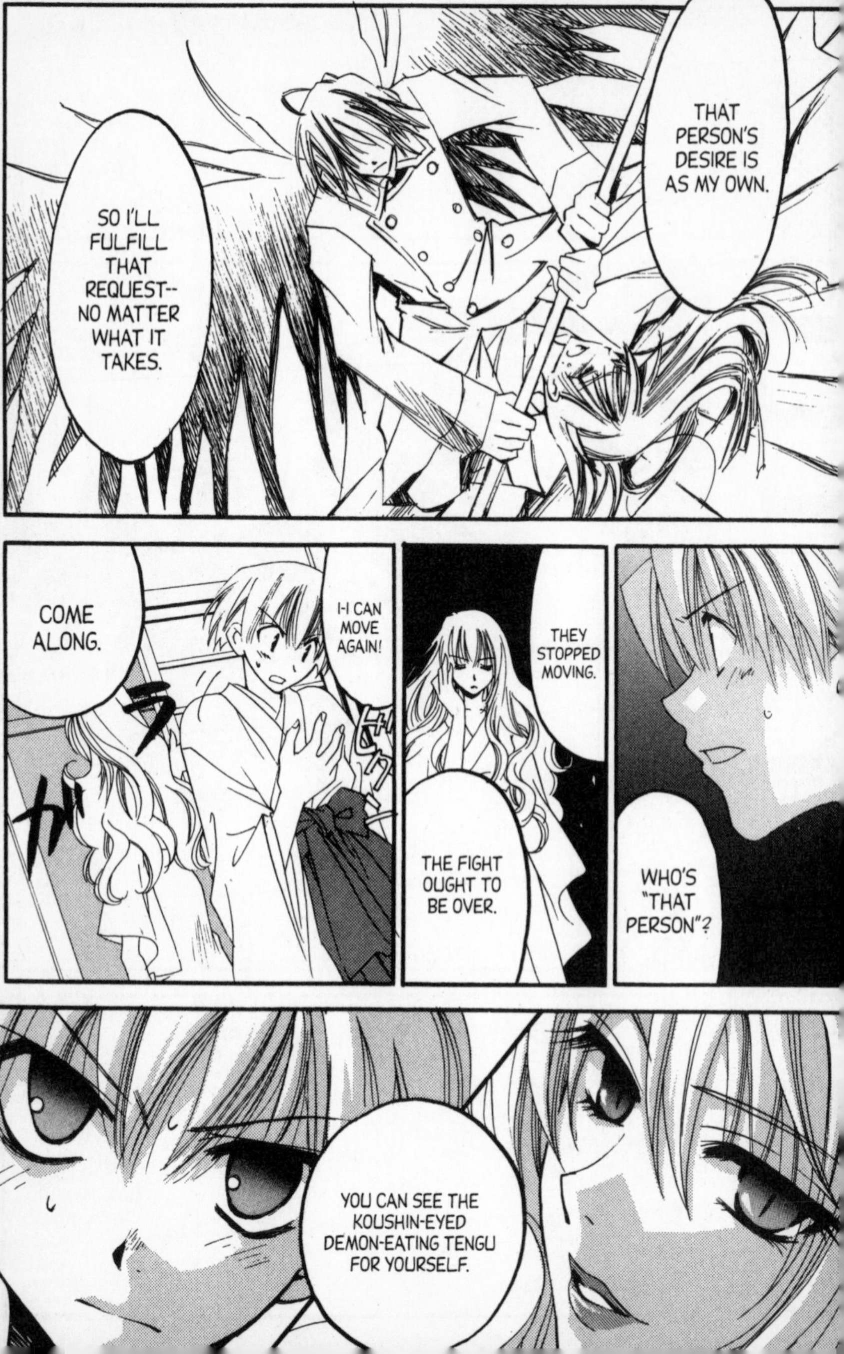
THAT PERSON'S DESIRE IS AS MY OWN.
SO I'LL FULFILL THAT REQUEST--NO MATTER WHAT IT TAKES.
WHO'S "THAT PERSON"?
THEY STOPPED MOVING.
THE FIGHT OUGHT TO BE OVER.
I-I CAN MOVE AGAIN!
COME ALONG.
YOU CAN SEE THE KOUSHIN-EYED DEMON-EATING TENGU FOR YOURSELF.

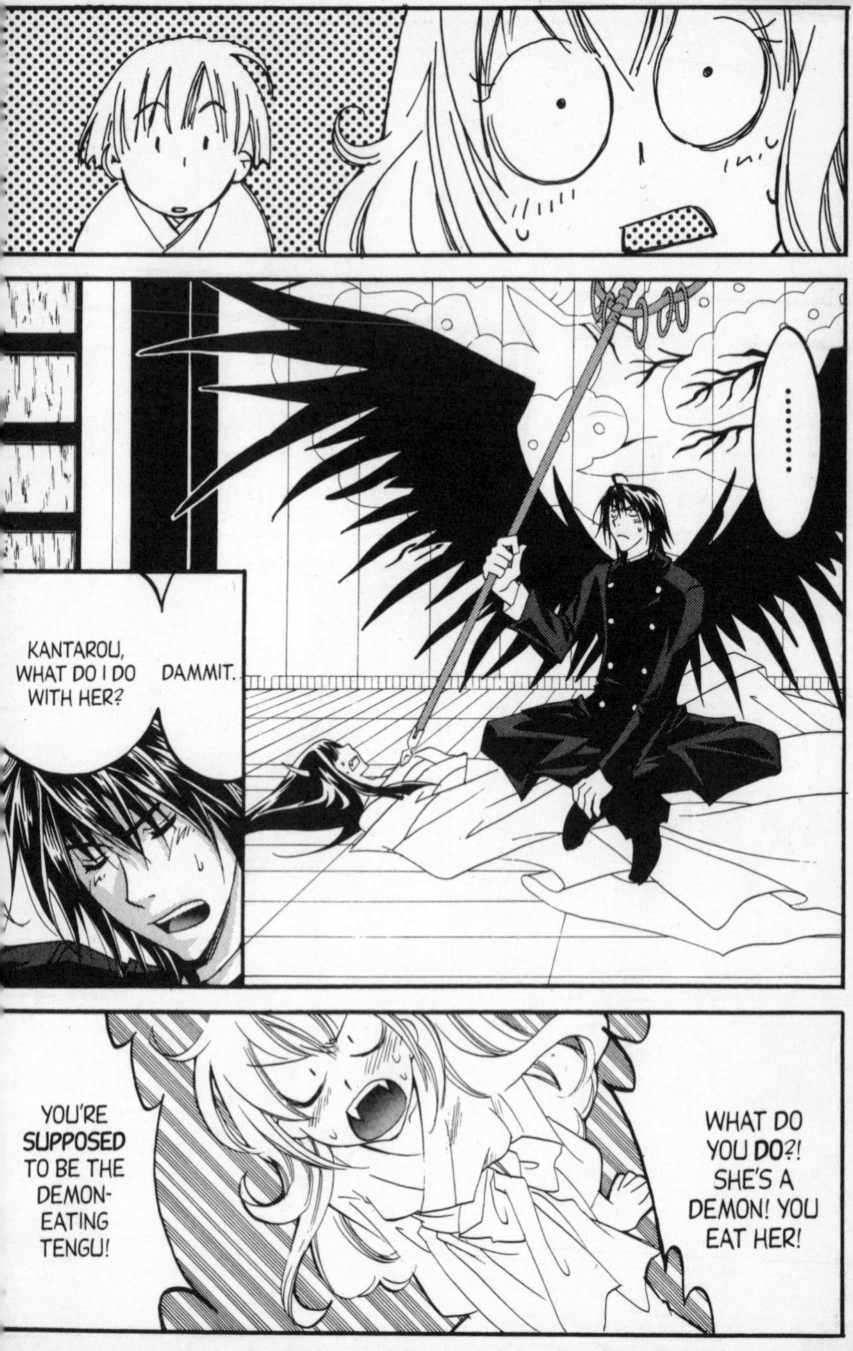
......
DAMMIT.
KANTAROU, WHAT DO I DO WITH HER?
WHAT DO YOU **DO**?! SHE'S A DEMON! YOU EAT HER!
YOU'RE **SUPPOSED** TO BE THE DEMON-EATING TENGU!

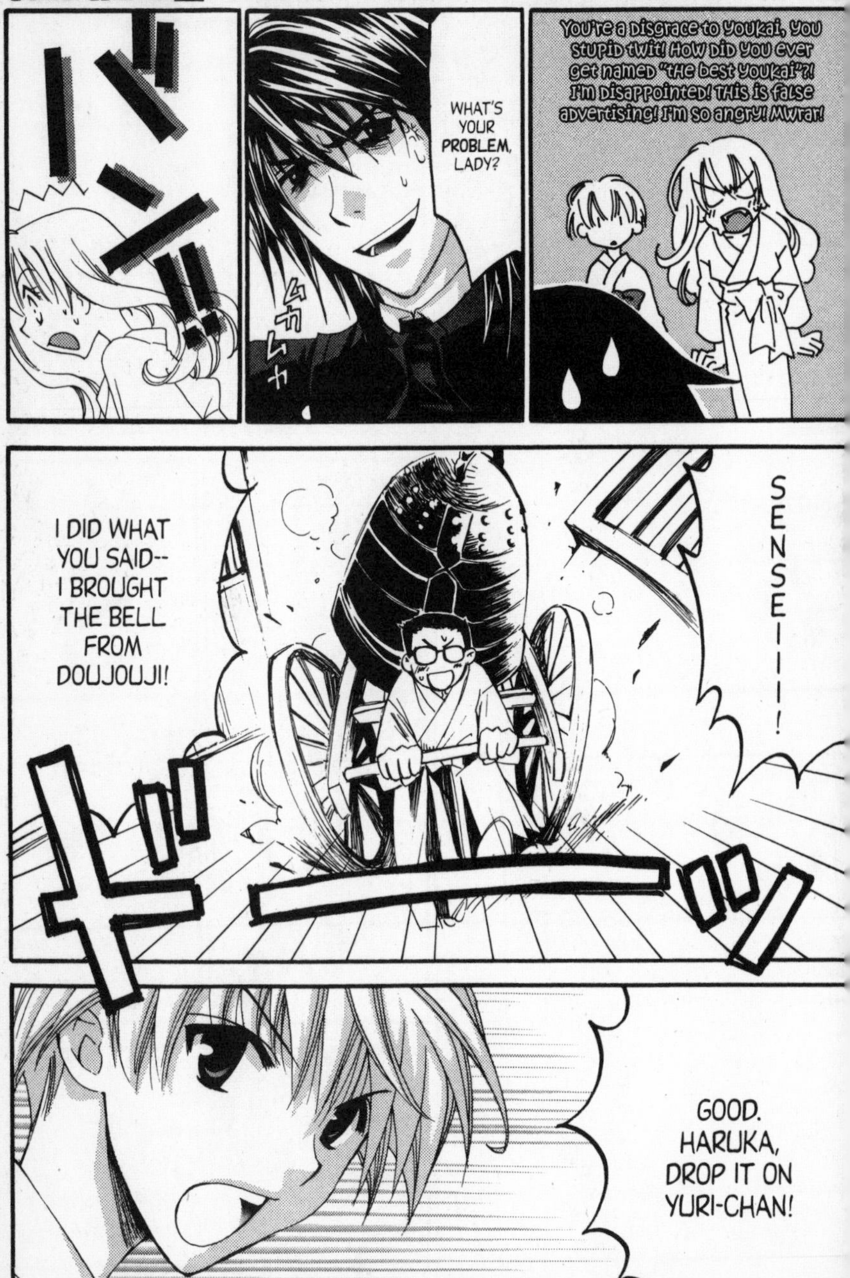
You're a disgrace to youkai, you stupid twit! How did you ever get named "the best youkai"?! I'm disappointed! This is false advertising! I'm so angry! Mwrar!
WHAT'S YOUR PROBLEM, LADY?
SENSEI--!
I DID WHAT YOU SAID-- I BROUGHT THE BELL FROM DOUJOUJI!
GOOD. HARUKA, DROP IT ON YURI-CHAN!

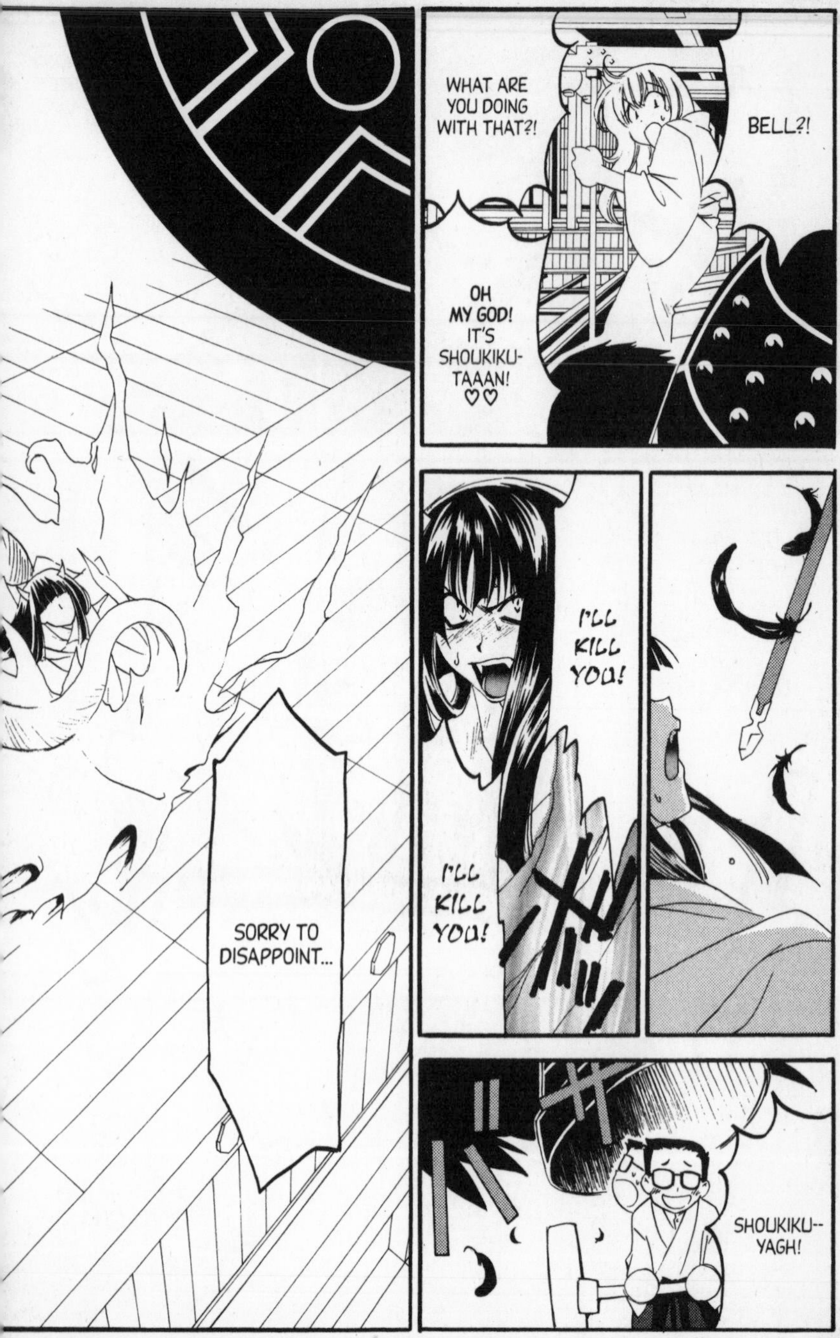
BELL?!
WHAT ARE YOU DOING WITH THAT?!
OH MY GOD! IT'S SHOUKIKU-TAAAN! ♡♡
I'LL KILL YOU!
I'LL KILL YOU!
SHOUKIKU--YAGH!
SORRY TO DISAPPOINT...

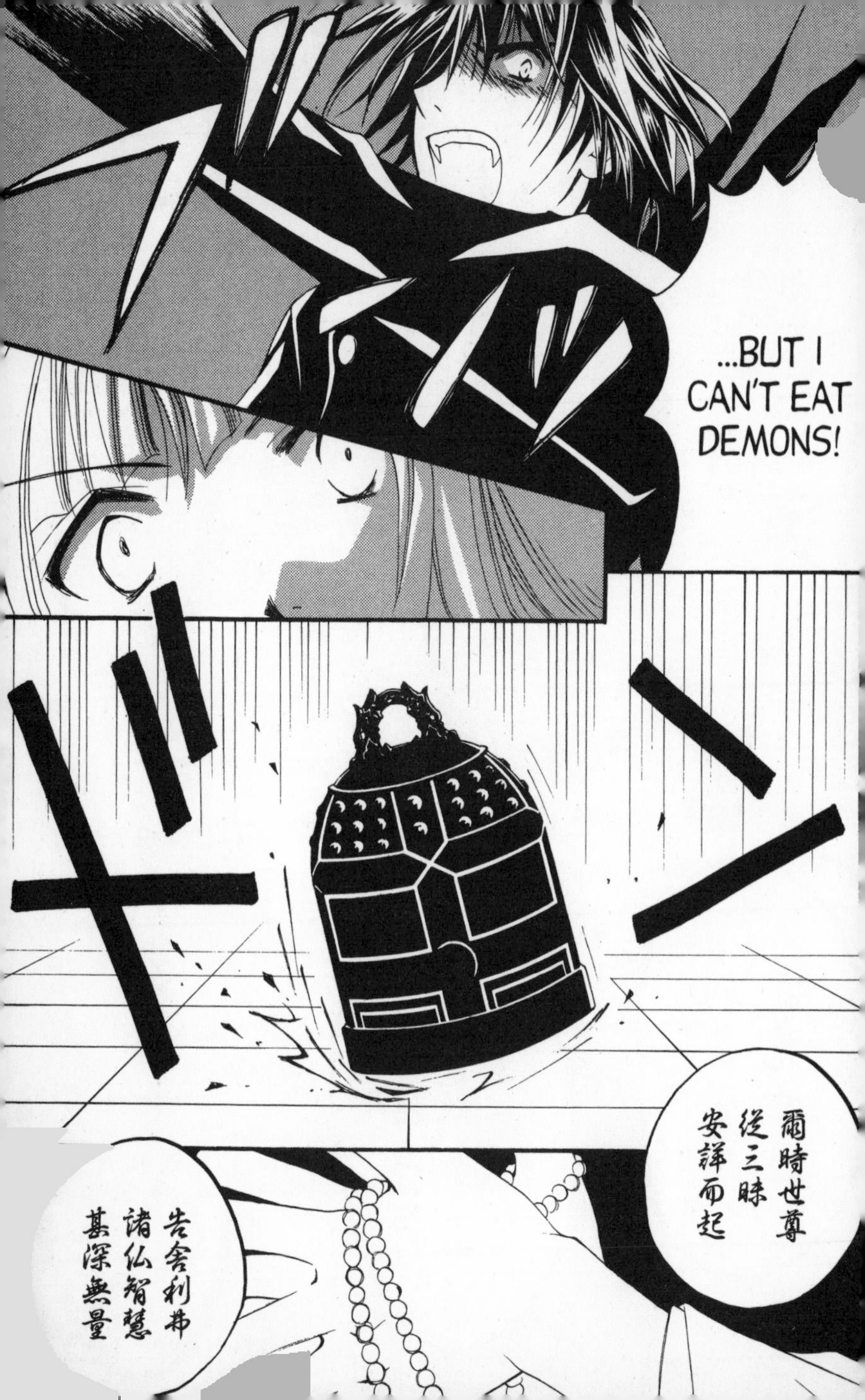
...BUT I CAN'T EAT DEMONS!
爾時世尊從三昧安詳而起
告舍利弗諸仏智慧甚深無量

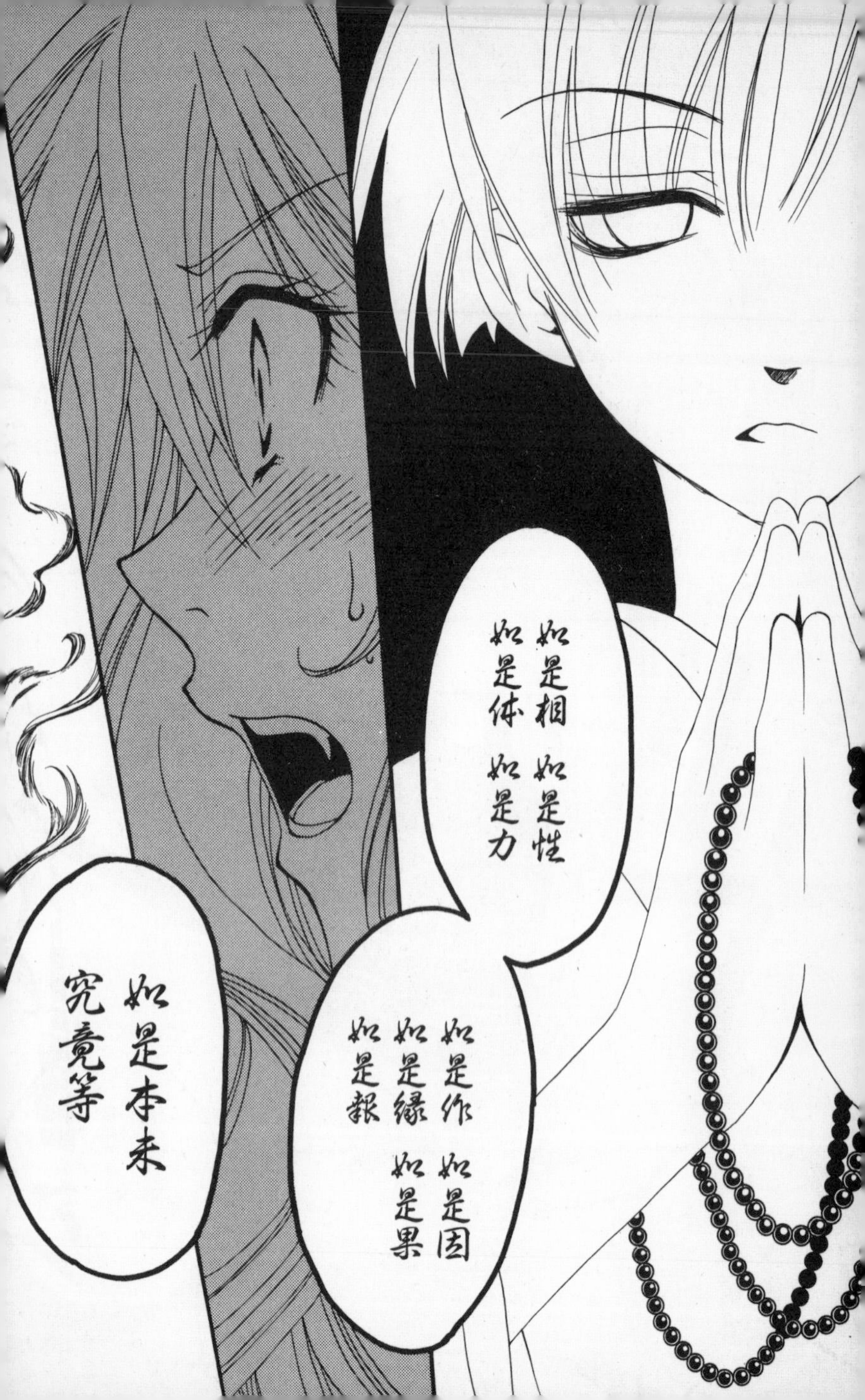
如是相 如是性 如是体 如是力
如是作 如是因 如是缘 如是果 如是報
如是本末究竟等

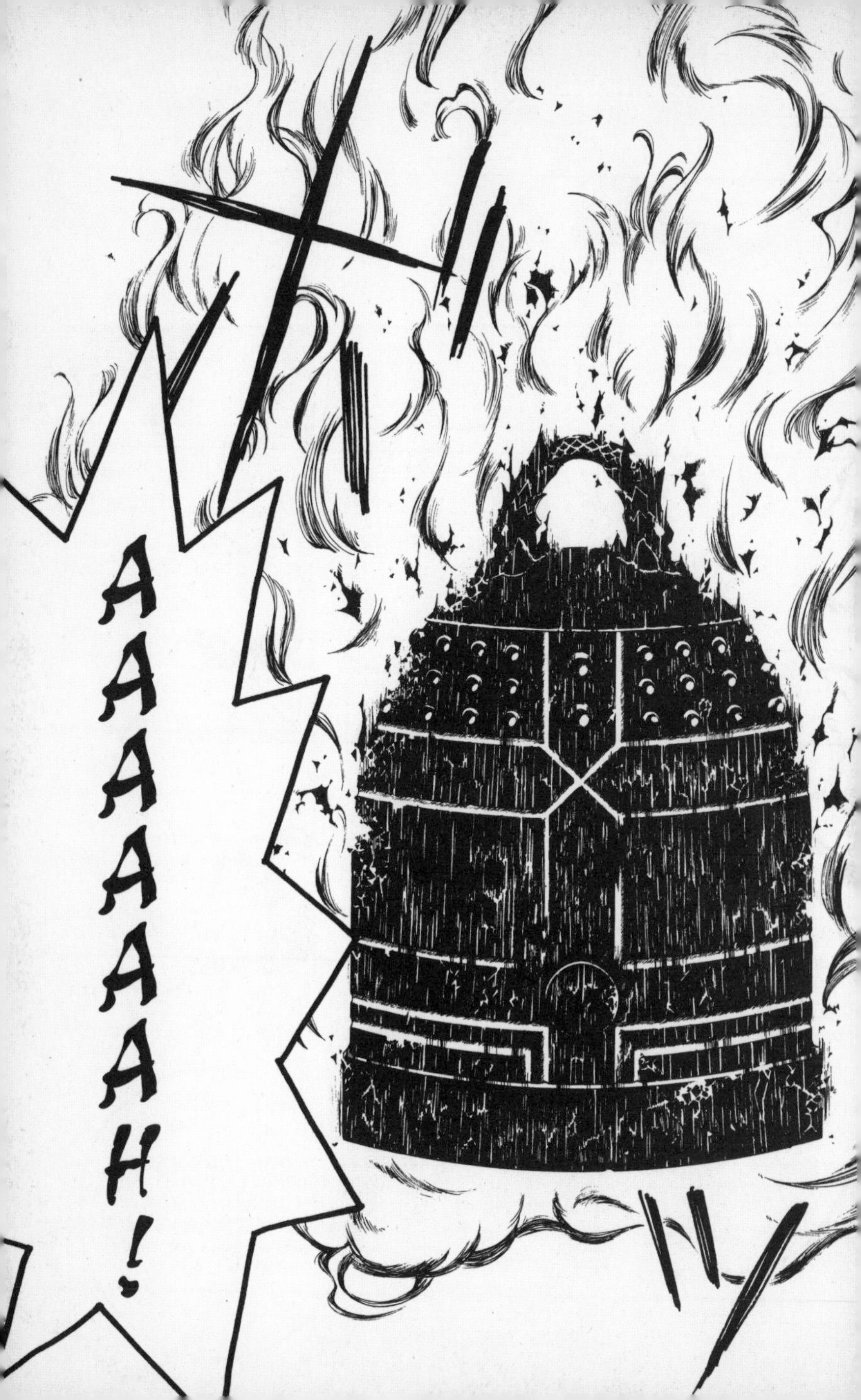
AAAAAAAH!

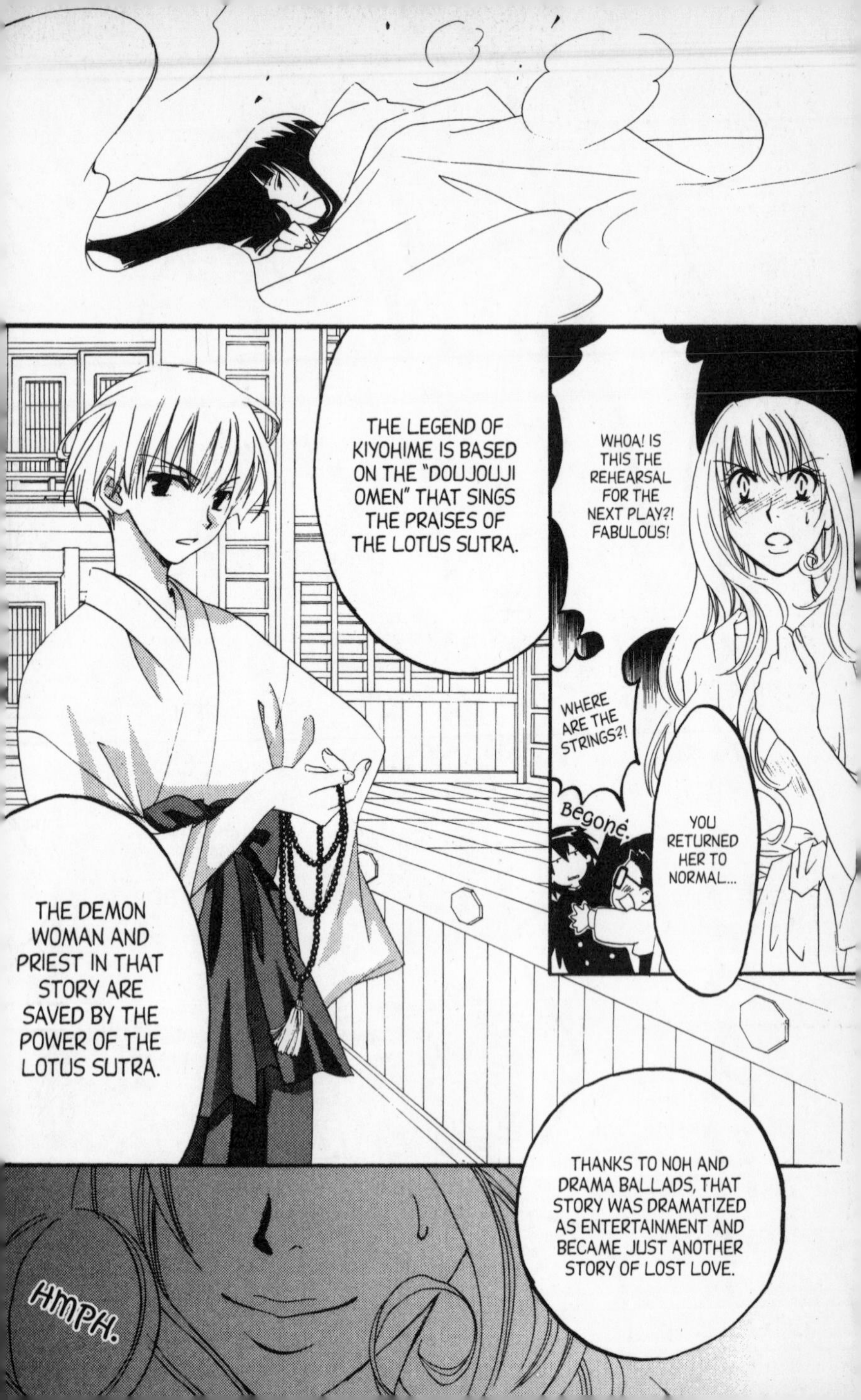
WHOA! IS THIS THE REHEARSAL FOR THE NEXT PLAY?! FABULOUS!
YOU RETURNED HER TO NORMAL...
WHERE ARE THE STRINGS?!
Begone.
THE LEGEND OF KIYOHIME IS BASED ON THE "DOUJOUJI OMEN" THAT SINGS THE PRAISES OF THE LOTUS SUTRA.
THE DEMON WOMAN AND PRIEST IN THAT STORY ARE SAVED BY THE POWER OF THE LOTUS SUTRA.
THANKS TO NOH AND DRAMA BALLADS, THAT STORY WAS DRAMATIZED AS ENTERTAINMENT AND BECAME JUST ANOTHER STORY OF LOST LOVE.
HMPH.

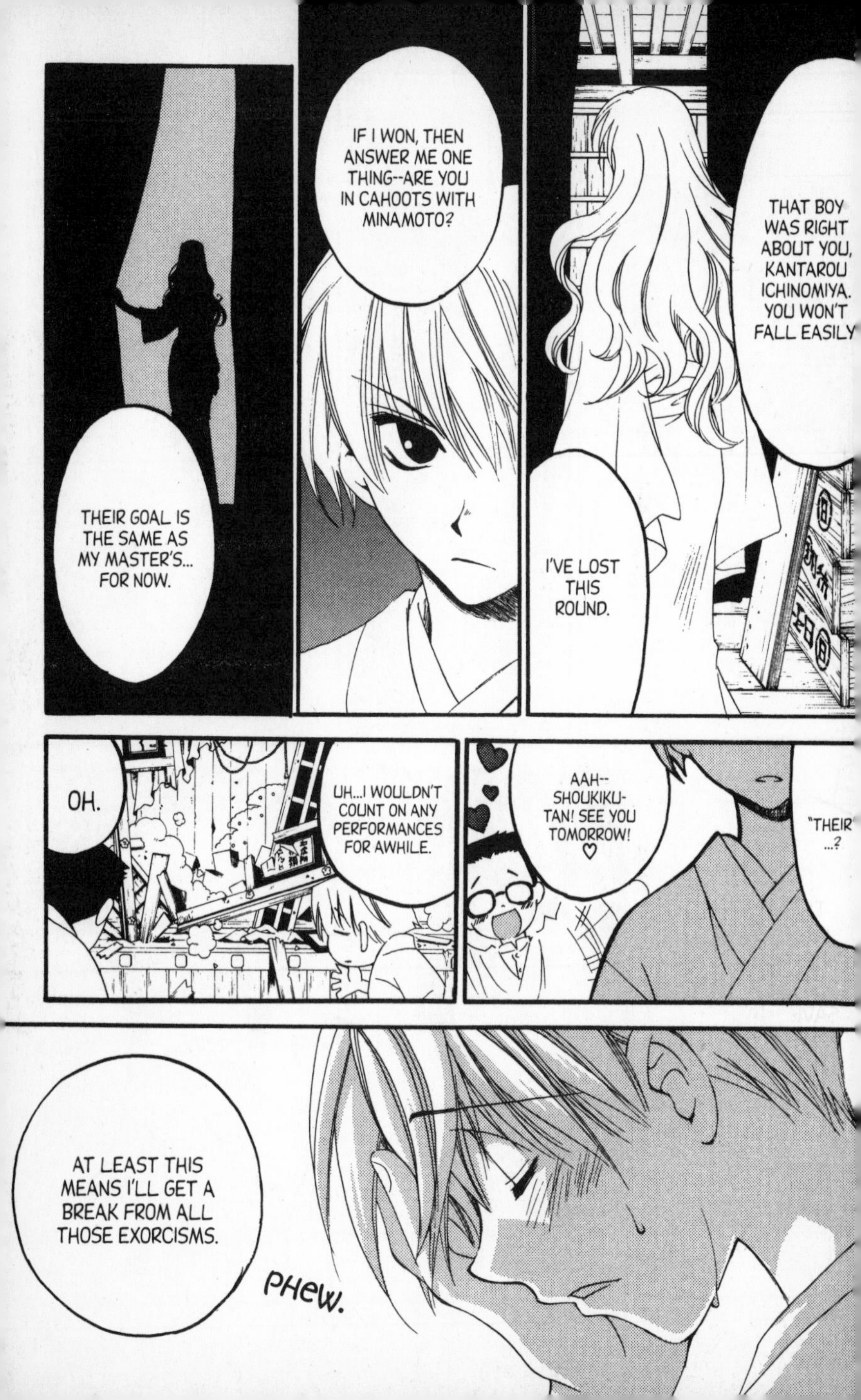
THAT BOY WAS RIGHT ABOUT YOU, KANTAROU ICHINOMIYA. YOU WON'T FALL EASILY
I'VE LOST THIS ROUND.
IF I WON, THEN ANSWER ME ONE THING--ARE YOU IN CAHOOTS WITH MINAMOTO?
THEIR GOAL IS THE SAME AS MY MASTER'S... FOR NOW.
"THEIR" ...?
AAH-- SHOUKIKU-TAN! SEE YOU TOMORROW! ♡
UH...I WOULDN'T COUNT ON ANY PERFORMANCES FOR AWHILE.
OH.
AT LEAST THIS MEANS I'LL GET A BREAK FROM ALL THOSE EXORCISMS.
PHEW.

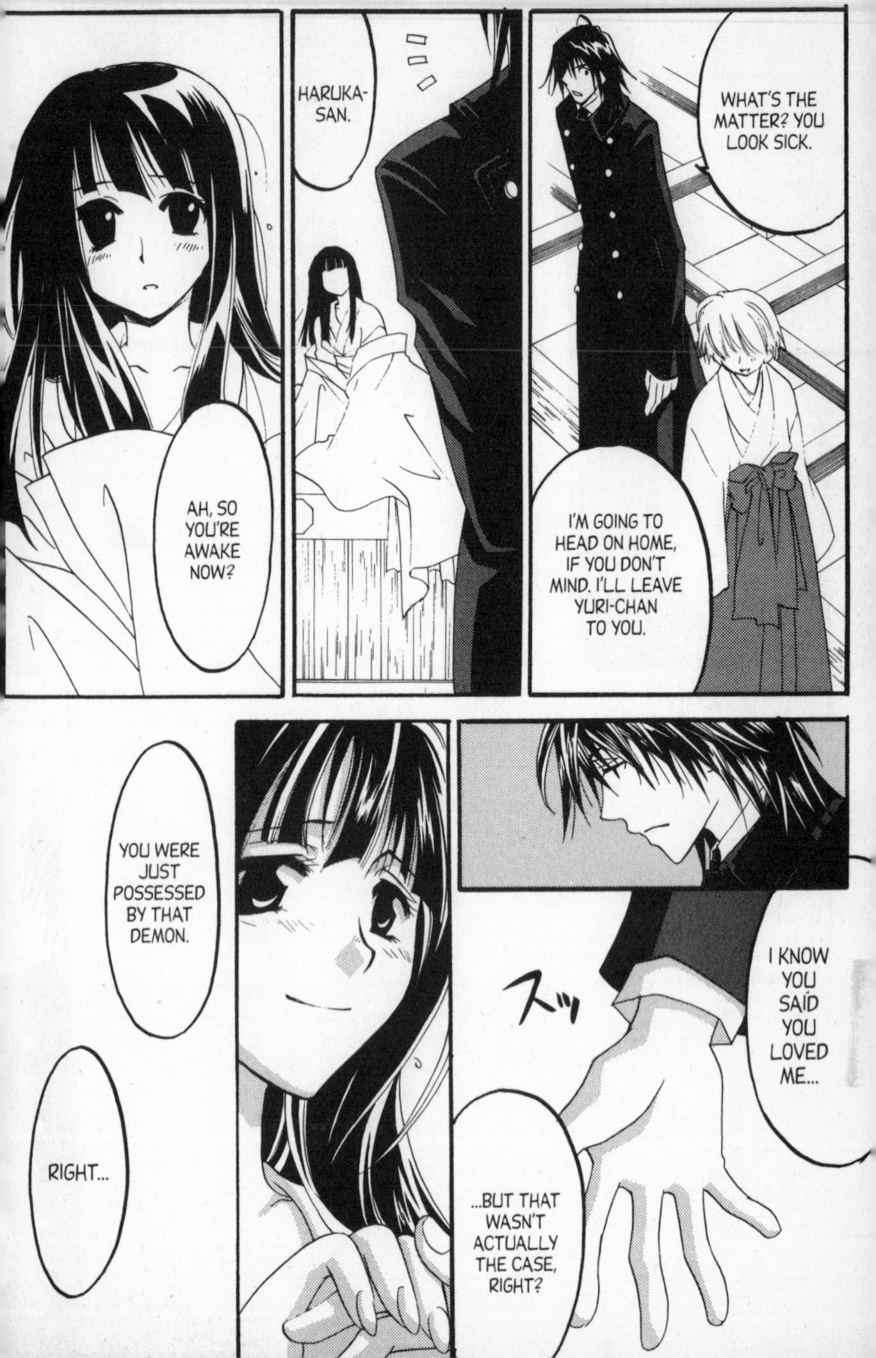
WHAT'S THE MATTER? YOU LOOK SICK.
I'M GOING TO HEAD ON HOME, IF YOU DON'T MIND. I'LL LEAVE YURI-CHAN TO YOU.
HARUKA-SAN.
AH, SO YOU'RE AWAKE NOW?
I KNOW YOU SAID YOU LOVED ME...
スッ
...BUT THAT WASN'T ACTUALLY THE CASE, RIGHT?
YOU WERE JUST POSSESSED BY THAT DEMON.
RIGHT...

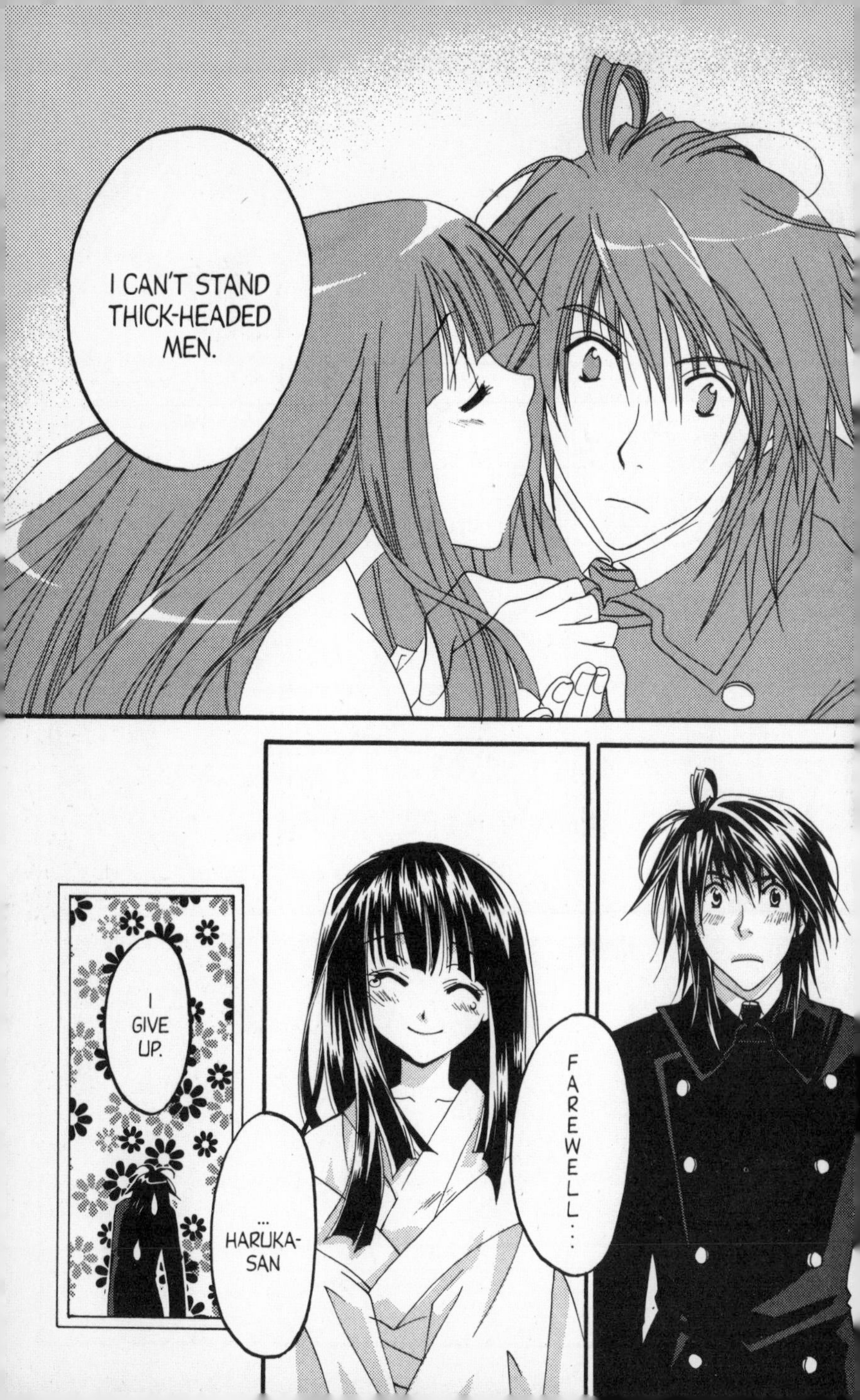
I CAN'T STAND THICK-HEADED MEN.
FAREWELL...
...HARUKA-SAN
I GIVE UP.

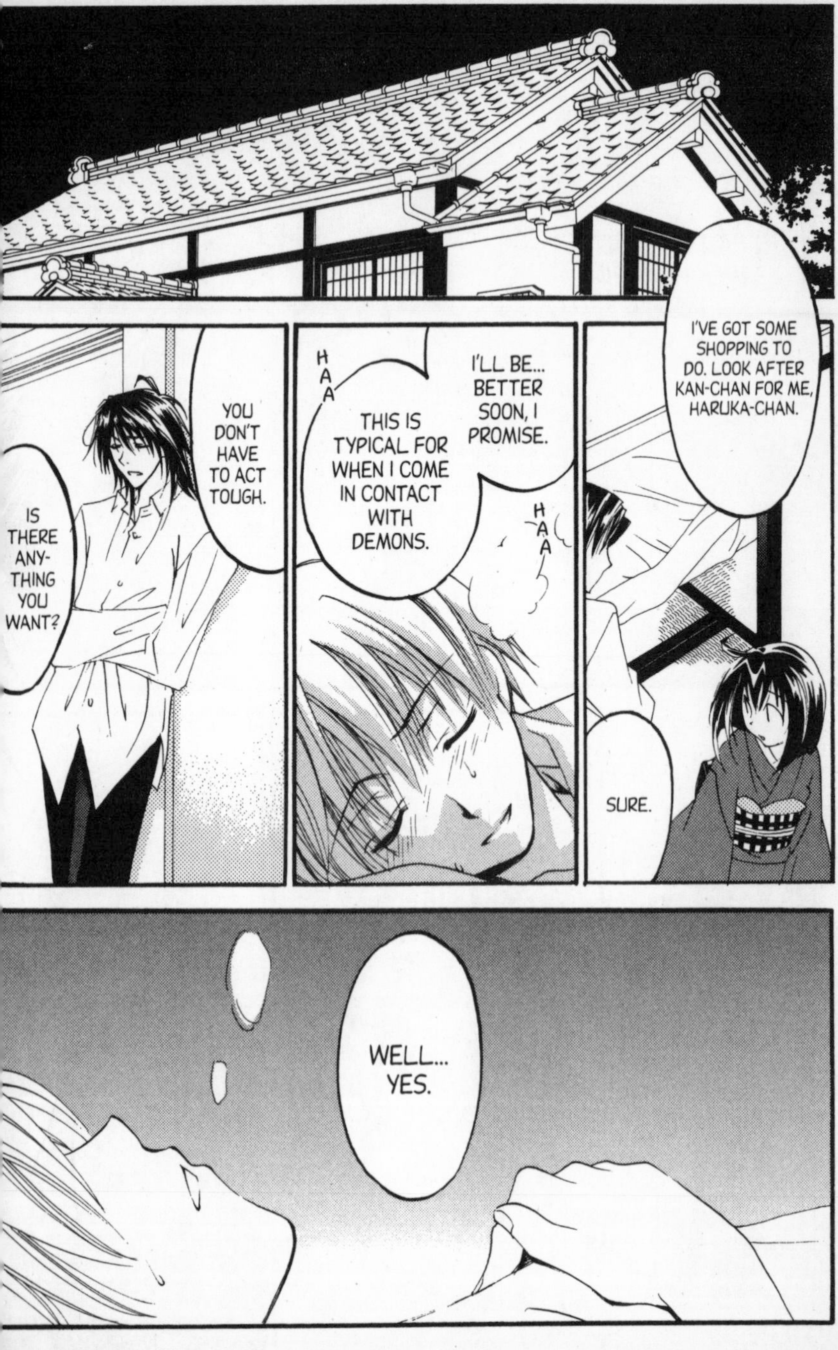
I'VE GOT SOME SHOPPING TO DO. LOOK AFTER KAN-CHAN FOR ME, HARUKA-CHAN.
SURE.
I'LL BE... BETTER SOON, I PROMISE.
HAA
THIS IS TYPICAL FOR WHEN I COME IN CONTACT WITH DEMONS.
HAA
YOU DON'T HAVE TO ACT TOUGH.
IS THERE ANYTHING YOU WANT?
WELL... YES.

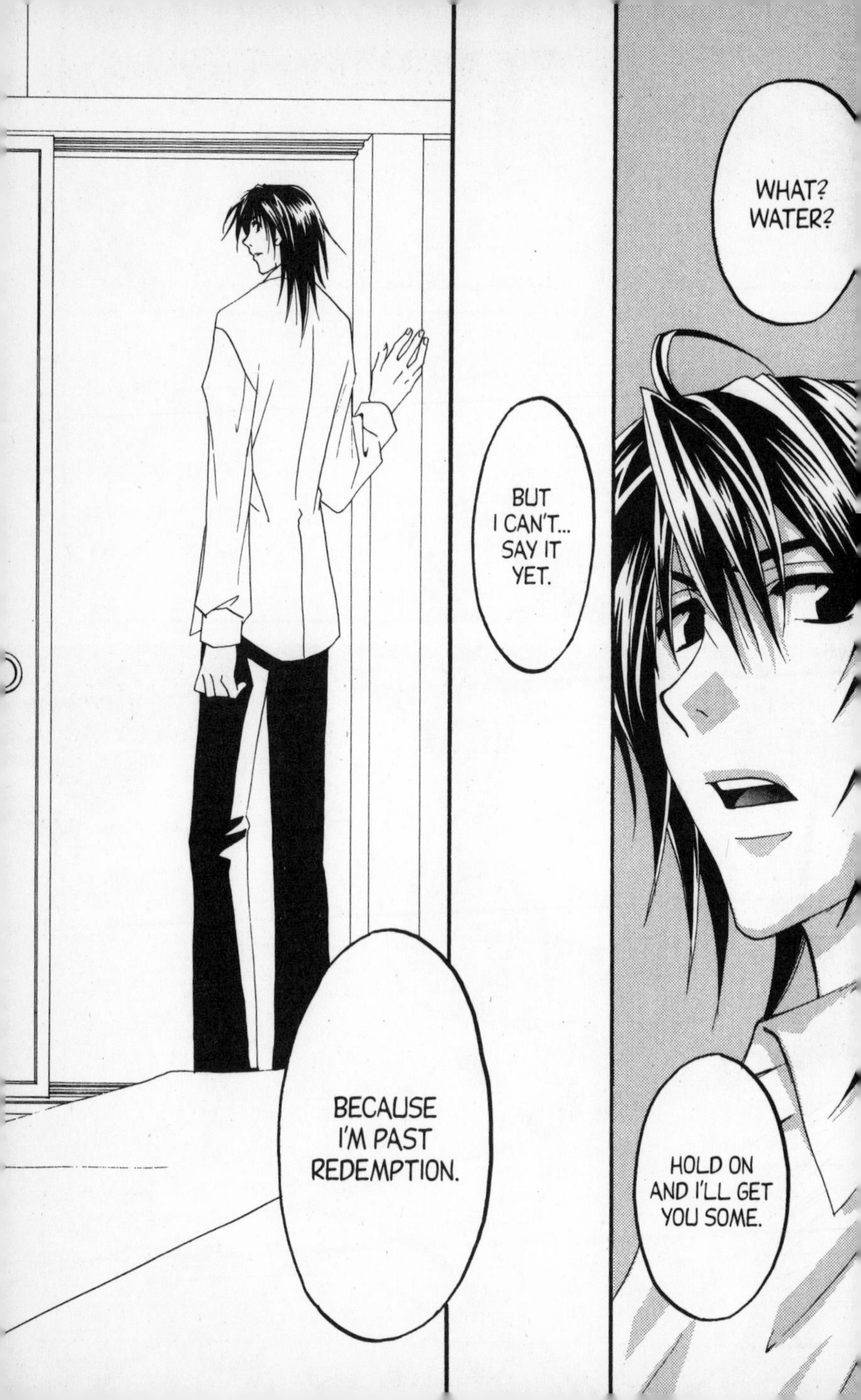
WHAT? WATER?
HOLD ON AND I'LL GET YOU SOME.
BUT I CAN'T... SAY IT YET.
BECAUSE I'M PAST REDEMPTION.

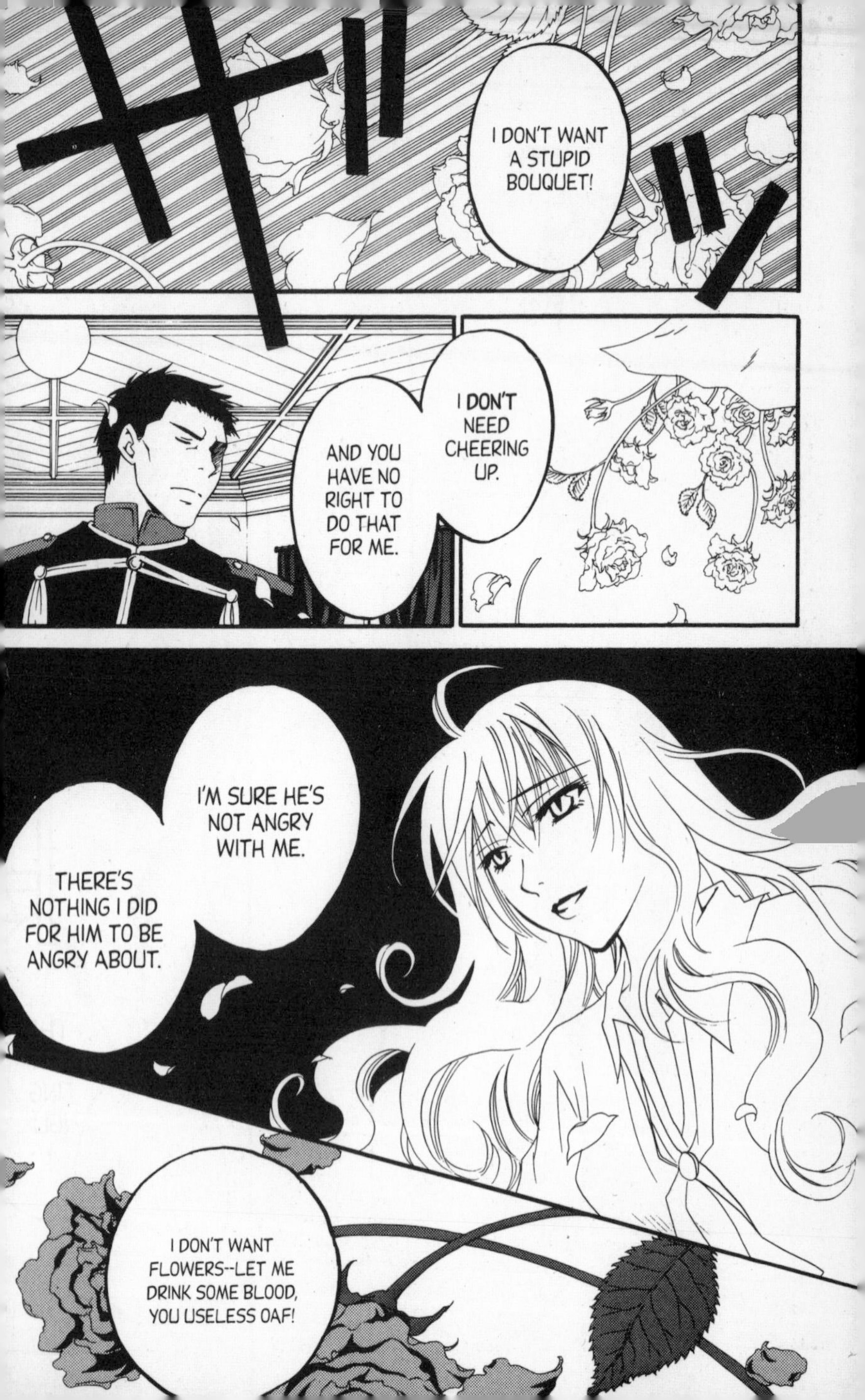
I DON'T WANT A STUPID BOUQUET!
I DON'T NEED CHEERING UP.
AND YOU HAVE NO RIGHT TO DO THAT FOR ME.
I'M SURE HE'S NOT ANGRY WITH ME.
THERE'S NOTHING I DID FOR HIM TO BE ANGRY ABOUT.
I DON'T WANT FLOWERS--LET ME DRINK SOME BLOOD, YOU USELESS OAF!

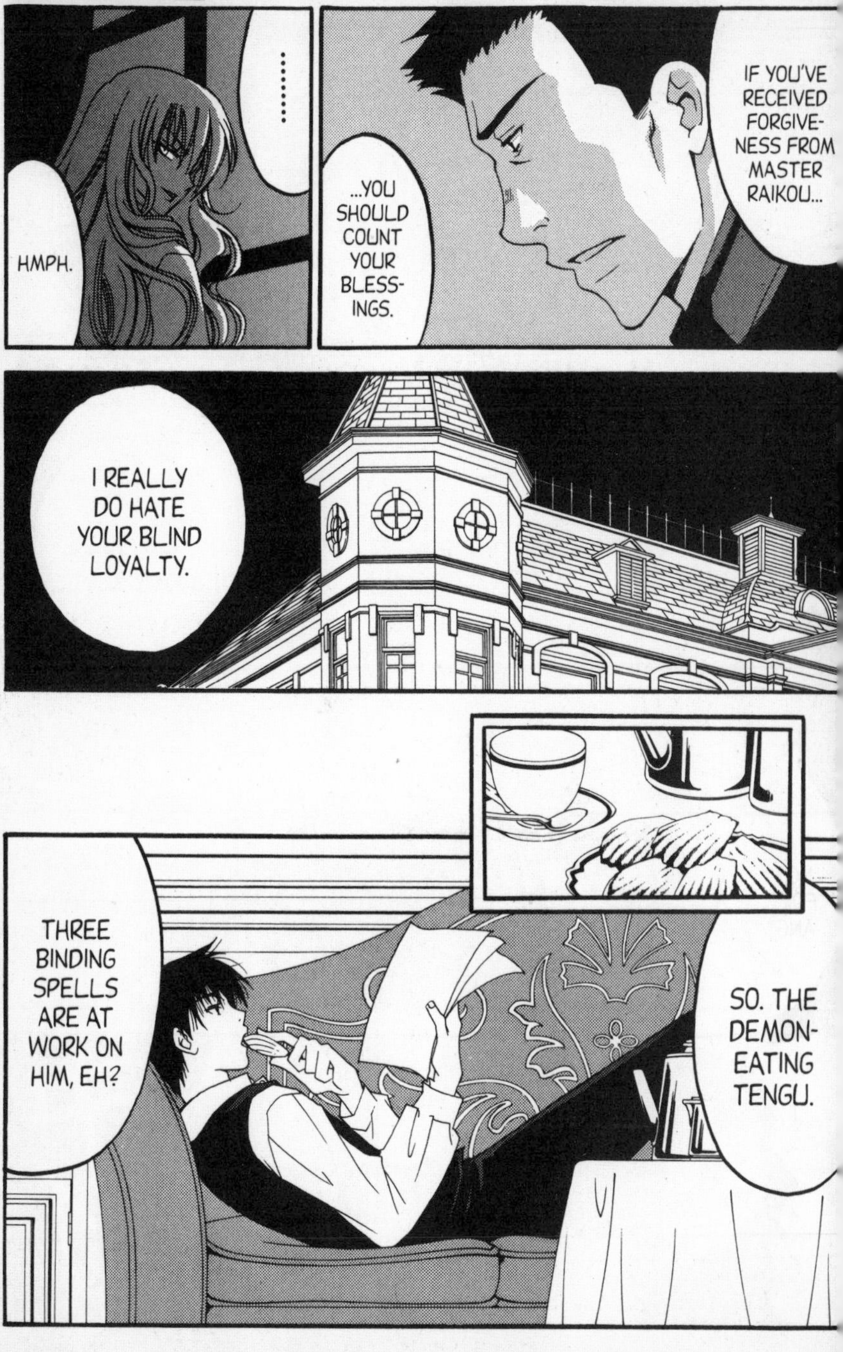
IF YOU'VE RECEIVED FORGIVE-NESS FROM MASTER RAIKOU...
...YOU SHOULD COUNT YOUR BLESS-INGS.
......
HMPH.
I REALLY DO HATE YOUR BLIND LOYALTY.
SO. THE DEMON-EATING TENGU.
THREE BINDING SPELLS ARE AT WORK ON HIM, EH?

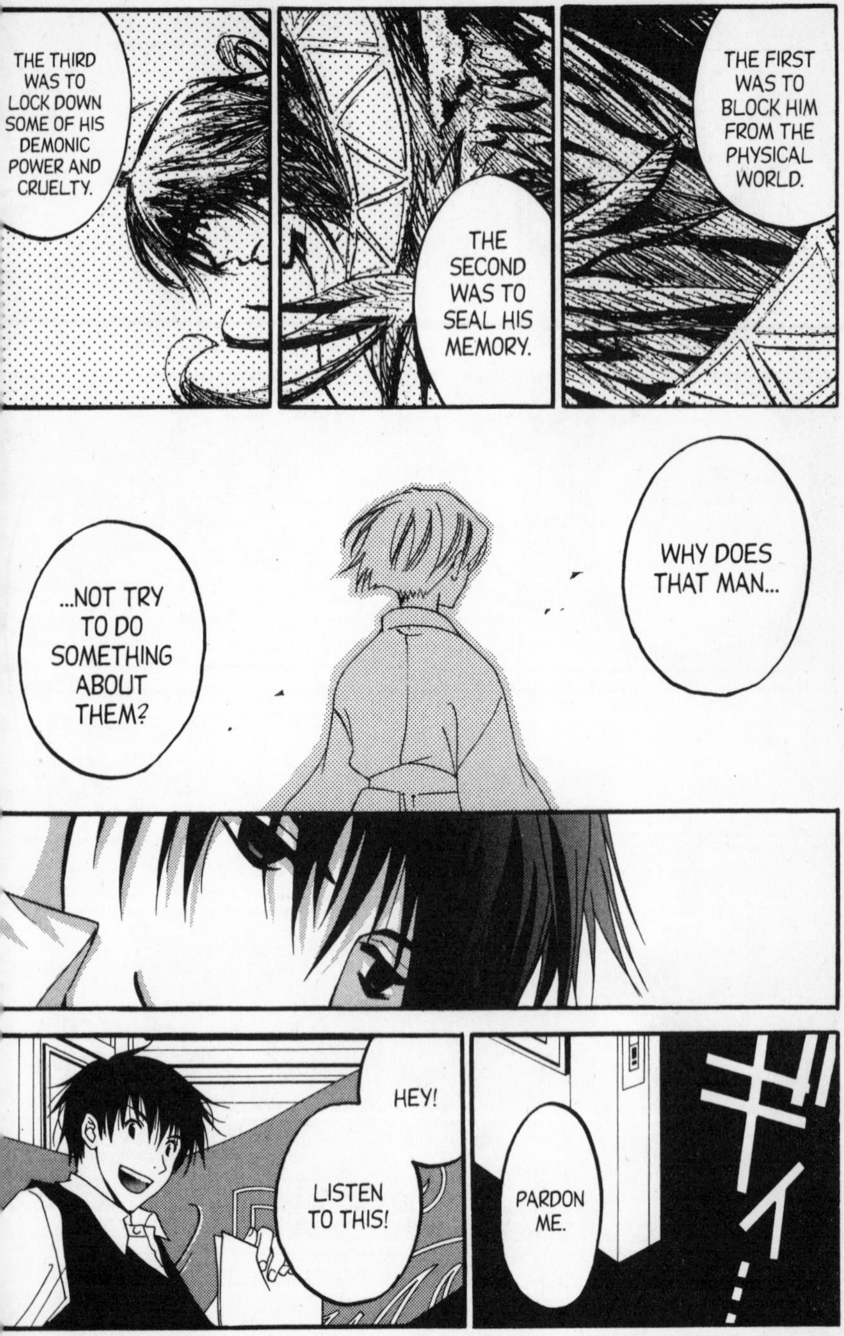
THE FIRST WAS TO BLOCK HIM FROM THE PHYSICAL WORLD.
THE SECOND WAS TO SEAL HIS MEMORY.
THE THIRD WAS TO LOCK DOWN SOME OF HIS DEMONIC POWER AND CRUELTY.
WHY DOES THAT MAN...
...NOT TRY TO DO SOMETHING ABOUT THEM?
ギイ…
PARDON ME.
HEY!
LISTEN TO THIS!

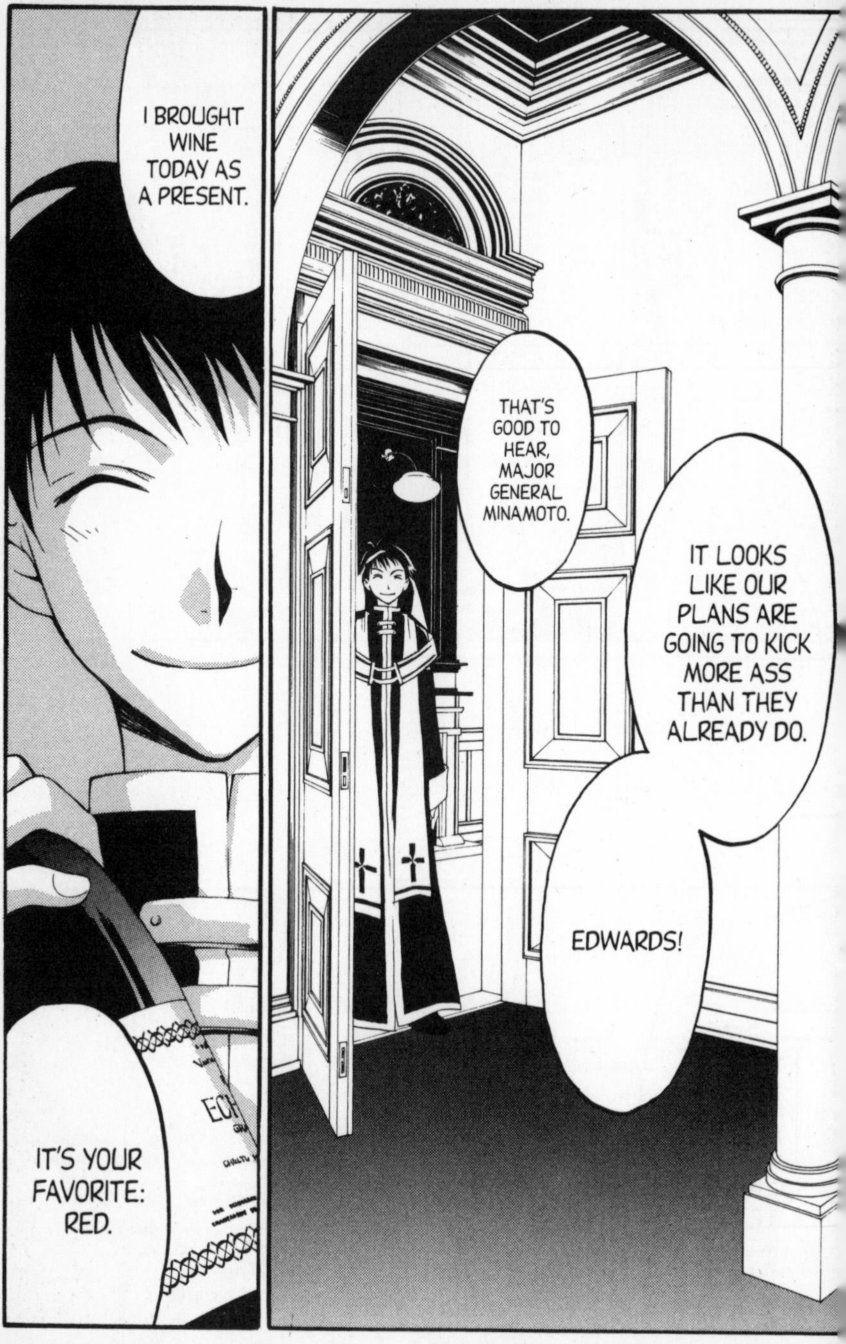
THAT'S GOOD TO HEAR, MAJOR GENERAL MINAMOTO.
IT LOOKS LIKE OUR PLANS ARE GOING TO KICK MORE ASS THAN THEY ALREADY DO.
EDWARDS!
I BROUGHT WINE TODAY AS A PRESENT.
IT'S YOUR FAVORITE: RED.

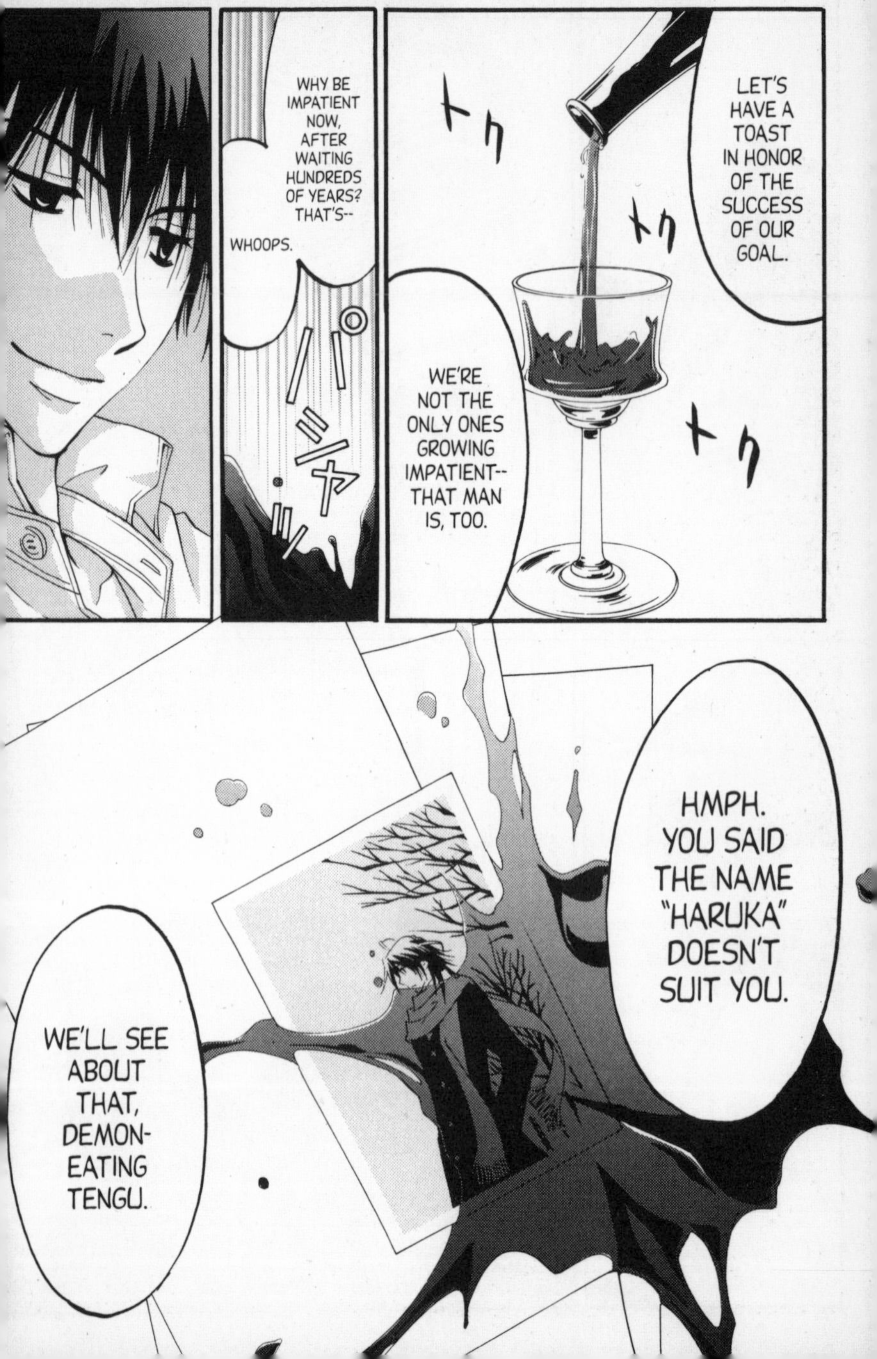
LET'S HAVE A TOAST IN HONOR OF THE SUCCESS OF OUR GOAL.
トク
トク
トク
WE'RE NOT THE ONLY ONES GROWING IMPATIENT-- THAT MAN IS, TOO.
WHY BE IMPATIENT NOW, AFTER WAITING HUNDREDS OF YEARS? THAT'S--
WHOOPS.
パシャ
HMPH. YOU SAID THE NAME "HARUKA" DOESN'T SUIT YOU.
WE'LL SEE ABOUT THAT, DEMON-EATING TENGU.

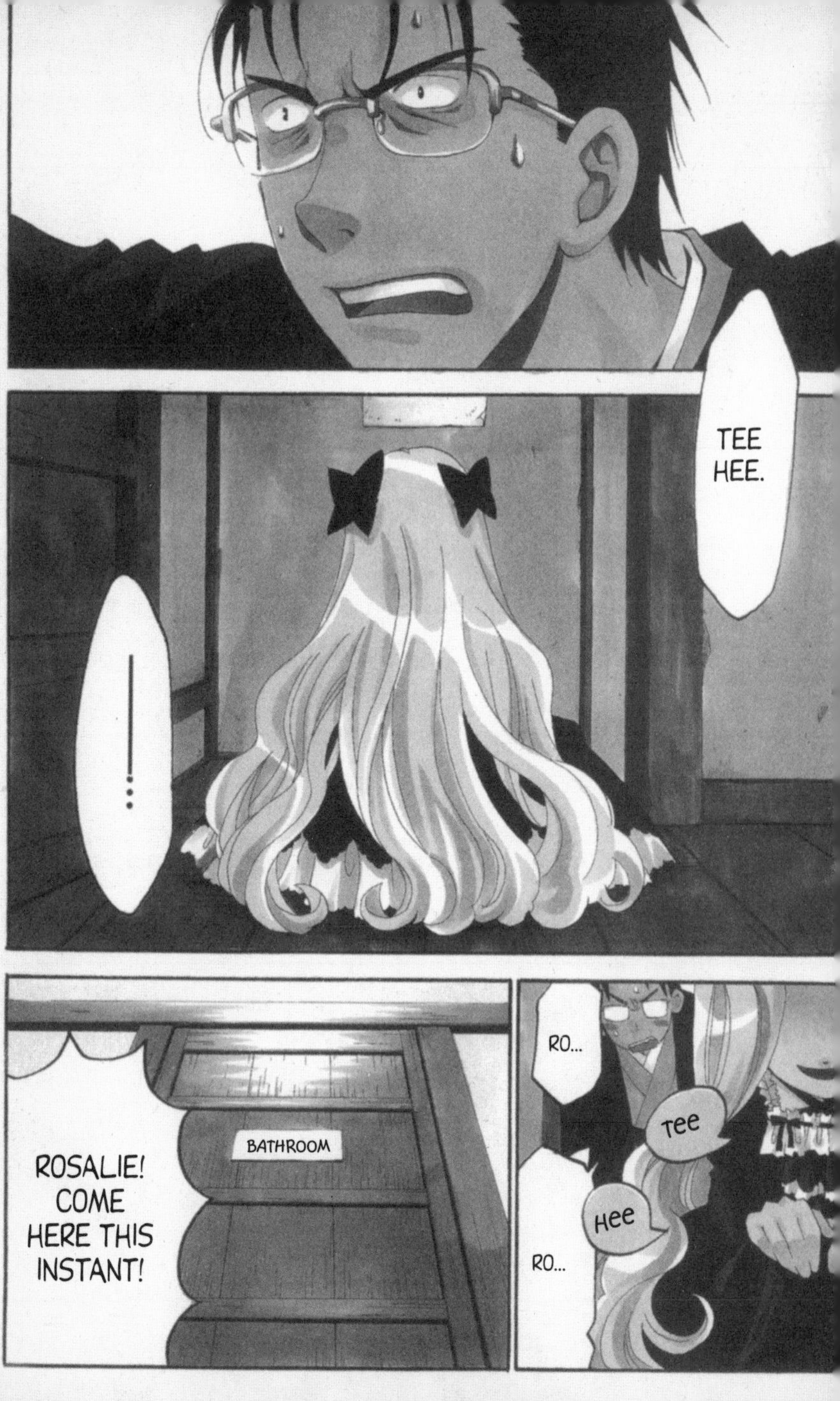
TEE HEE.
—...!
RO...
Tee
Hee
RO...
BATHROOM
ROSALIE! COME HERE THIS INSTANT!

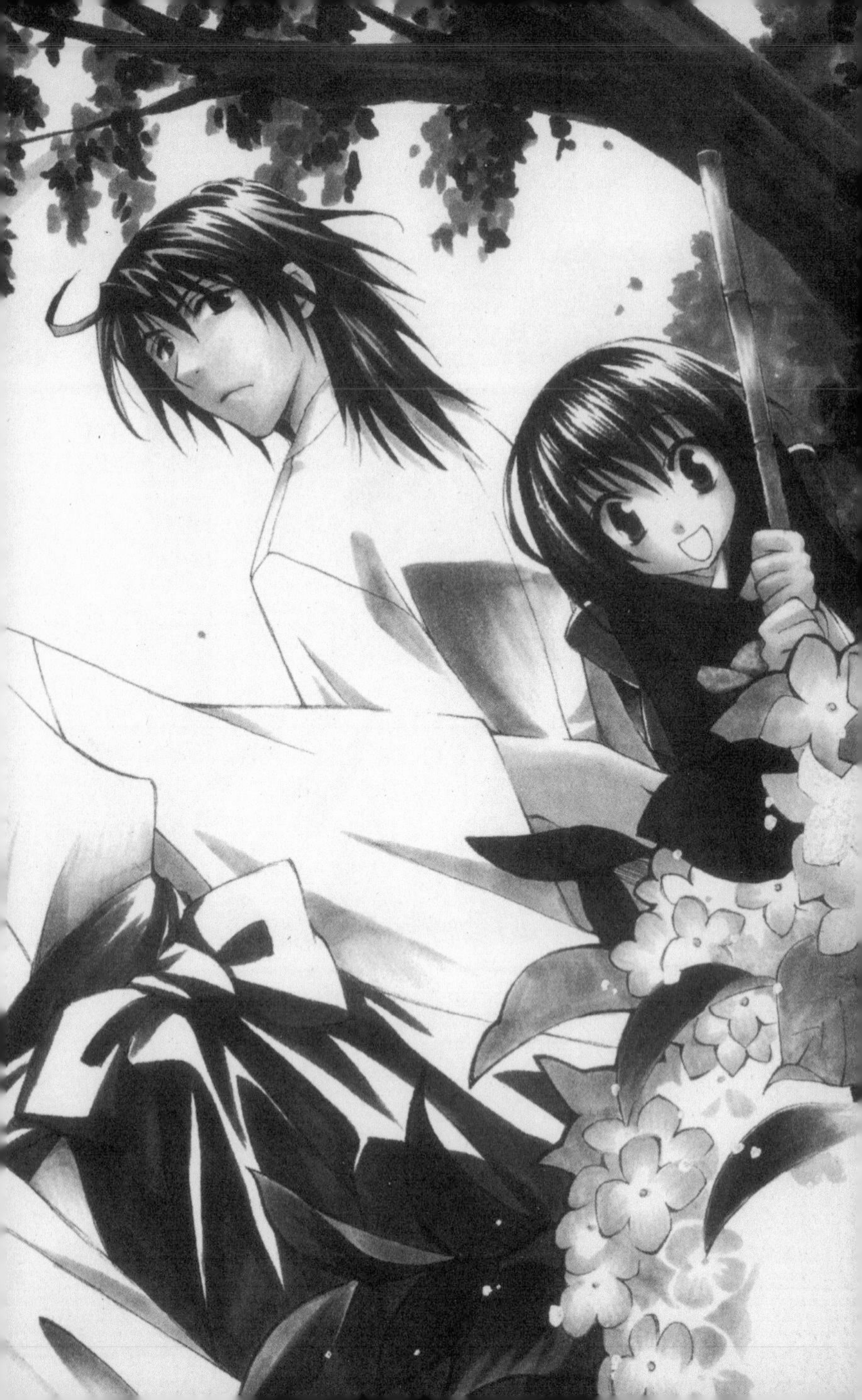

KANBARINYUUDOU STAGE PART I

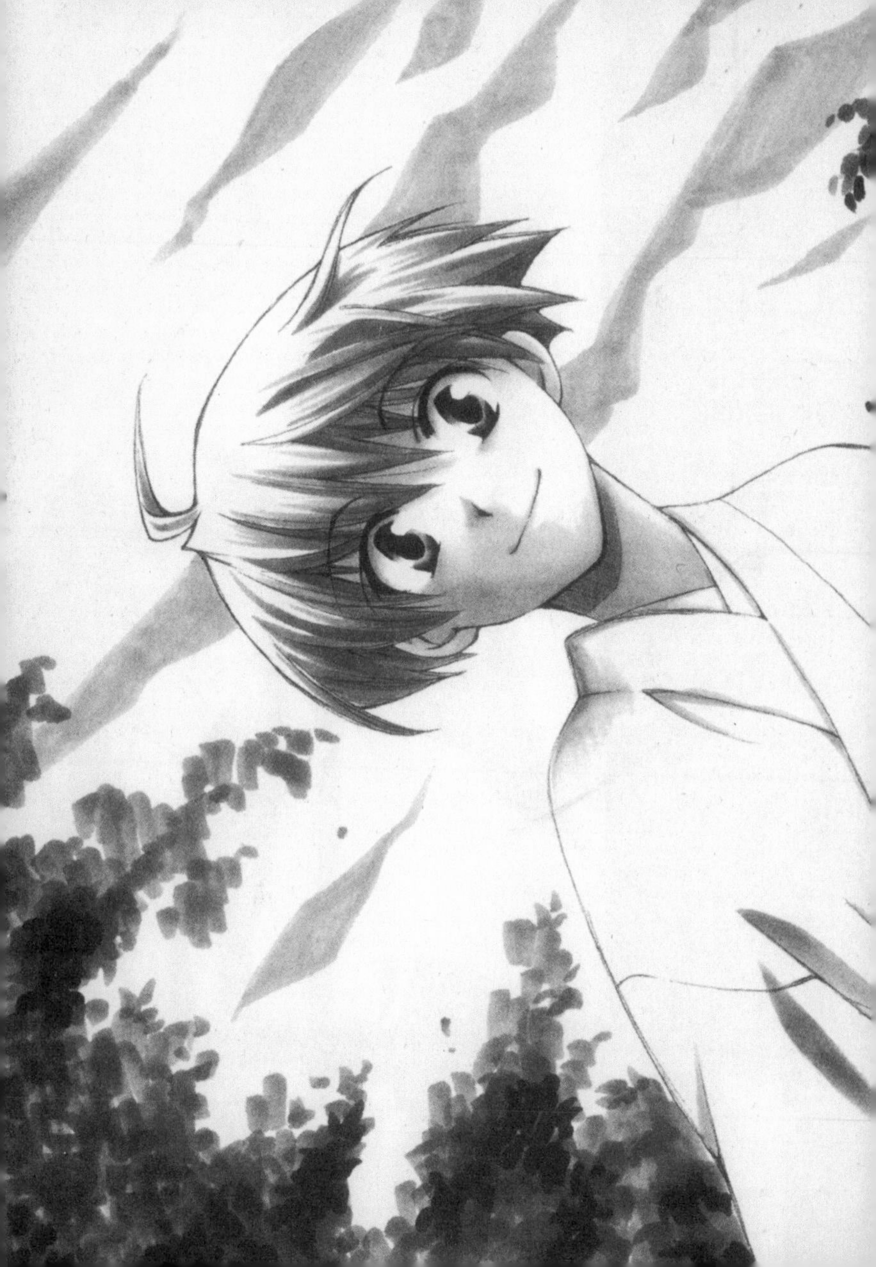

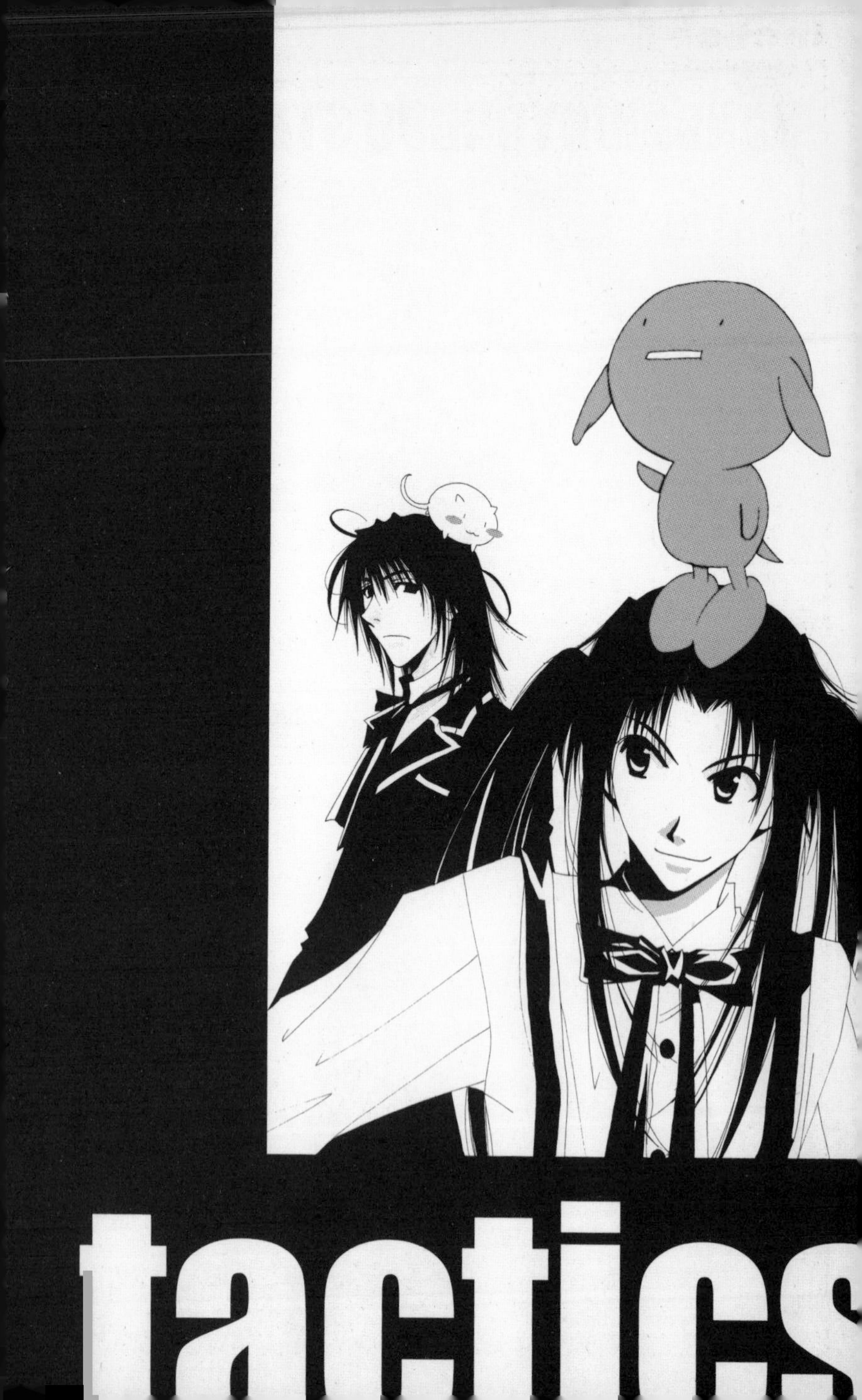
tactics

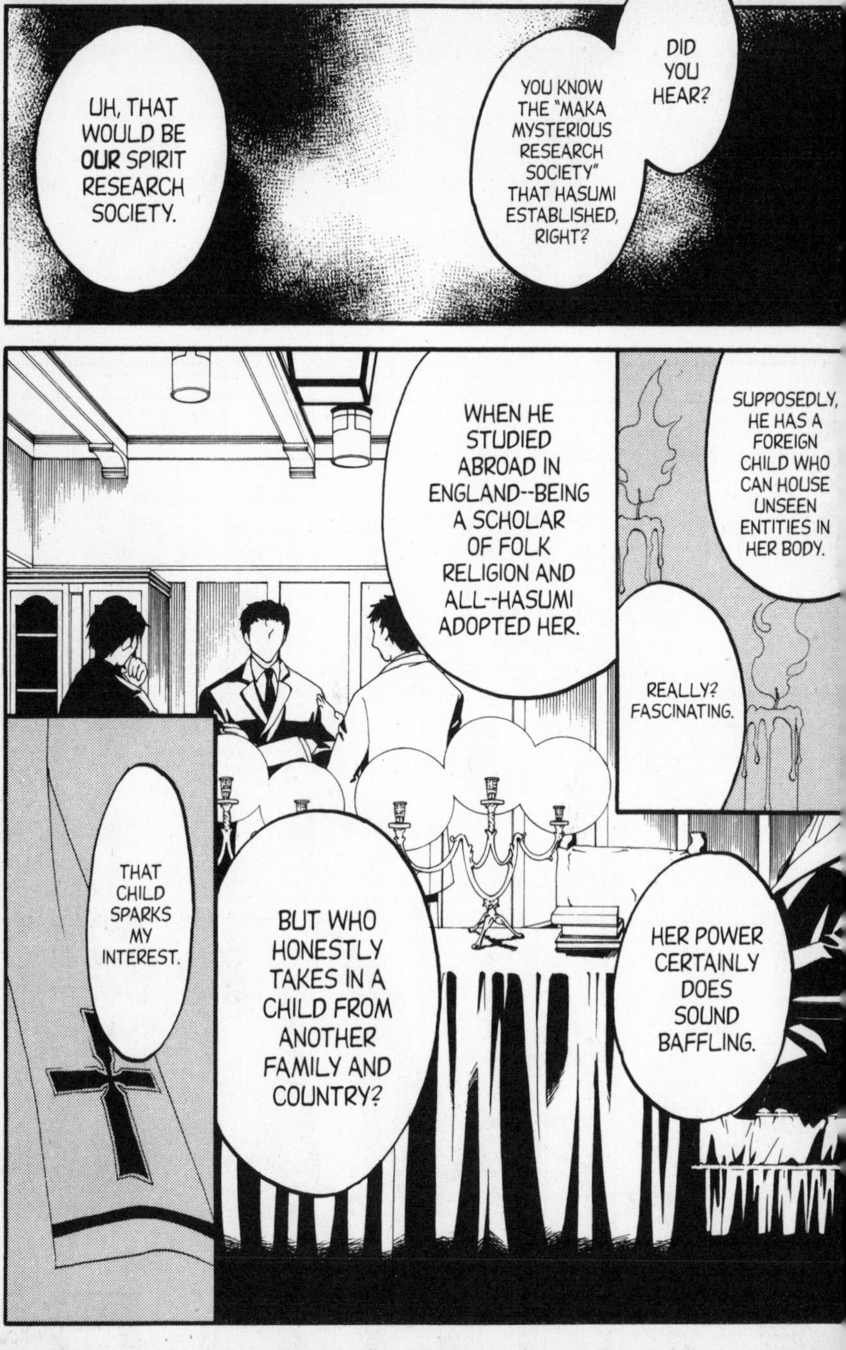
DID YOU HEAR?
YOU KNOW THE "MAKA MYSTERIOUS RESEARCH SOCIETY" THAT HASUMI ESTABLISHED, RIGHT?
UH, THAT WOULD BE **OUR** SPIRIT RESEARCH SOCIETY.
SUPPOSEDLY, HE HAS A FOREIGN CHILD WHO CAN HOUSE UNSEEN ENTITIES IN HER BODY.
WHEN HE STUDIED ABROAD IN ENGLAND--BEING A SCHOLAR OF FOLK RELIGION AND ALL--HASUMI ADOPTED HER.
REALLY? FASCINATING.
HER POWER CERTAINLY DOES SOUND BAFFLING.
BUT WHO HONESTLY TAKES IN A CHILD FROM ANOTHER FAMILY AND COUNTRY?
THAT CHILD SPARKS MY INTEREST.

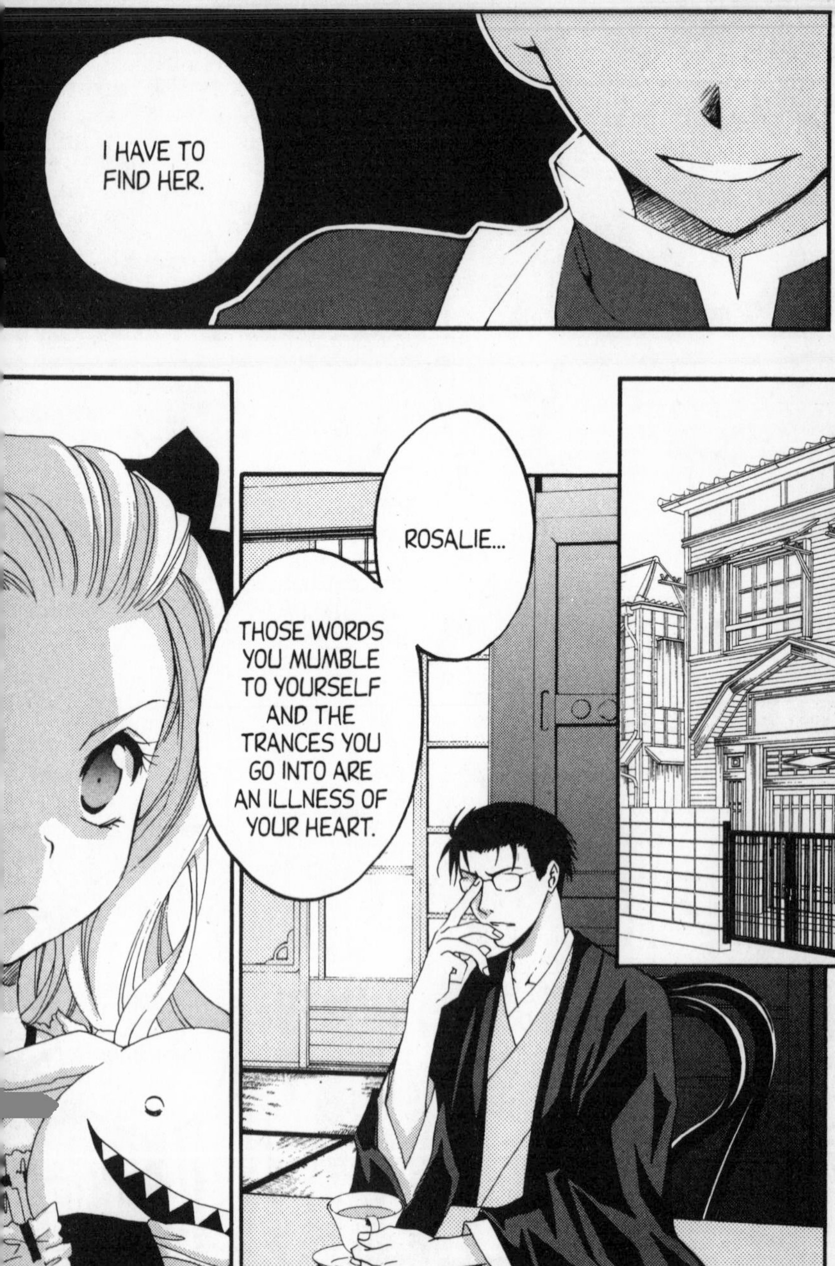
I HAVE TO FIND HER.
ROSALIE...
THOSE WORDS YOU MUMBLE TO YOURSELF AND THE TRANCES YOU GO INTO ARE AN ILLNESS OF YOUR HEART.

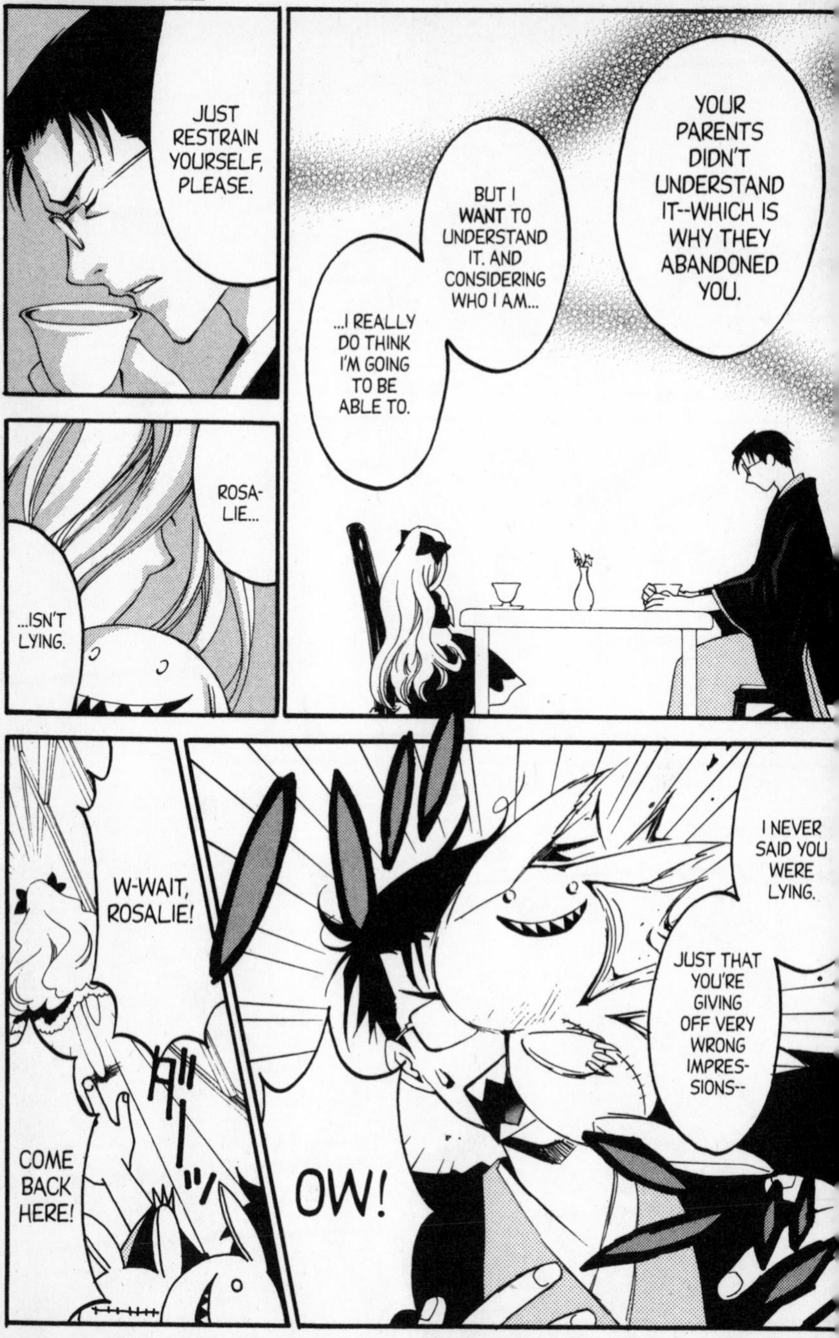
YOUR PARENTS DIDN'T UNDERSTAND IT--WHICH IS WHY THEY ABANDONED YOU.
BUT I WANT TO UNDERSTAND IT. AND CONSIDERING WHO I AM...
...I REALLY DO THINK I'M GOING TO BE ABLE TO.
JUST RESTRAIN YOURSELF, PLEASE.
ROSALIE...
...ISN'T LYING.
I NEVER SAID YOU WERE LYING.
JUST THAT YOU'RE GIVING OFF VERY WRONG IMPRESSIONS--
OW!
W-WAIT, ROSALIE!
COME BACK HERE!

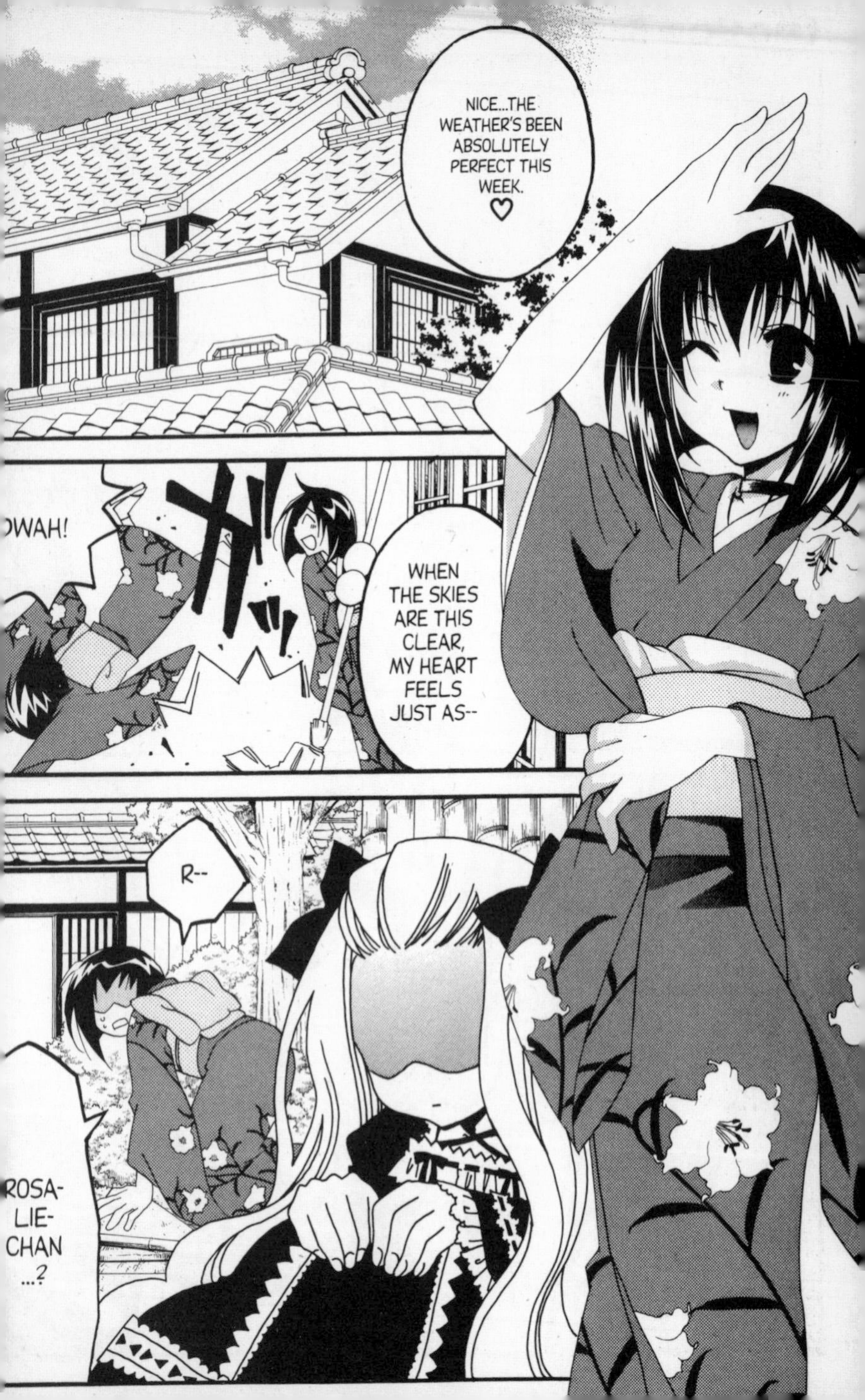
NICE...THE WEATHER'S BEEN ABSOLUTELY PERFECT THIS WEEK. ♡
WHEN THE SKIES ARE THIS CLEAR, MY HEART FEELS JUST AS--
OWAH!
R--
ROSA-LIE-CHAN ...?

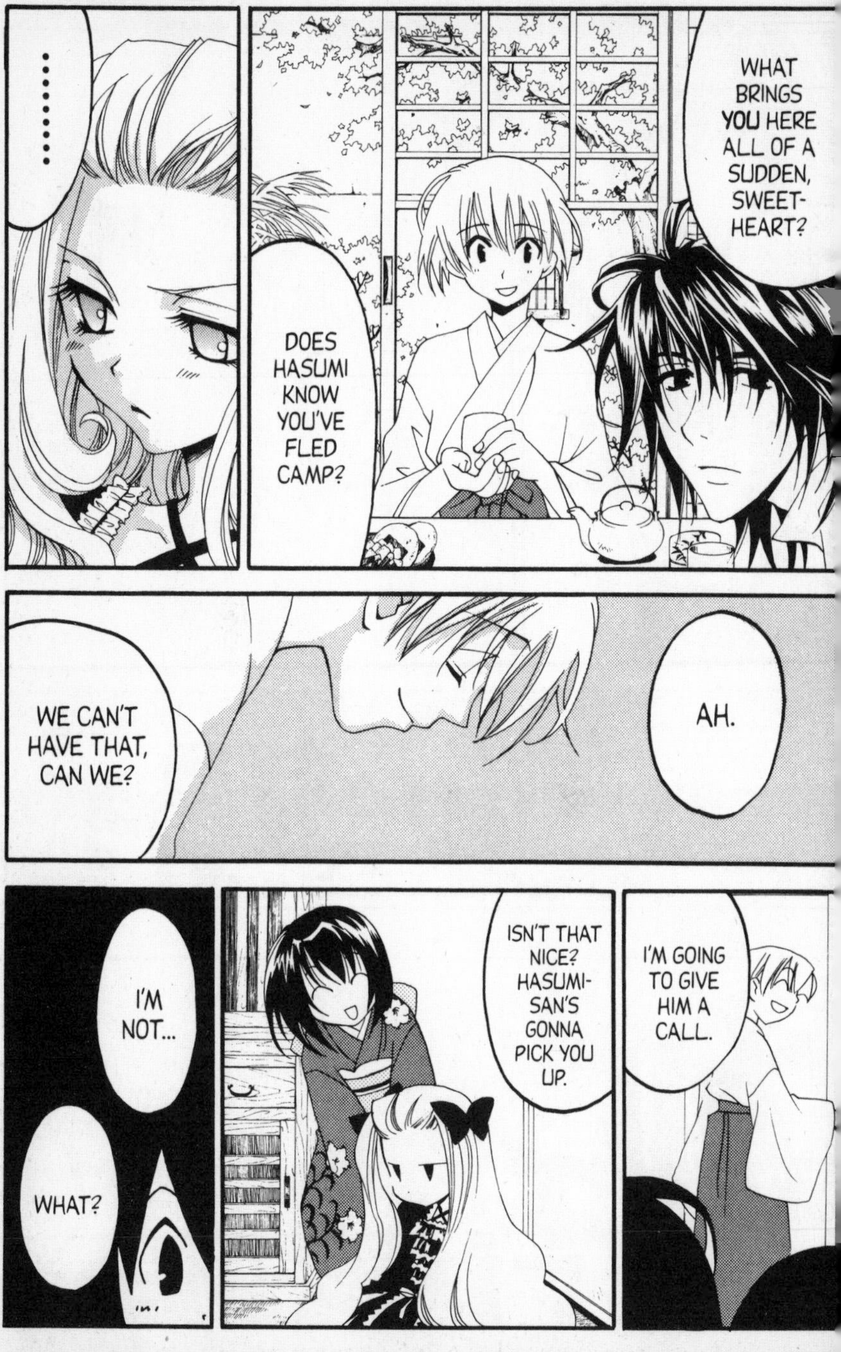

WHAT BRINGS YOU HERE ALL OF A SUDDEN, SWEET-HEART?
DOES HASUMI KNOW YOU'VE FLED CAMP?
....
AH.
WE CAN'T HAVE THAT, CAN WE?
I'M GOING TO GIVE HIM A CALL.
ISN'T THAT NICE? HASUMI-SAN'S GONNA PICK YOU UP.
I'M NOT...
WHAT?

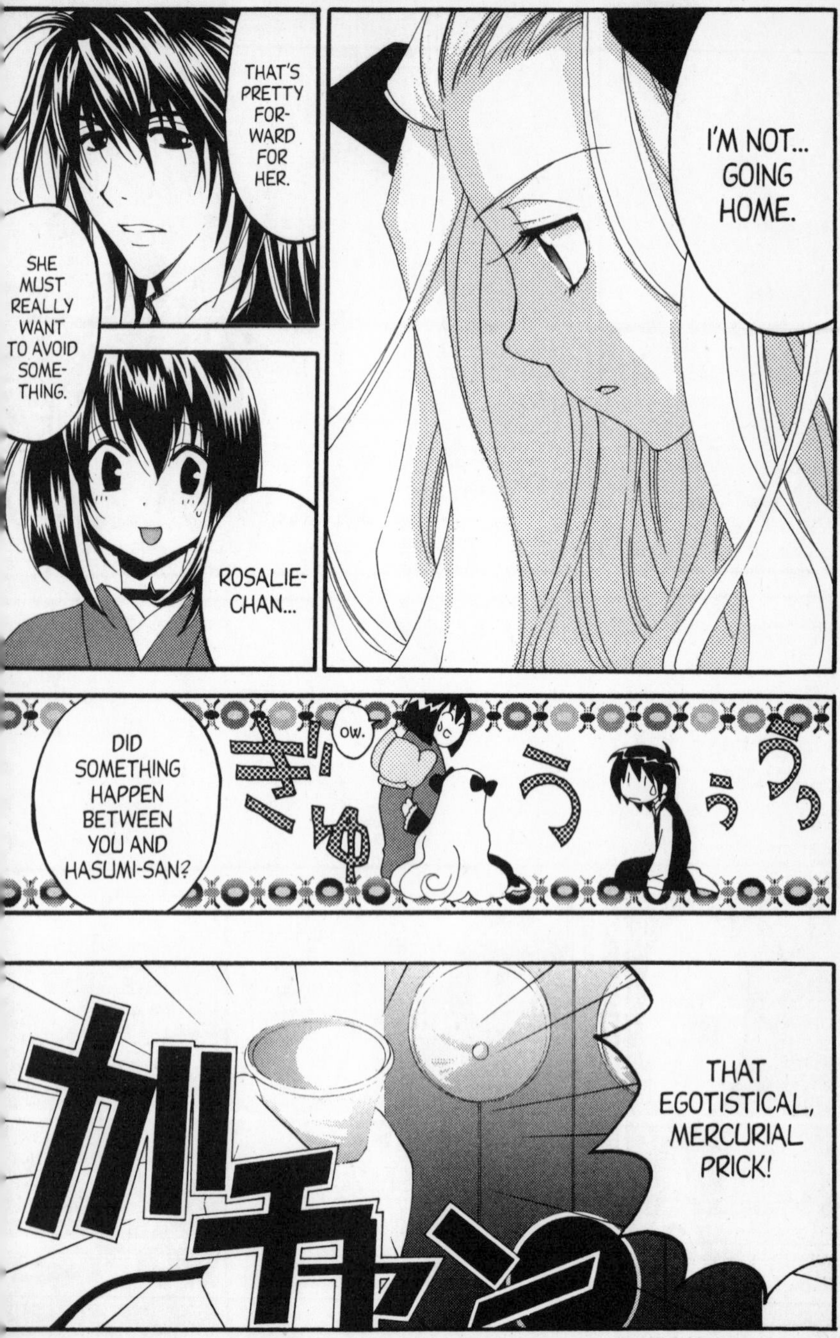
I'M NOT... GOING HOME.
THAT'S PRETTY FOR-WARD FOR HER.
SHE MUST REALLY WANT TO AVOID SOME-THING.
ROSALIE-CHAN...
OW.
DID SOMETHING HAPPEN BETWEEN YOU AND HASUMI-SAN?
THAT EGOTISTICAL, MERCURIAL PRICK!

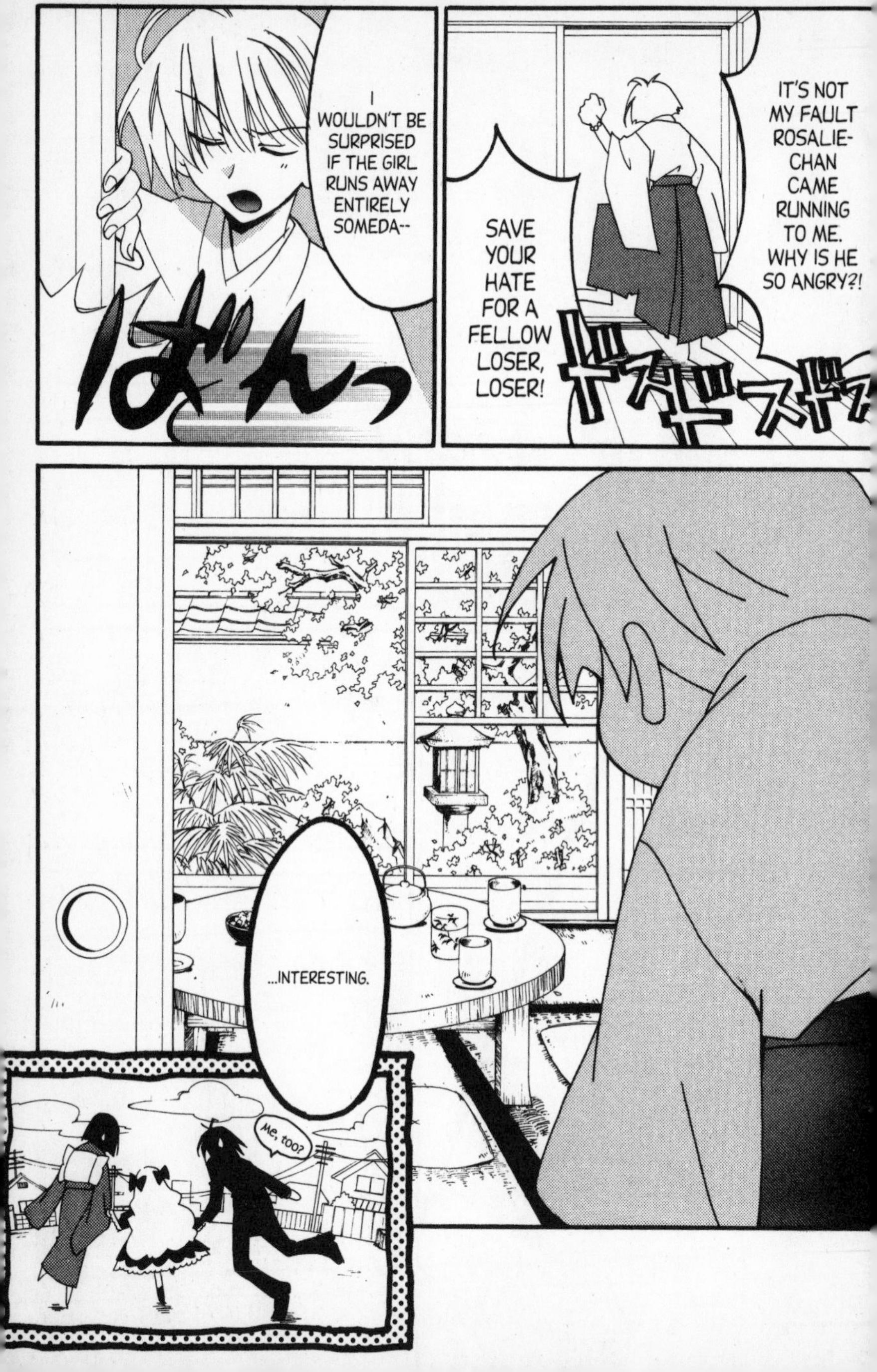
IT'S NOT MY FAULT ROSALIE-CHAN CAME RUNNING TO ME. WHY IS HE SO ANGRY?!
SAVE YOUR HATE FOR A FELLOW LOSER, LOSER!
I WOULDN'T BE SURPRISED IF THE GIRL RUNS AWAY ENTIRELY SOMEDA--
ばんっ
...INTERESTING.
Me, too?

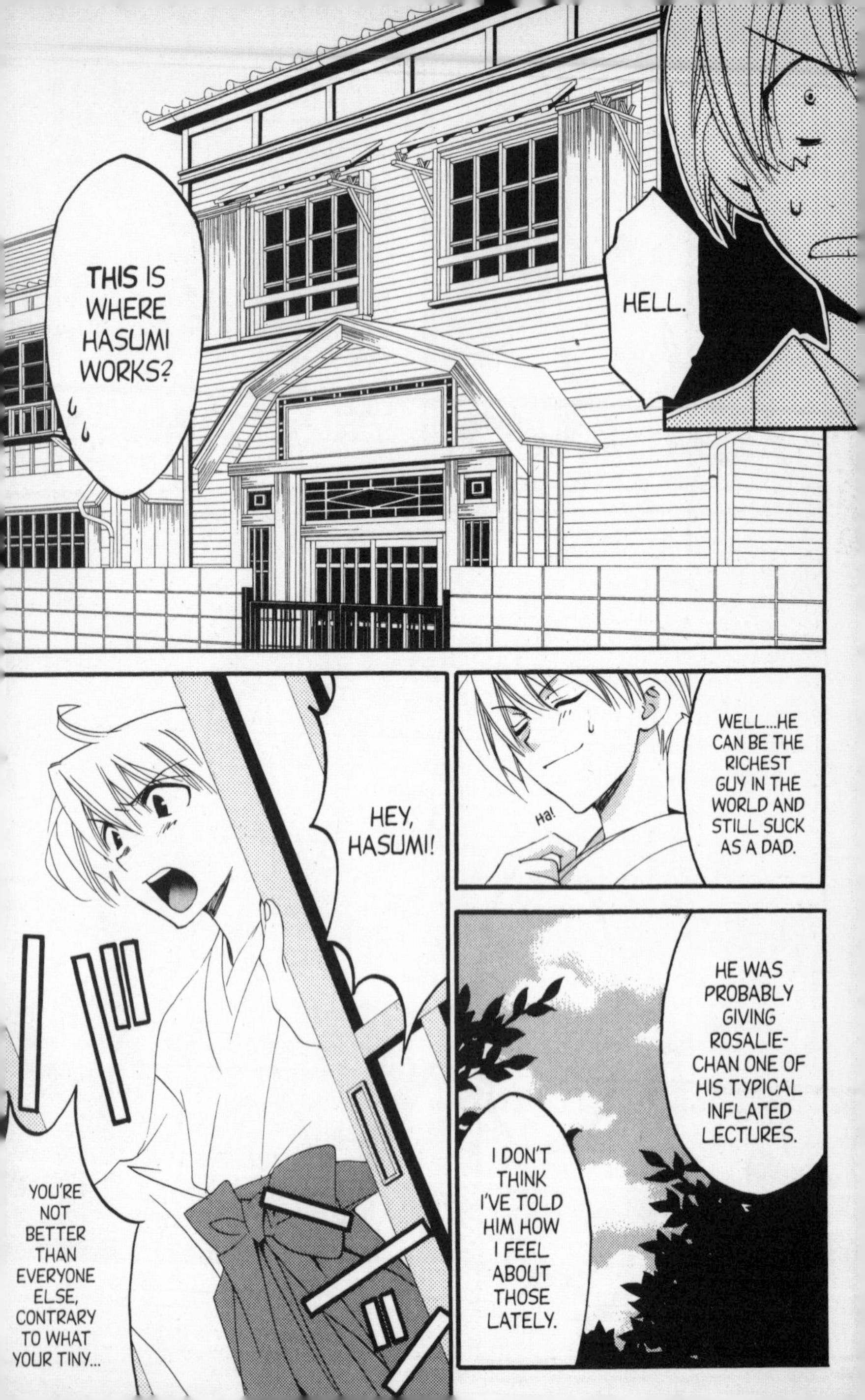
HELL.
THIS IS WHERE HASUMI WORKS?
WELL...HE CAN BE THE RICHEST GUY IN THE WORLD AND STILL SUCK AS A DAD.
Ha!
HE WAS PROBABLY GIVING ROSALIE-CHAN ONE OF HIS TYPICAL INFLATED LECTURES.
I DON'T THINK I'VE TOLD HIM HOW I FEEL ABOUT THOSE LATELY.
HEY, HASUMI!
YOU'RE NOT BETTER THAN EVERYONE ELSE, CONTRARY TO WHAT YOUR TINY...

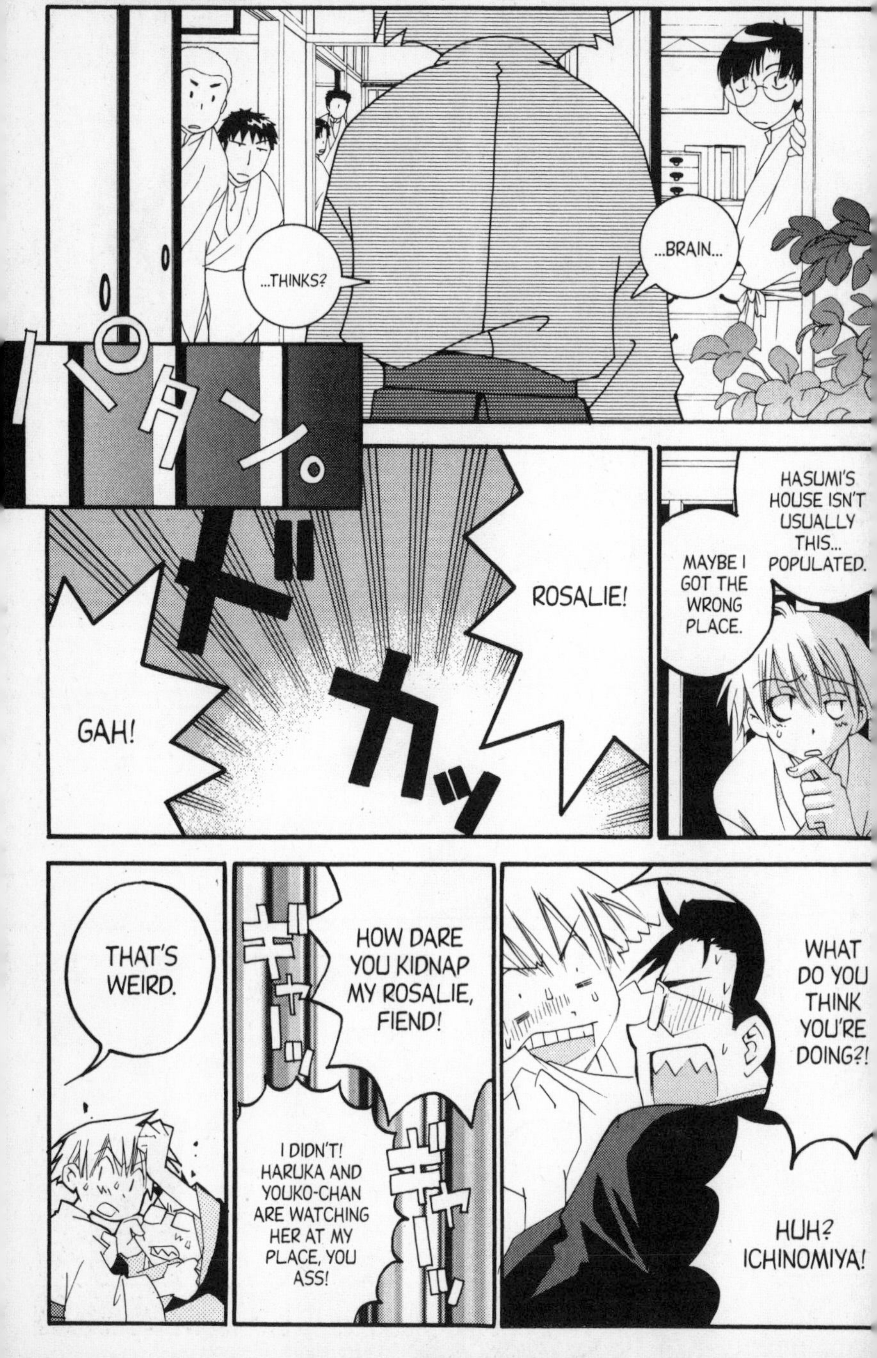
...BRAIN...
...THINKS?
パタン。
HASUMI'S HOUSE ISN'T USUALLY THIS... POPULATED.
MAYBE I GOT THE WRONG PLACE.
ROSALIE!
ドカッ
GAH!
WHAT DO YOU THINK YOU'RE DOING?!
HUH? ICHINOMIYA!
HOW DARE YOU KIDNAP MY ROSALIE, FIEND!
ギャー
I DIDN'T! HARUKA AND YOUKO-CHAN ARE WATCHING HER AT MY PLACE, YOU ASS!
ギャー
THAT'S WEIRD.

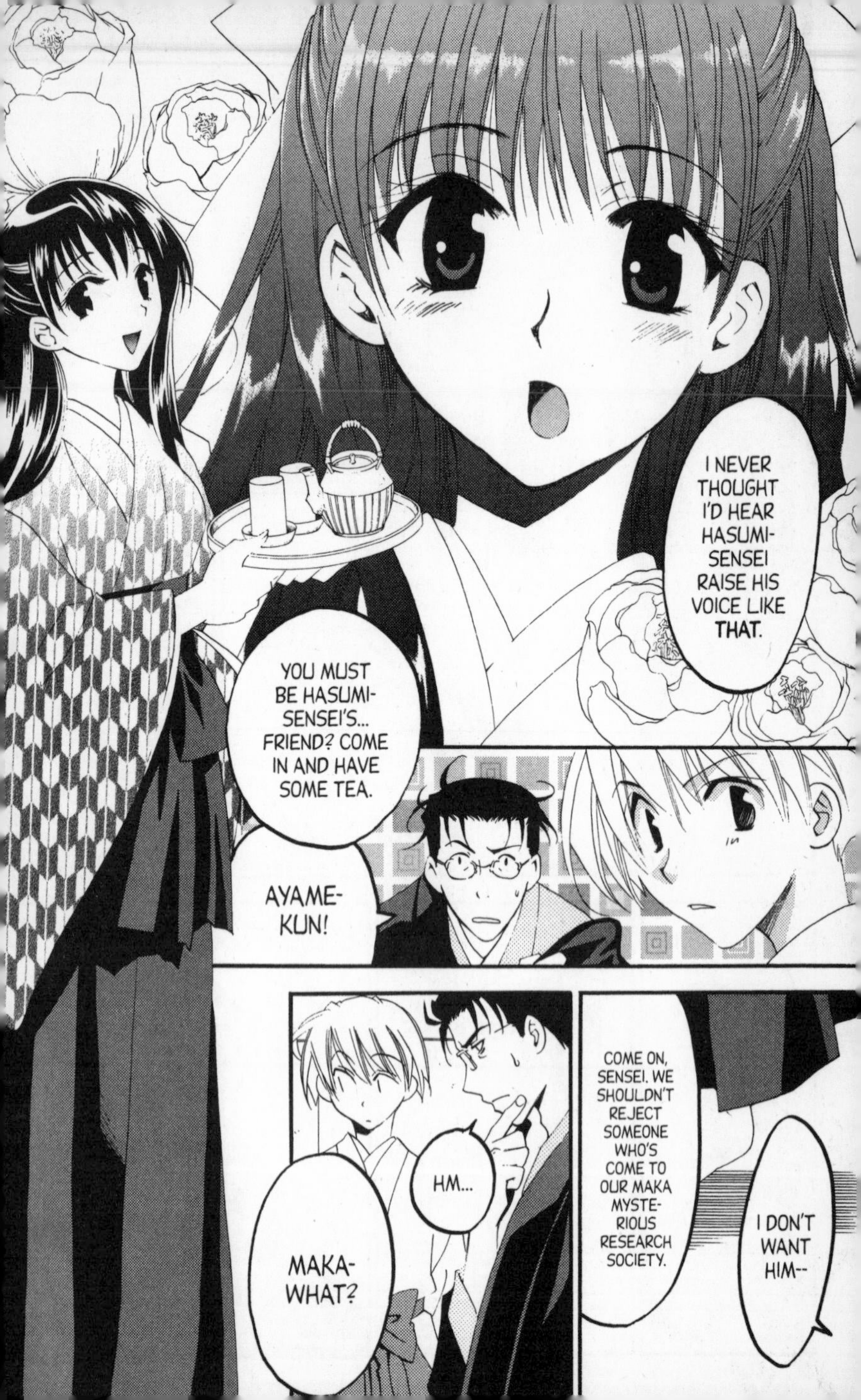

I NEVER THOUGHT I'D HEAR HASUMI-SENSEI RAISE HIS VOICE LIKE THAT.
YOU MUST BE HASUMI-SENSEI'S... FRIEND? COME IN AND HAVE SOME TEA.
AYAME-KUN!
I DON'T WANT HIM--
COME ON, SENSEI. WE SHOULDN'T REJECT SOMEONE WHO'S COME TO OUR MAKA MYSTERIOUS RESEARCH SOCIETY.
HM...
MAKA-WHAT?

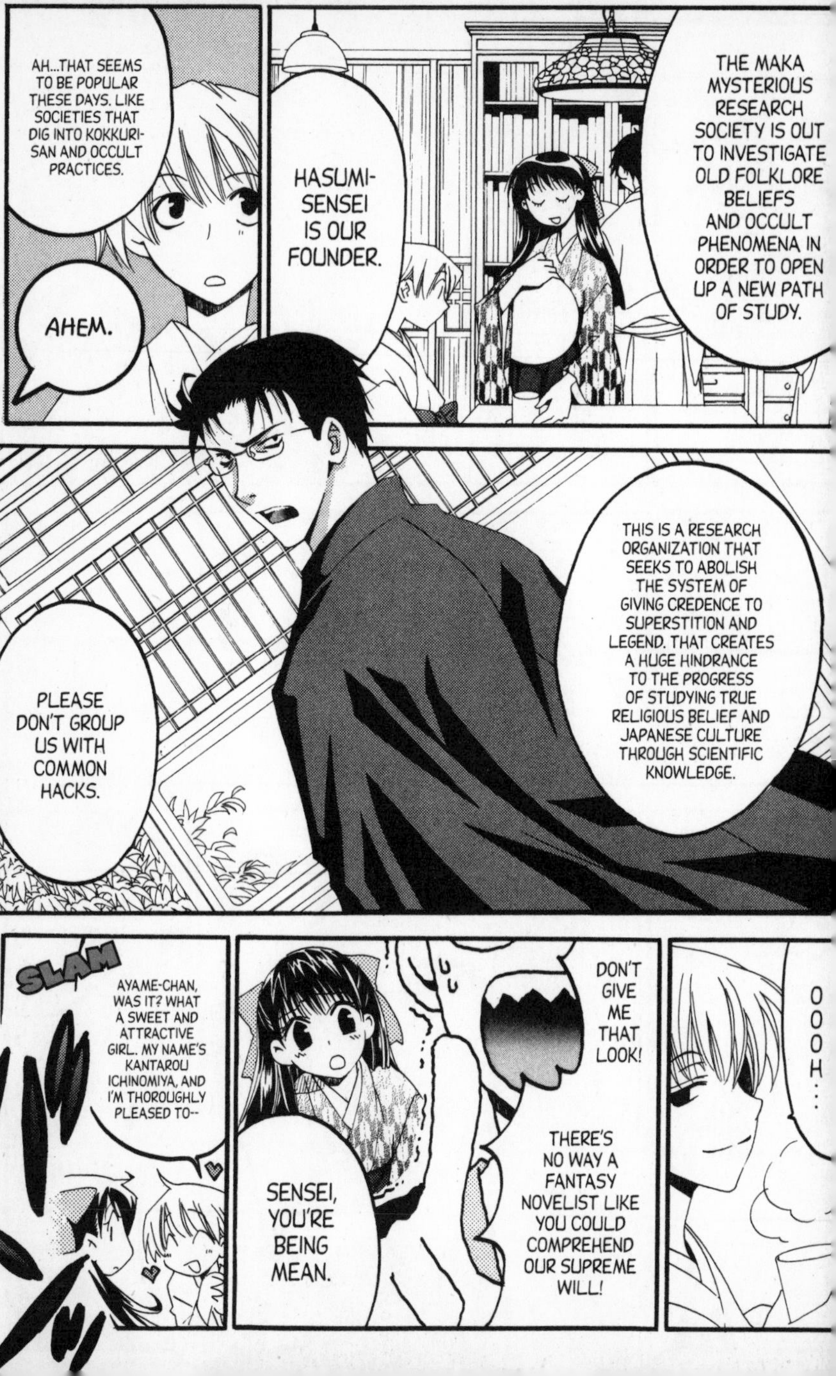
THE MAKA MYSTERIOUS RESEARCH SOCIETY IS OUT TO INVESTIGATE OLD FOLKLORE BELIEFS AND OCCULT PHENOMENA IN ORDER TO OPEN UP A NEW PATH OF STUDY.
HASUMI-SENSEI IS OUR FOUNDER.
AH...THAT SEEMS TO BE POPULAR THESE DAYS. LIKE SOCIETIES THAT DIG INTO KOKKURI-SAN AND OCCULT PRACTICES.
AHEM.
THIS IS A RESEARCH ORGANIZATION THAT SEEKS TO ABOLISH THE SYSTEM OF GIVING CREDENCE TO SUPERSTITION AND LEGEND. THAT CREATES A HUGE HINDRANCE TO THE PROGRESS OF STUDYING TRUE RELIGIOUS BELIEF AND JAPANESE CULTURE THROUGH SCIENTIFIC KNOWLEDGE.
PLEASE DON'T GROUP US WITH COMMON HACKS.
OOOH...
DON'T GIVE ME THAT LOOK!
THERE'S NO WAY A FANTASY NOVELIST LIKE YOU COULD COMPREHEND OUR SUPREME WILL!
SENSEI, YOU'RE BEING MEAN.
SLAM
AYAME-CHAN, WAS IT? WHAT A SWEET AND ATTRACTIVE GIRL. MY NAME'S KANTAROU ICHINOMIYA, AND I'M THOROUGHLY PLEASED TO--

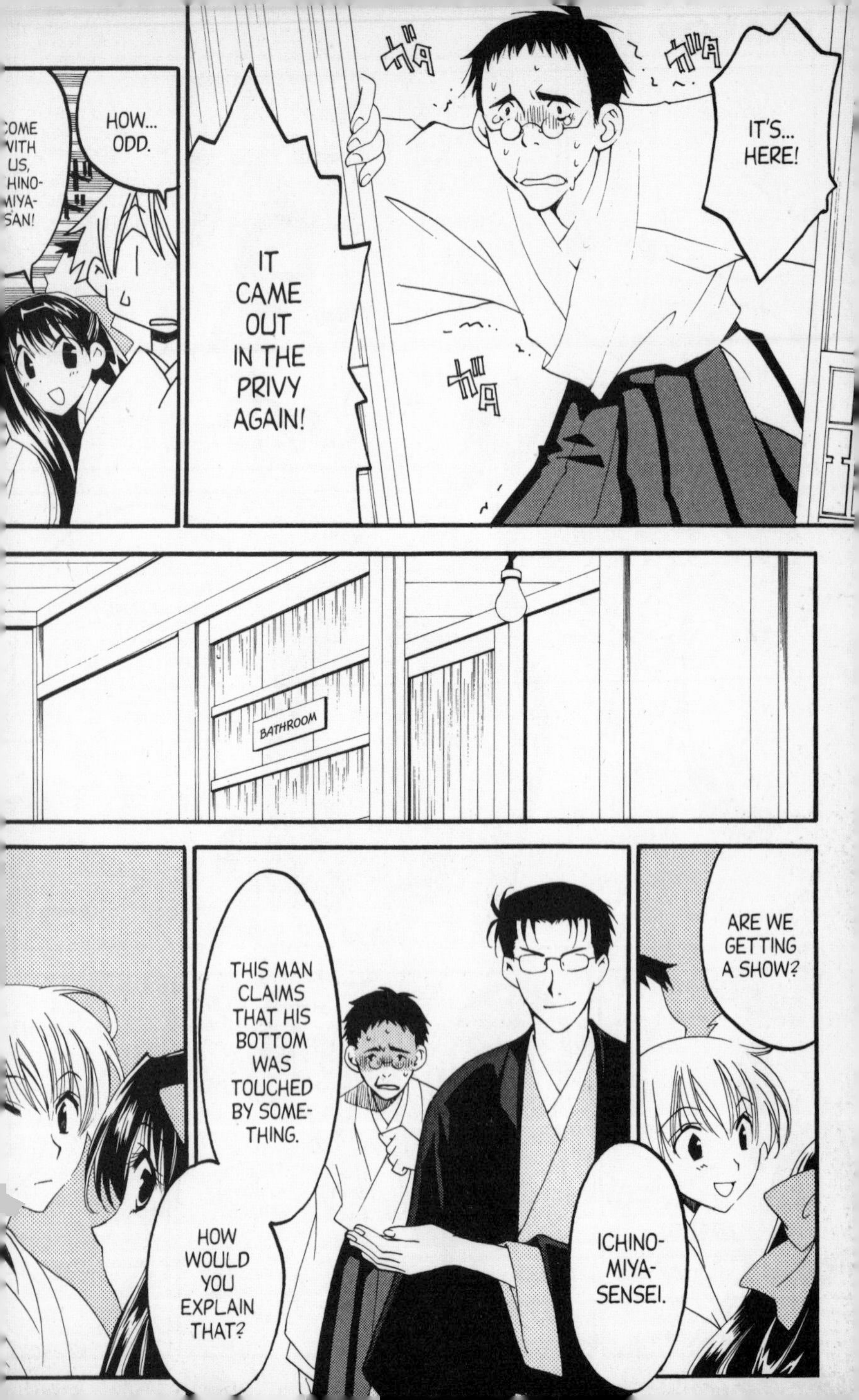
IT'S... HERE!
IT CAME OUT IN THE PRIVY AGAIN!
HOW... ODD.
COME WITH US, HINO-MIYA-SAN!
BATHROOM
ARE WE GETTING A SHOW?
ICHINO-MIYA-SENSEI.
THIS MAN CLAIMS THAT HIS BOTTOM WAS TOUCHED BY SOME-THING.
HOW WOULD YOU EXPLAIN THAT?

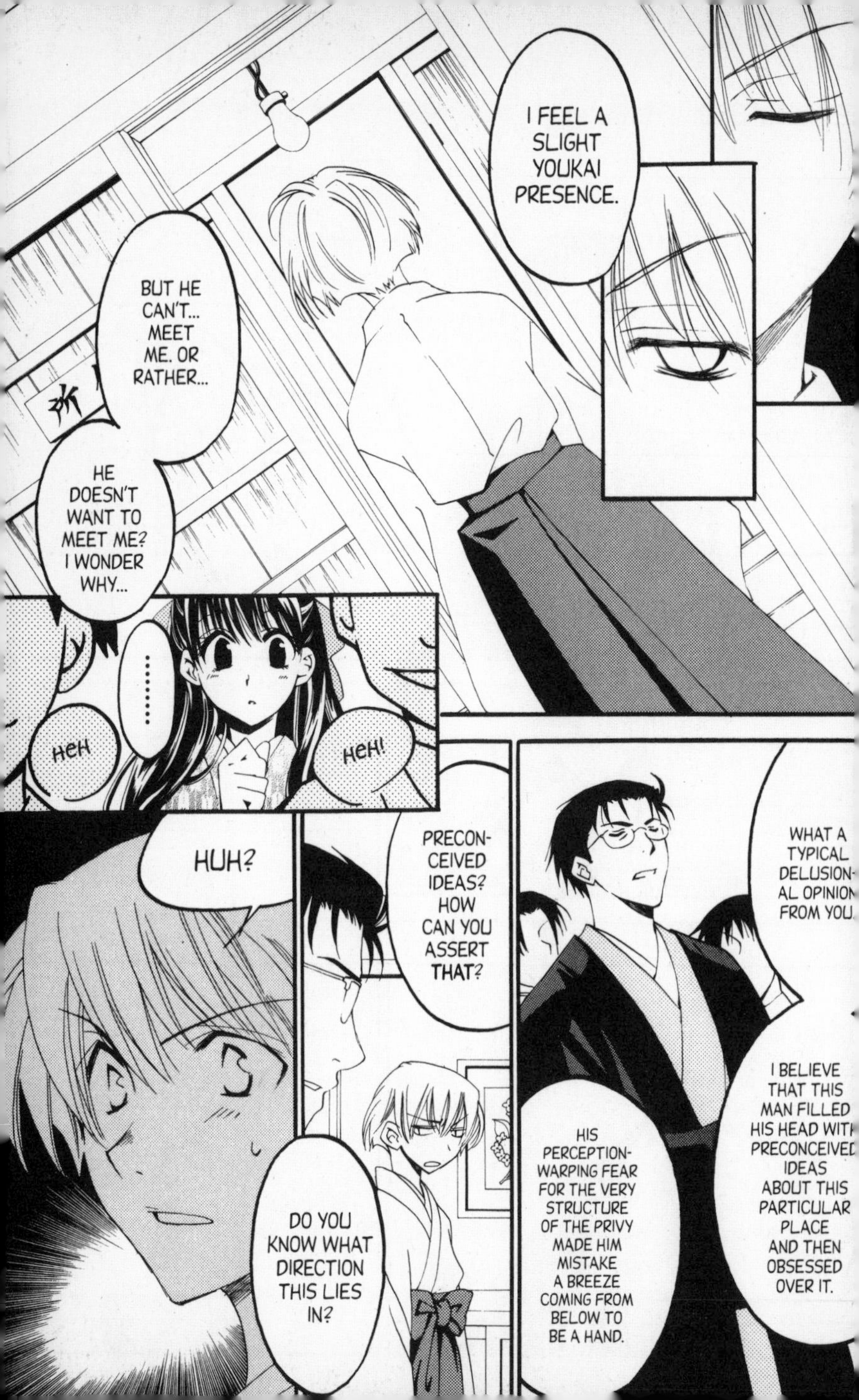
I FEEL A SLIGHT YOUKAI PRESENCE.
BUT HE CAN'T... MEET ME. OR RATHER...
HE DOESN'T WANT TO MEET ME? I WONDER WHY...
HEH!
......
HEH
WHAT A TYPICAL DELUSIONAL OPINION FROM YOU.
I BELIEVE THAT THIS MAN FILLED HIS HEAD WITH PRECONCEIVED IDEAS ABOUT THIS PARTICULAR PLACE AND THEN OBSESSED OVER IT.
HIS PERCEPTION-WARPING FEAR FOR THE VERY STRUCTURE OF THE PRIVY MADE HIM MISTAKE A BREEZE COMING FROM BELOW TO BE A HAND.
PRECONCEIVED IDEAS? HOW CAN YOU ASSERT THAT?
DO YOU KNOW WHAT DIRECTION THIS LIES IN?
HUH?

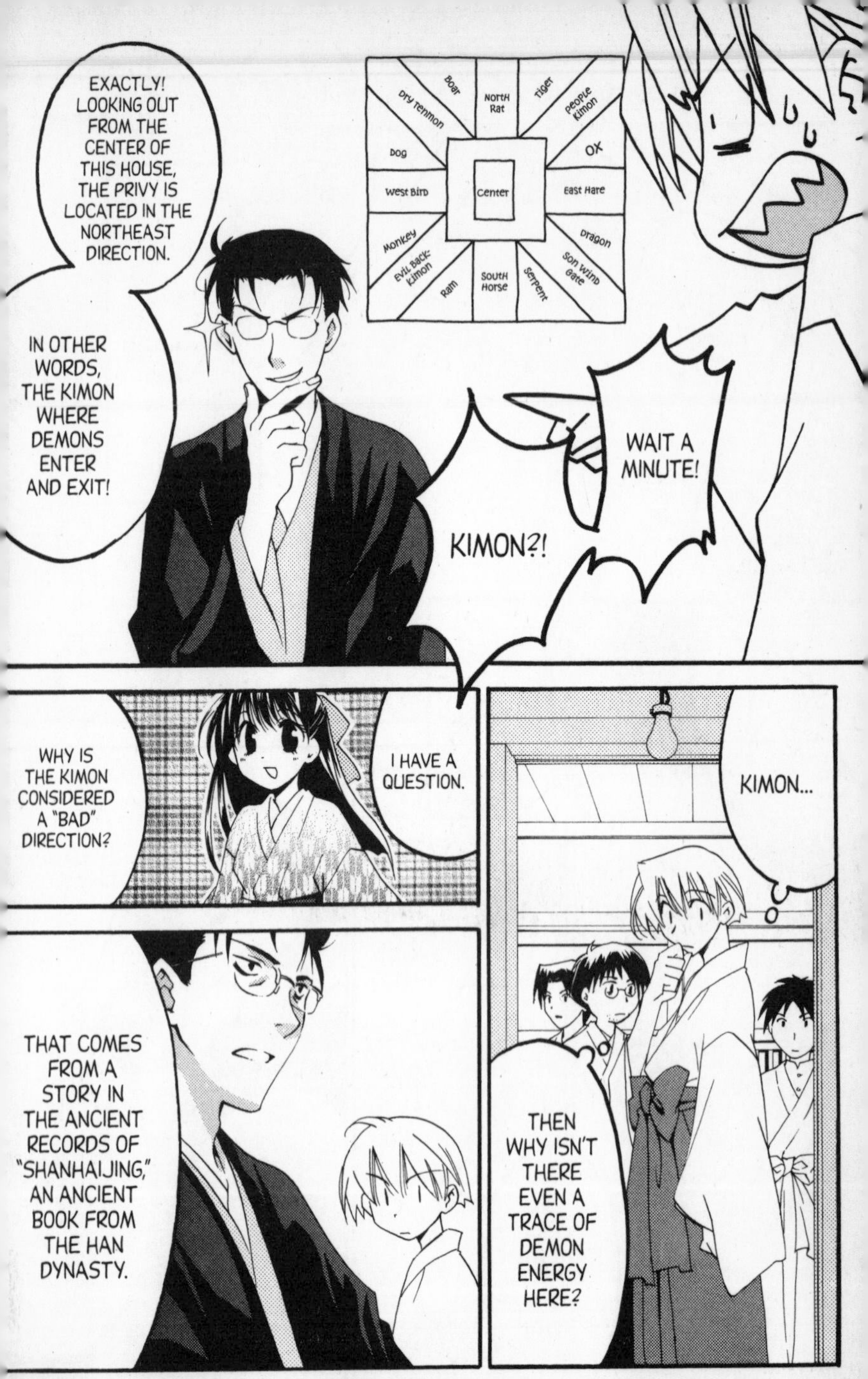
North Rat
Tiger
People Kimon
Ox
East Hare
Dragon
Son Wind Gate
Serpent
South Horse
Ram
Evil Back-Kimon
Monkey
West Bird
Dog
Dry Tenmon
Boar
Center
EXACTLY! LOOKING OUT FROM THE CENTER OF THIS HOUSE, THE PRIVY IS LOCATED IN THE NORTHEAST DIRECTION.
IN OTHER WORDS, THE KIMON WHERE DEMONS ENTER AND EXIT!
WAIT A MINUTE!
KIMON?!
KIMON...
THEN WHY ISN'T THERE EVEN A TRACE OF DEMON ENERGY HERE?
I HAVE A QUESTION.
WHY IS THE KIMON CONSIDERED A "BAD" DIRECTION?
THAT COMES FROM A STORY IN THE ANCIENT RECORDS OF "SHANHAIJING," AN ANCIENT BOOK FROM THE HAN DYNASTY.

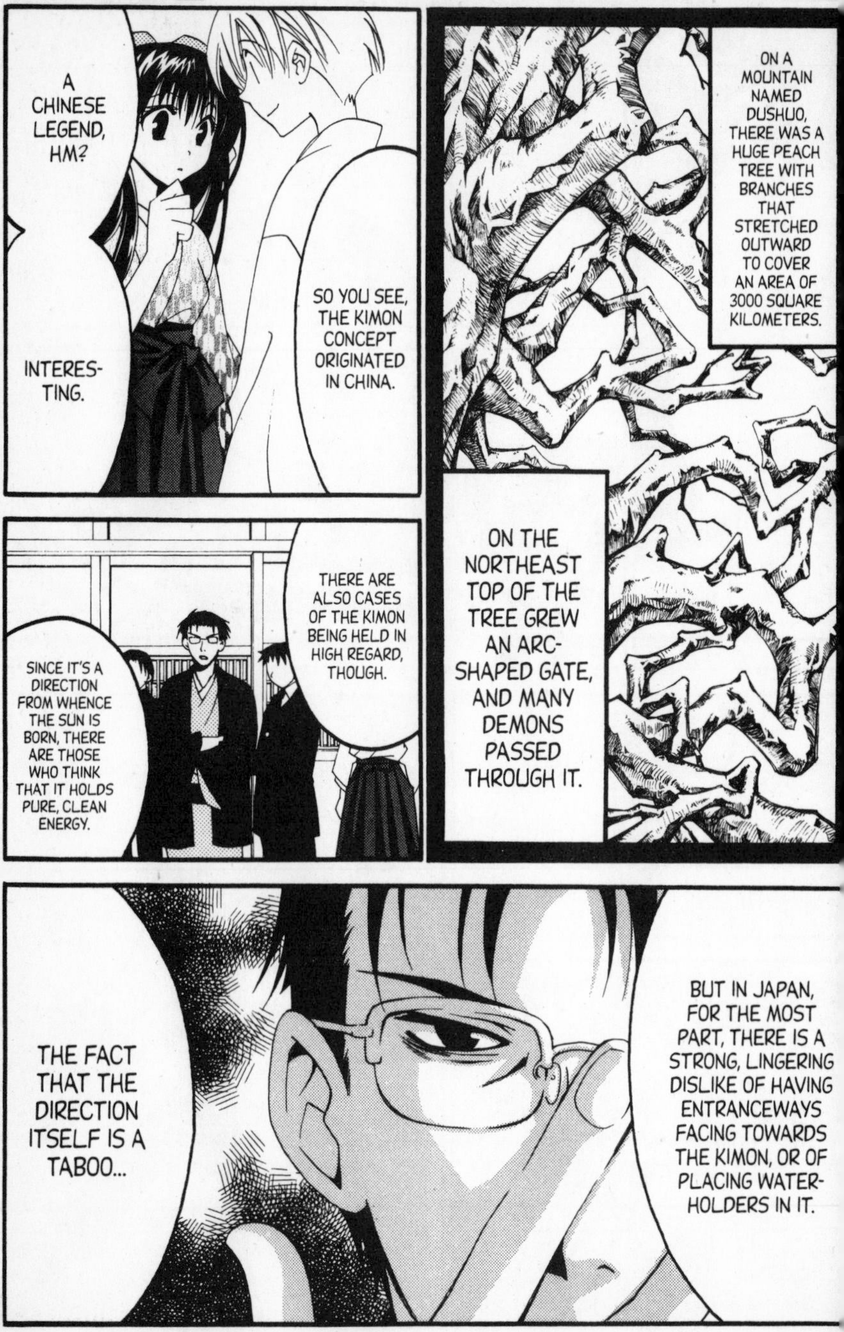
ON A MOUNTAIN NAMED DUSHUO, THERE WAS A HUGE PEACH TREE WITH BRANCHES THAT STRETCHED OUTWARD TO COVER AN AREA OF 3000 SQUARE KILOMETERS.
ON THE NORTHEAST TOP OF THE TREE GREW AN ARC-SHAPED GATE, AND MANY DEMONS PASSED THROUGH IT.
A CHINESE LEGEND, HM?
SO YOU SEE, THE KIMON CONCEPT ORIGINATED IN CHINA.
INTERES-TING.
THERE ARE ALSO CASES OF THE KIMON BEING HELD IN HIGH REGARD, THOUGH.
SINCE IT'S A DIRECTION FROM WHENCE THE SUN IS BORN, THERE ARE THOSE WHO THINK THAT IT HOLDS PURE, CLEAN ENERGY.
BUT IN JAPAN, FOR THE MOST PART, THERE IS A STRONG, LINGERING DISLIKE OF HAVING ENTRANCEWAYS FACING TOWARDS THE KIMON, OR OF PLACING WATER-HOLDERS IN IT.
THE FACT THAT THE DIRECTION ITSELF IS A TABOO...

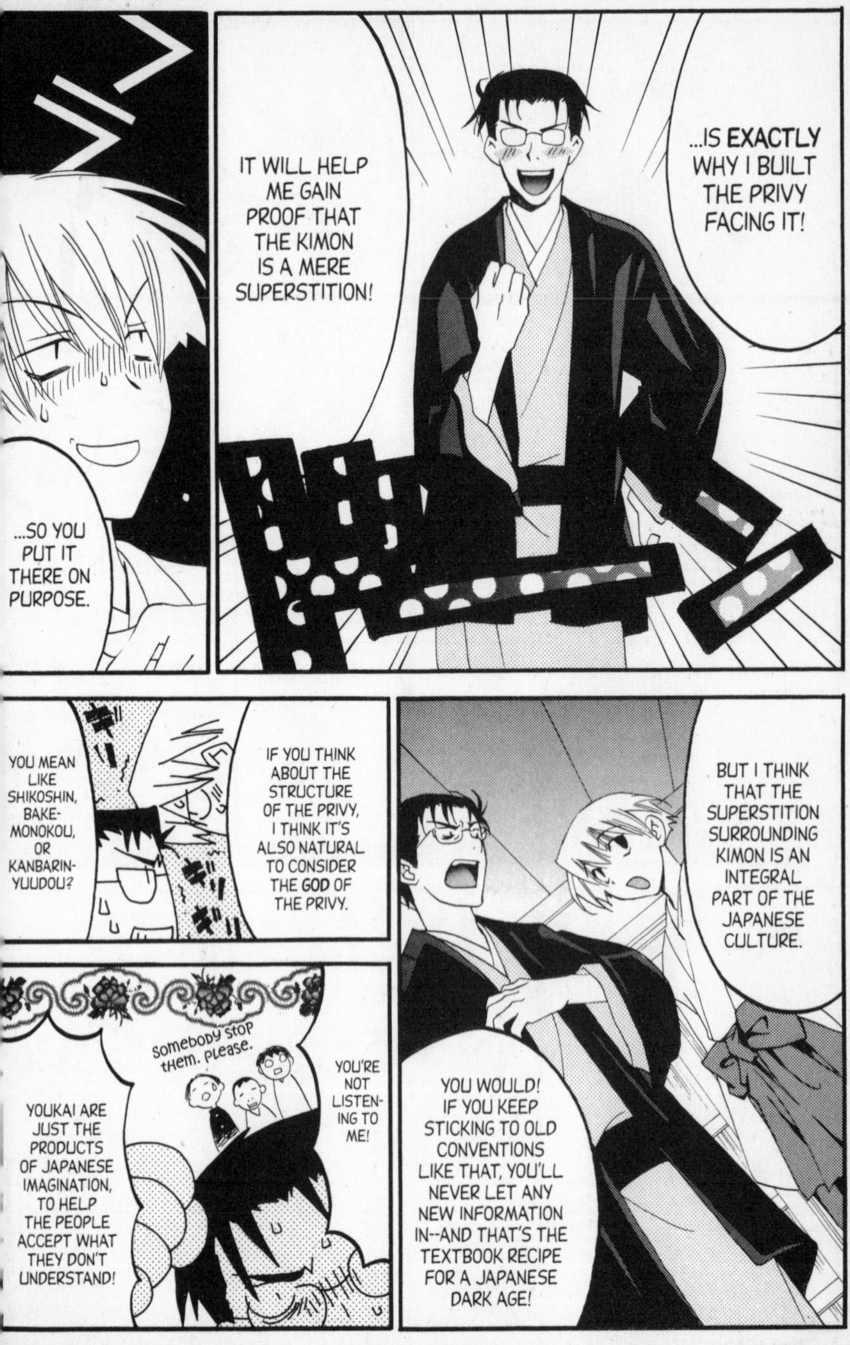
...IS EXACTLY WHY I BUILT THE PRIVY FACING IT!
IT WILL HELP ME GAIN PROOF THAT THE KIMON IS A MERE SUPERSTITION!
...SO YOU PUT IT THERE ON PURPOSE.
BUT I THINK THAT THE SUPERSTITION SURROUNDING KIMON IS AN INTEGRAL PART OF THE JAPANESE CULTURE.
YOU WOULD! IF YOU KEEP STICKING TO OLD CONVENTIONS LIKE THAT, YOU'LL NEVER LET ANY NEW INFORMATION IN--AND THAT'S THE TEXTBOOK RECIPE FOR A JAPANESE DARK AGE!
IF YOU THINK ABOUT THE STRUCTURE OF THE PRIVY, I THINK IT'S ALSO NATURAL TO CONSIDER THE GOD OF THE PRIVY.
YOU MEAN LIKE SHIKOSHIN, BAKE-MONOKOU, OR KANBARIN-YUUDOU?
YOU'RE NOT LISTEN-ING TO ME!
Somebody stop them. Please.
YOUKAI ARE JUST THE PRODUCTS OF JAPANESE IMAGINATION, TO HELP THE PEOPLE ACCEPT WHAT THEY DON'T UNDERSTAND!

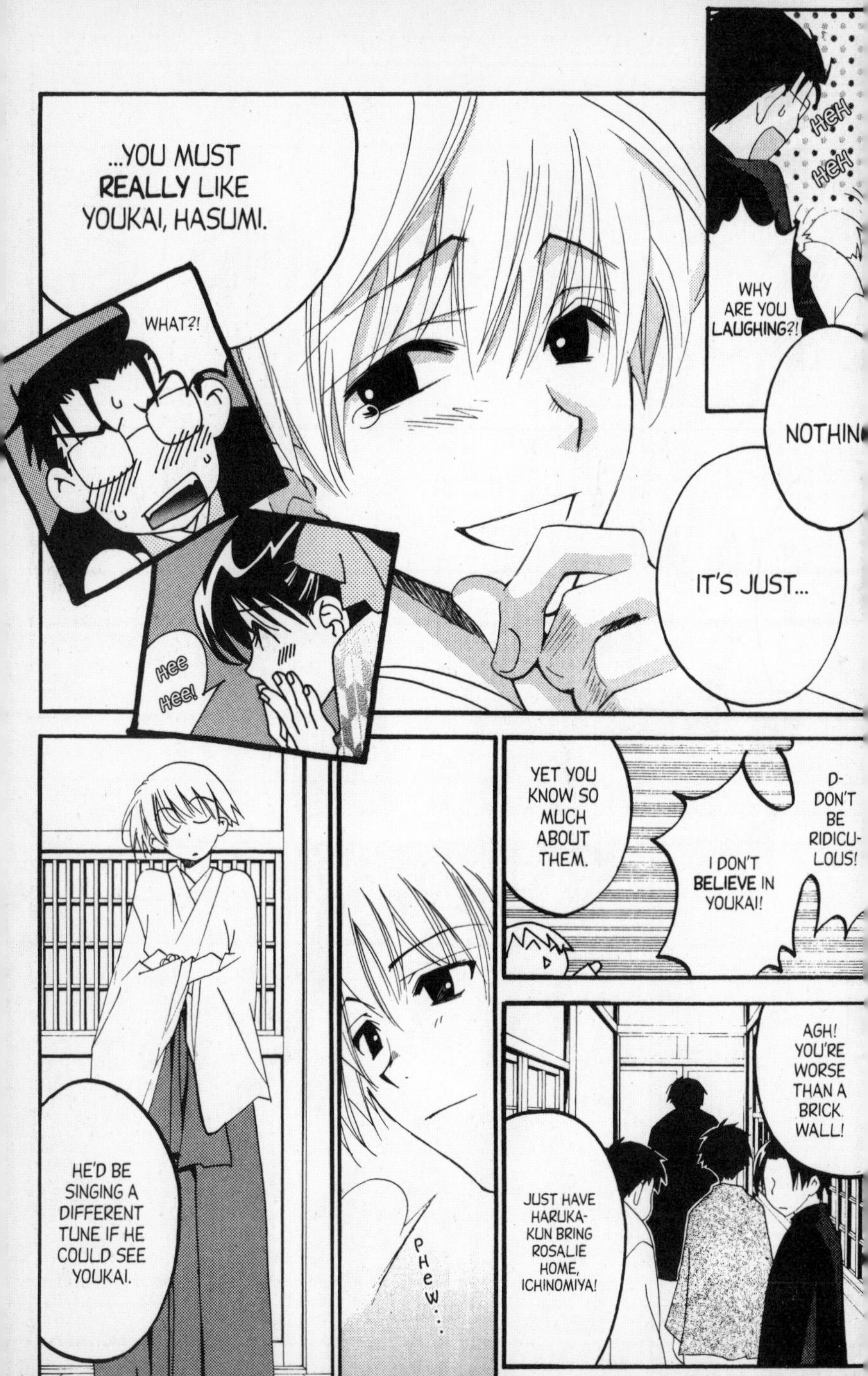
HEH
HEH
WHY ARE YOU LAUGHING?!
NOTHIN
IT'S JUST...
...YOU MUST REALLY LIKE YOUKAI, HASUMI.
WHAT?!
Hee Hee!
D-DON'T BE RIDICU-LOUS!
I DON'T BELIEVE IN YOUKAI!
YET YOU KNOW SO MUCH ABOUT THEM.
AGH! YOU'RE WORSE THAN A BRICK WALL!
JUST HAVE HARUKA-KUN BRING ROSALIE HOME, ICHINOMIYA!
PHEW...
HE'D BE SINGING A DIFFERENT TUNE IF HE COULD SEE YOUKAI.

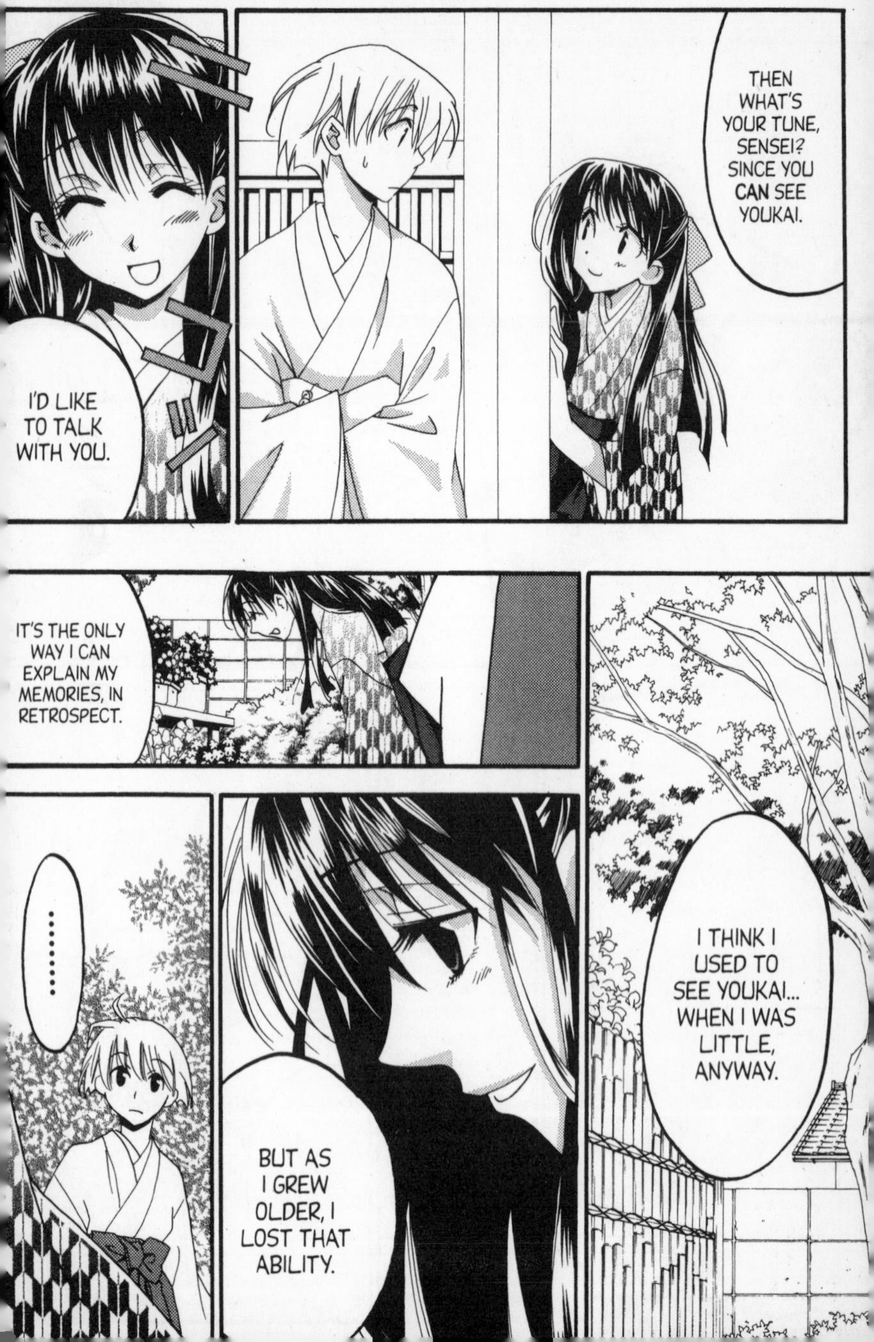
THEN WHAT'S YOUR TUNE, SENSEI? SINCE YOU CAN SEE YOUKAI.
I'D LIKE TO TALK WITH YOU.
I THINK I USED TO SEE YOUKAI... WHEN I WAS LITTLE, ANYWAY.
IT'S THE ONLY WAY I CAN EXPLAIN MY MEMORIES, IN RETROSPECT.
BUT AS I GREW OLDER, I LOST THAT ABILITY.
....

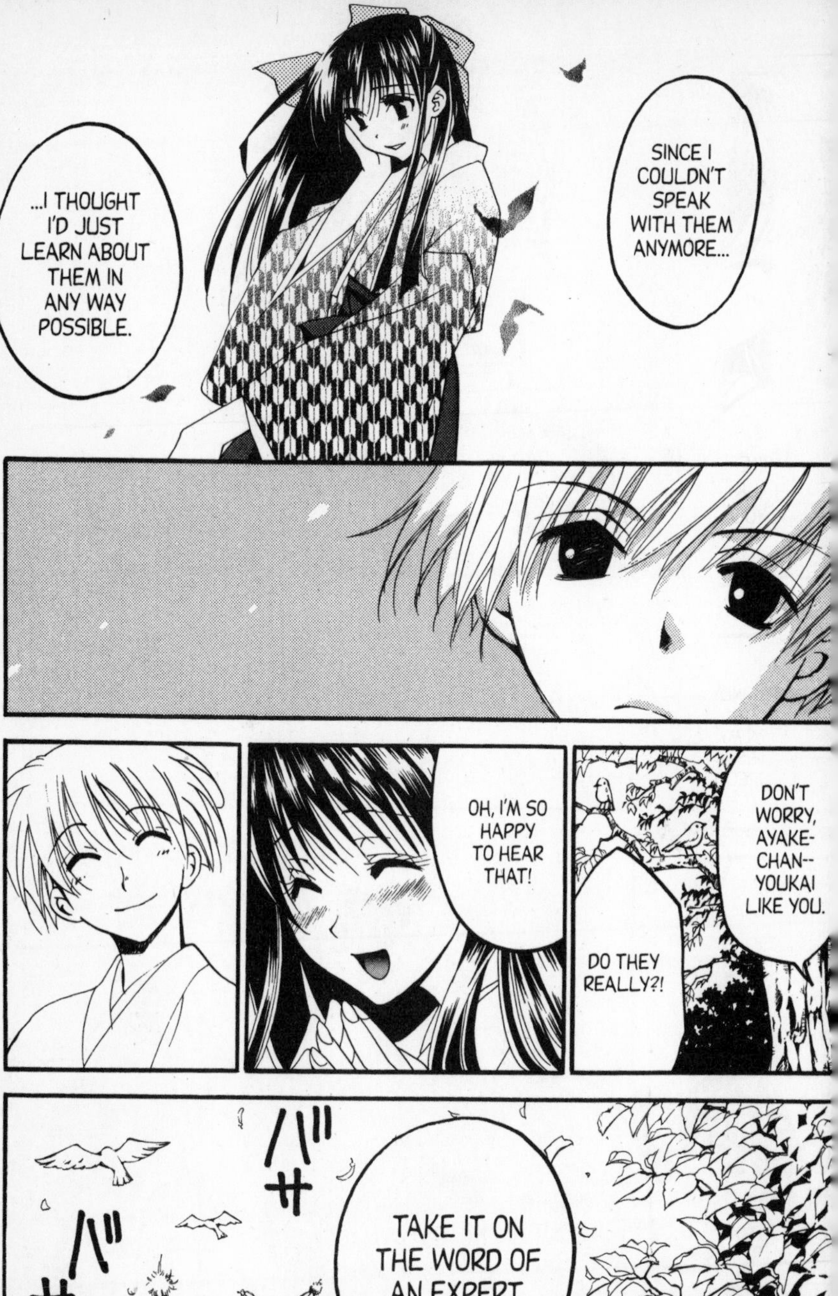
SINCE I COULDN'T SPEAK WITH THEM ANYMORE...
...I THOUGHT I'D JUST LEARN ABOUT THEM IN ANY WAY POSSIBLE.
DON'T WORRY, AYAKE-CHAN-- YOUKAI LIKE YOU.
DO THEY REALLY?!
OH, I'M SO HAPPY TO HEAR THAT!
バサ
TAKE IT ON THE WORD OF AN EXPERT.
バサ

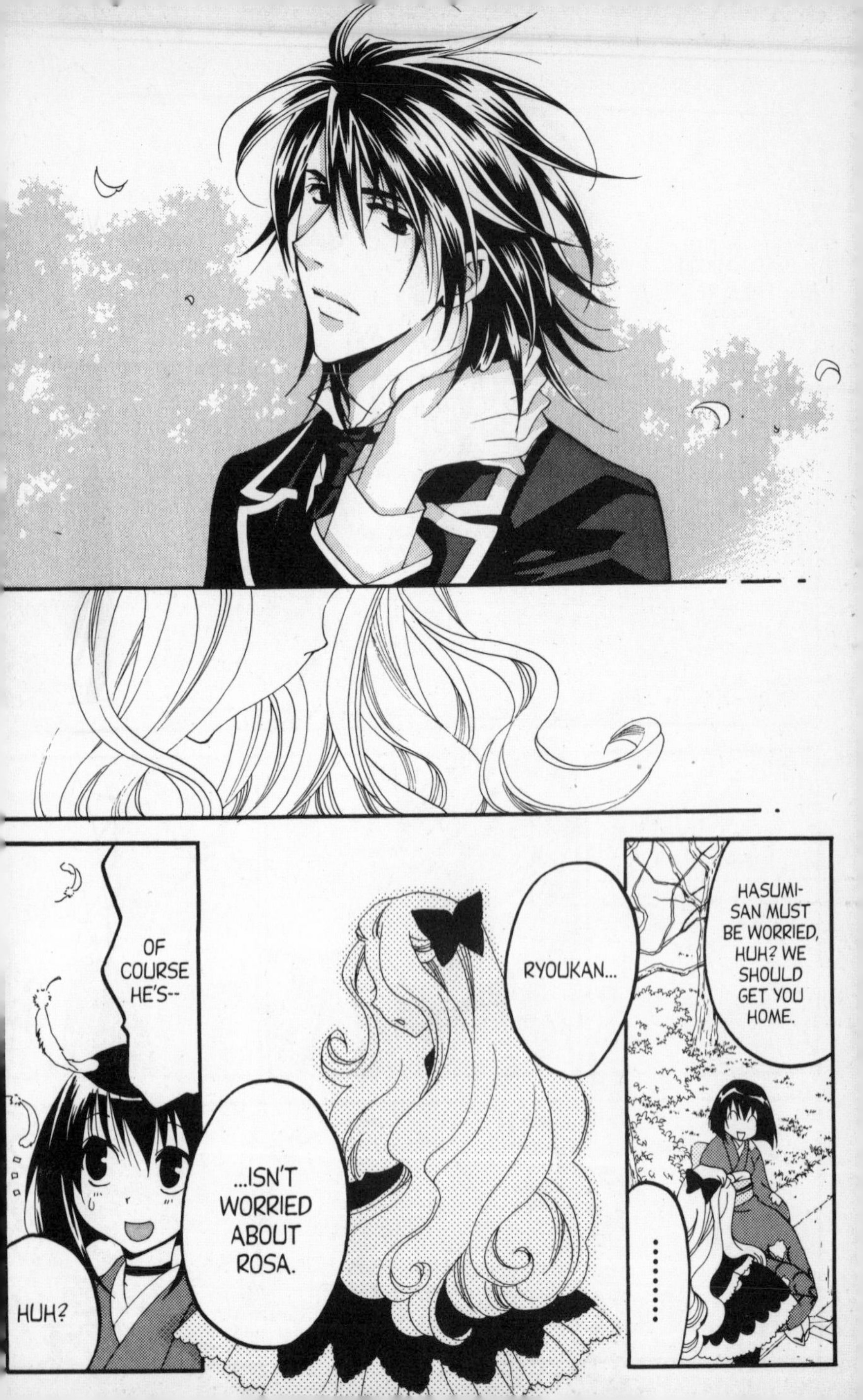
HASUMI-SAN MUST BE WORRIED, HUH? WE SHOULD GET YOU HOME.
......
RYOUKAN...
OF COURSE HE'S--
...ISN'T WORRIED ABOUT ROSA.
HUH?

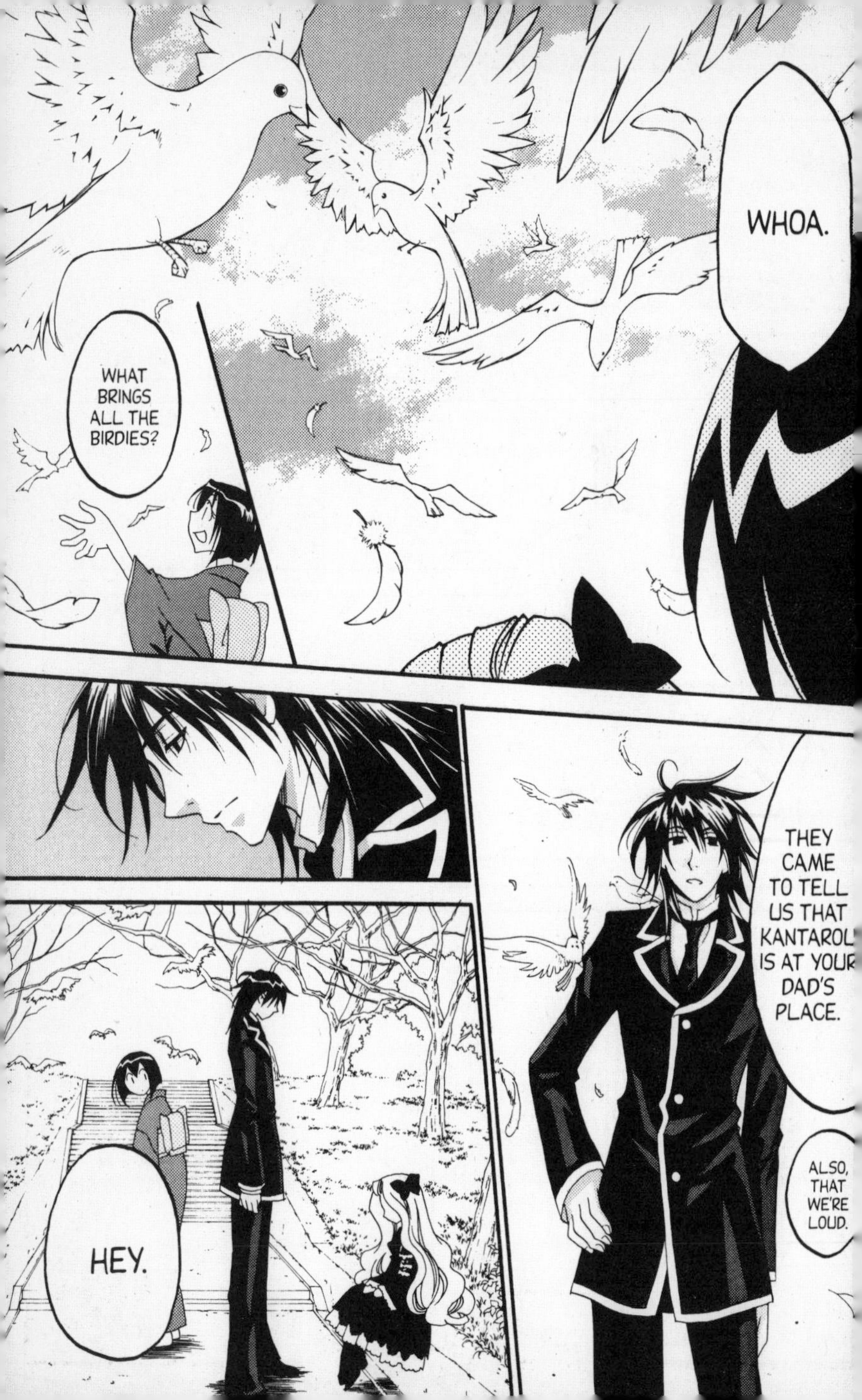
WHOA.
WHAT BRINGS ALL THE BIRDIES?
THEY CAME TO TELL US THAT KANTAROU IS AT YOUR DAD'S PLACE.
ALSO, THAT WE'RE LOUD.
HEY.

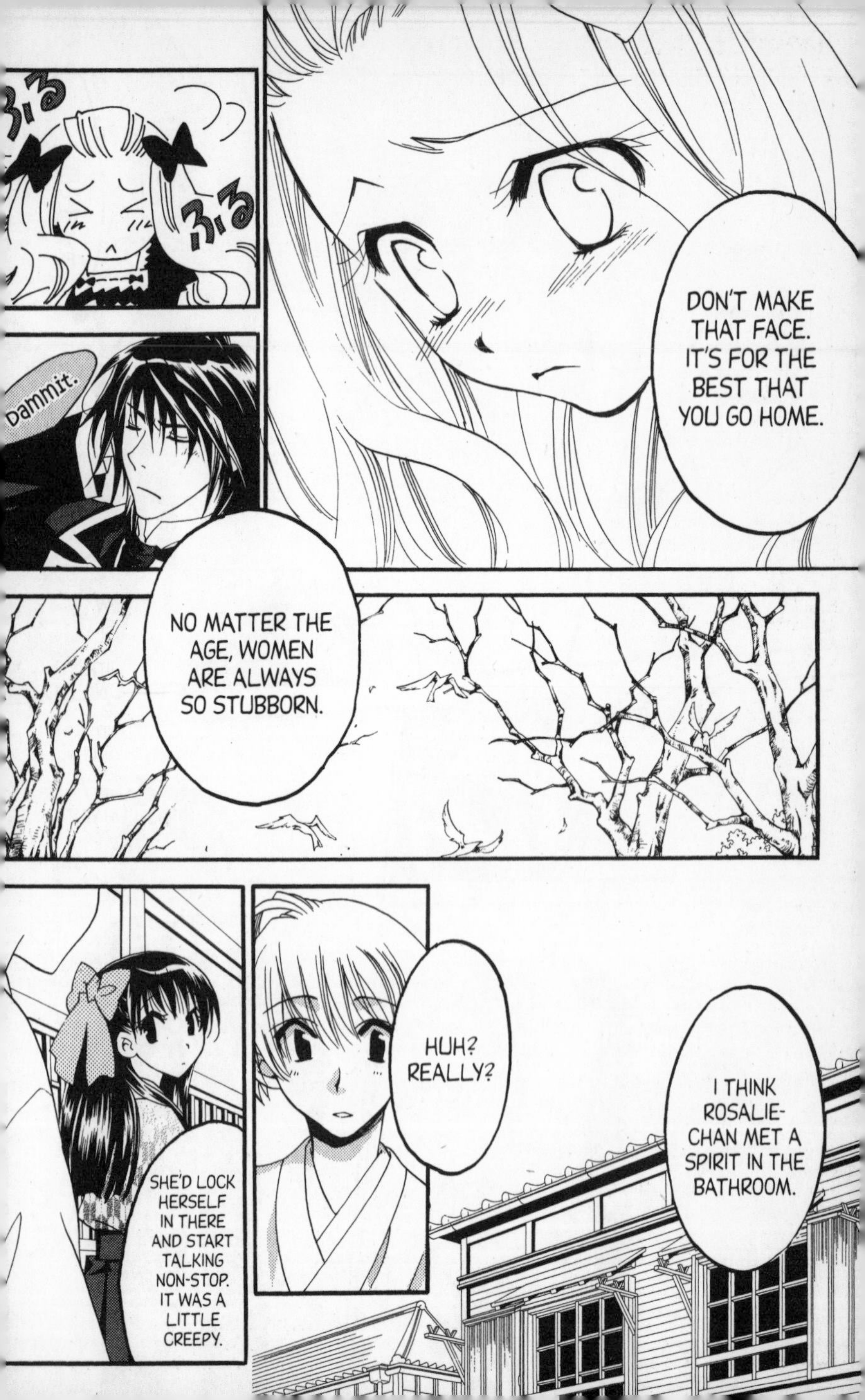
DON'T MAKE THAT FACE. IT'S FOR THE BEST THAT YOU GO HOME.
ふる
ふる
Dammit.
NO MATTER THE AGE, WOMEN ARE ALWAYS SO STUBBORN.
I THINK ROSALIE-CHAN MET A SPIRIT IN THE BATHROOM.
HUH? REALLY?
SHE'D LOCK HERSELF IN THERE AND START TALKING NON-STOP. IT WAS A LITTLE CREEPY.

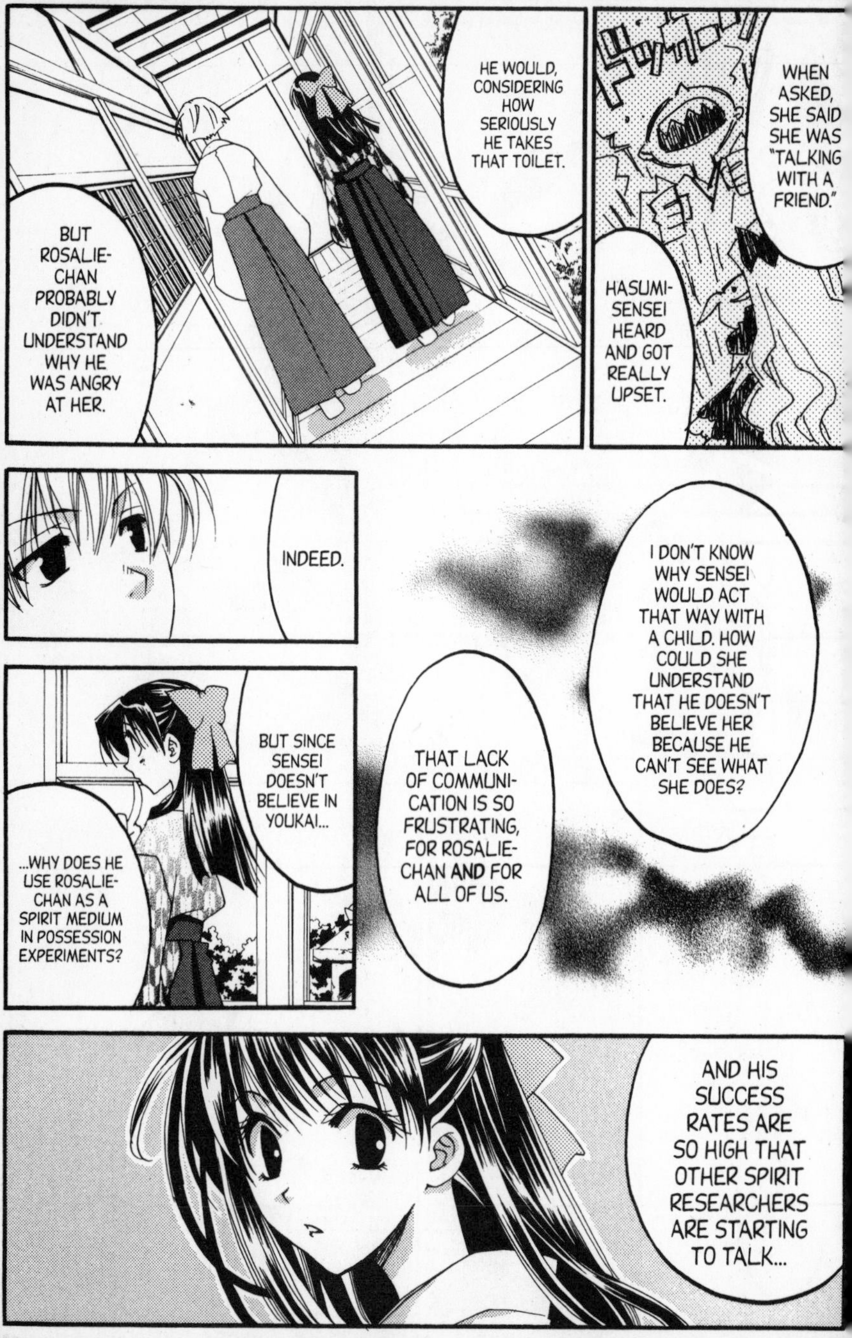
WHEN ASKED, SHE SAID SHE WAS "TALKING WITH A FRIEND."
HASUMI-SENSEI HEARD AND GOT REALLY UPSET.
HE WOULD, CONSIDERING HOW SERIOUSLY HE TAKES THAT TOILET.
BUT ROSALIE-CHAN PROBABLY DIDN'T UNDERSTAND WHY HE WAS ANGRY AT HER.
I DON'T KNOW WHY SENSEI WOULD ACT THAT WAY WITH A CHILD. HOW COULD SHE UNDERSTAND THAT HE DOESN'T BELIEVE HER BECAUSE HE CAN'T SEE WHAT SHE DOES?
THAT LACK OF COMMUNICATION IS SO FRUSTRATING, FOR ROSALIE-CHAN AND FOR ALL OF US.
INDEED.
BUT SINCE SENSEI DOESN'T BELIEVE IN YOUKAI...
...WHY DOES HE USE ROSALIE-CHAN AS A SPIRIT MEDIUM IN POSSESSION EXPERIMENTS?
AND HIS SUCCESS RATES ARE SO HIGH THAT OTHER SPIRIT RESEARCHERS ARE STARTING TO TALK...

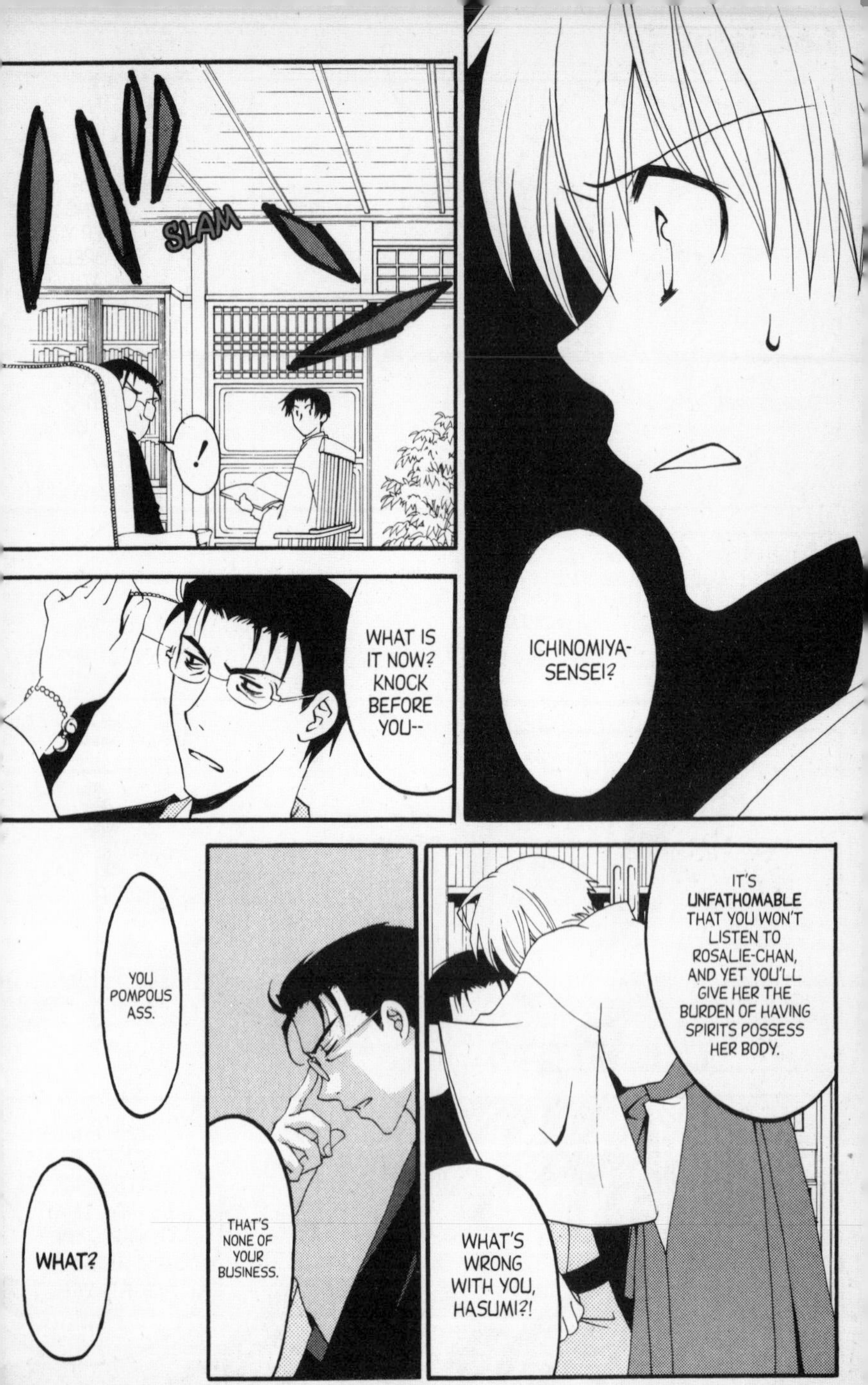
ICHINOMIYA-SENSEI?
SLAM
!
WHAT IS IT NOW? KNOCK BEFORE YOU--
IT'S **UNFATHOMABLE** THAT YOU WON'T LISTEN TO ROSALIE-CHAN, AND YET YOU'LL GIVE HER THE BURDEN OF HAVING SPIRITS POSSESS HER BODY.
WHAT'S WRONG WITH YOU, HASUMI?!
THAT'S NONE OF YOUR BUSINESS.
YOU POMPOUS ASS.
WHAT?

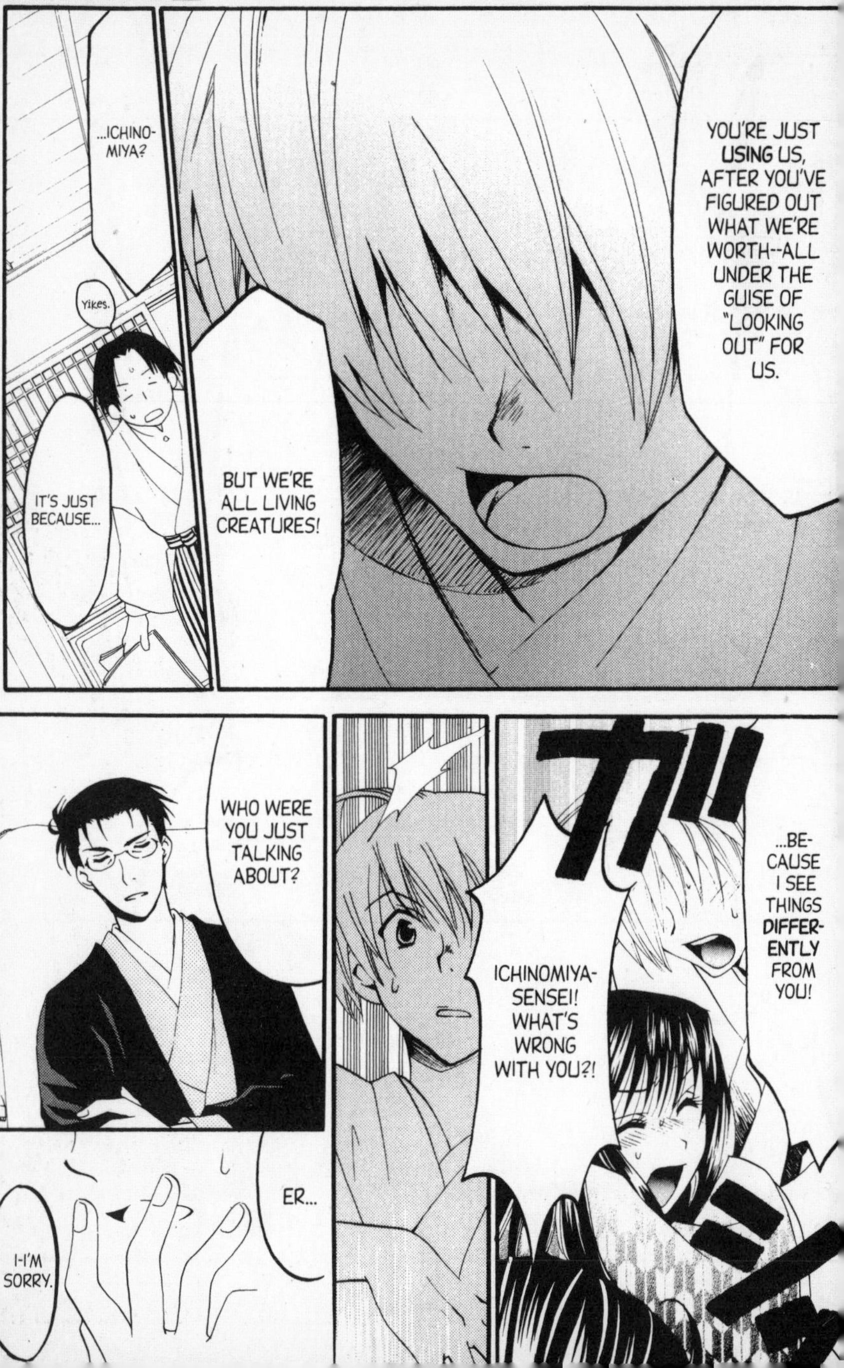
YOU'RE JUST USING US, AFTER YOU'VE FIGURED OUT WHAT WE'RE WORTH--ALL UNDER THE GUISE OF "LOOKING OUT" FOR US.
BUT WE'RE ALL LIVING CREATURES!
...ICHINO-MIYA?
Yikes.
IT'S JUST BECAUSE...
...BE-CAUSE I SEE THINGS DIFFER-ENTLY FROM YOU!
ICHINOMIYA-SENSEI! WHAT'S WRONG WITH YOU?!
WHO WERE YOU JUST TALKING ABOUT?
ER...
I-I'M SORRY.

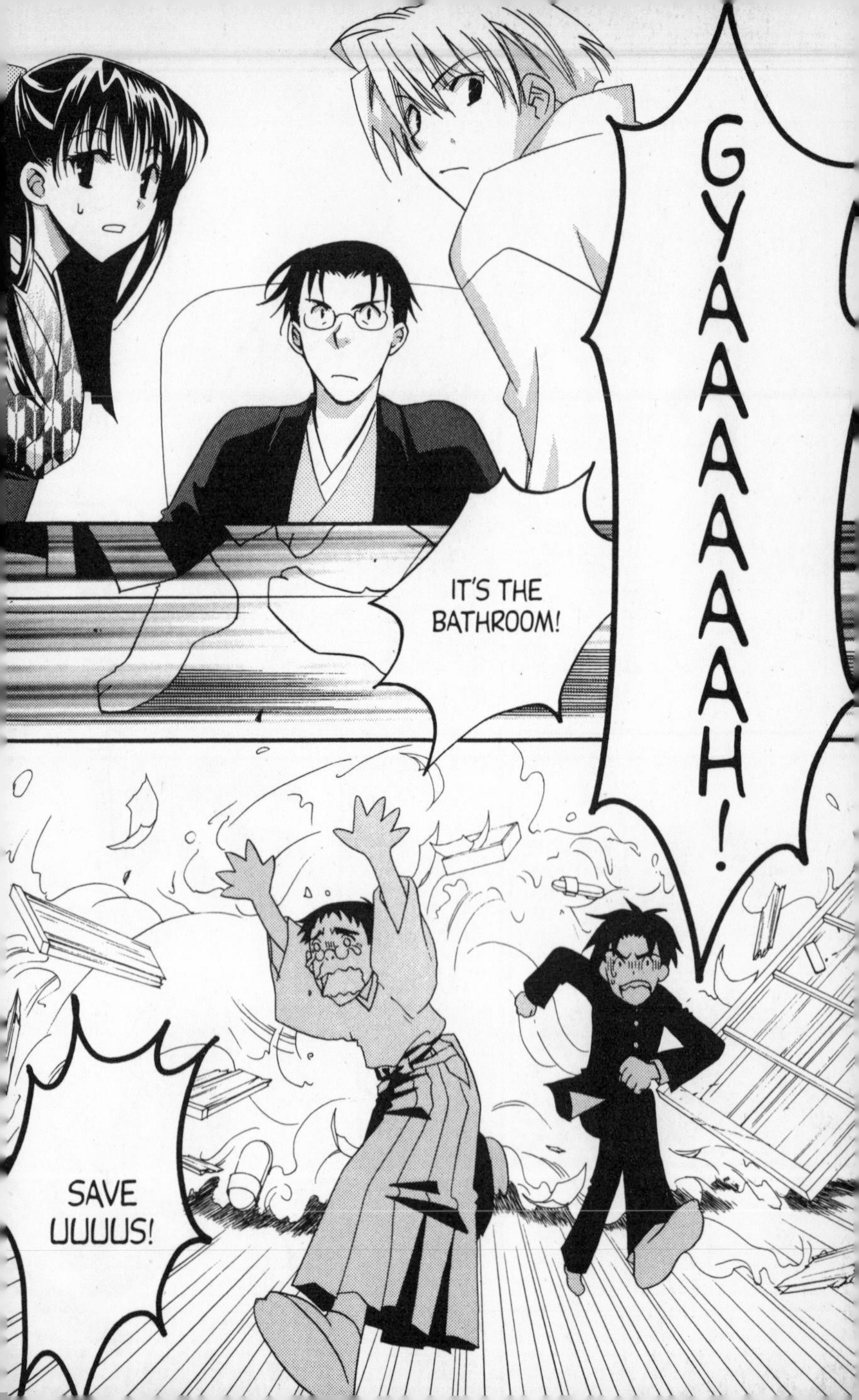
GYAAAAAAH!
IT'S THE BATHROOM!
SAVE UUUUS!

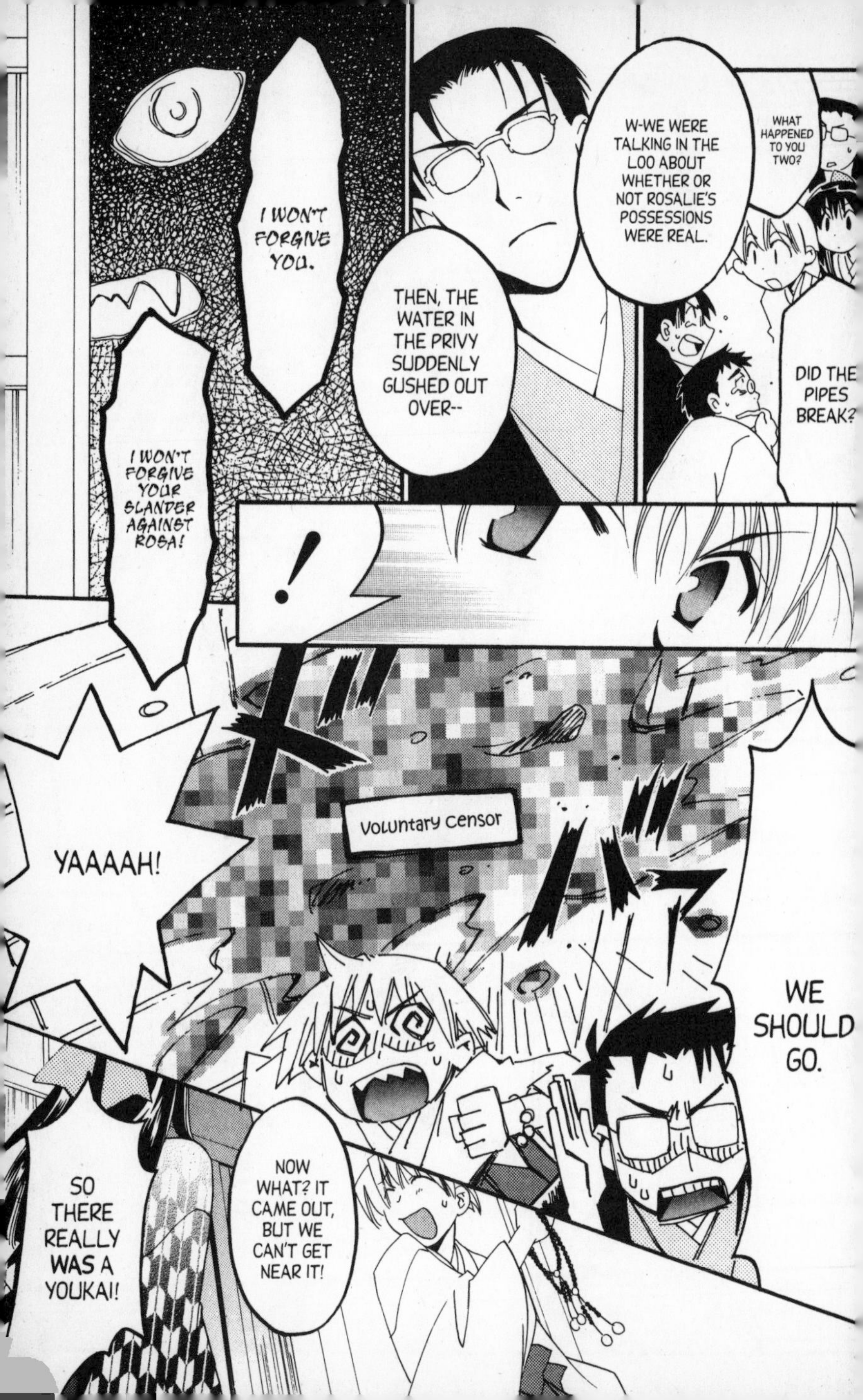
WHAT HAPPENED TO YOU TWO?
DID THE PIPES BREAK?
W-WE WERE TALKING IN THE LOO ABOUT WHETHER OR NOT ROSALIE'S POSSESSIONS WERE REAL.
THEN, THE WATER IN THE PRIVY SUDDENLY GUSHED OUT OVER--
I WON'T FORGIVE YOU.
I WON'T FORGIVE YOUR SLANDER AGAINST ROSA!
!
Voluntary Censor
YAAAAH!
WE SHOULD GO.
NOW WHAT? IT CAME OUT, BUT WE CAN'T GET NEAR IT!
SO THERE REALLY WAS A YOUKAI!

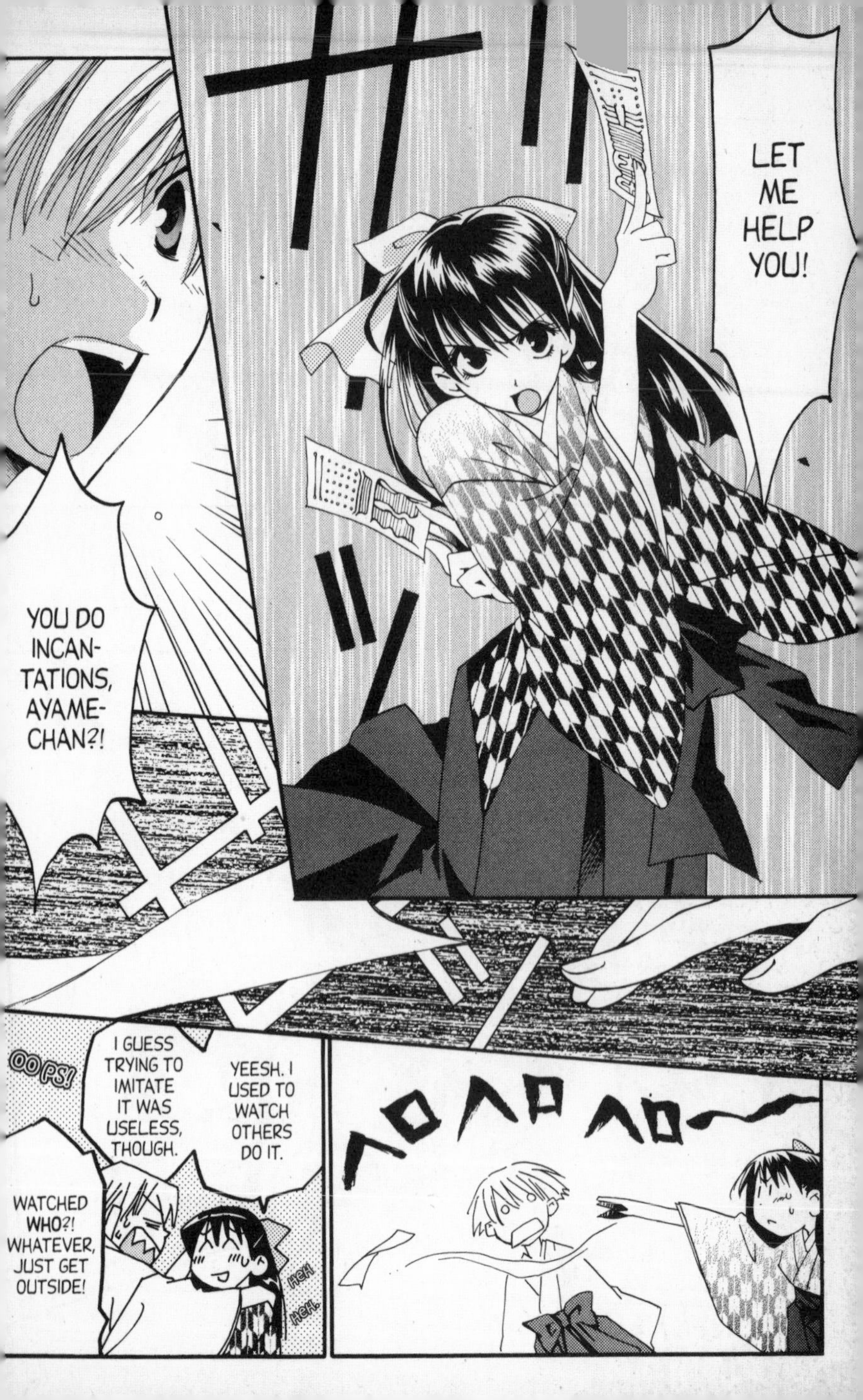
LET ME HELP YOU!
YOU DO INCANTATIONS, AYAME-CHAN?!
YEESH. I USED TO WATCH OTHERS DO IT.
I GUESS TRYING TO IMITATE IT WAS USELESS, THOUGH.
OOPS!
WATCHED WHO?! WHATEVER, JUST GET OUTSIDE!
HEH HEH.

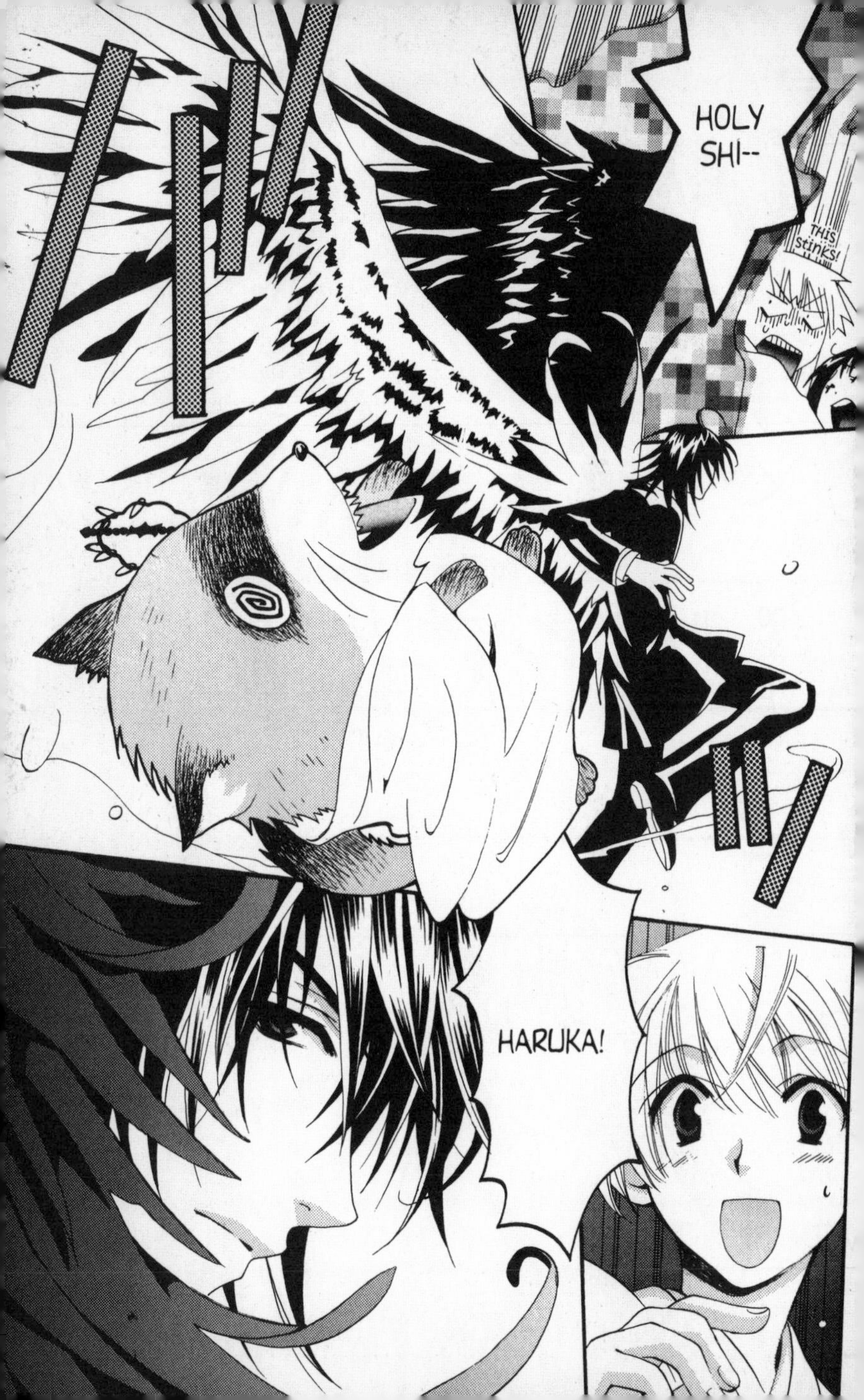
HOLY SHI--
THIS stinks!
HARUKA!

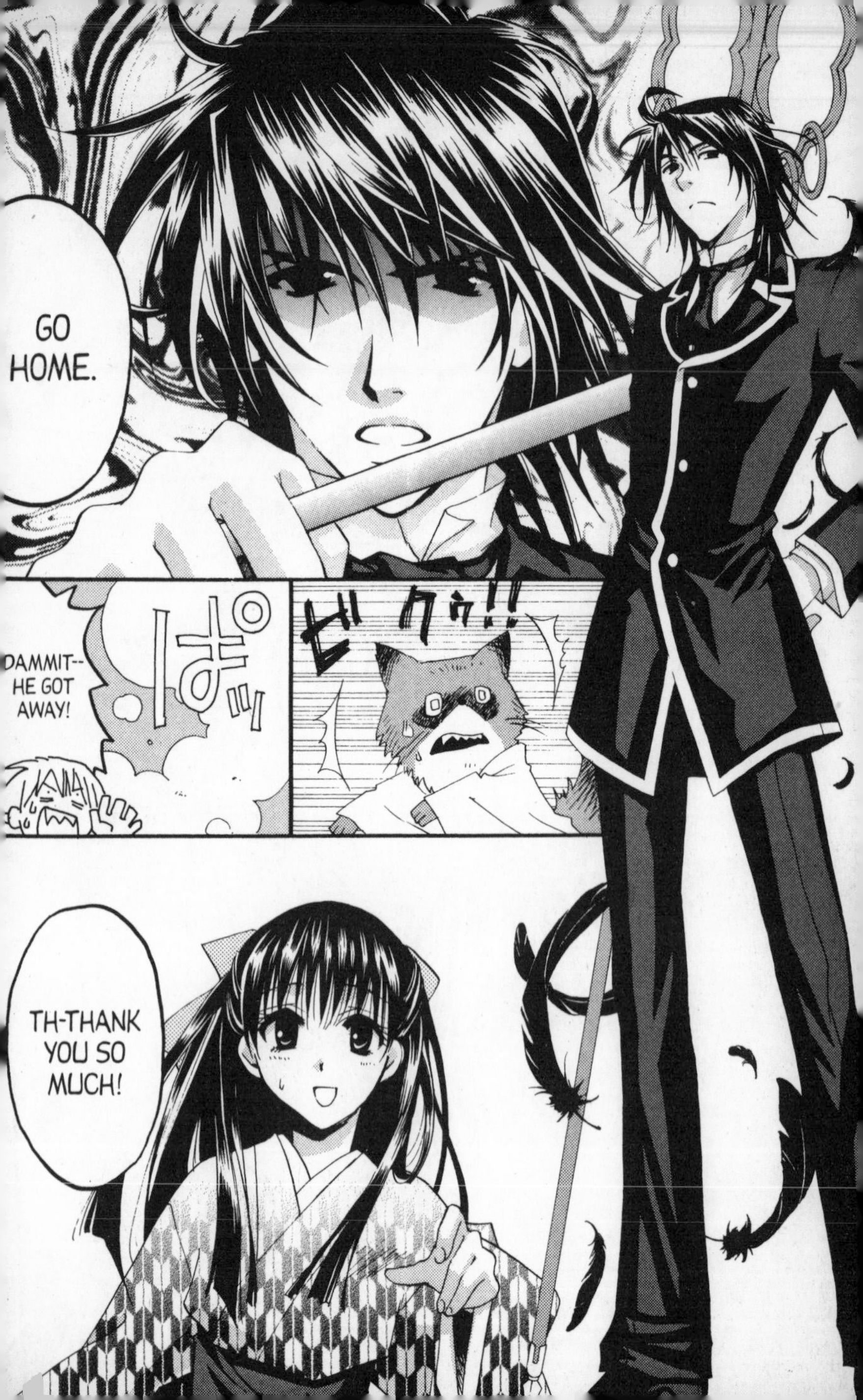
GO HOME.
ビクゥ!!
ぽ
DAMMIT-- HE GOT AWAY!
TH-THANK YOU SO MUCH!

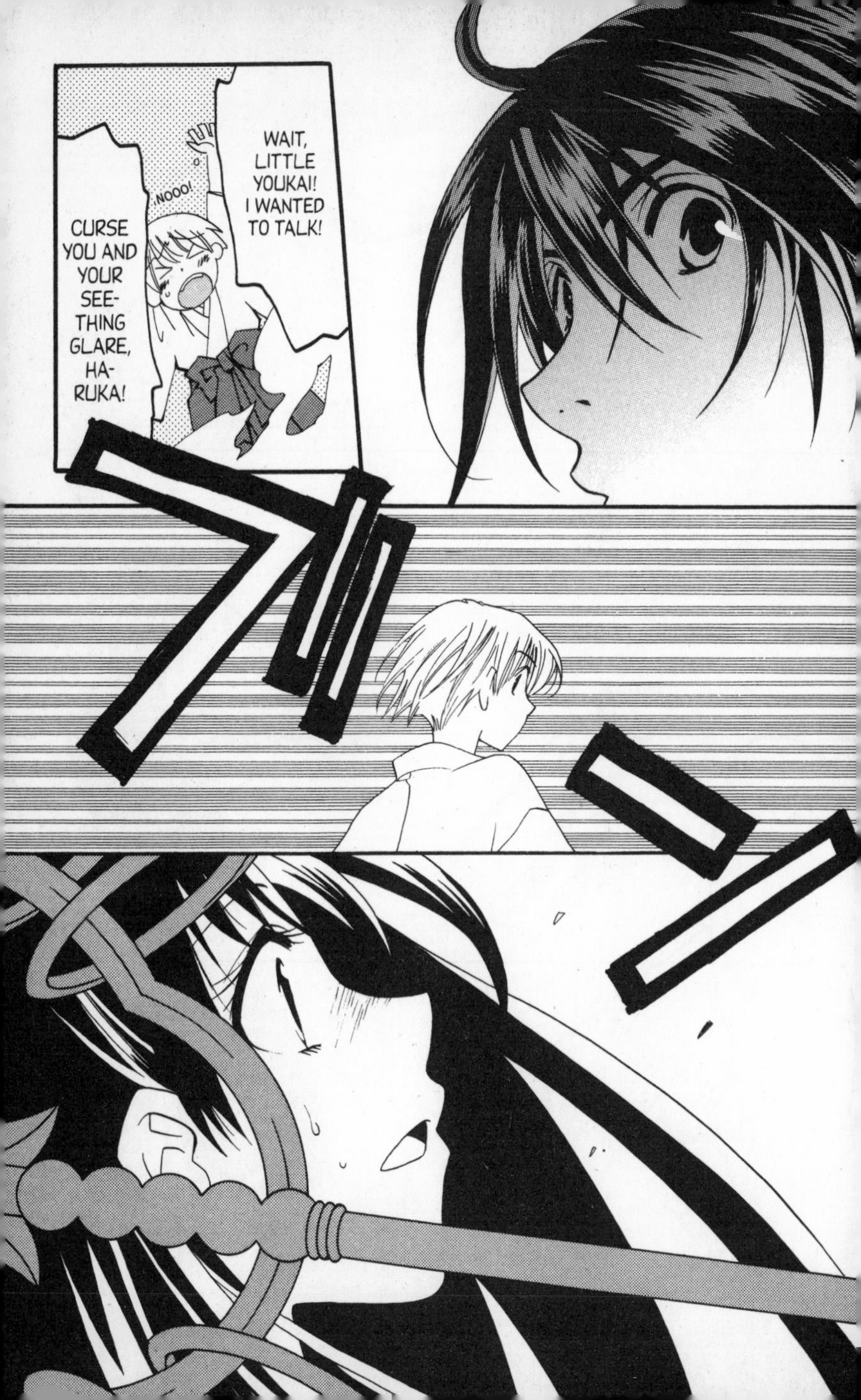
WAIT, LITTLE YOUKAI! I WANTED TO TALK!
NOOO!
CURSE YOU AND YOUR SEE-THING GLARE, HA-RUKA!

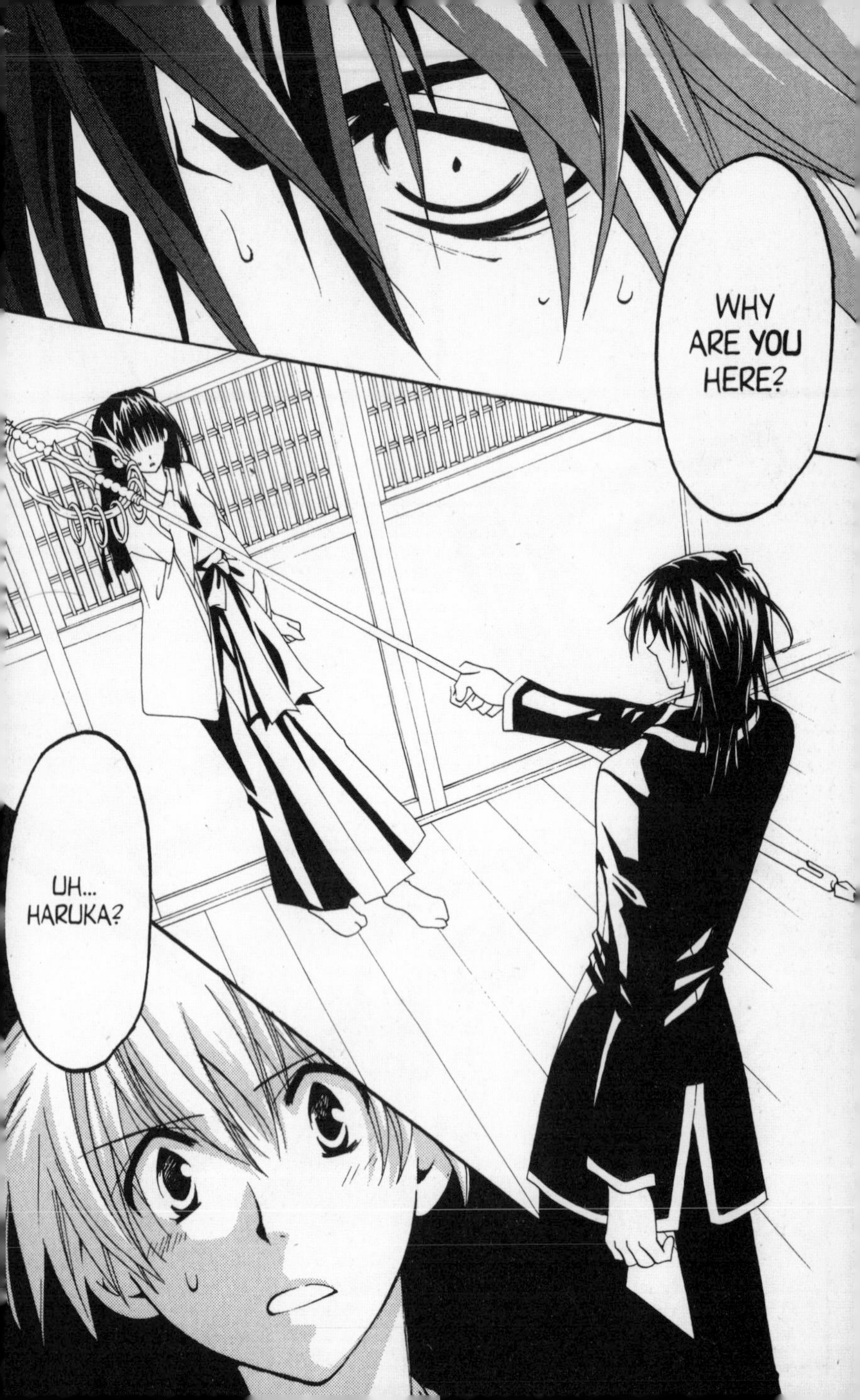
WHY ARE YOU HERE?
UH... HARUKA?

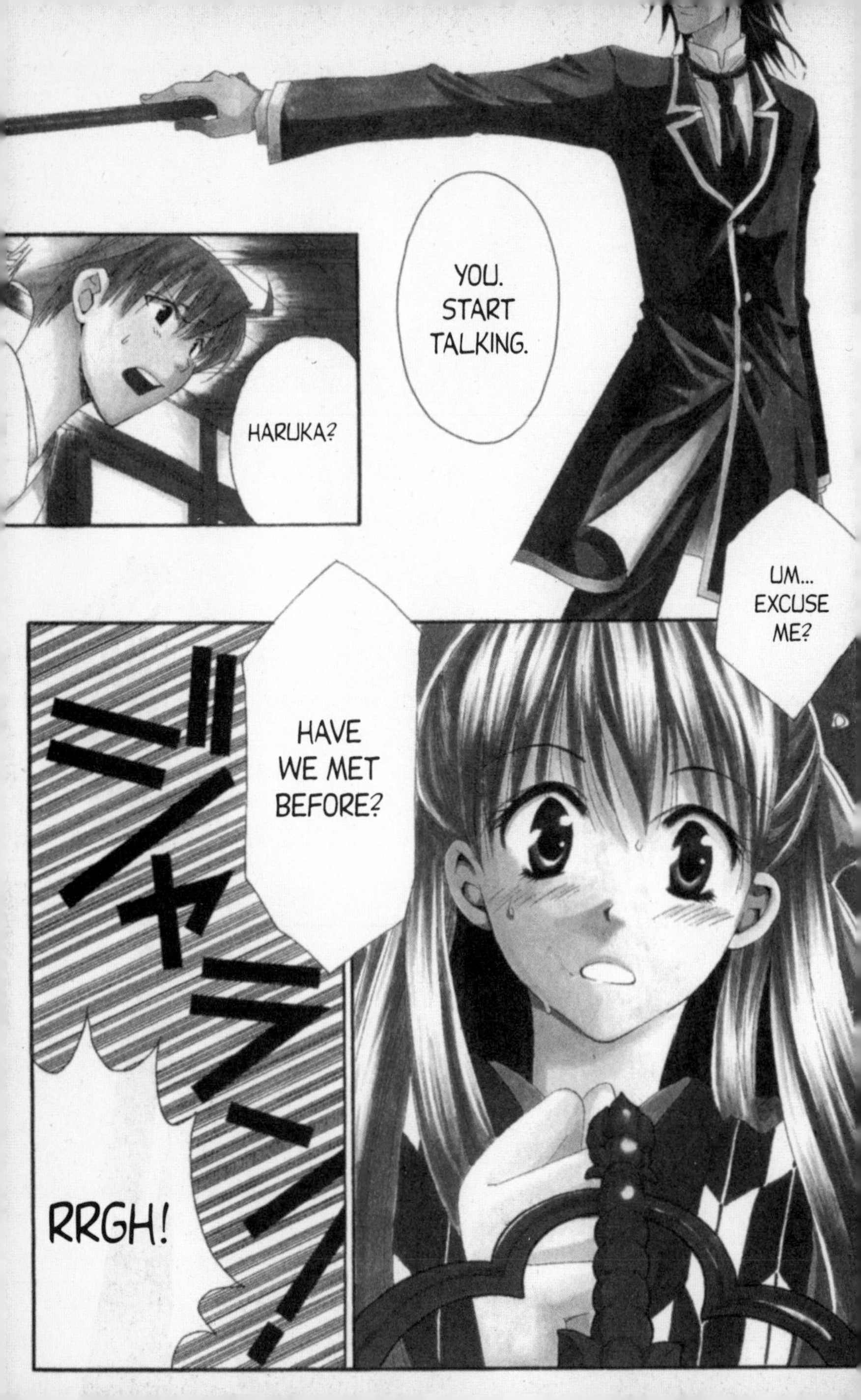
YOU. START TALKING.
HARUKA?
UM... EXCUSE ME?
HAVE WE MET BEFORE?
RRGH!

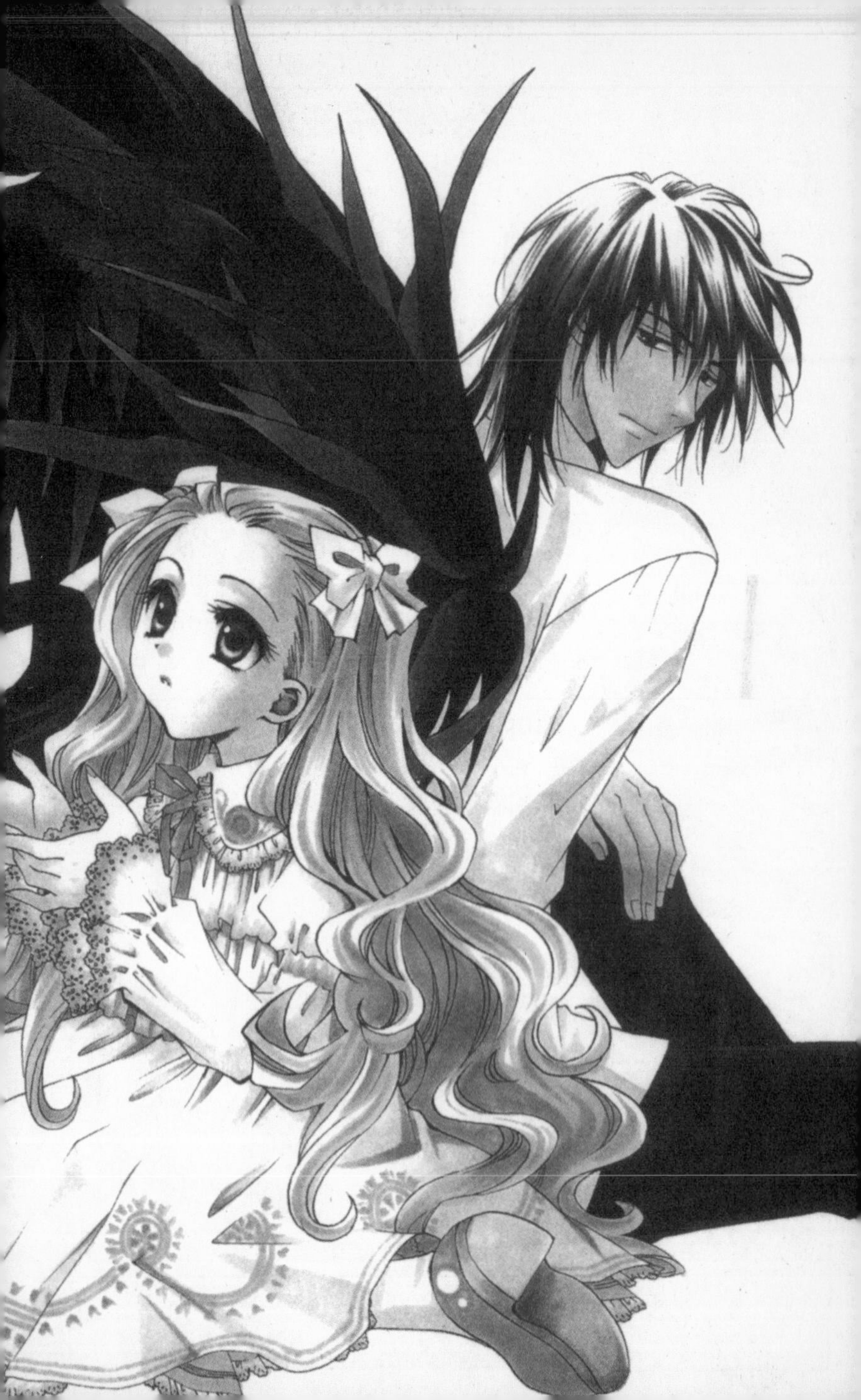

KANBARINYUUDOU STAGE PART II

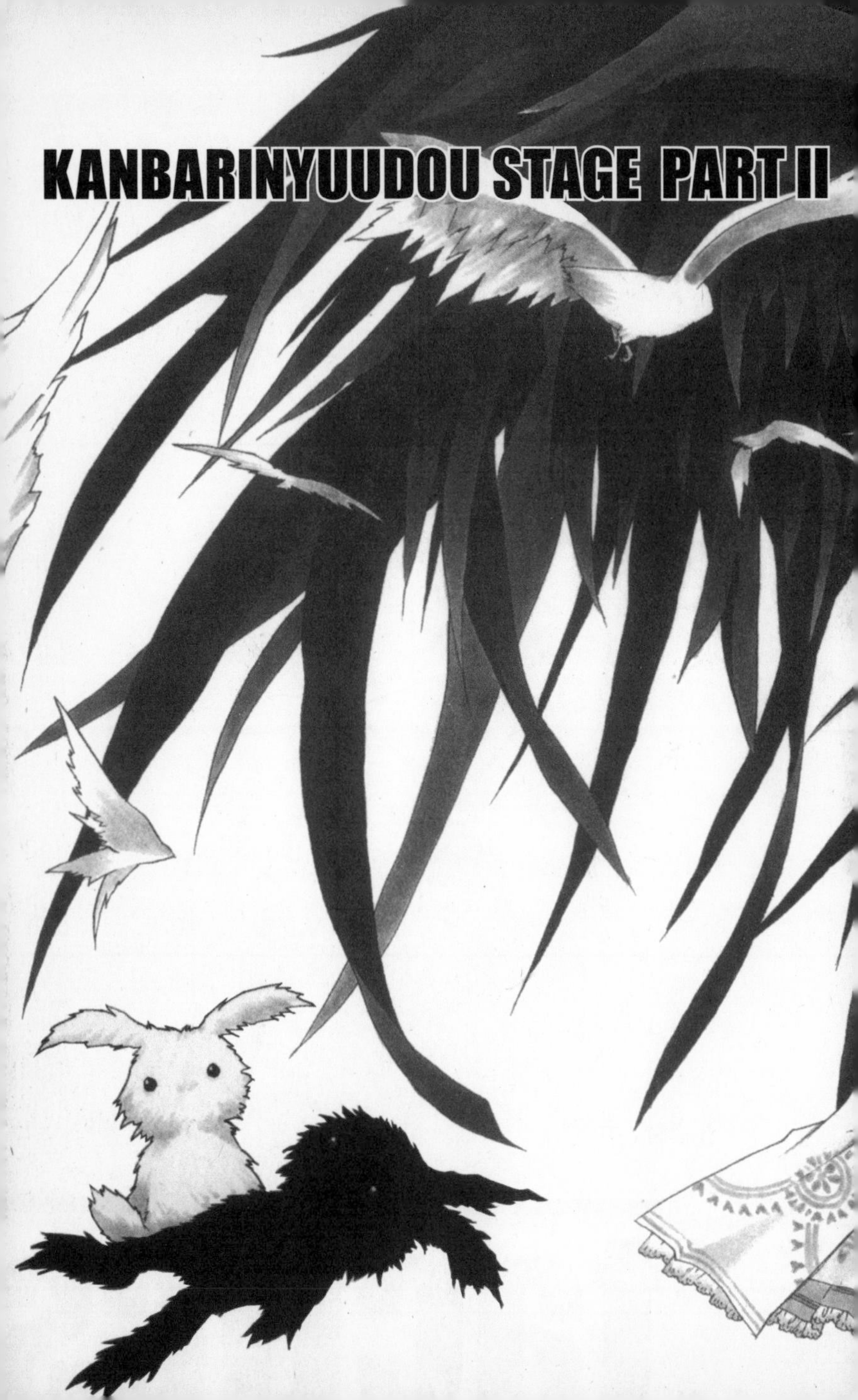

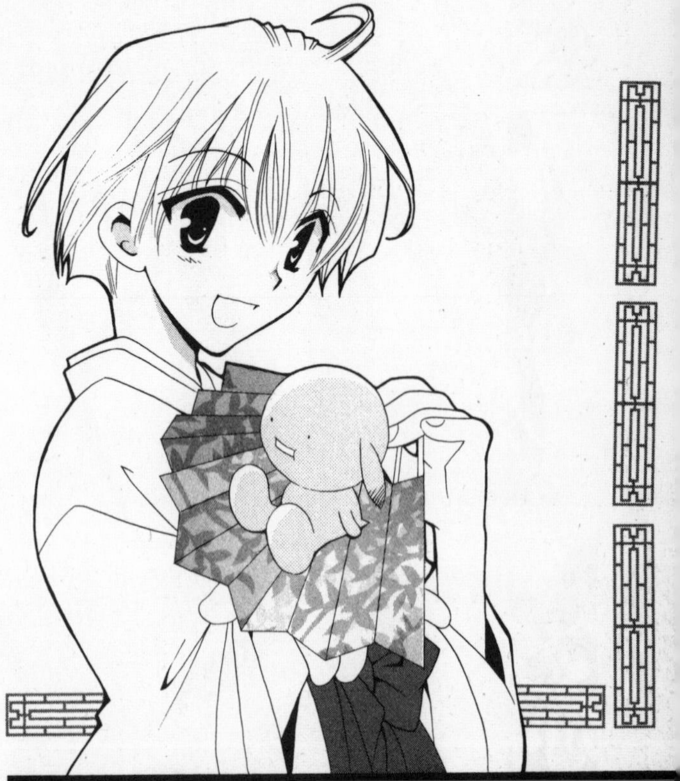

tactics

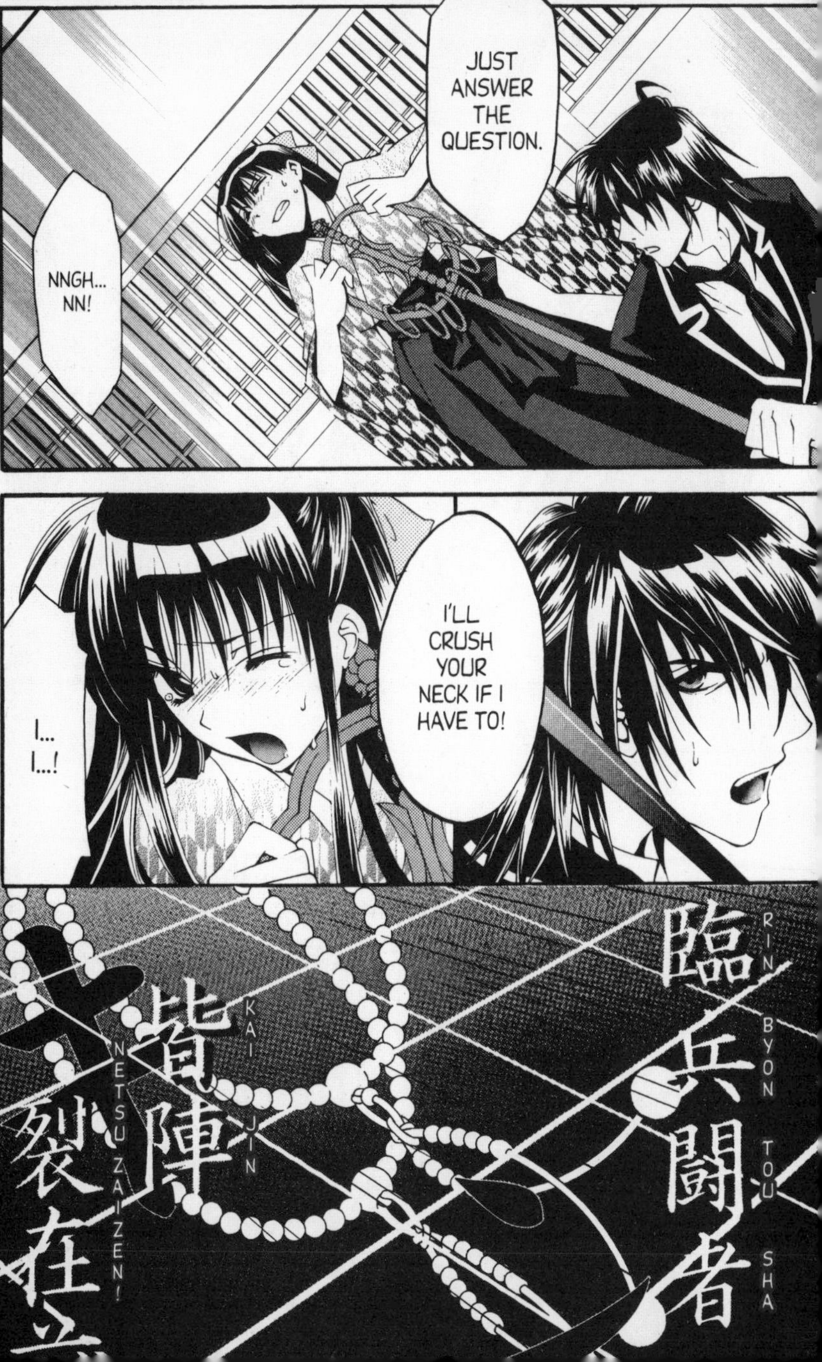
JUST ANSWER THE QUESTION.
NNGH... NN!
I'LL CRUSH YOUR NECK IF I HAVE TO!
I... I...!
臨兵闘者
RIN BYON TOU SHA
皆陣
KAI JIN
裂在
NETSU ZAIZEN!

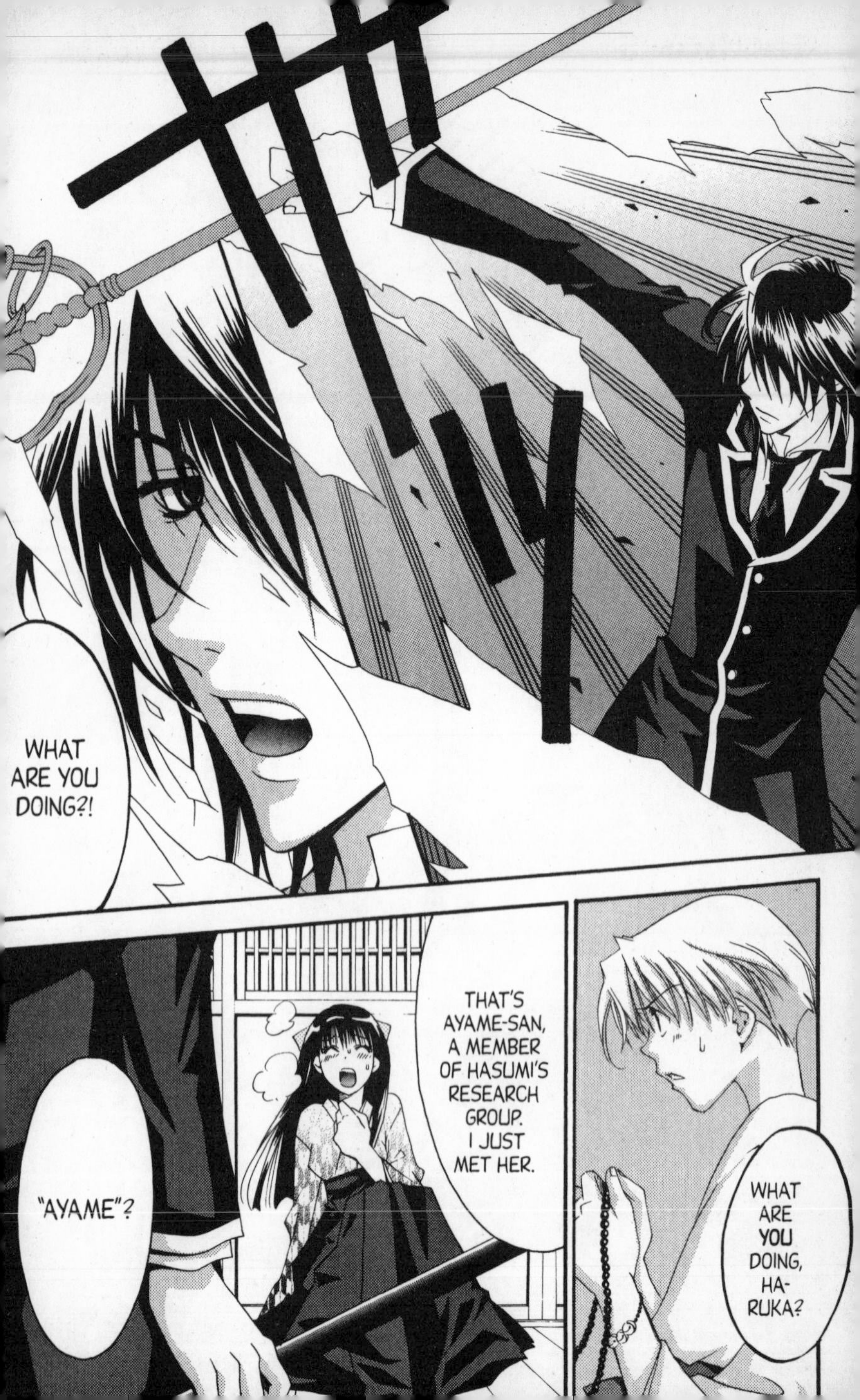
WHAT ARE YOU DOING?!
WHAT ARE YOU DOING, HA-RUKA?
THAT'S AYAME-SAN, A MEMBER OF HASUMI'S RESEARCH GROUP. I JUST MET HER.
"AYAME"?

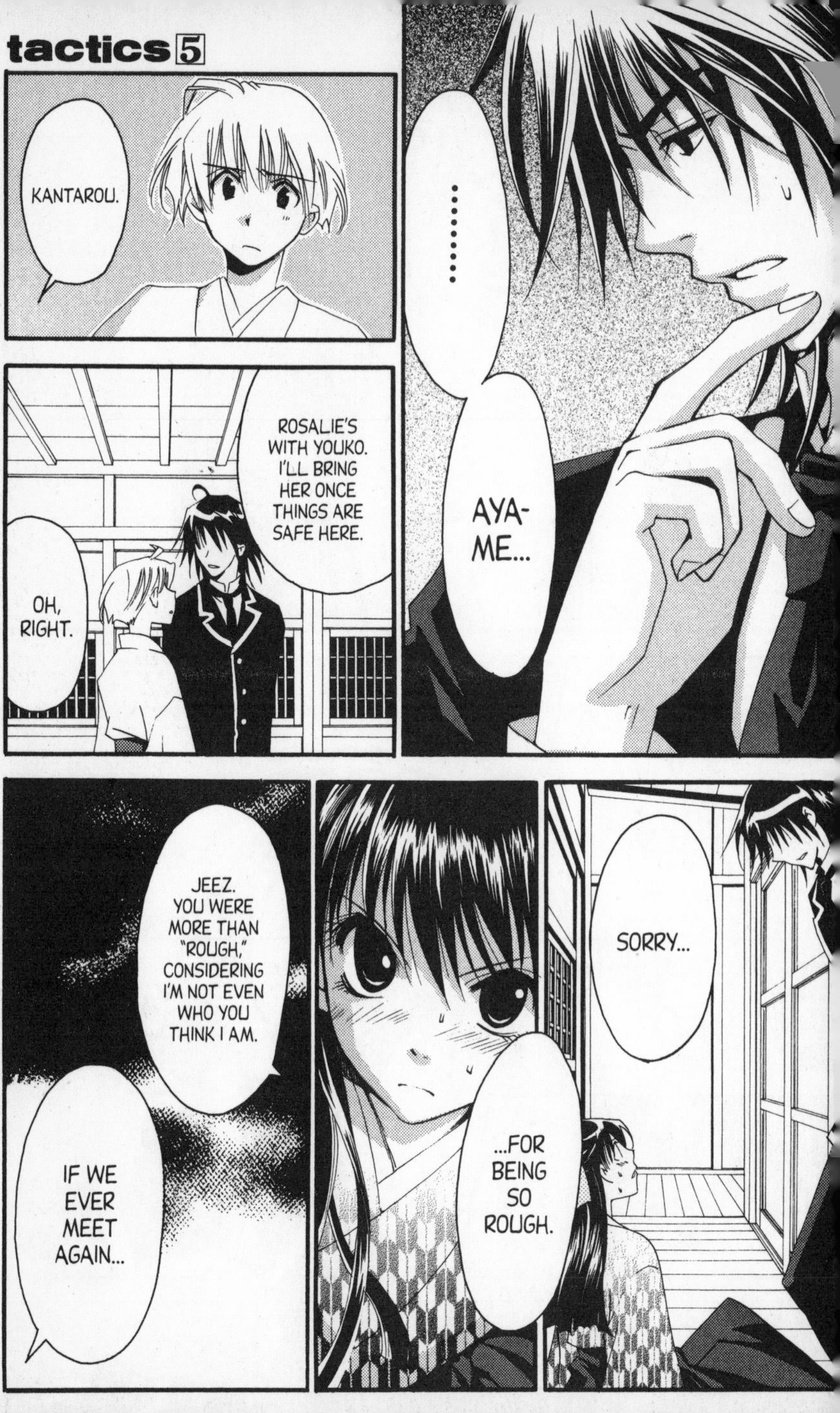
......
AYA-ME...
KANTAROU.
ROSALIE'S WITH YOUKO. I'LL BRING HER ONCE THINGS ARE SAFE HERE.
OH, RIGHT.
SORRY...
...FOR BEING SO ROUGH.
JEEZ. YOU WERE MORE THAN "ROUGH," CONSIDERING I'M NOT EVEN WHO YOU THINK I AM.
IF WE EVER MEET AGAIN...

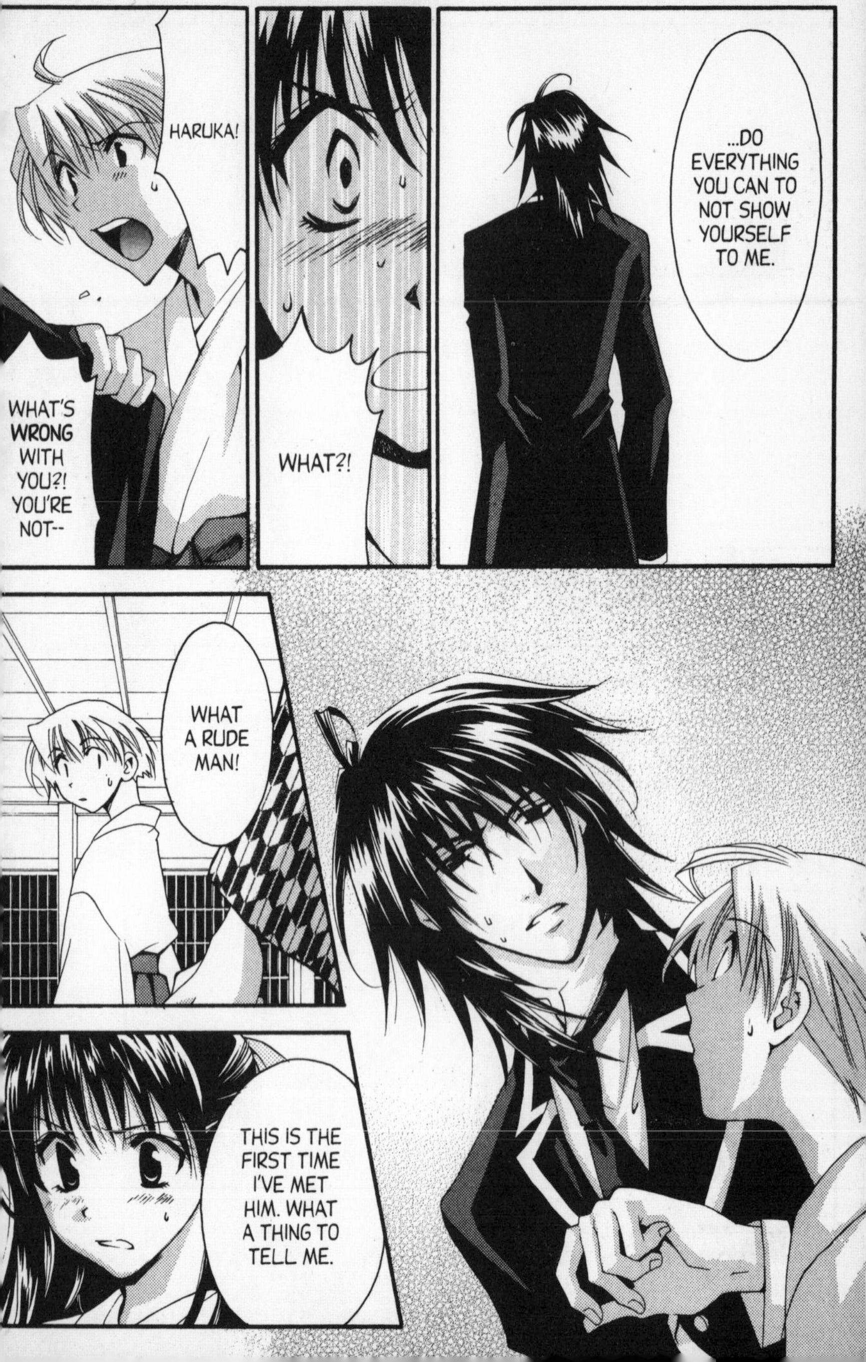
...DO EVERYTHING YOU CAN TO NOT SHOW YOURSELF TO ME.
WHAT?!
HARUKA!
WHAT'S **WRONG** WITH YOU?! YOU'RE NOT--
WHAT A RUDE MAN!
THIS IS THE FIRST TIME I'VE MET HIM. WHAT A THING TO TELL ME.

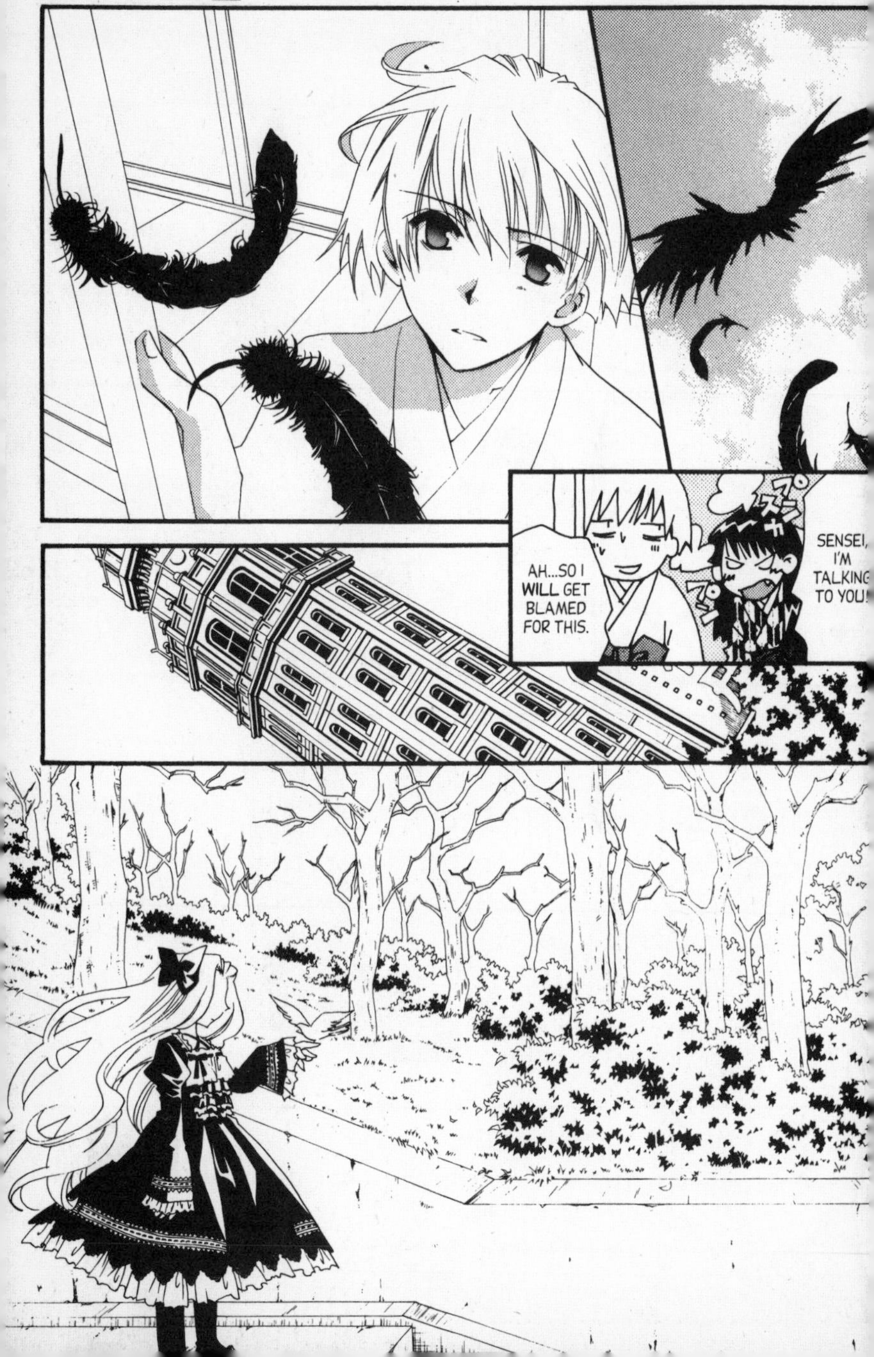
SENSEI, I'M TALKING TO YOU!
AH...SO I WILL GET BLAMED FOR THIS.

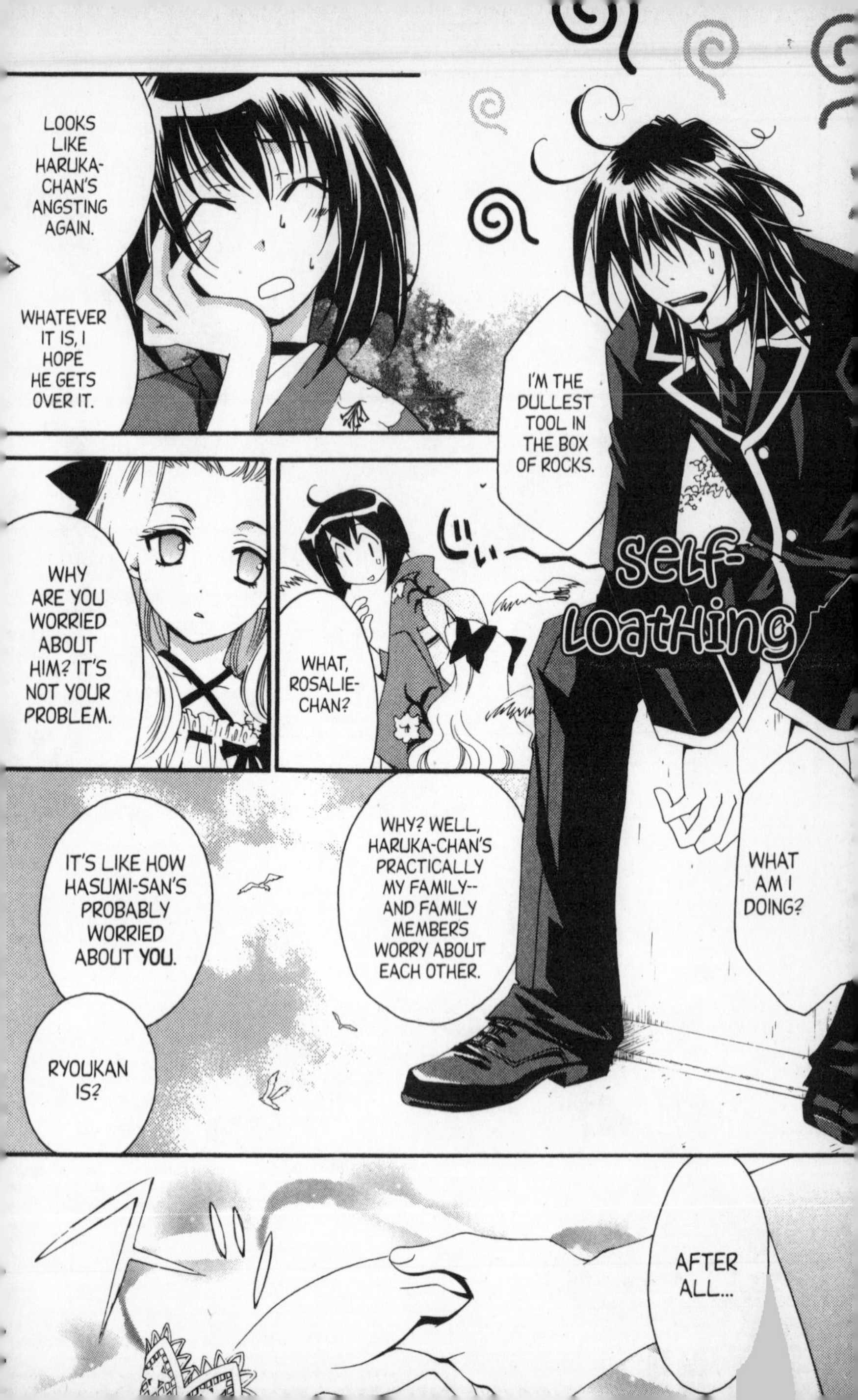
I'M THE DULLEST TOOL IN THE BOX OF ROCKS.
SELF-LOATHING
LOOKS LIKE HARUKA-CHAN'S ANGSTING AGAIN.
WHATEVER IT IS, I HOPE HE GETS OVER IT.
じぃ
WHAT, ROSALIE-CHAN?
WHY ARE YOU WORRIED ABOUT HIM? IT'S NOT YOUR PROBLEM.
WHAT AM I DOING?
WHY? WELL, HARUKA-CHAN'S PRACTICALLY MY FAMILY-- AND FAMILY MEMBERS WORRY ABOUT EACH OTHER.
IT'S LIKE HOW HASUMI-SAN'S PROBABLY WORRIED ABOUT **YOU**.
RYOUKAN IS?
AFTER ALL...

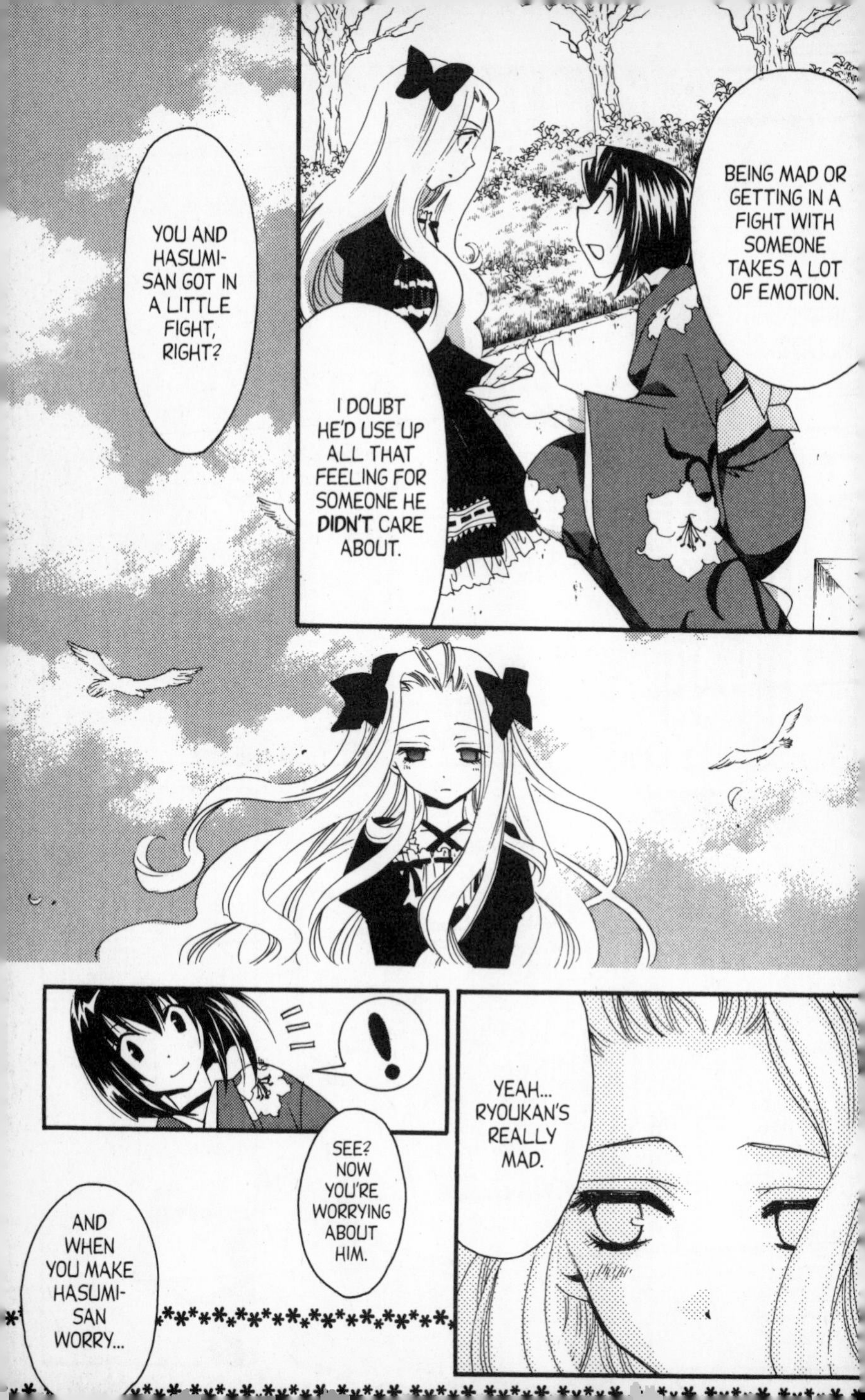
BEING MAD OR GETTING IN A FIGHT WITH SOMEONE TAKES A LOT OF EMOTION.
I DOUBT HE'D USE UP ALL THAT FEELING FOR SOMEONE HE **DIDN'T** CARE ABOUT.
YOU AND HASUMI-SAN GOT IN A LITTLE FIGHT, RIGHT?
YEAH... RYOUKAN'S REALLY MAD.
!
SEE? NOW YOU'RE WORRYING ABOUT HIM.
AND WHEN YOU MAKE HASUMI-SAN WORRY...

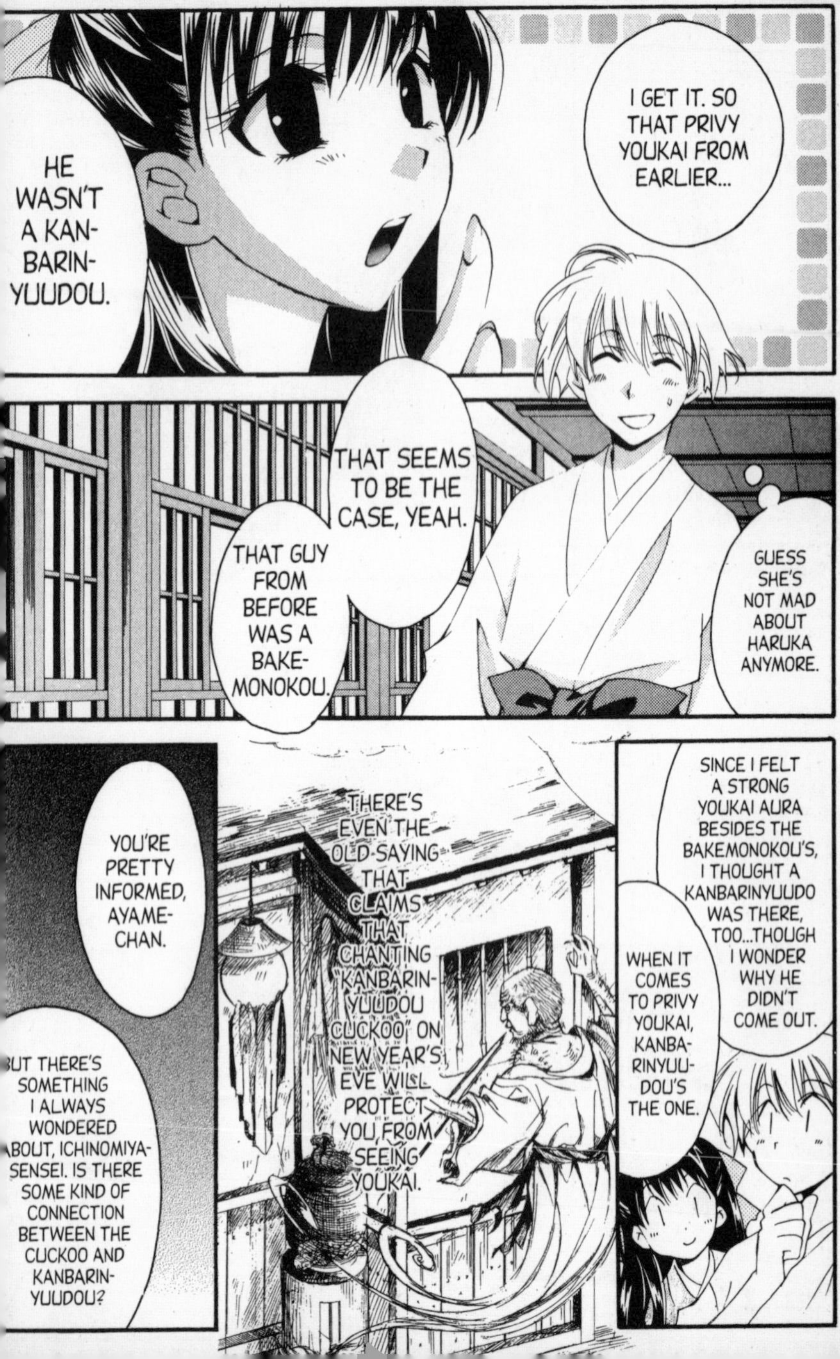
I GET IT. SO THAT PRIVY YOUKAI FROM EARLIER...
HE WASN'T A KANBARINYUUDOU.
THAT SEEMS TO BE THE CASE, YEAH.
THAT GUY FROM BEFORE WAS A BAKEMONOKOU.
GUESS SHE'S NOT MAD ABOUT HARUKA ANYMORE.
SINCE I FELT A STRONG YOUKAI AURA BESIDES THE BAKEMONOKOU'S, I THOUGHT A KANBARINYUUDO WAS THERE, TOO...THOUGH I WONDER WHY HE DIDN'T COME OUT.
WHEN IT COMES TO PRIVY YOUKAI, KANBARINYUUDOU'S THE ONE.
THERE'S EVEN THE OLD SAYING THAT CLAIMS THAT CHANTING "KANBARINYUUDOU CUCKOO" ON NEW YEAR'S EVE WILL PROTECT YOU FROM SEEING YOUKAI.
YOU'RE PRETTY INFORMED, AYAME-CHAN.
UT THERE'S SOMETHING I ALWAYS WONDERED BOUT, ICHINOMIYA-SENSEI. IS THERE SOME KIND OF CONNECTION BETWEEN THE CUCKOO AND KANBARINYUUDOU?

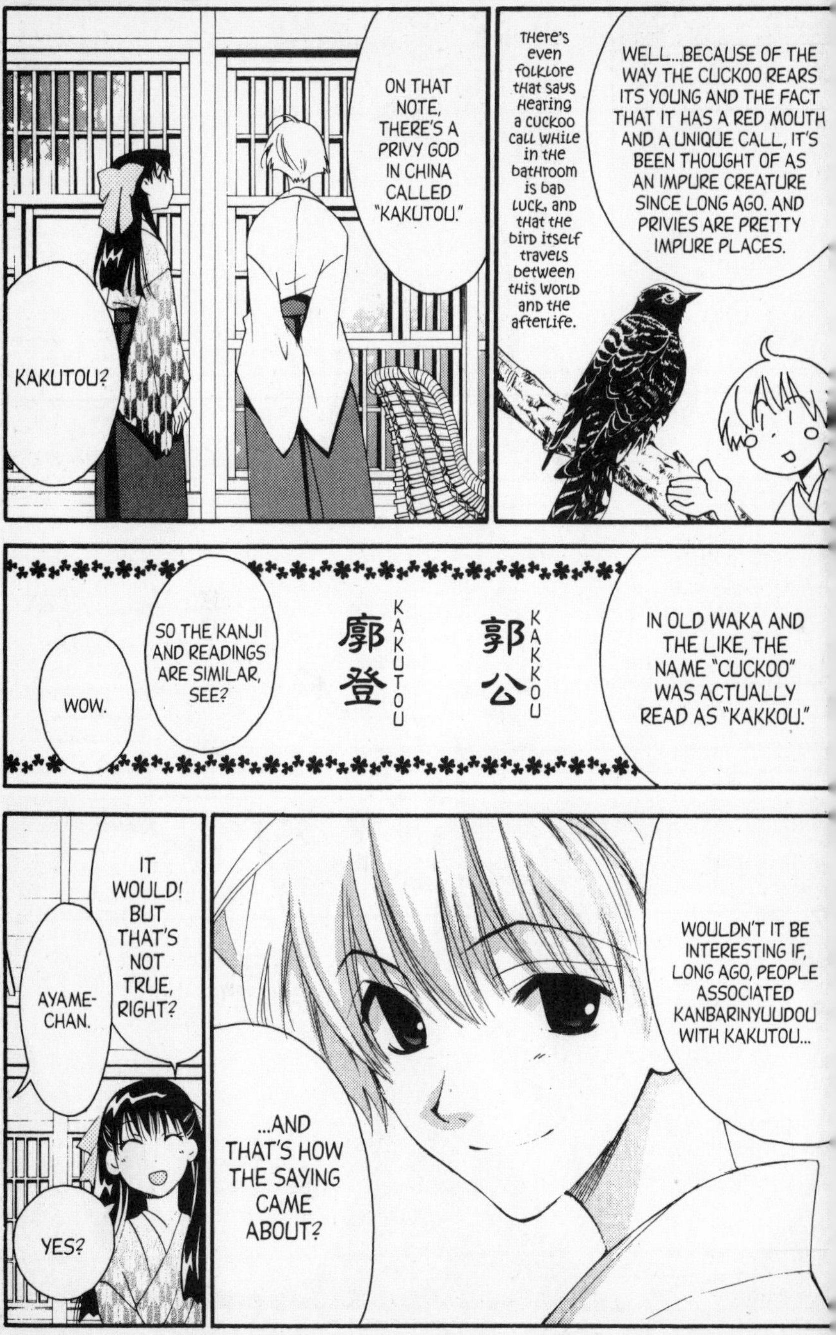
WELL...BECAUSE OF THE WAY THE CUCKOO REARS ITS YOUNG AND THE FACT THAT IT HAS A RED MOUTH AND A UNIQUE CALL, IT'S BEEN THOUGHT OF AS AN IMPURE CREATURE SINCE LONG AGO. AND PRIVIES ARE PRETTY IMPURE PLACES.
There's even folklore that says hearing a cuckoo call while in the bathroom is bad luck, and that the bird itself travels between this world and the afterlife.
ON THAT NOTE, THERE'S A PRIVY GOD IN CHINA CALLED "KAKUTOU."
KAKUTOU?
IN OLD WAKA AND THE LIKE, THE NAME "CUCKOO" WAS ACTUALLY READ AS "KAKKOU."
郭公 KAKKOU
廓登 KAKUTOU
SO THE KANJI AND READINGS ARE SIMILAR, SEE?
WOW.
WOULDN'T IT BE INTERESTING IF, LONG AGO, PEOPLE ASSOCIATED KANBARINYUUDOU WITH KAKUTOU...
...AND THAT'S HOW THE SAYING CAME ABOUT?
IT WOULD! BUT THAT'S NOT TRUE, RIGHT?
AYAME-CHAN.
YES?

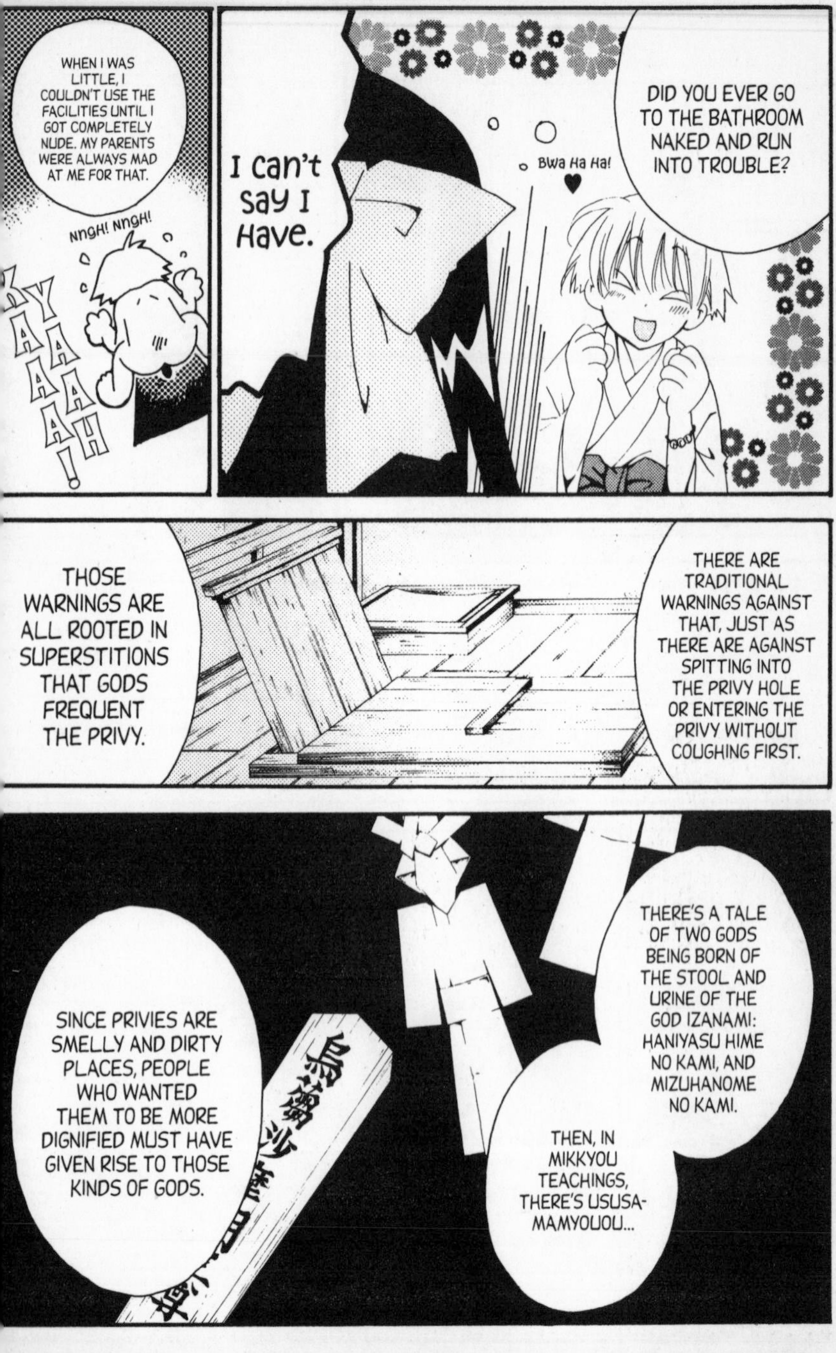
DID YOU EVER GO TO THE BATHROOM NAKED AND RUN INTO TROUBLE?
BWA HA HA! ♥
I can't say I Have.
WHEN I WAS LITTLE, I COULDN'T USE THE FACILITIES UNTIL I GOT COMPLETELY NUDE. MY PARENTS WERE ALWAYS MAD AT ME FOR THAT.
NNGH! NNGH!
KYAAAAAH!
THERE ARE TRADITIONAL WARNINGS AGAINST THAT, JUST AS THERE ARE AGAINST SPITTING INTO THE PRIVY HOLE OR ENTERING THE PRIVY WITHOUT COUGHING FIRST.
THOSE WARNINGS ARE ALL ROOTED IN SUPERSTITIONS THAT GODS FREQUENT THE PRIVY.
THERE'S A TALE OF TWO GODS BEING BORN OF THE STOOL AND URINE OF THE GOD IZANAMI: HANIYASU HIME NO KAMI, AND MIZUHANOME NO KAMI.
THEN, IN MIKKYOU TEACHINGS, THERE'S USUSA-MAMYOUOU...
SINCE PRIVIES ARE SMELLY AND DIRTY PLACES, PEOPLE WHO WANTED THEM TO BE MORE DIGNIFIED MUST HAVE GIVEN RISE TO THOSE KINDS OF GODS.

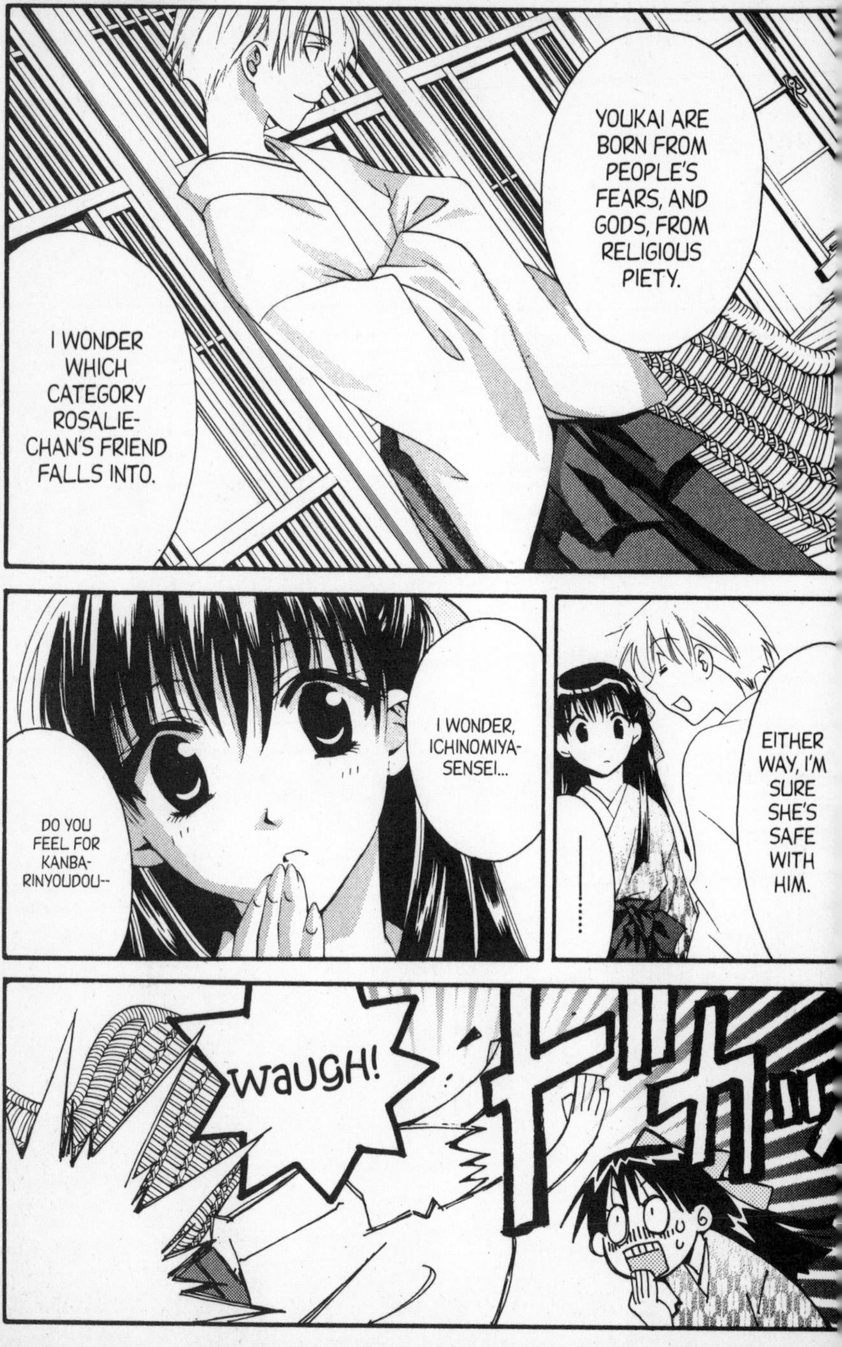
YOUKAI ARE BORN FROM PEOPLE'S FEARS, AND GODS, FROM RELIGIOUS PIETY.
I WONDER WHICH CATEGORY ROSALIE-CHAN'S FRIEND FALLS INTO.
EITHER WAY, I'M SURE SHE'S SAFE WITH HIM.
I WONDER, ICHINOMIYA-SENSEI...
DO YOU FEEL FOR KANBA-RINYOUDOU--
WAUGH!

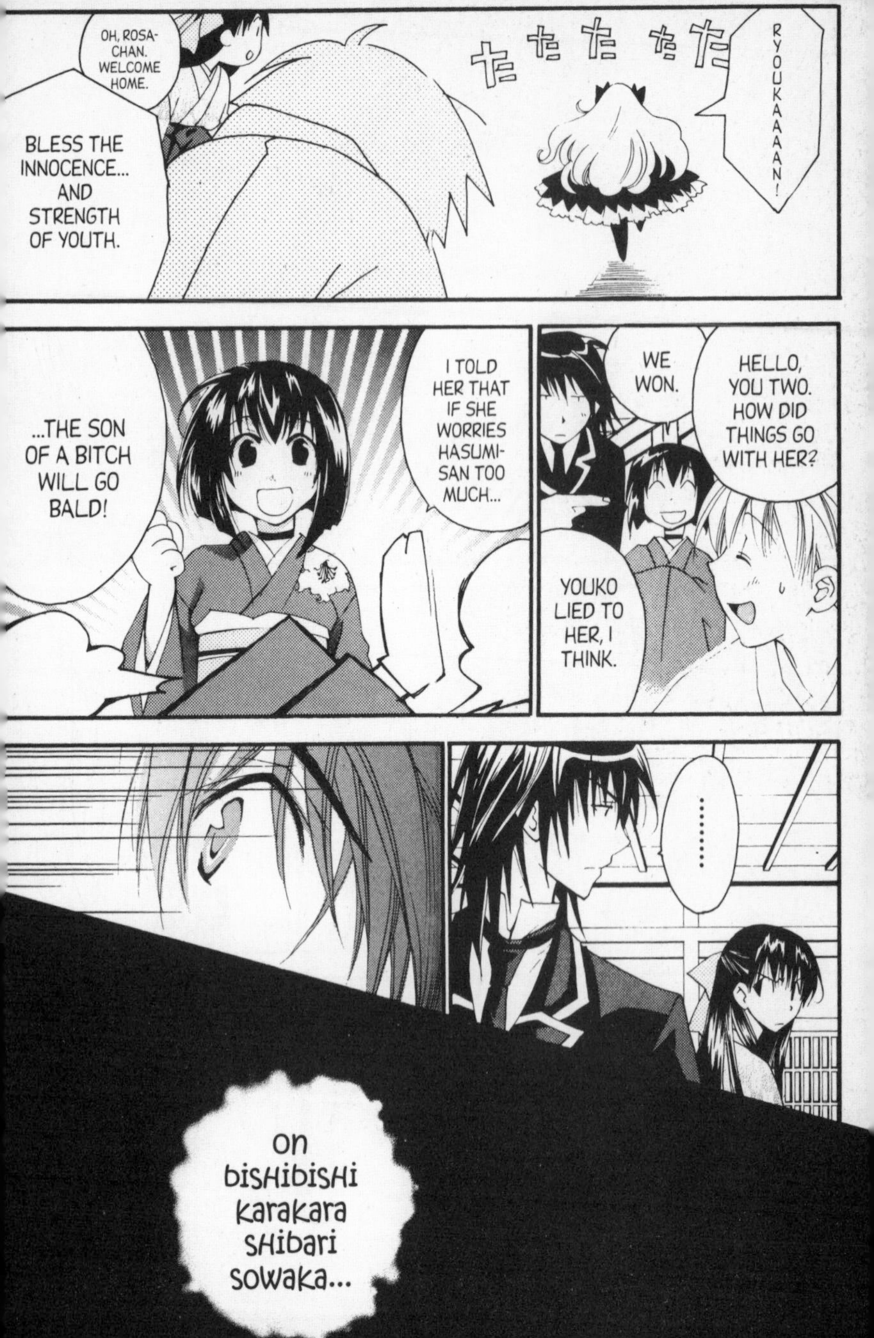
RYOUKAAAAAN!
たたたたた
OH, ROSA-CHAN. WELCOME HOME.
BLESS THE INNOCENCE... AND STRENGTH OF YOUTH.
HELLO, YOU TWO. HOW DID THINGS GO WITH HER?
WE WON.
YOUKO LIED TO HER, I THINK.
I TOLD HER THAT IF SHE WORRIES HASUMI-SAN TOO MUCH...
...THE SON OF A BITCH WILL GO BALD!
......
on bishibishi karakara shibari sowaka...

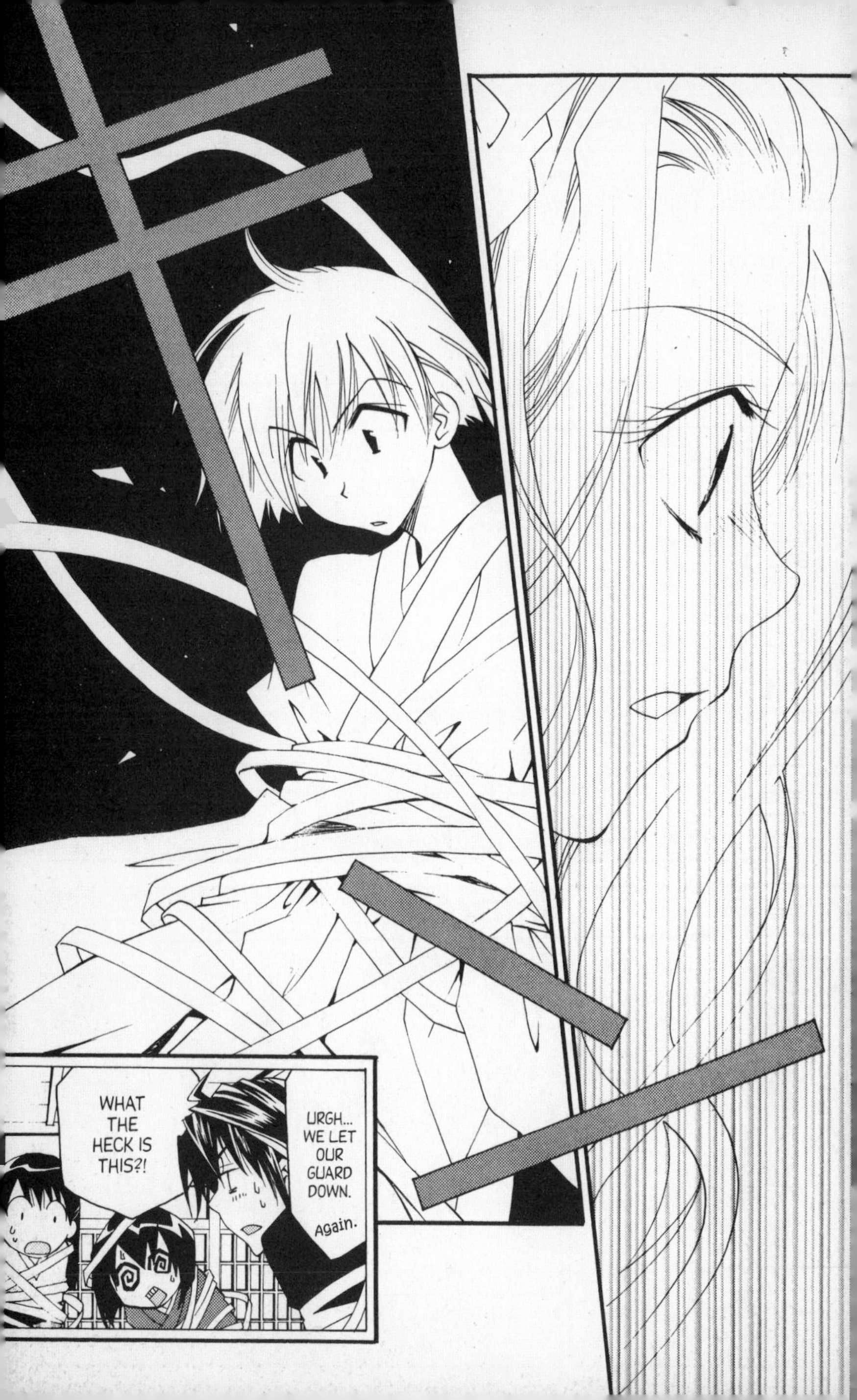
URGH... WE LET OUR GUARD DOWN.
Again.
WHAT THE HECK IS THIS?!

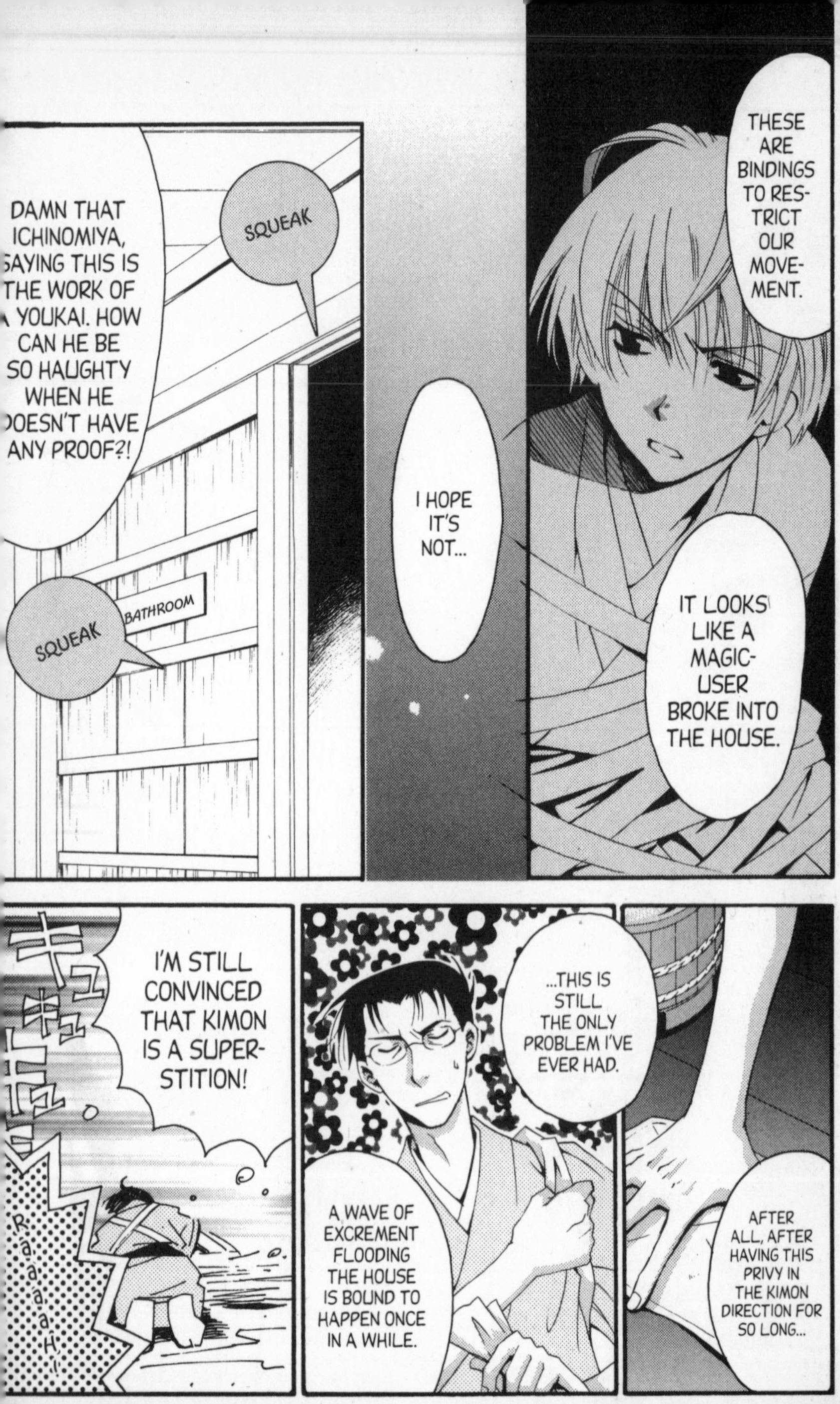
THESE ARE BINDINGS TO RESTRICT OUR MOVEMENT.
IT LOOKS LIKE A MAGIC-USER BROKE INTO THE HOUSE.
I HOPE IT'S NOT...
SQUEAK
DAMN THAT ICHINOMIYA, SAYING THIS IS THE WORK OF A YOUKAI. HOW CAN HE BE SO HAUGHTY WHEN HE DOESN'T HAVE ANY PROOF?!
SQUEAK
BATHROOM
AFTER ALL, AFTER HAVING THIS PRIVY IN THE KIMON DIRECTION FOR SO LONG...
...THIS IS STILL THE ONLY PROBLEM I'VE EVER HAD.
A WAVE OF EXCREMENT FLOODING THE HOUSE IS BOUND TO HAPPEN ONCE IN A WHILE.
I'M STILL CONVINCED THAT KIMON IS A SUPERSTITION!
Raaaaah!!

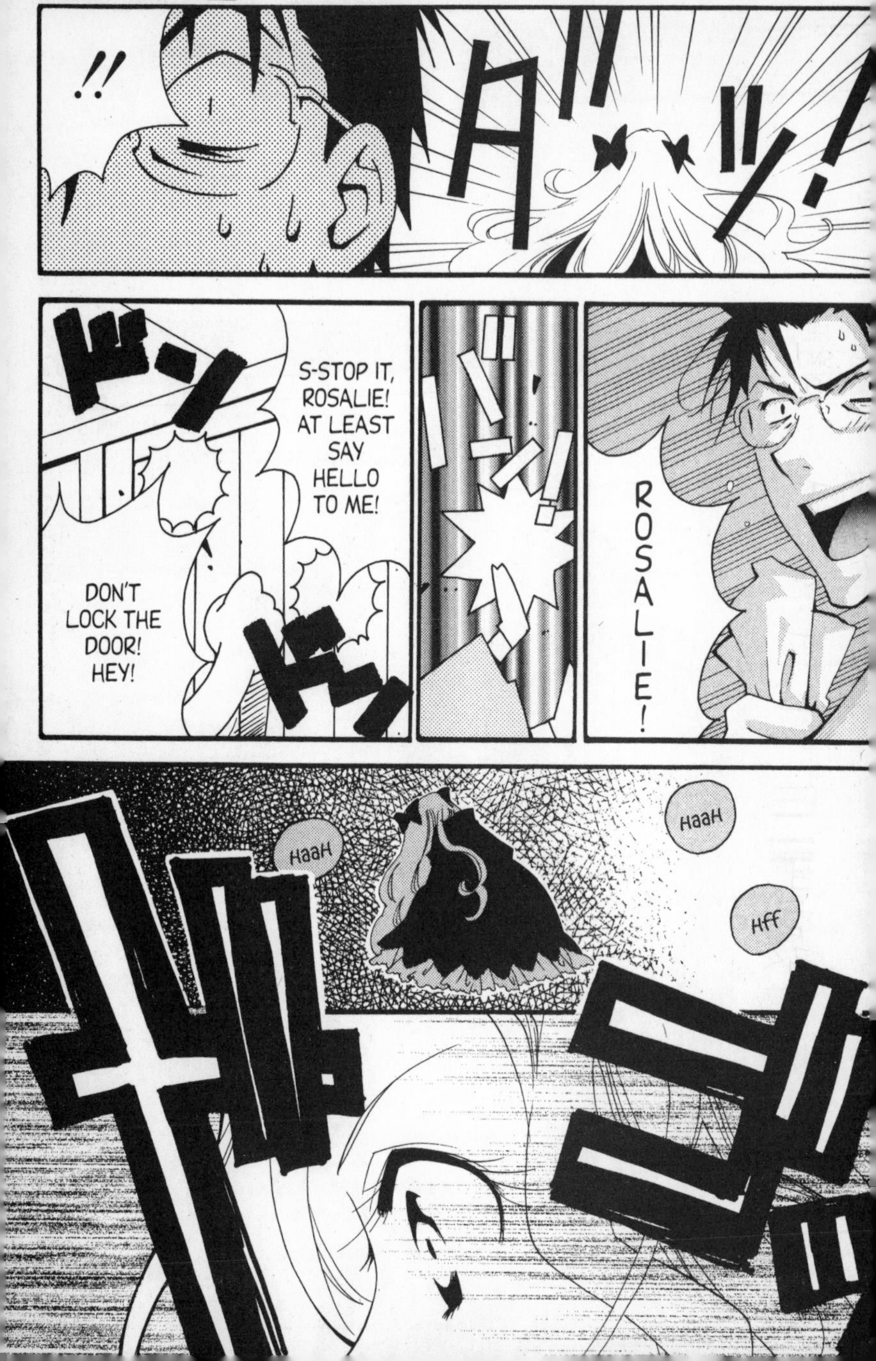
!!
ROSALIE!
S-STOP IT, ROSALIE! AT LEAST SAY HELLO TO ME!
DON'T LOCK THE DOOR! HEY!
HaaH
Hff
HaaH

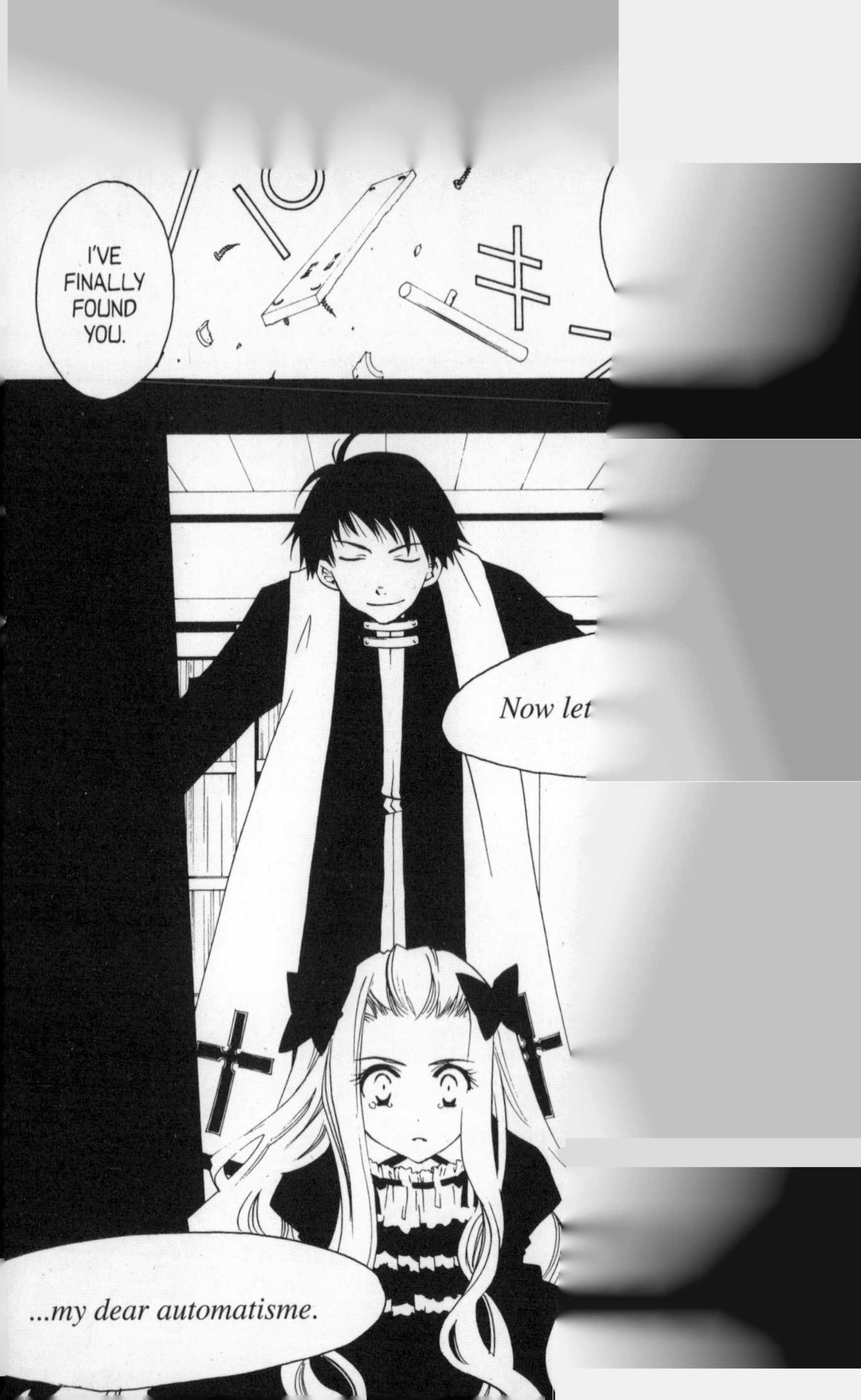
I'VE FINALLY FOUND YOU.
Now let
...my dear automatisme.

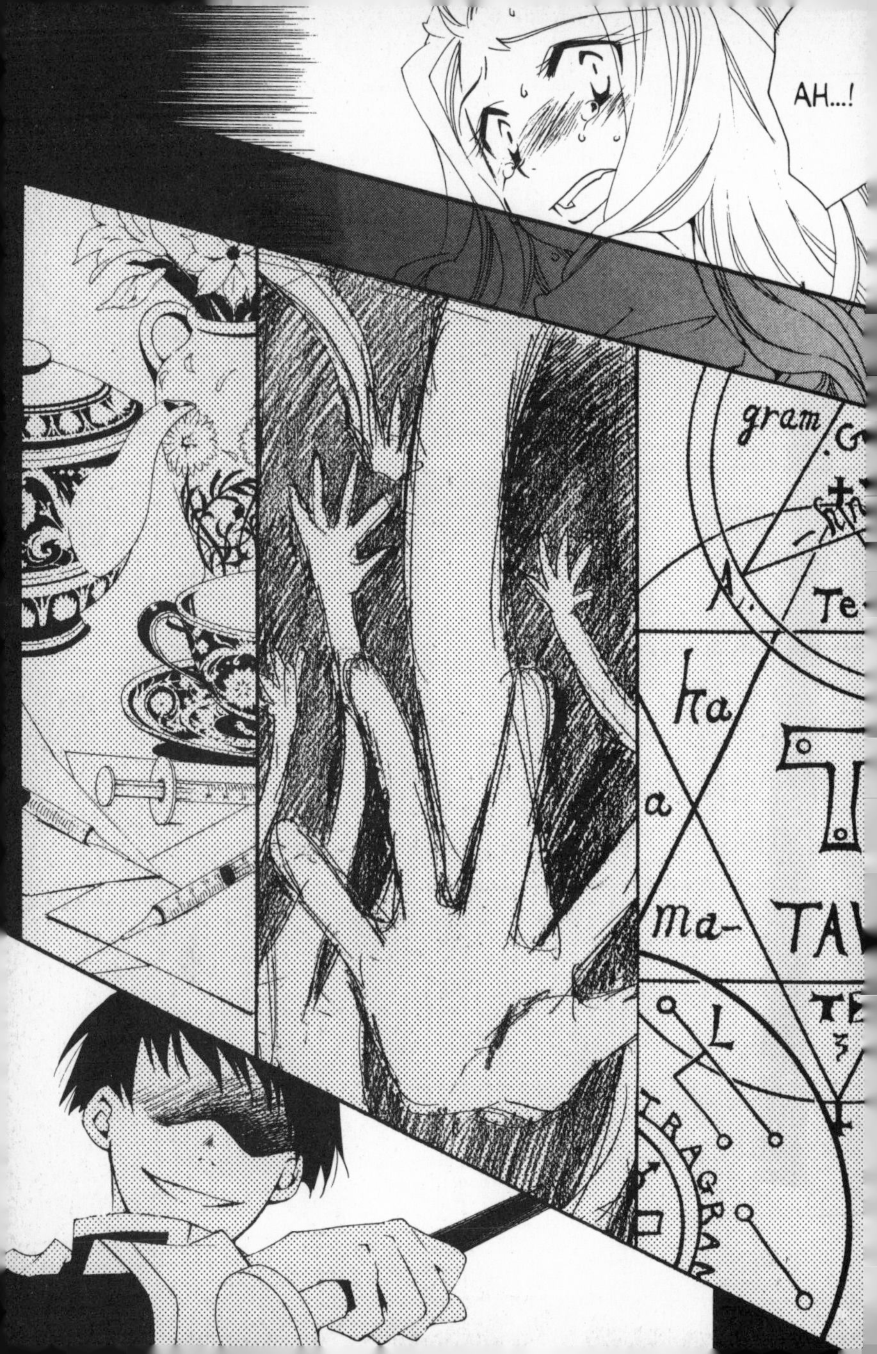
AH...!

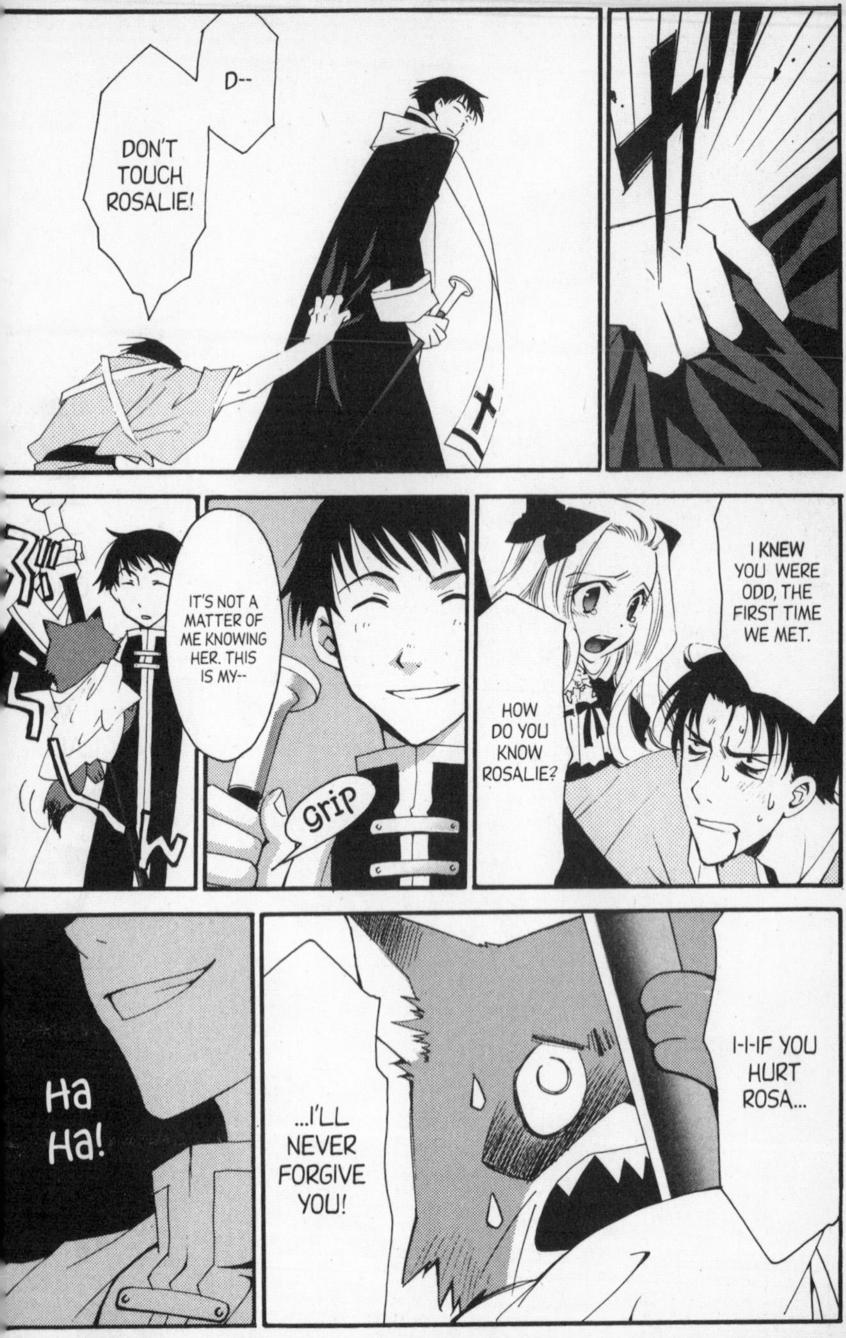
D--
DON'T TOUCH ROSALIE!
I KNEW YOU WERE ODD, THE FIRST TIME WE MET.
HOW DO YOU KNOW ROSALIE?
IT'S NOT A MATTER OF ME KNOWING HER. THIS IS MY--
grip
I-I-IF YOU HURT ROSA...
...I'LL NEVER FORGIVE YOU!
Ha Ha!

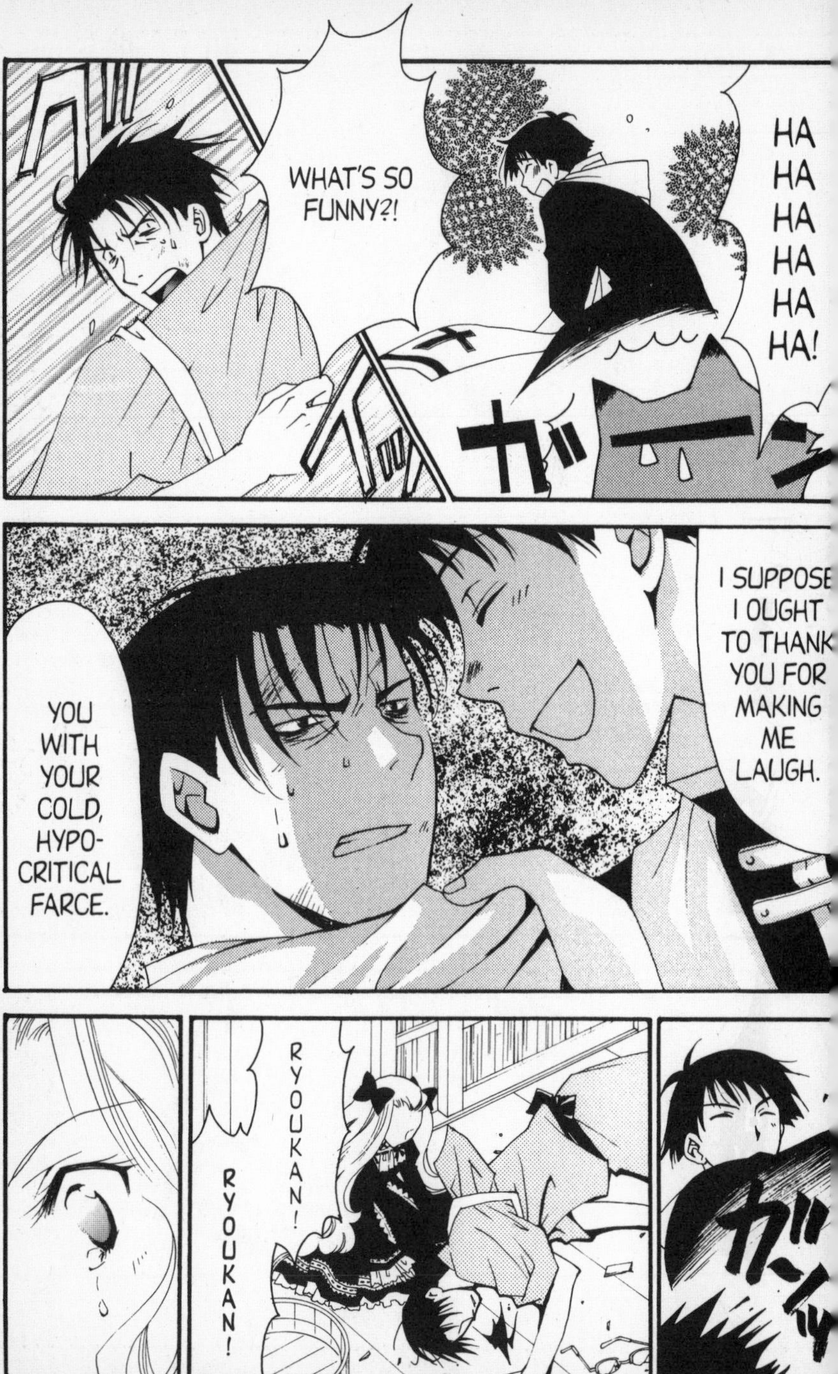
HA HA HA HA HA HA!
WHAT'S SO FUNNY?!
I SUPPOSE I OUGHT TO THANK YOU FOR MAKING ME LAUGH.
YOU WITH YOUR COLD, HYPO-CRITICAL FARCE.
RYOUKAN!
RYOUKAN!

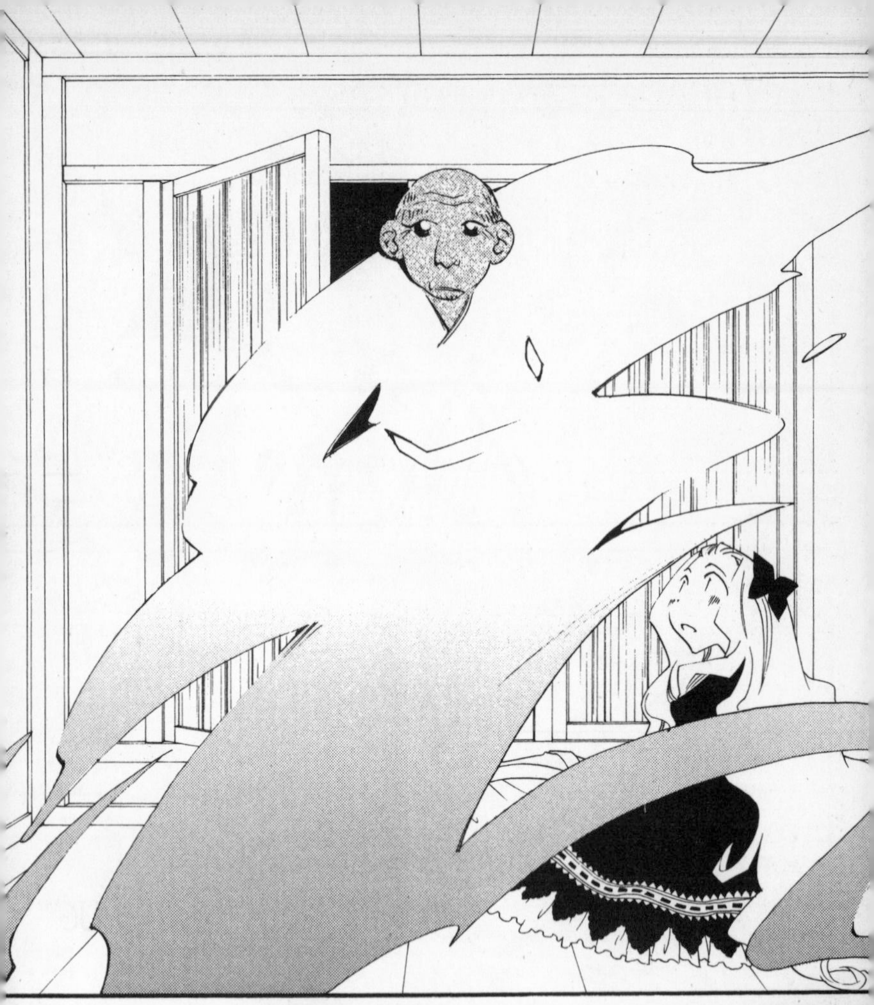
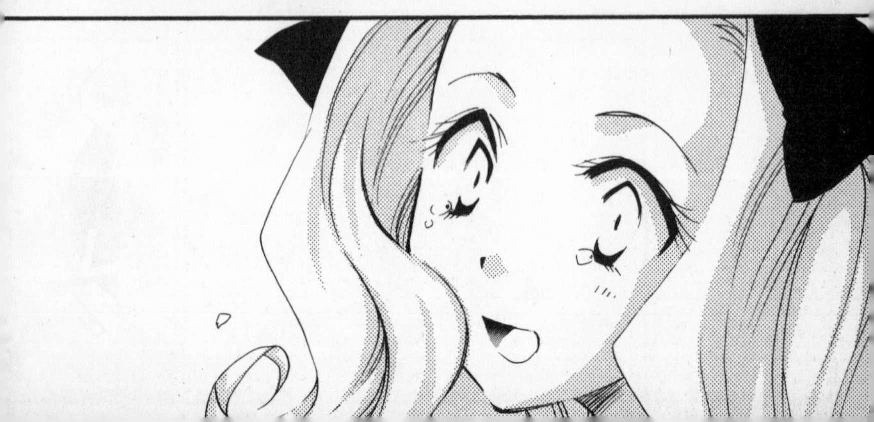

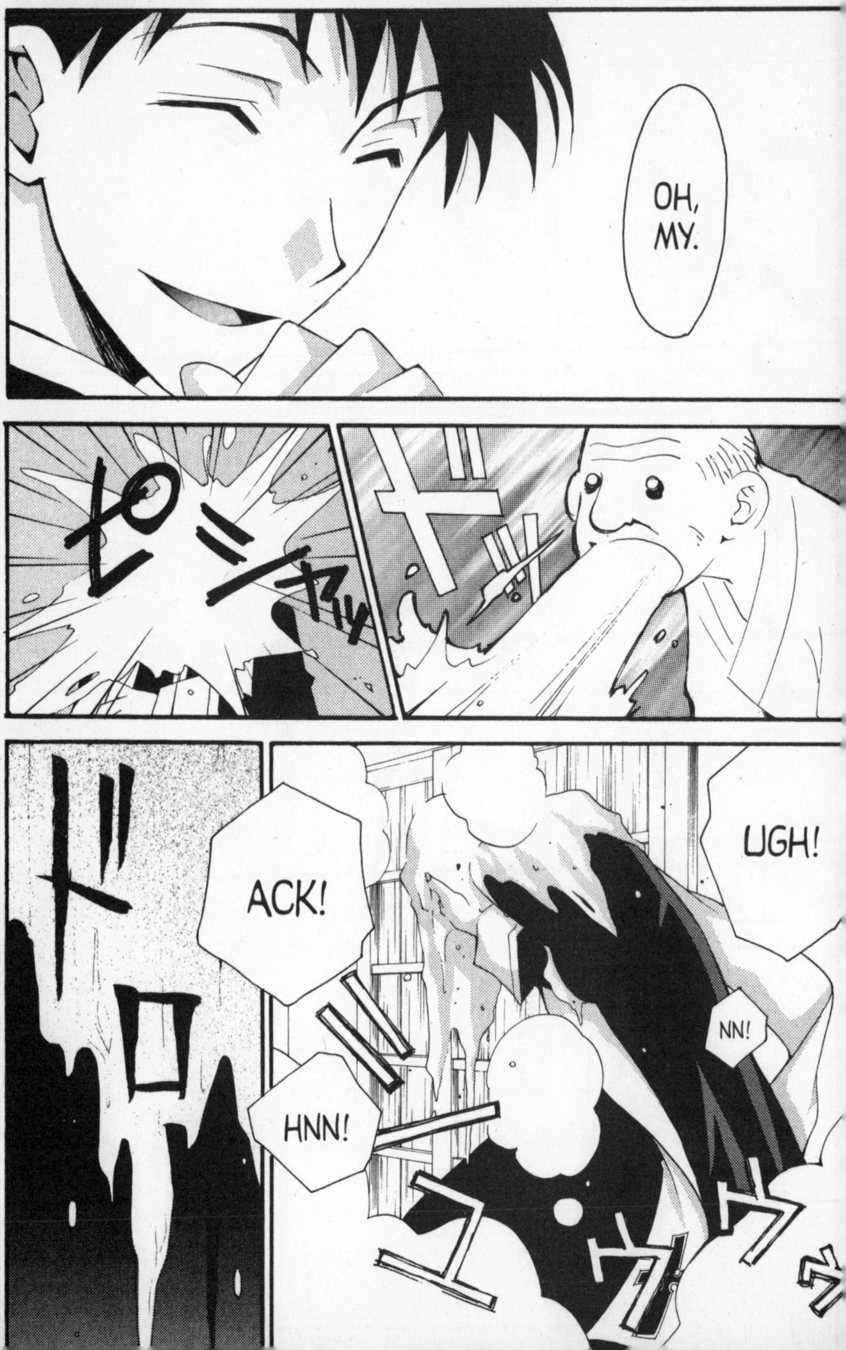
OH, MY.
UGH!
NN!
ACK!
HNN!

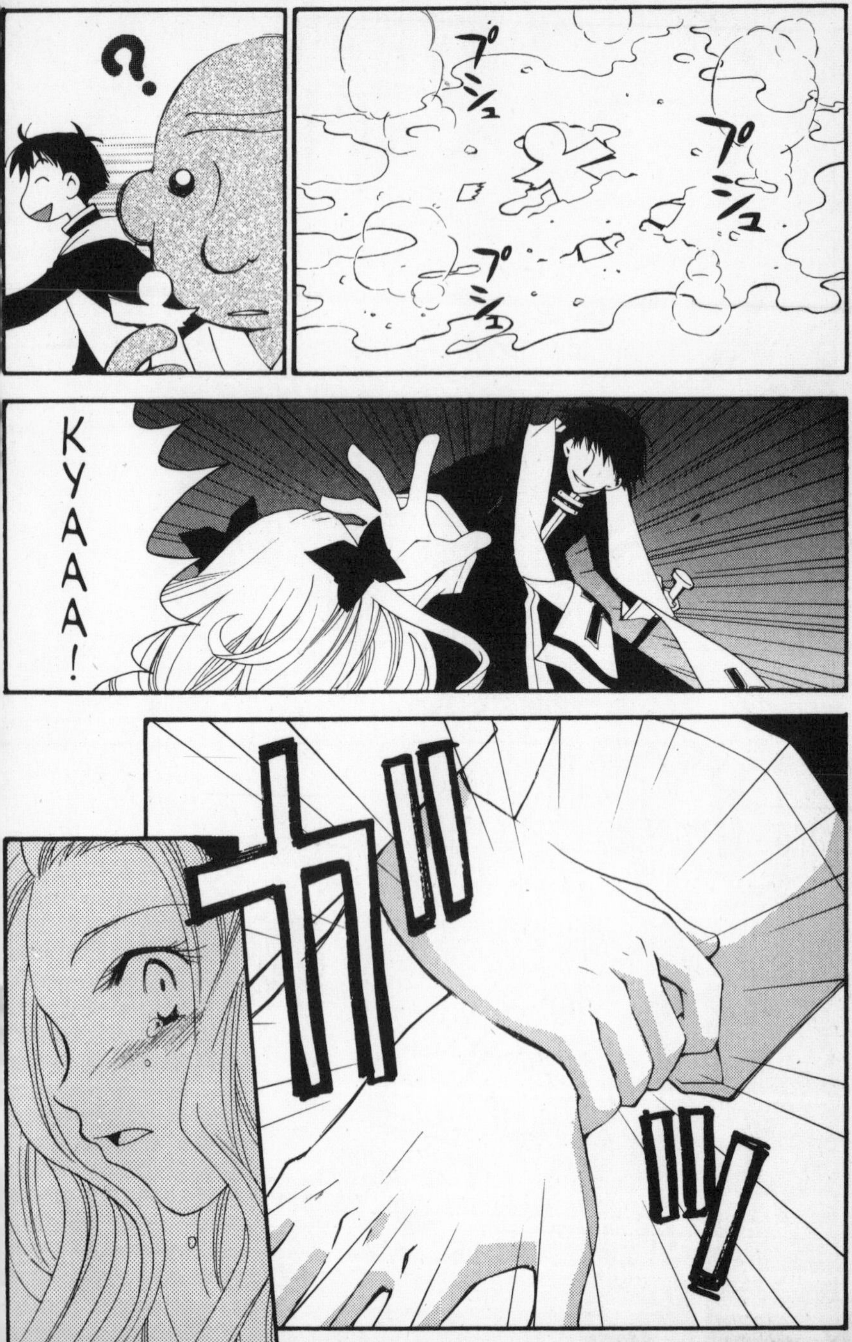
プシュ
プシュ
プシュ
?
KYAAAA!
ガッ

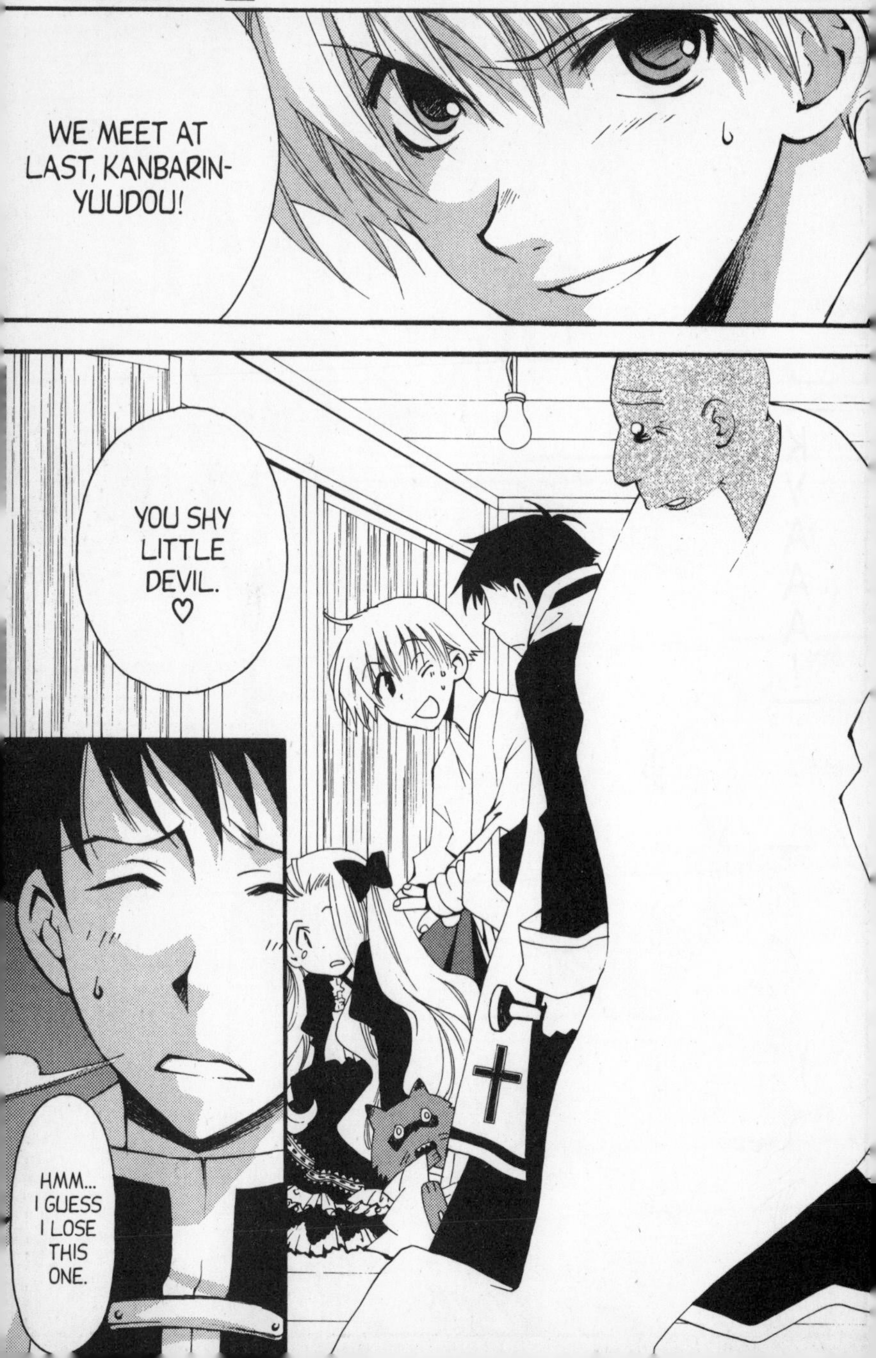
WE MEET AT LAST, KANBARIN-YUUDOU!
YOU SHY LITTLE DEVIL. ♡
HMM... I GUESS I LOSE THIS ONE.

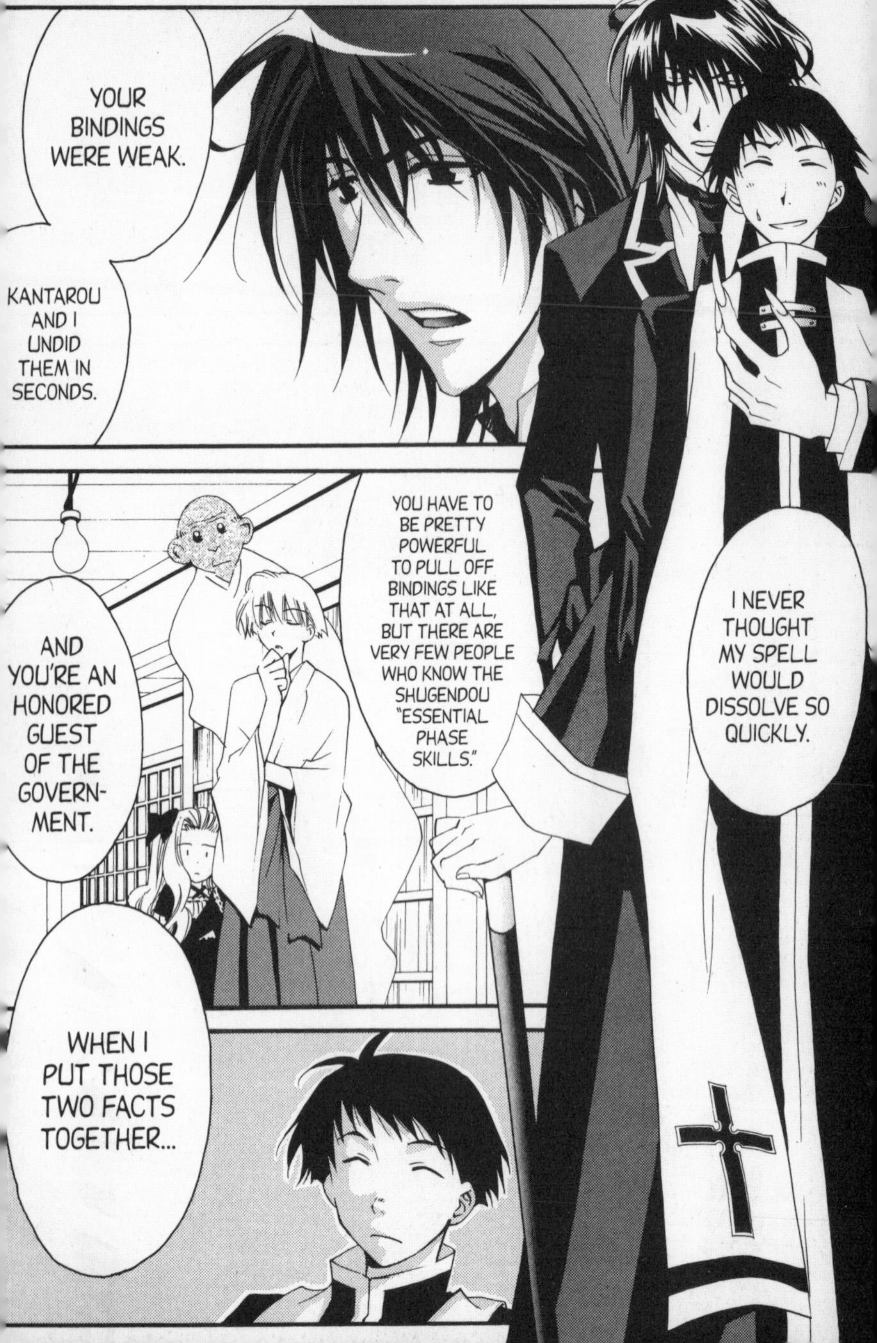
YOUR BINDINGS WERE WEAK.
KANTAROU AND I UNDID THEM IN SECONDS.
I NEVER THOUGHT MY SPELL WOULD DISSOLVE SO QUICKLY.
YOU HAVE TO BE PRETTY POWERFUL TO PULL OFF BINDINGS LIKE THAT AT ALL, BUT THERE ARE VERY FEW PEOPLE WHO KNOW THE SHUGENDOU "ESSENTIAL PHASE SKILLS."
AND YOU'RE AN HONORED GUEST OF THE GOVERN-MENT.
WHEN I PUT THOSE TWO FACTS TOGETHER...

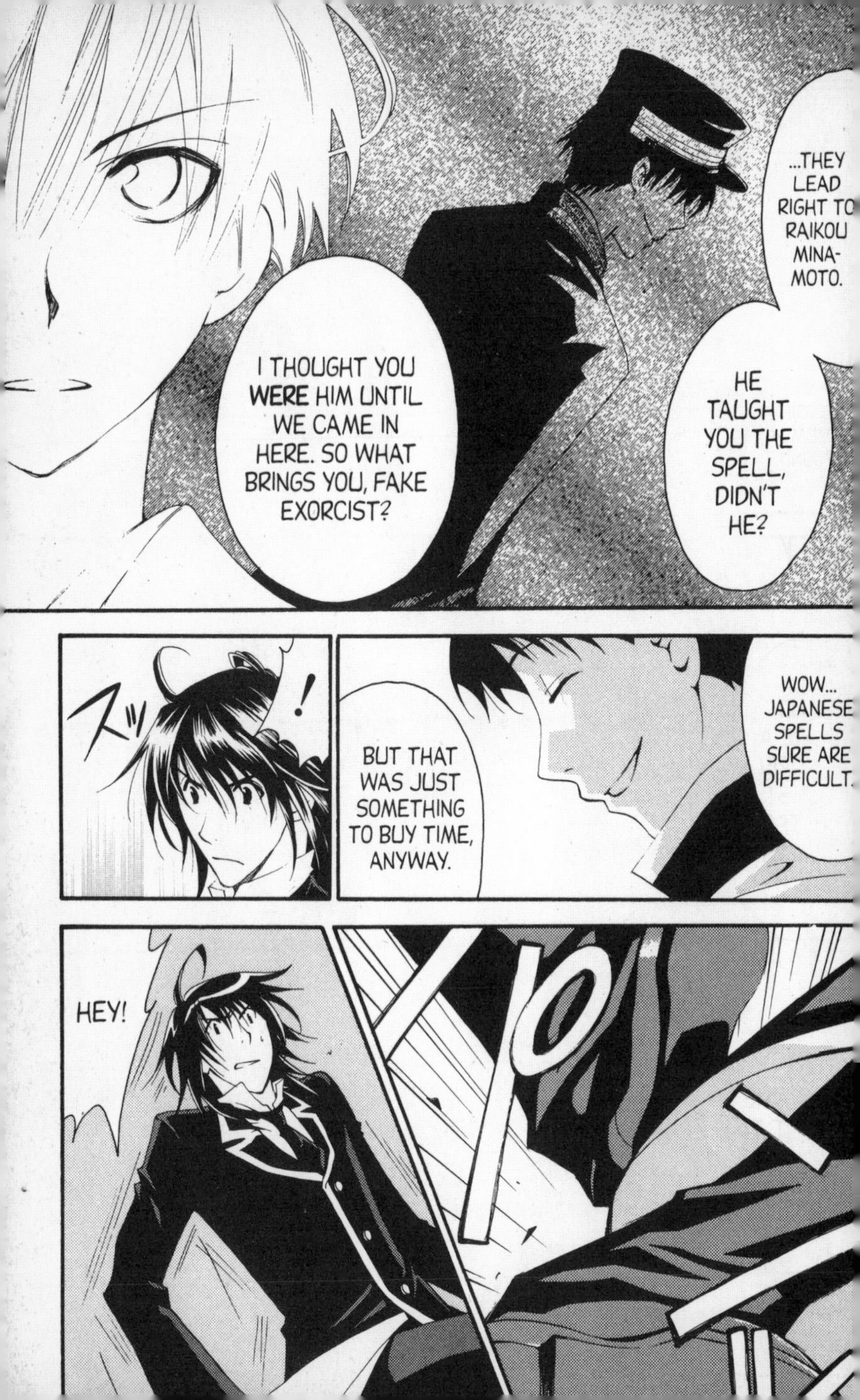
...THEY LEAD RIGHT TO RAIKOU MINA-MOTO.
HE TAUGHT YOU THE SPELL, DIDN'T HE?
I THOUGHT YOU **WERE** HIM UNTIL WE CAME IN HERE. SO WHAT BRINGS YOU, FAKE EXORCIST?
WOW... JAPANESE SPELLS SURE ARE DIFFICULT.
BUT THAT WAS JUST SOMETHING TO BUY TIME, ANYWAY.
スッ
!
HEY!

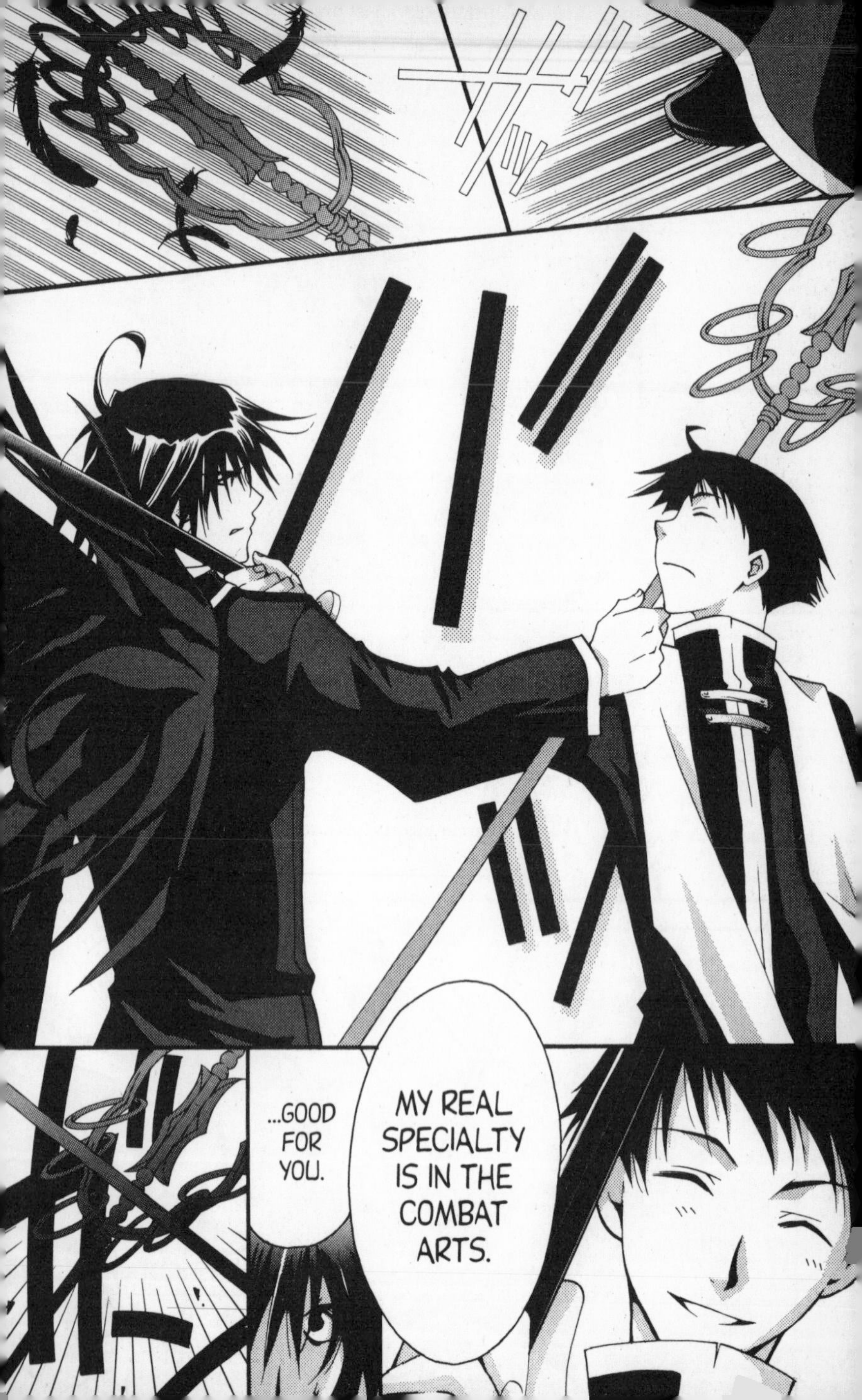
MY REAL SPECIALTY IS IN THE COMBAT ARTS.
...GOOD FOR YOU.

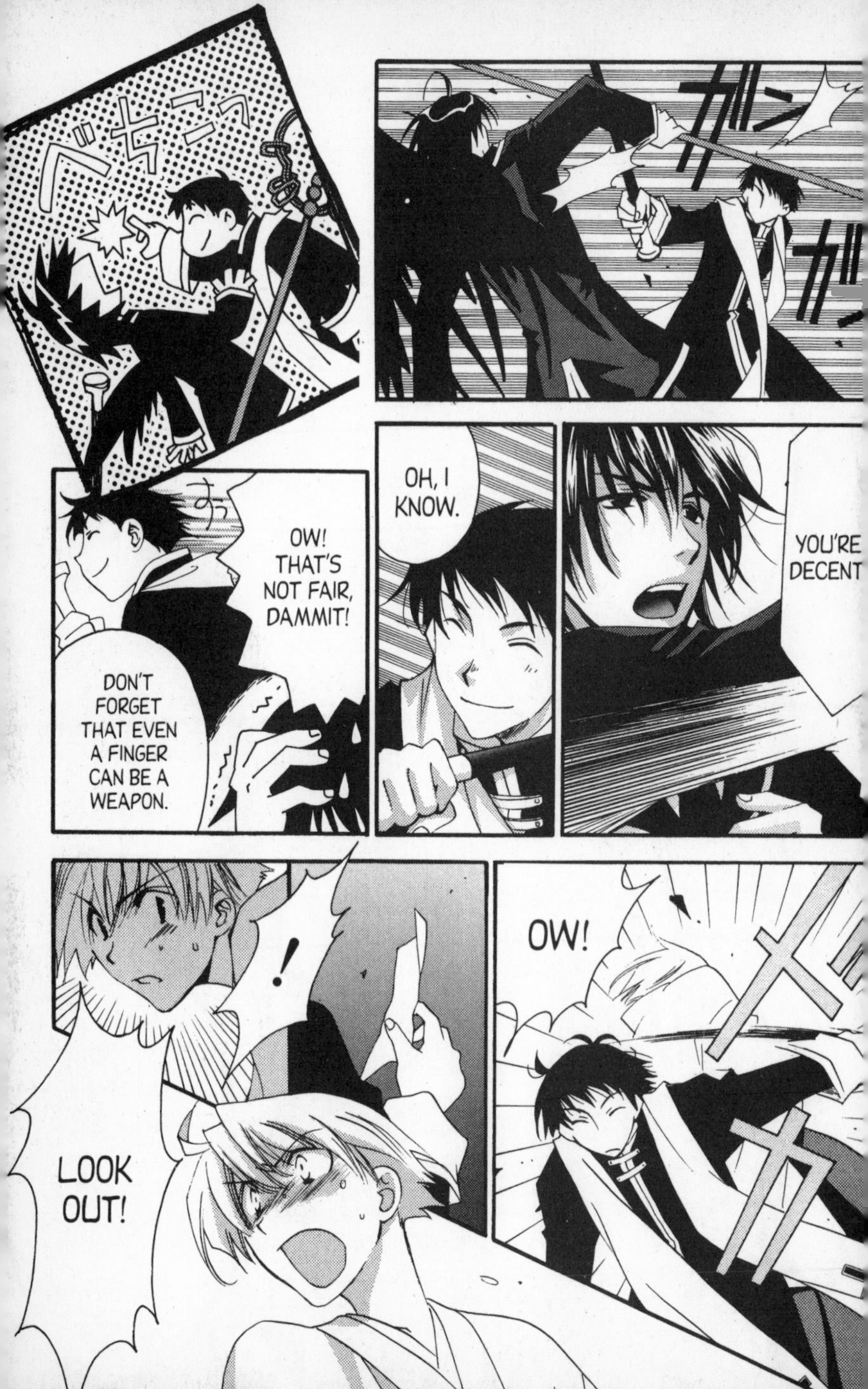

YOU'RE DECENT
OH, I KNOW.
OW! THAT'S NOT FAIR, DAMMIT!
DON'T FORGET THAT EVEN A FINGER CAN BE A WEAPON.
OW!
!
LOOK OUT!

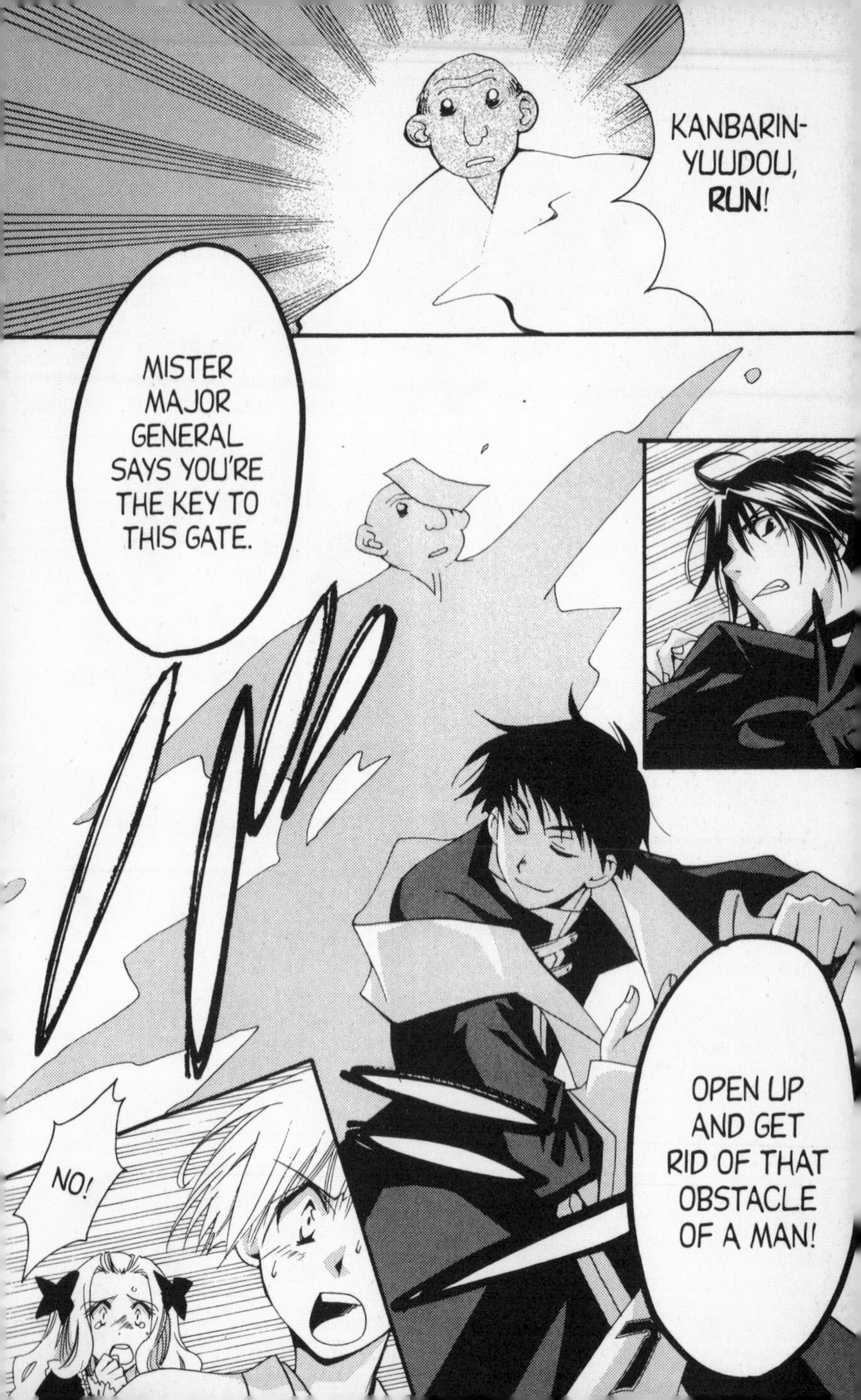
KANBARIN-YUUDOU, RUN!
MISTER MAJOR GENERAL SAYS YOU'RE THE KEY TO THIS GATE.
OPEN UP AND GET RID OF THAT OBSTACLE OF A MAN!
NO!

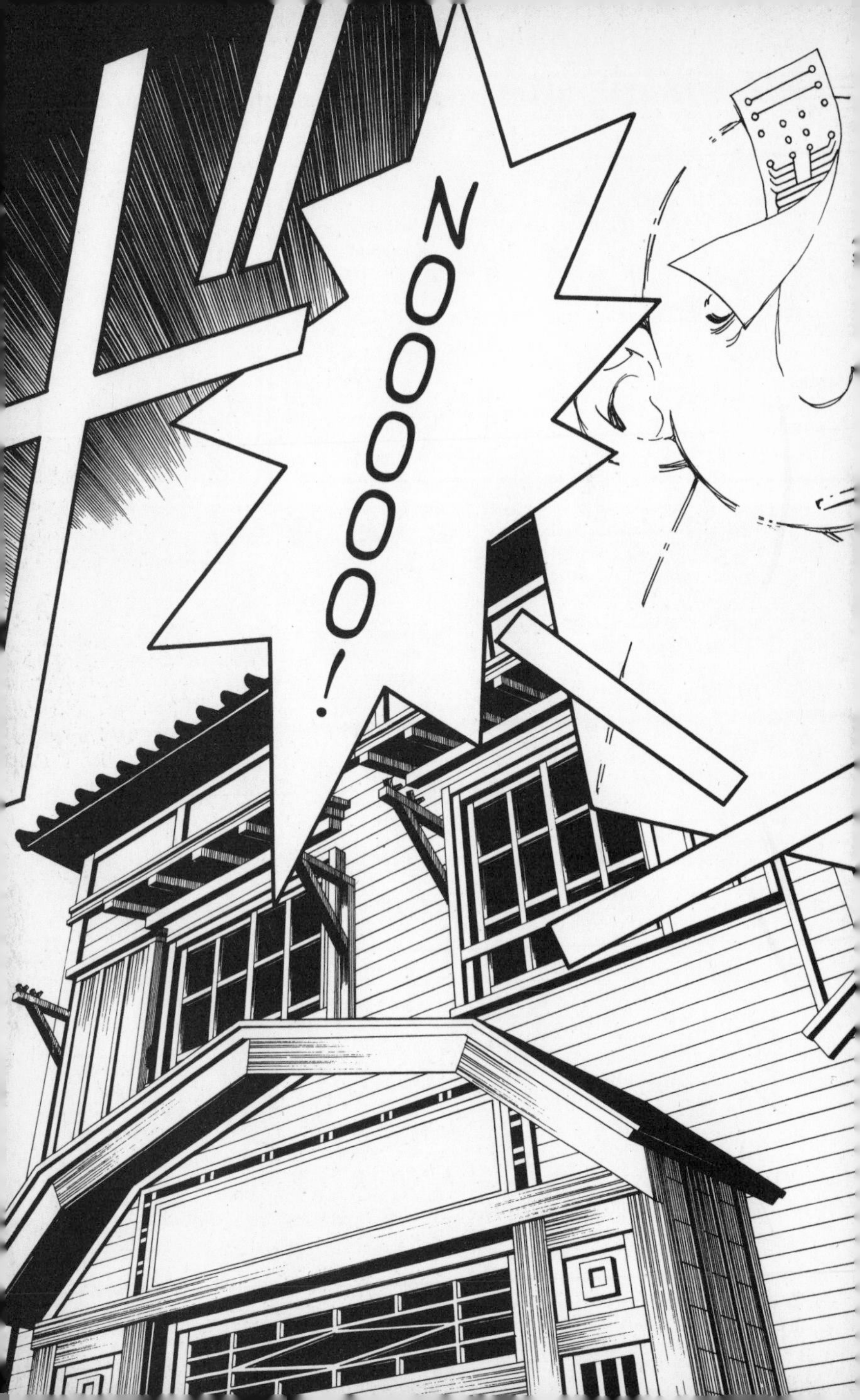
NOOOOOOO!

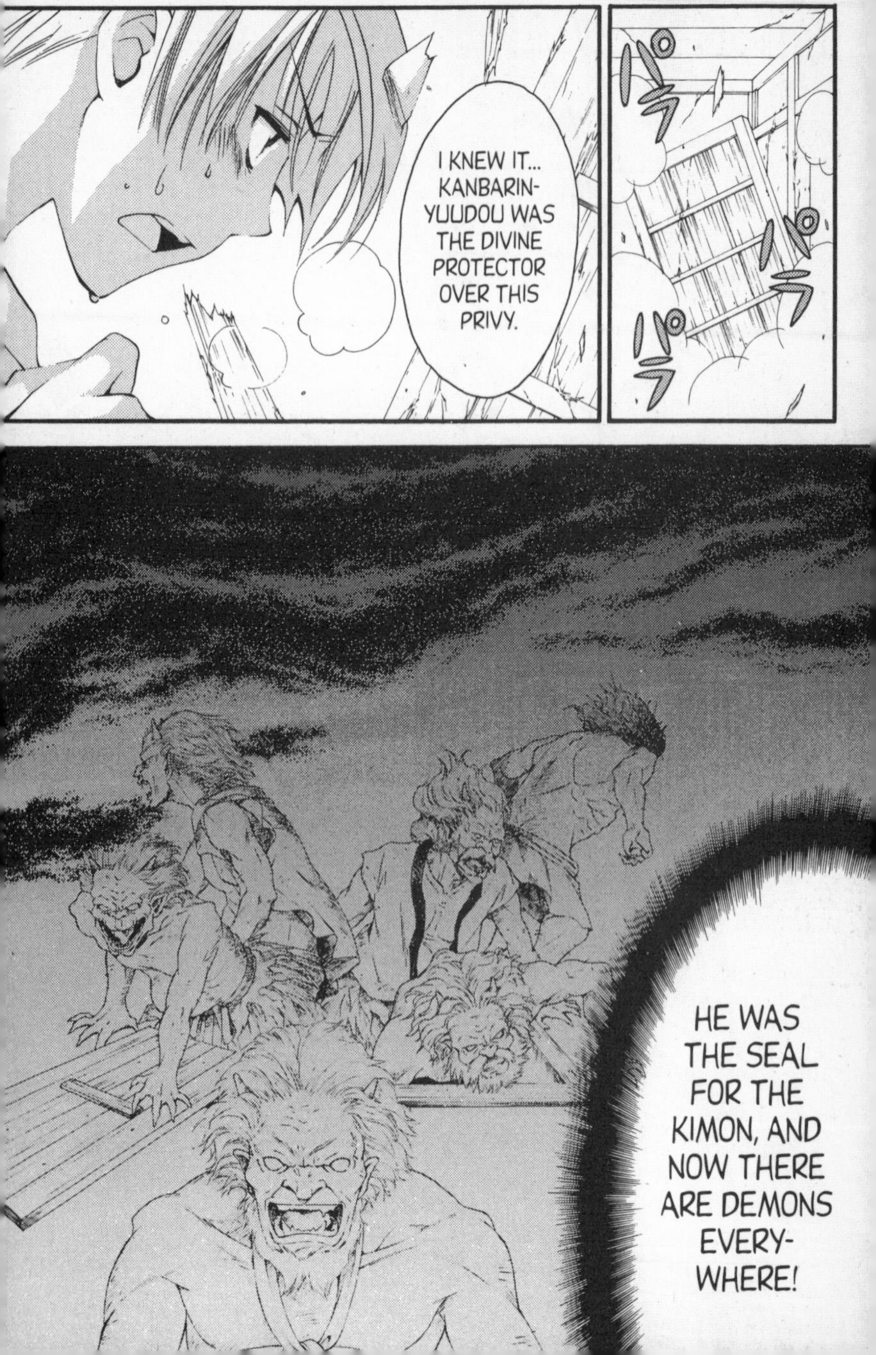
I KNEW IT... KANBARIN-YUUDOU WAS THE DIVINE PROTECTOR OVER THIS PRIVY.
HE WAS THE SEAL FOR THE KIMON, AND NOW THERE ARE DEMONS EVERY-WHERE!

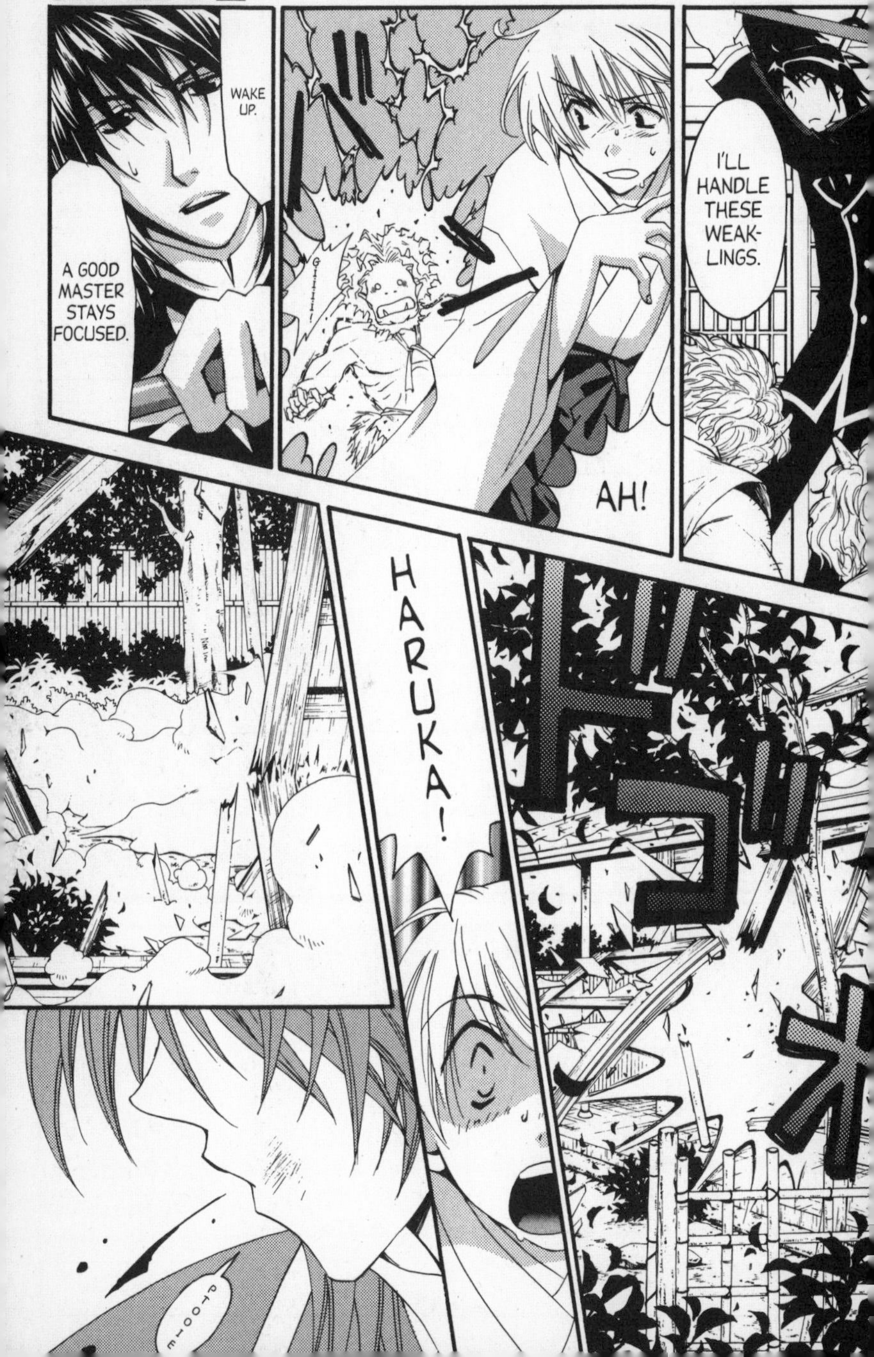
I'LL HANDLE THESE WEAK-LINGS.
AH!
WAKE UP.
A GOOD MASTER STAYS FOCUSED.
HARUKA!
PTOOIE

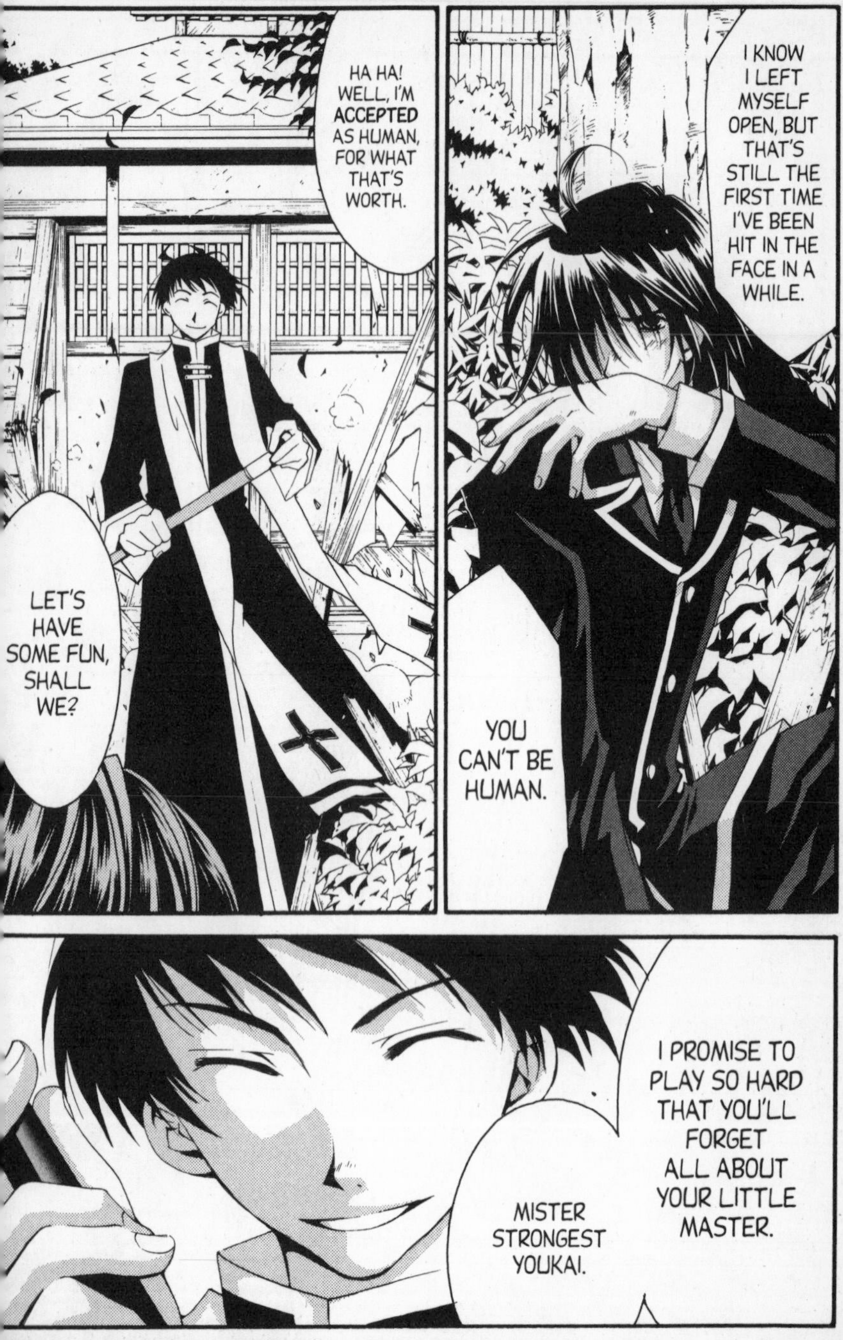
I KNOW I LEFT MYSELF OPEN, BUT THAT'S STILL THE FIRST TIME I'VE BEEN HIT IN THE FACE IN A WHILE.
YOU CAN'T BE HUMAN.
HA HA! WELL, I'M ACCEPTED AS HUMAN, FOR WHAT THAT'S WORTH.
LET'S HAVE SOME FUN, SHALL WE?
I PROMISE TO PLAY SO HARD THAT YOU'LL FORGET ALL ABOUT YOUR LITTLE MASTER.
MISTER STRONGEST YOUKAI.

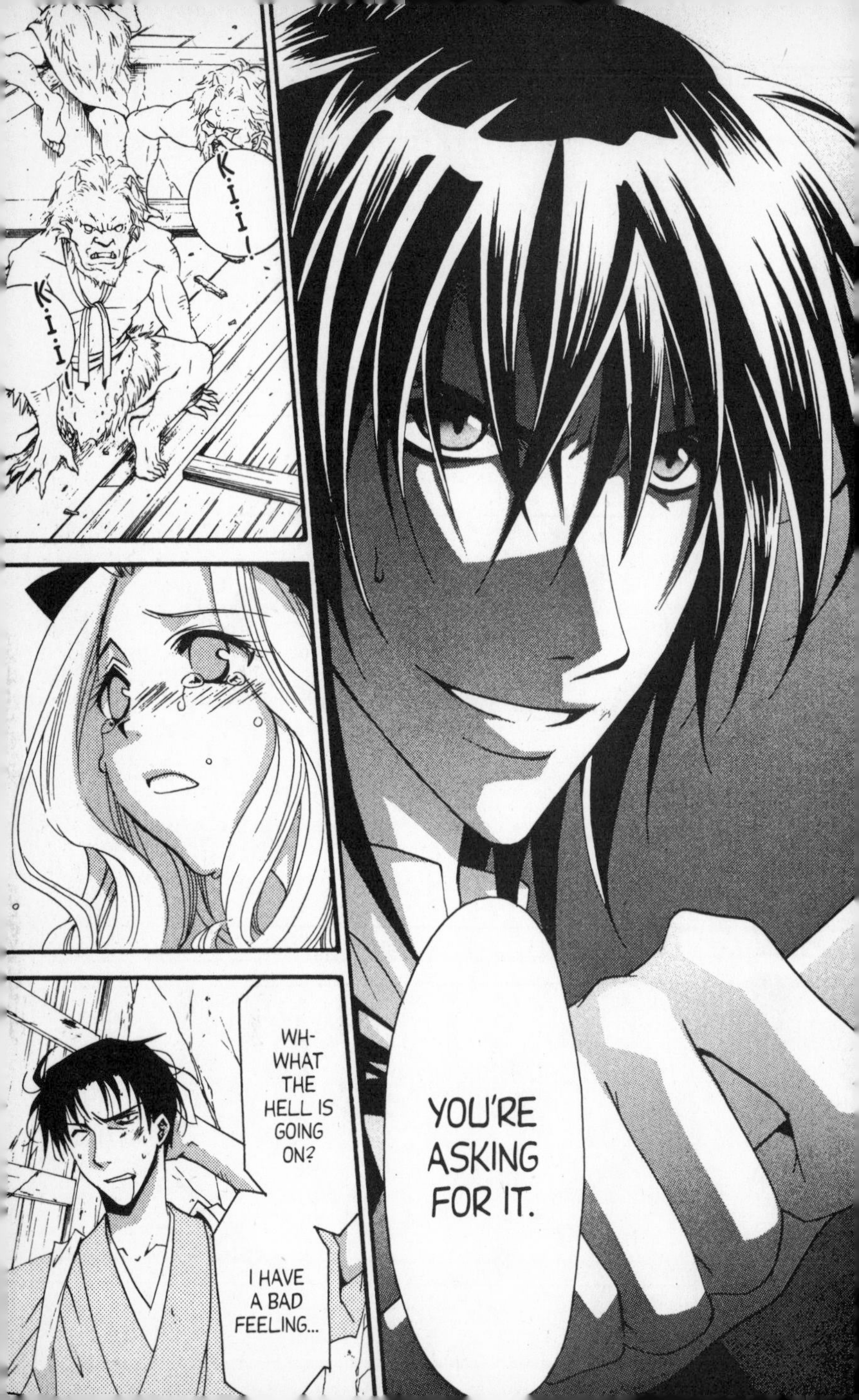
YOU'RE ASKING FOR IT.
K-I-I-I!
K-I-I-I!
WH-WHAT THE HELL IS GOING ON?
I HAVE A BAD FEELING...

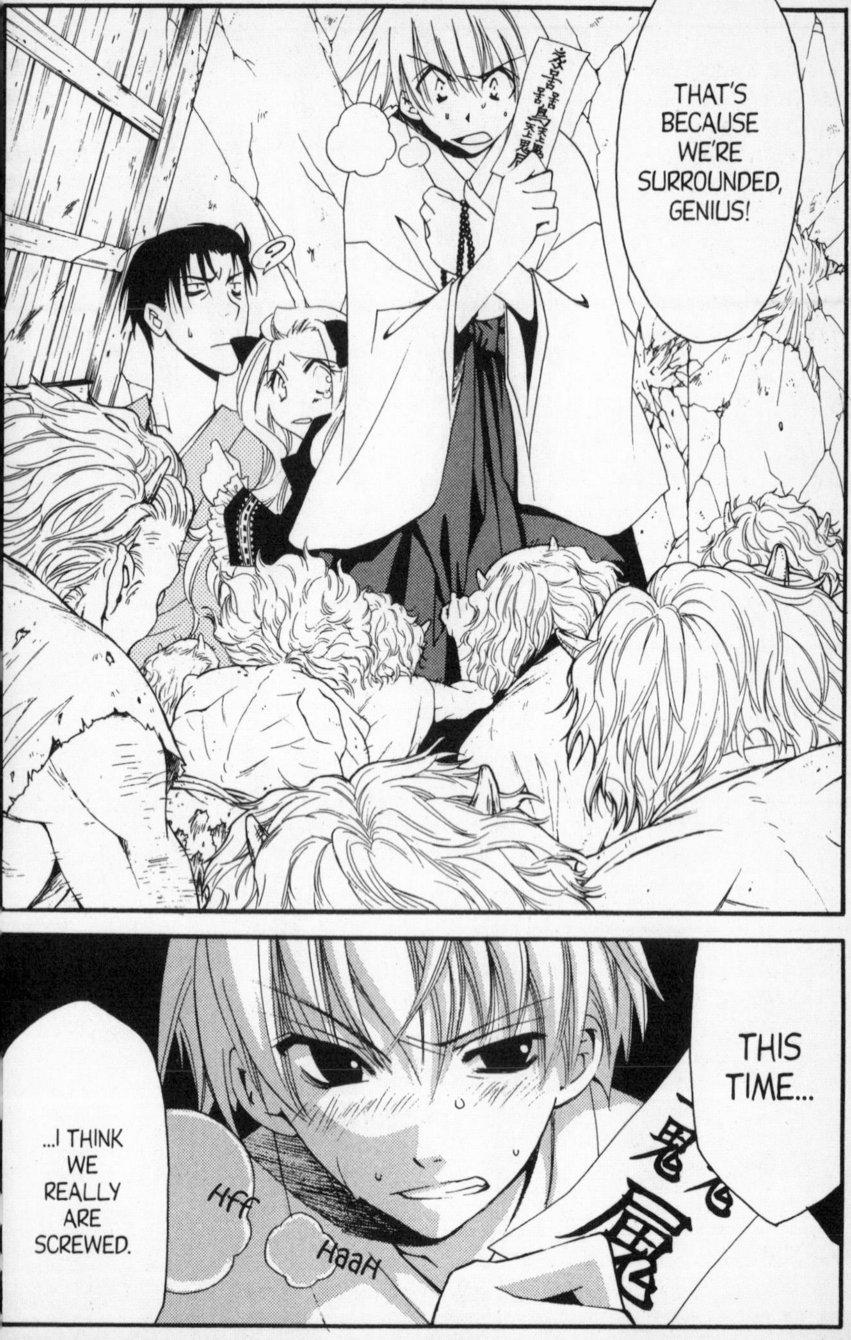
THAT'S BECAUSE WE'RE SURROUNDED, GENIUS!
THIS TIME...
...I THINK WE REALLY ARE SCREWED.
Hff
HaaH

Hello. This is Kazuko Higashiyama.

Thank you for buying *Tactics* Volume 5!

Lately it's felt like I have all this time, and yet no time at all. My sense of time has gotten all weird. Ah, well, it's not really worth caring about.

Now as for the actual reading of Volume 5...

It's all about Edwards-san, isn't it? And we used to think he was just a blockhead of a priest.

Then there's Rosa and Hasumi.

The spotlight's finally shifted to these three people.

But that decreased the number of times Haruka made an appearance...

Also, the bonus material in this particular volume is a manga!

Sorry, Kinoshita-san, for always having you carry me on your back or in your arms.

I'll give you clothes as a present so just please forgive me... (weep).

I got to see snapshots of the work in progress through a cell phone camera, but I still have no clue as to the actual content. This is going to be my first time seeing it, along with all of you.

But just the great images made it look fun enough!

Along with the limited-edition drama CD...I'm so looking forward to it!

Starting in this volume, the loooong subtitle of "Demon-Eating Tengu Shinobuyo Fuji Soushi" gets added and the story takes a clean shift in focus to Haruka's past and the goings-on within Kantarou.

I'm also thinking I want to open up new sides to the sub-characters as well.

The story is overall going to get more serious, but I'll never forget to include the funny stuff.

So please stick along for the ride.

Well, I hope to see you again in Volume 6!

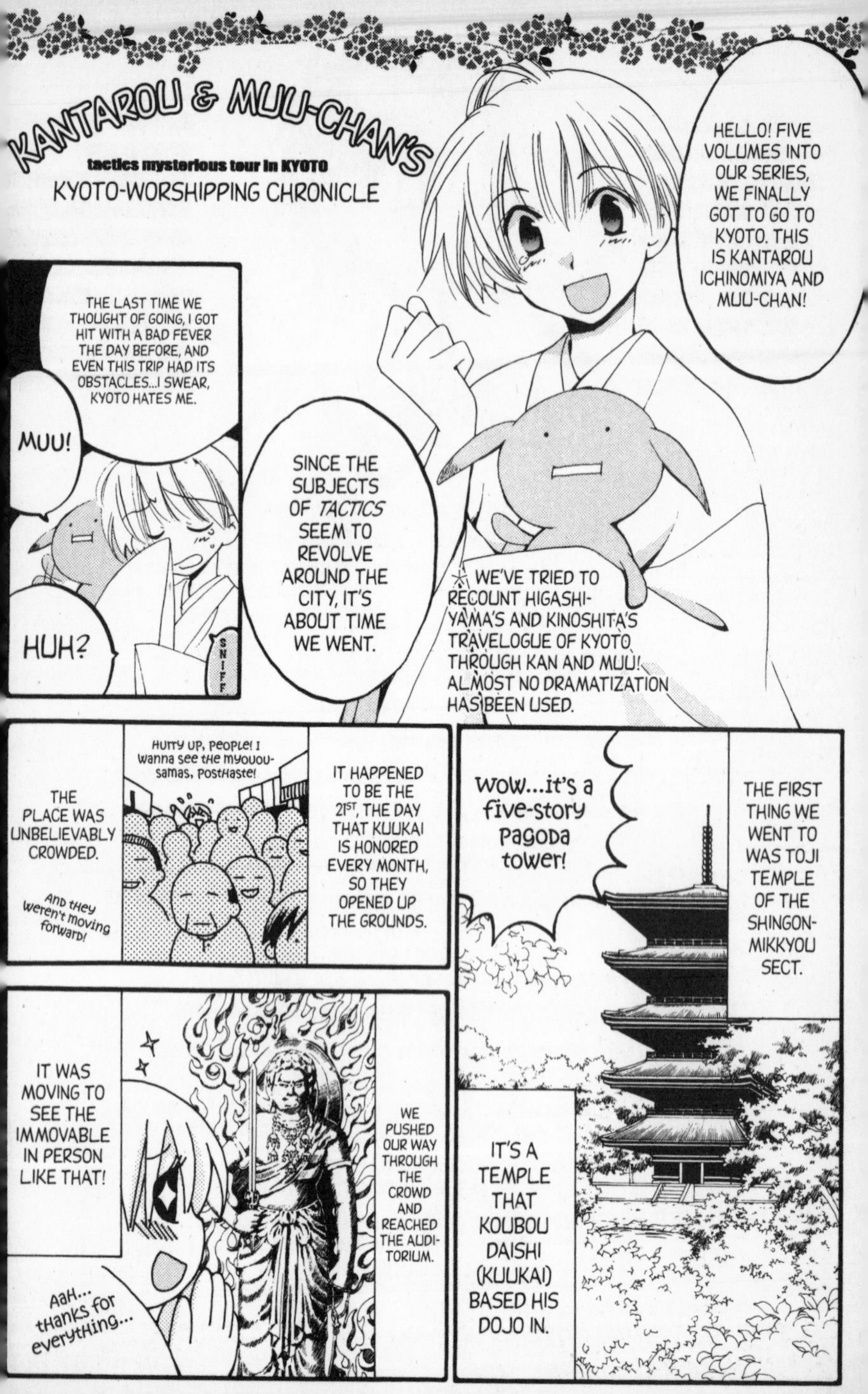
KANTAROU & MUU-CHAN'S
tactics mysterious tour in KYOTO
KYOTO-WORSHIPPING CHRONICLE
HELLO! FIVE VOLUMES INTO OUR SERIES, WE FINALLY GOT TO GO TO KYOTO. THIS IS KANTAROU ICHINOMIYA AND MUU-CHAN!
SINCE THE SUBJECTS OF TACTICS SEEM TO REVOLVE AROUND THE CITY, IT'S ABOUT TIME WE WENT.
※ WE'VE TRIED TO RECOUNT HIGASHIYAMA'S AND KINOSHITA'S TRAVELOGUE OF KYOTO THROUGH KAN AND MUU! ALMOST NO DRAMATIZATION HAS BEEN USED.
THE LAST TIME WE THOUGHT OF GOING, I GOT HIT WITH A BAD FEVER THE DAY BEFORE, AND EVEN THIS TRIP HAD ITS OBSTACLES...I SWEAR, KYOTO HATES ME.
MUU!
HUH?
SNIFF
THE FIRST THING WE WENT TO WAS TOJI TEMPLE OF THE SHINGON-MIKKYOU SECT.
wow...it's a five-story pagoda tower!
IT'S A TEMPLE THAT KOUBOU DAISHI (KUUKAI) BASED HIS DOJO IN.
IT HAPPENED TO BE THE 21ST, THE DAY THAT KUUKAI IS HONORED EVERY MONTH, SO THEY OPENED UP THE GROUNDS.
Hurry up, people! I wanna see the myouou-samas, posthaste!
THE PLACE WAS UNBELIEVABLY CROWDED.
And they weren't moving forward!
WE PUSHED OUR WAY THROUGH THE CROWD AND REACHED THE AUDITORIUM.
IT WAS MOVING TO SEE THE IMMOVABLE IN PERSON LIKE THAT!
Aah... thanks for everything...

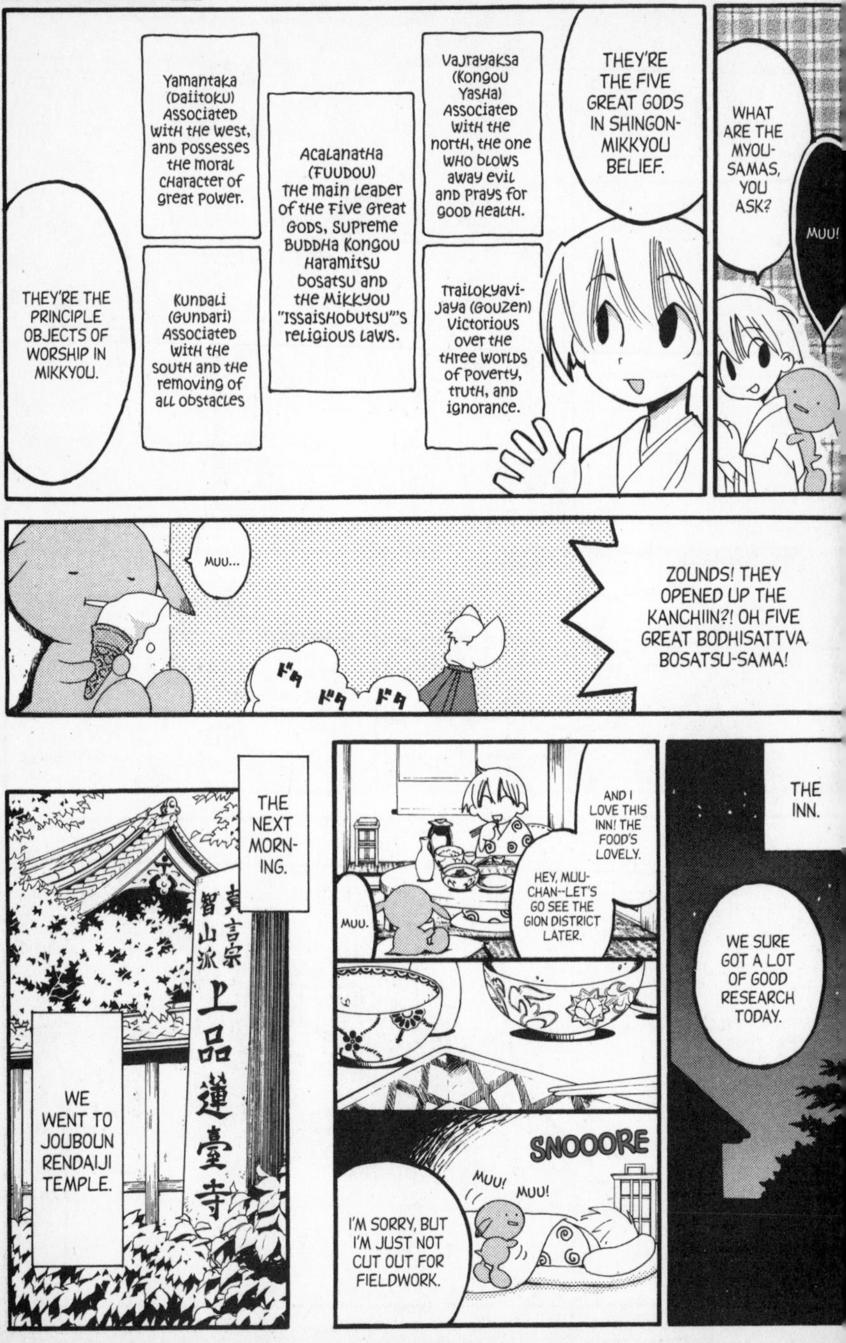
WHAT ARE THE MYOU-SAMAS, YOU ASK?
MUU!
THEY'RE THE FIVE GREAT GODS IN SHINGON-MIKKYOU BELIEF.
Vajrayaksa (Kongou Yasha) Associated with the north, the one who blows away evil and prays for good health.
Trailokyavijaya (Gouzen) Victorious over the three worlds of poverty, truth, and ignorance.
Acalanatha (Fuudou) The main leader of the Five Great Gods, Supreme Buddha Kongou Haramitsu bosatsu and the Mikkyou "Issaishobutsu"'s religious laws.
Yamantaka (Daiitoku) Associated with the west, and possesses the moral character of great power.
Kundali (Gundari) Associated with the south and the removing of all obstacles
THEY'RE THE PRINCIPLE OBJECTS OF WORSHIP IN MIKKYOU.
ZOUNDS! THEY OPENED UP THE KANCHIIN?! OH FIVE GREAT BODHISATTVA BOSATSU-SAMA!
ドタ ドタ ドタ
MUU...
THE INN.
WE SURE GOT A LOT OF GOOD RESEARCH TODAY.
AND I LOVE THIS INN! THE FOOD'S LOVELY.
HEY, MUU-CHAN--LET'S GO SEE THE GION DISTRICT LATER.
MUU.
SNOOORE
MUU! MUU!
I'M SORRY, BUT I'M JUST NOT CUT OUT FOR FIELDWORK.
THE NEXT MORNING.
真言宗 智山派 上品蓮臺寺
WE WENT TO JOUBOUN RENDAIJI TEMPLE.

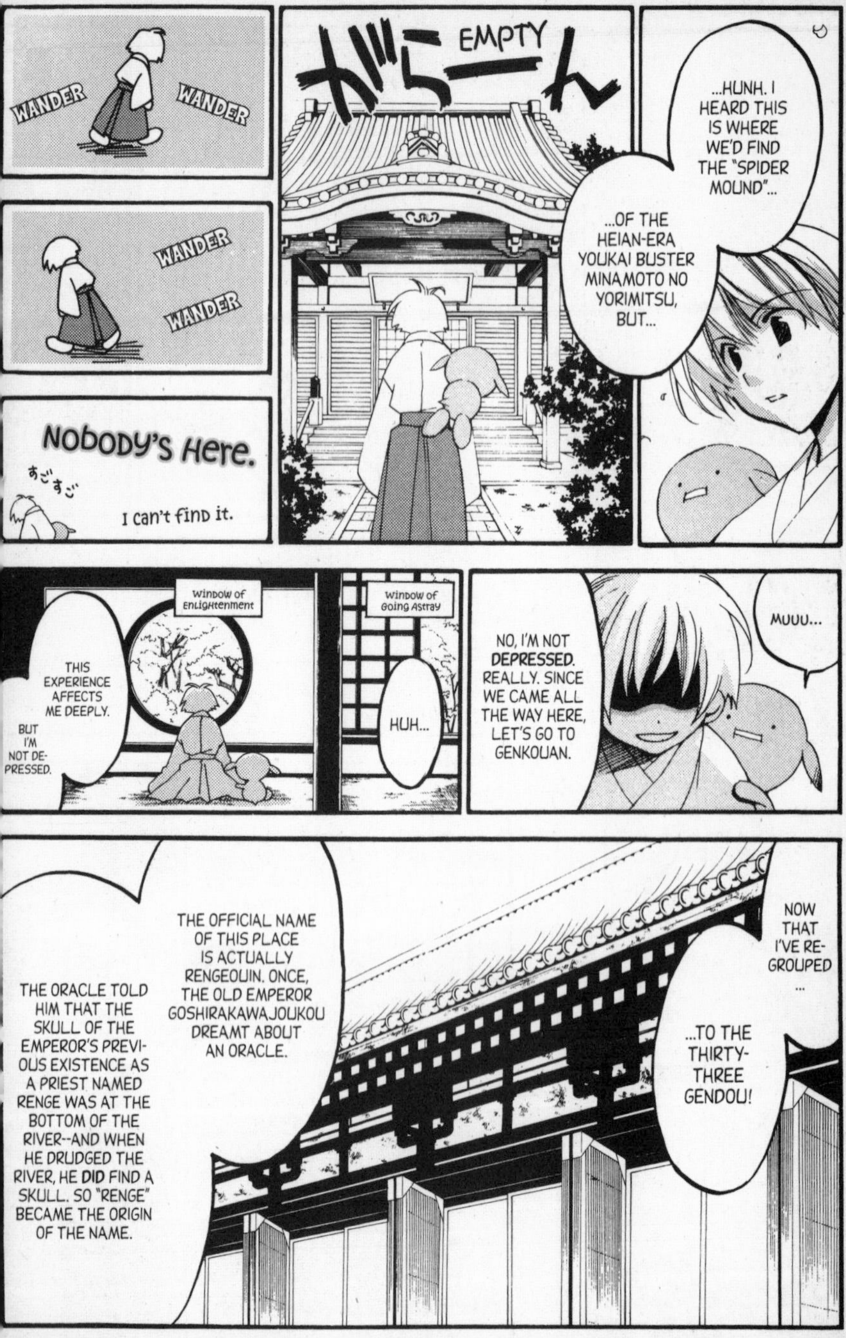
...HUNH. I HEARD THIS IS WHERE WE'D FIND THE "SPIDER MOUND"...
...OF THE HEIAN-ERA YOUKAI BUSTER MINAMOTO NO YORIMITSU, BUT...
がらーん
EMPTY
WANDER
WANDER
WANDER
WANDER
Nobody's Here.
すごすご
I can't find it.
MUUU...
NO, I'M NOT DEPRESSED. REALLY. SINCE WE CAME ALL THE WAY HERE, LET'S GO TO GENKOUAN.
Window of Going Astray
HUH...
Window of Enlightenment
THIS EXPERIENCE AFFECTS ME DEEPLY.
BUT I'M NOT DE-PRESSED.
NOW THAT I'VE RE-GROUPED ...
...TO THE THIRTY-THREE GENDOU!
THE OFFICIAL NAME OF THIS PLACE IS ACTUALLY RENGEOUIN. ONCE, THE OLD EMPEROR GOSHIRAKAWAJOUKOU DREAMT ABOUT AN ORACLE.
THE ORACLE TOLD HIM THAT THE SKULL OF THE EMPEROR'S PREVI-OUS EXISTENCE AS A PRIEST NAMED RENGE WAS AT THE BOTTOM OF THE RIVER--AND WHEN HE DRUDGED THE RIVER, HE DID FIND A SKULL. SO "RENGE" BECAME THE ORIGIN OF THE NAME.

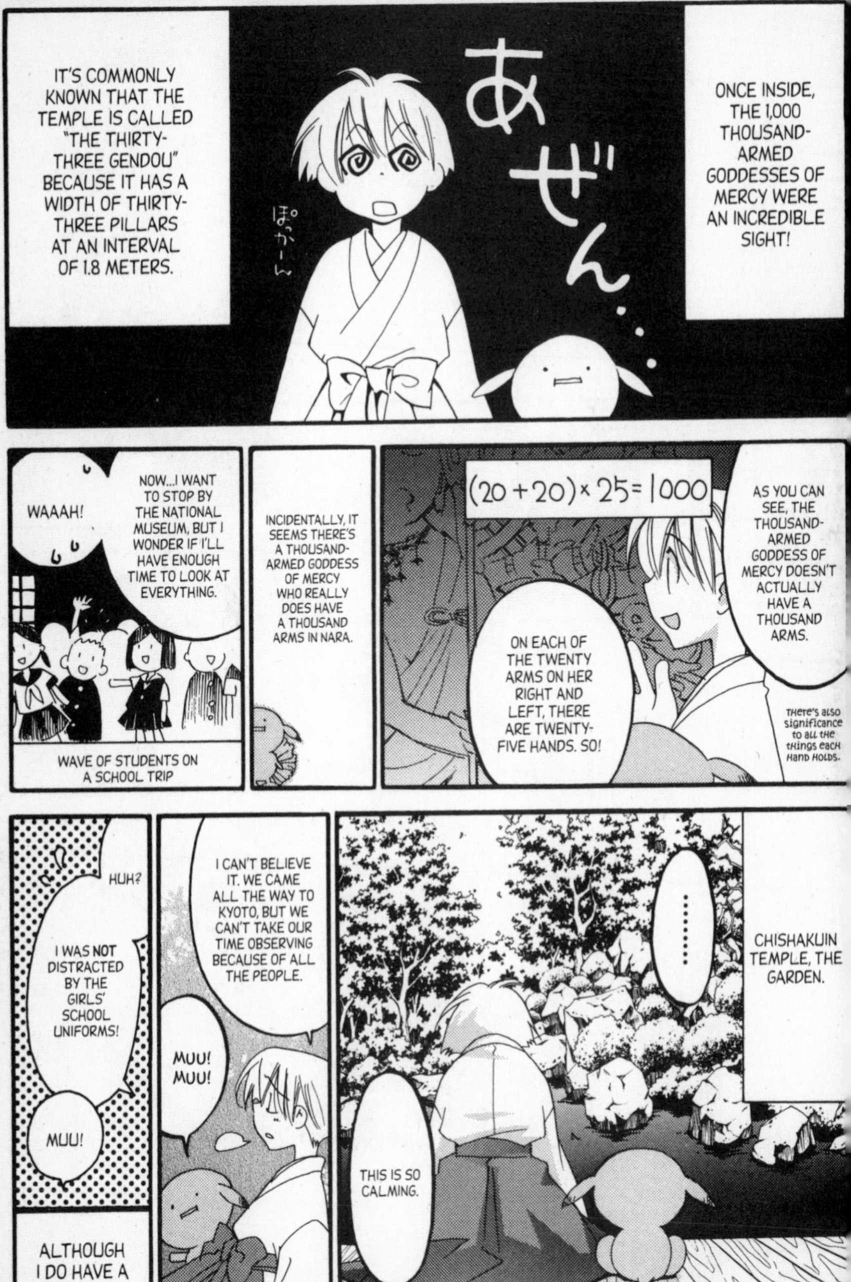
ONCE INSIDE, THE 1,000 THOUSAND-ARMED GODDESSES OF MERCY WERE AN INCREDIBLE SIGHT!
あぜん...
ぽかーん
IT'S COMMONLY KNOWN THAT THE TEMPLE IS CALLED "THE THIRTY-THREE GENDOU" BECAUSE IT HAS A WIDTH OF THIRTY-THREE PILLARS AT AN INTERVAL OF 1.8 METERS.
AS YOU CAN SEE, THE THOUSAND-ARMED GODDESS OF MERCY DOESN'T ACTUALLY HAVE A THOUSAND ARMS.
ON EACH OF THE TWENTY ARMS ON HER RIGHT AND LEFT, THERE ARE TWENTY-FIVE HANDS. SO!
(20 + 20) × 25 = 1000
There's also significance to all the things each hand holds.
INCIDENTALLY, IT SEEMS THERE'S A THOUSAND-ARMED GODDESS OF MERCY WHO REALLY DOES HAVE A THOUSAND ARMS IN NARA.
NOW...I WANT TO STOP BY THE NATIONAL MUSEUM, BUT I WONDER IF I'LL HAVE ENOUGH TIME TO LOOK AT EVERYTHING.
WAAAH!
WAVE OF STUDENTS ON A SCHOOL TRIP
CHISHAKUIN TEMPLE, THE GARDEN.
......
THIS IS SO CALMING.
I CAN'T BELIEVE IT. WE CAME ALL THE WAY TO KYOTO, BUT WE CAN'T TAKE OUR TIME OBSERVING BECAUSE OF ALL THE PEOPLE.
MUU! MUU!
HUH?
I WAS NOT DISTRACTED BY THE GIRLS' SCHOOL UNIFORMS!
MUU!
ALTHOUGH I DO HAVE A DIRTY MIND.

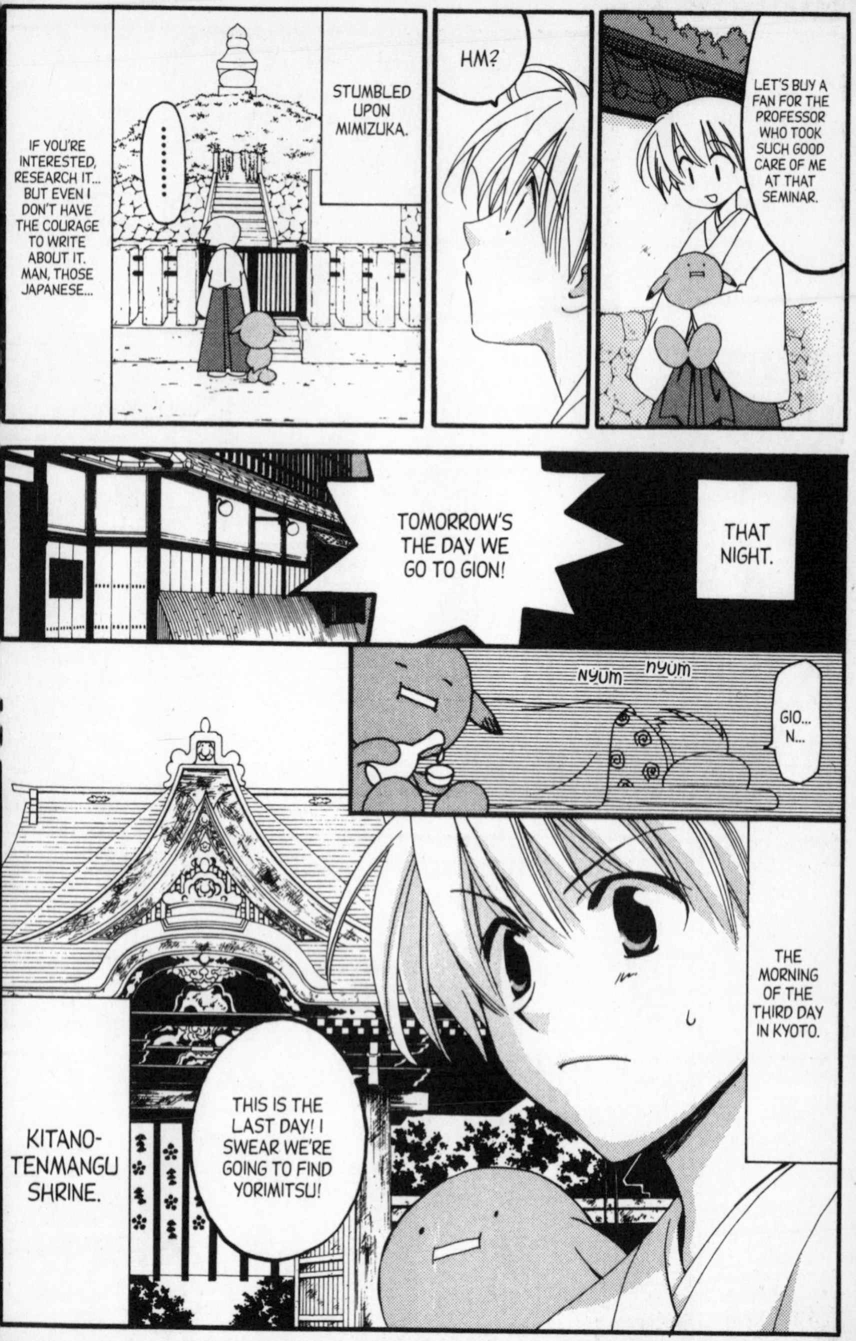
LET'S BUY A FAN FOR THE PROFESSOR WHO TOOK SUCH GOOD CARE OF ME AT THAT SEMINAR.
HM?
STUMBLED UPON MIMIZUKA.
......
IF YOU'RE INTERESTED, RESEARCH IT... BUT EVEN I DON'T HAVE THE COURAGE TO WRITE ABOUT IT. MAN, THOSE JAPANESE...
THAT NIGHT.
TOMORROW'S THE DAY WE GO TO GION!
GIO... N...
NYUM
NYUM
THE MORNING OF THE THIRD DAY IN KYOTO.
THIS IS THE LAST DAY! I SWEAR WE'RE GOING TO FIND YORIMITSU!
KITANO-TENMANGU SHRINE.

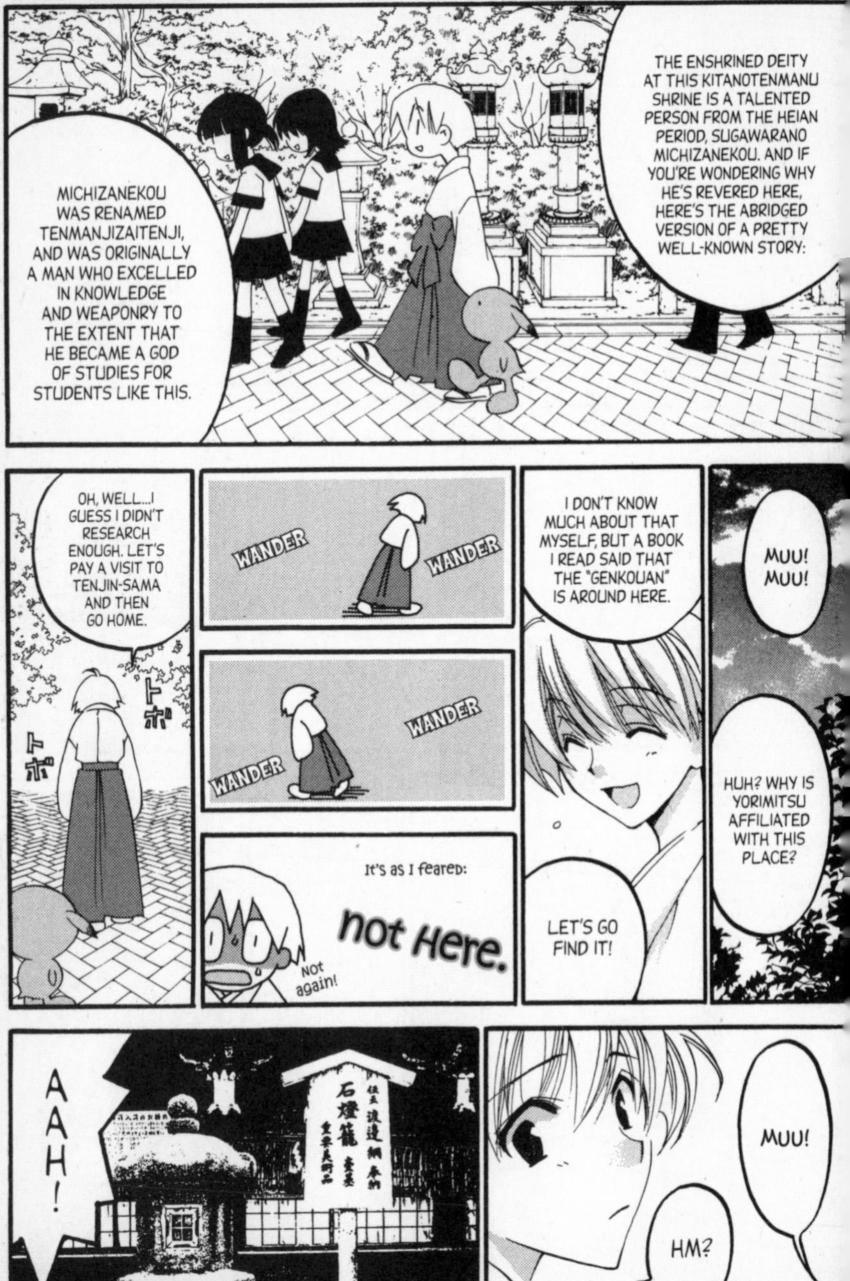
THE ENSHRINED DEITY AT THIS KITANOTENMANU SHRINE IS A TALENTED PERSON FROM THE HEIAN PERIOD, SUGAWARANO MICHIZANEKOU. AND IF YOU'RE WONDERING WHY HE'S REVERED HERE, HERE'S THE ABRIDGED VERSION OF A PRETTY WELL-KNOWN STORY:
MICHIZANEKOU WAS RENAMED TENMANJIZAITENJI, AND WAS ORIGINALLY A MAN WHO EXCELLED IN KNOWLEDGE AND WEAPONRY TO THE EXTENT THAT HE BECAME A GOD OF STUDIES FOR STUDENTS LIKE THIS.
MUU! MUU!
HUH? WHY IS YORIMITSU AFFILIATED WITH THIS PLACE?
I DON'T KNOW MUCH ABOUT THAT MYSELF, BUT A BOOK I READ SAID THAT THE "GENKOUAN" IS AROUND HERE.
LET'S GO FIND IT!
WANDER
WANDER
WANDER
WANDER
It's as I feared:
not Here.
Not again!
OH, WELL...I GUESS I DIDN'T RESEARCH ENOUGH. LET'S PAY A VISIT TO TENJIN-SAMA AND THEN GO HOME.
トボ
トボ
MUU!
HM?
AAH!
石燈籠

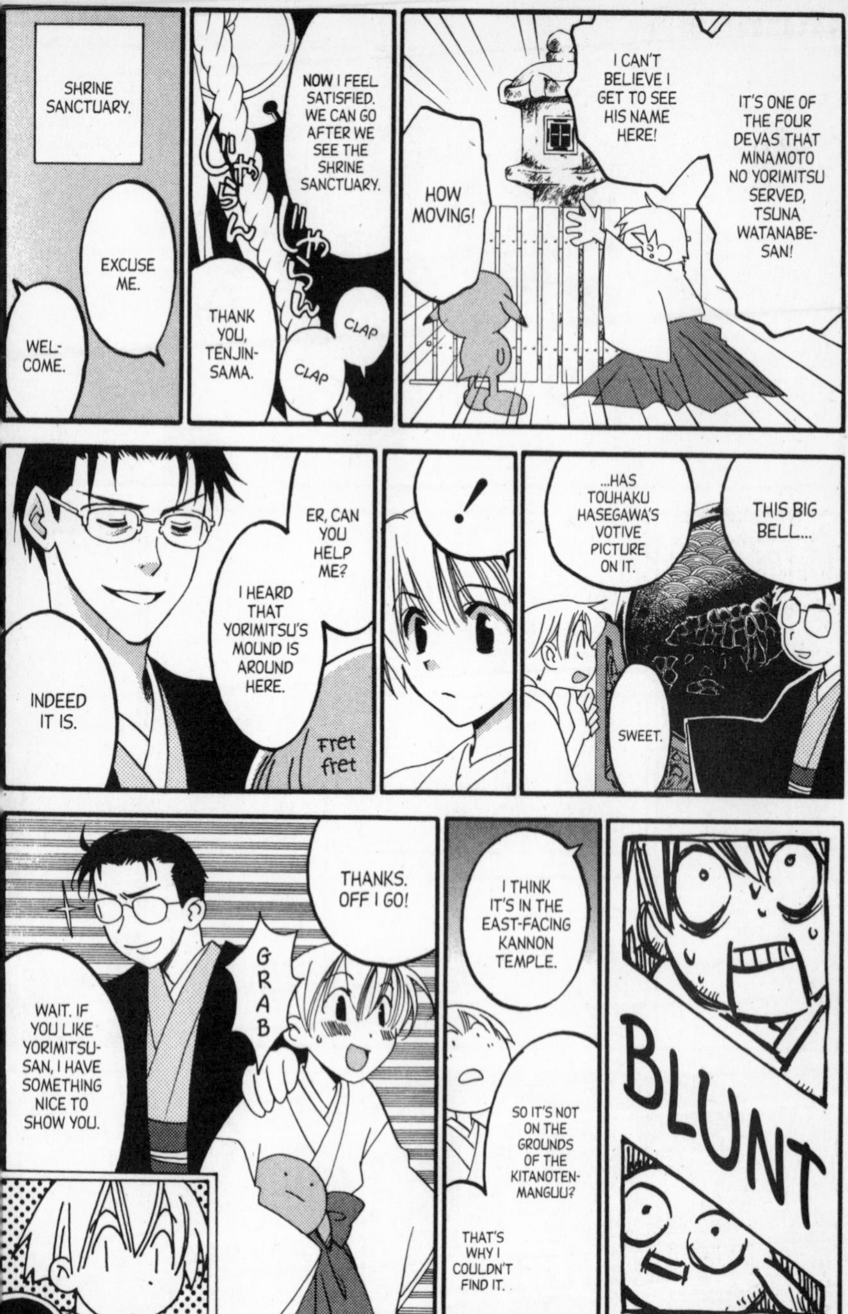
IT'S ONE OF THE FOUR DEVAS THAT MINAMOTO NO YORIMITSU SERVED, TSUNA WATANABE-SAN!
I CAN'T BELIEVE I GET TO SEE HIS NAME HERE!
HOW MOVING!
NOW I FEEL SATISFIED. WE CAN GO AFTER WE SEE THE SHRINE SANCTUARY.
CLAP
CLAP
THANK YOU, TENJIN-SAMA.
SHRINE SANCTUARY.
EXCUSE ME.
WEL-COME.
THIS BIG BELL...
...HAS TOUHAKU HASEGAWA'S VOTIVE PICTURE ON IT.
SWEET.
!
ER, CAN YOU HELP ME?
I HEARD THAT YORIMITSU'S MOUND IS AROUND HERE.
Fret fret
INDEED IT IS.
BLUNT
I THINK IT'S IN THE EAST-FACING KANNON TEMPLE.
SO IT'S NOT ON THE GROUNDS OF THE KITANOTEN-MANGUU?
THAT'S WHY I COULDN'T FIND IT.
THANKS. OFF I GO!
GRAB
WAIT. IF YOU LIKE YORIMITSU-SAN, I HAVE SOMETHING NICE TO SHOW YOU.
HUH?

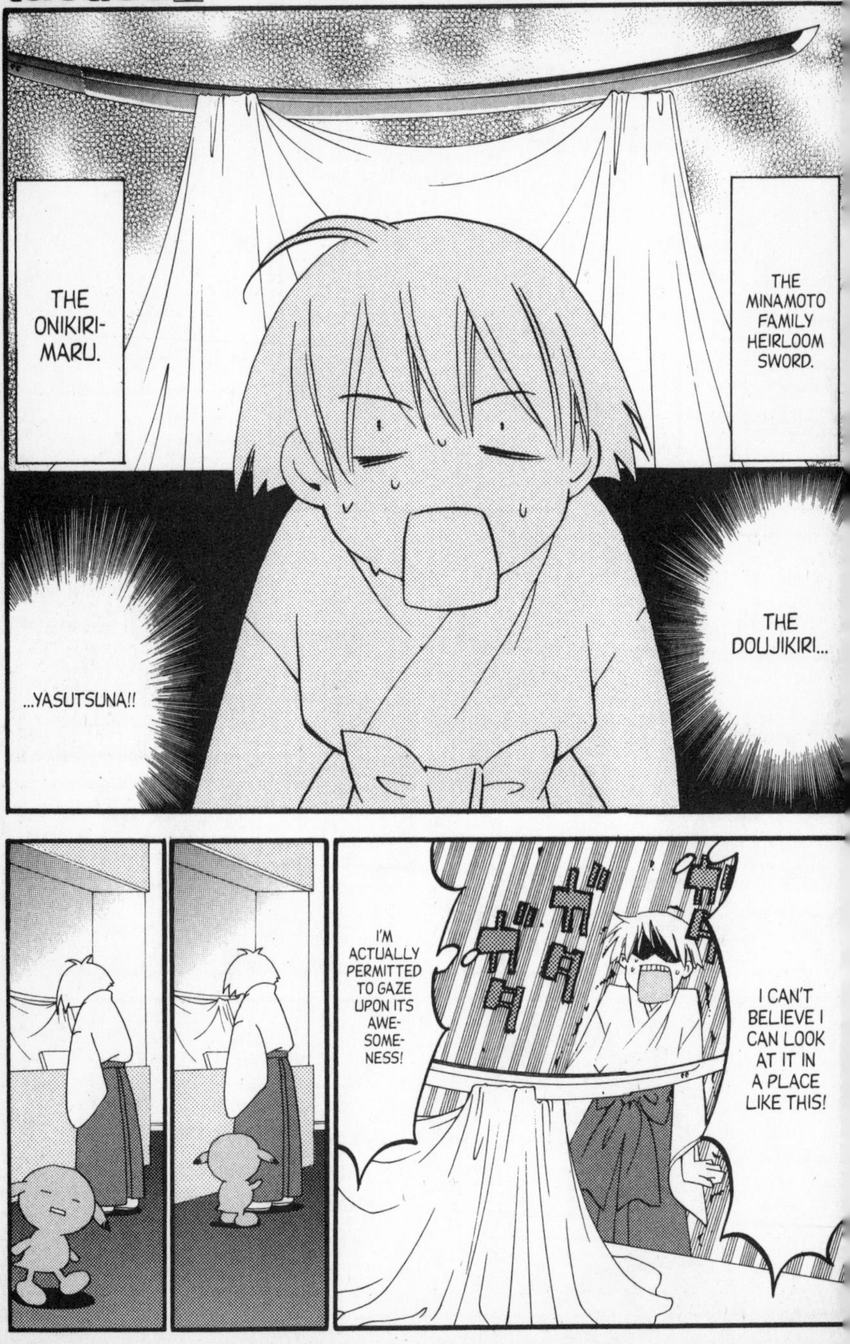
THE MINAMOTO FAMILY HEIRLOOM SWORD.
THE ONIKIRI-MARU.
THE DOUJIKIRI...
...YASUTSUNA!!
I CAN'T BELIEVE I CAN LOOK AT IT IN A PLACE LIKE THIS!
I'M ACTUALLY PERMITTED TO GAZE UPON ITS AWE-SOME-NESS!

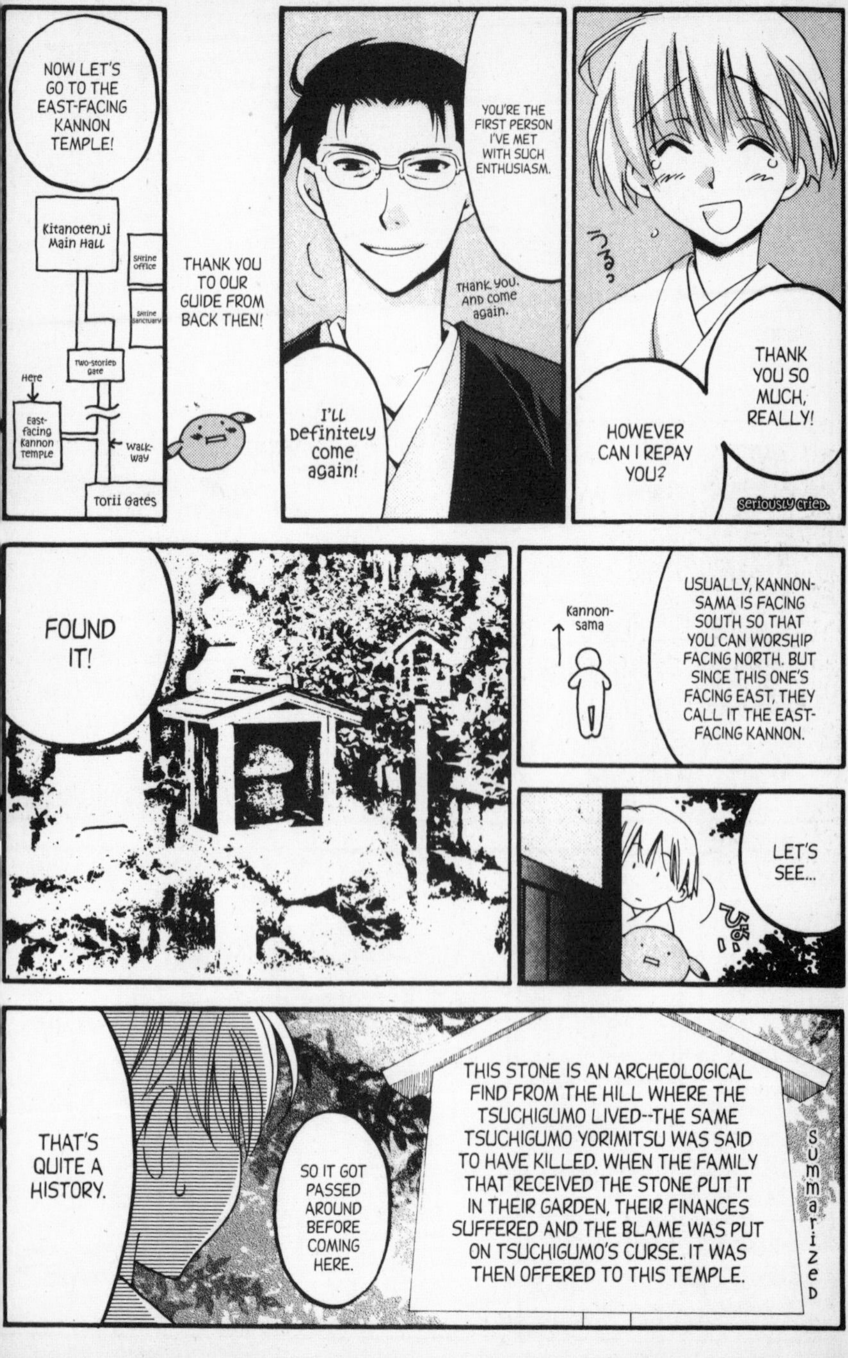
THANK YOU SO MUCH, REALLY!
HOWEVER CAN I REPAY YOU?
seriously cried.
YOU'RE THE FIRST PERSON I'VE MET WITH SUCH ENTHUSIASM.
Thank you. And come again.
I'll definitely come again!
NOW LET'S GO TO THE EAST-FACING KANNON TEMPLE!
Kitanotenji Main Hall
Shrine Office
Shrine Sanctuary
Two-storied Gate
Here
East-facing Kannon Temple
Walk-way
Torii Gates
THANK YOU TO OUR GUIDE FROM BACK THEN!
USUALLY, KANNON-SAMA IS FACING SOUTH SO THAT YOU CAN WORSHIP FACING NORTH. BUT SINCE THIS ONE'S FACING EAST, THEY CALL IT THE EAST-FACING KANNON.
Kannon-sama
LET'S SEE...
FOUND IT!
THIS STONE IS AN ARCHEOLOGICAL FIND FROM THE HILL WHERE THE TSUCHIGUMO LIVED--THE SAME TSUCHIGUMO YORIMITSU WAS SAID TO HAVE KILLED. WHEN THE FAMILY THAT RECEIVED THE STONE PUT IT IN THEIR GARDEN, THEIR FINANCES SUFFERED AND THE BLAME WAS PUT ON TSUCHIGUMO'S CURSE. IT WAS THEN OFFERED TO THIS TEMPLE.
summarized
SO IT GOT PASSED AROUND BEFORE COMING HERE.
THAT'S QUITE A HISTORY.

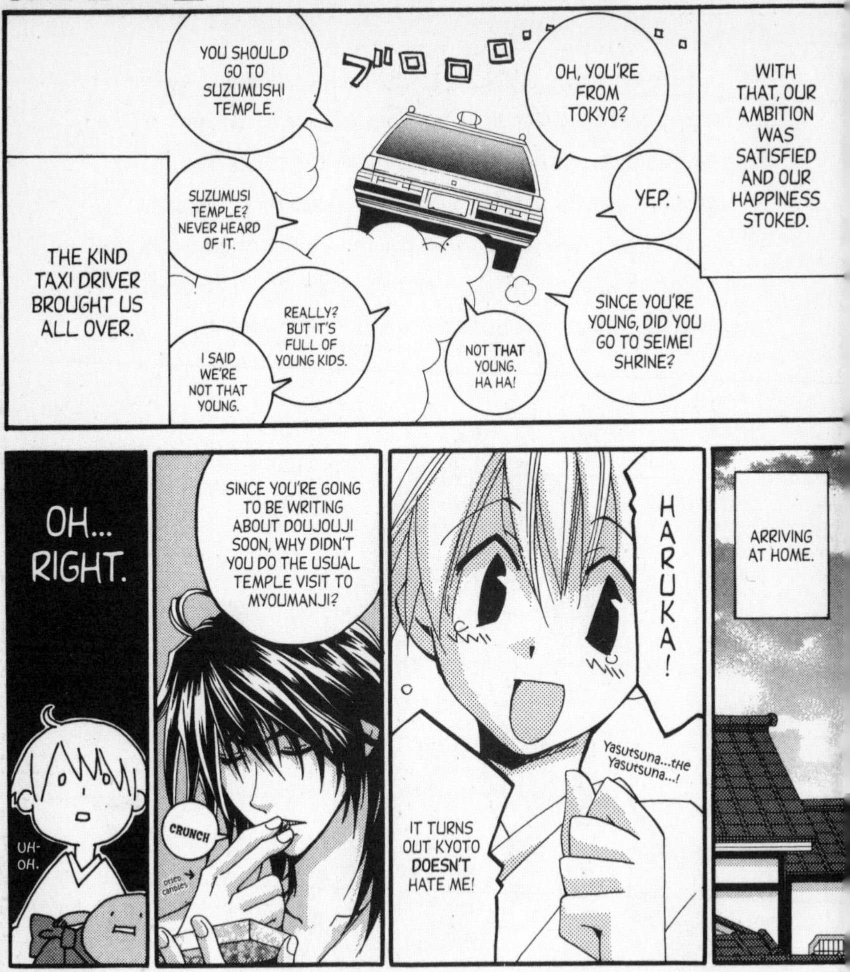
WITH THAT, OUR AMBITION WAS SATISFIED AND OUR HAPPINESS STOKED.
OH, YOU'RE FROM TOKYO?
YEP.
ブロロロ
YOU SHOULD GO TO SUZUMUSHI TEMPLE.
SUZUMUSI TEMPLE? NEVER HEARD OF IT.
SINCE YOU'RE YOUNG, DID YOU GO TO SEIMEI SHRINE?
NOT THAT YOUNG. HA HA!
REALLY? BUT IT'S FULL OF YOUNG KIDS.
I SAID WE'RE NOT THAT YOUNG.
THE KIND TAXI DRIVER BROUGHT US ALL OVER.
ARRIVING AT HOME.
HARUKA!
Yasutsuna...the Yasutsuna...!
IT TURNS OUT KYOTO DOESN'T HATE ME!
SINCE YOU'RE GOING TO BE WRITING ABOUT DOUJOUJI SOON, WHY DIDN'T YOU DO THE USUAL TEMPLE VISIT TO MYOUMANJI?
CRUNCH
dried candies
OH... RIGHT.
UH-OH.

IN THE END, AFTER RESEARCHING IT AT HOME, IT SEEMS THE "SPIDER MOUND" IS IN FACT IN RENDAIJI. WE WERE BAD AT FINDING IT. NEXT TIME, WE WANT TO BUILD UP OUR PHYSICAL ENDURANCE AND HIT KURAMA TEMPLE, TOO!

WE'RE GOING AGAIN! TO KYOTO!

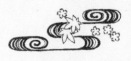

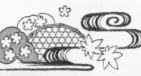

tactics 5 THE END

Hello, everyone. This is Sakura Kinoshita. Thank you so much for buying *Tactics* Volume 5. I can't believe we're this far already. Score! I finally got to write the true person behind the mysterious character that is Edwards-shi. Good luck, Edwards! *Tactics* is a marsh where all these bad guys keep coming out, but I won't forget to keep the lighthearted elements in place--so please look forward to Volume 6. It's coming right up!

September 2004
Sakura Kinoshita

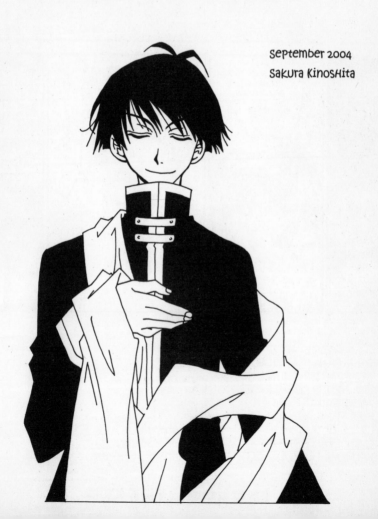

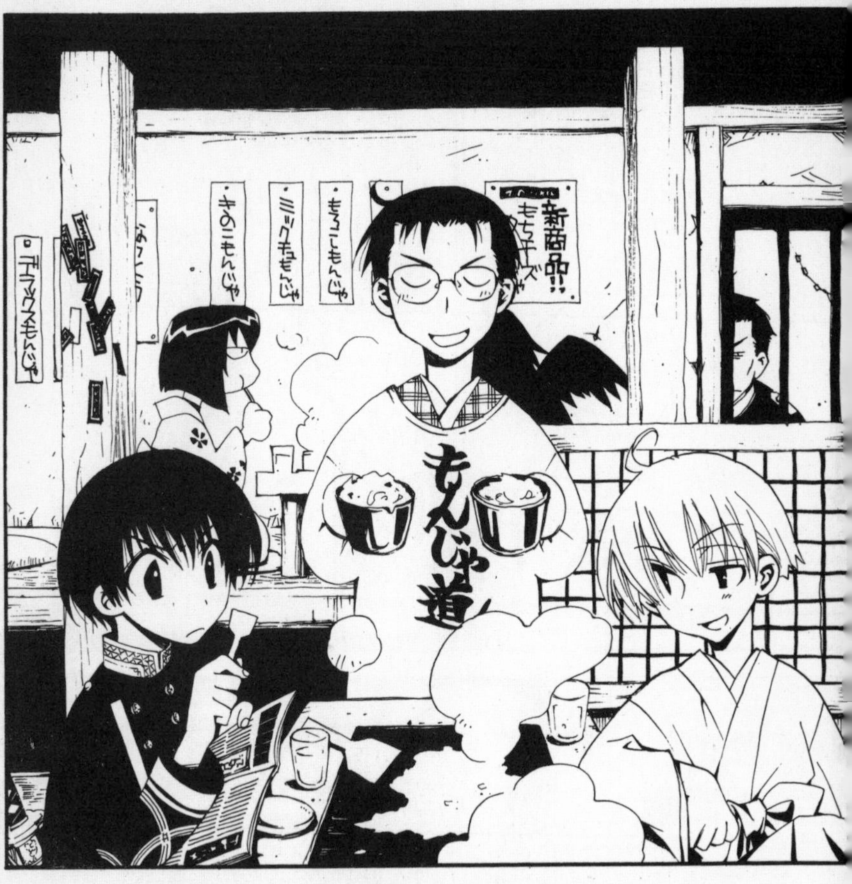
新商品!!
もろこしもんじゃ
きのこもんじゃ
もんじゃ道

Tactics Volume 5 Limited Edition Drama CD

This is the first scene from it. After the recording was done, I couldn't take it anymore and went to eat monja at Tsukishima (Ha Ha!).

Starting on the next page is the continuation manga of what happens in the drama CD.
It's just a lot of silliness, so don't go asking, "Why's Hasumi working at a monja restaurant?!" and the like...best regards!

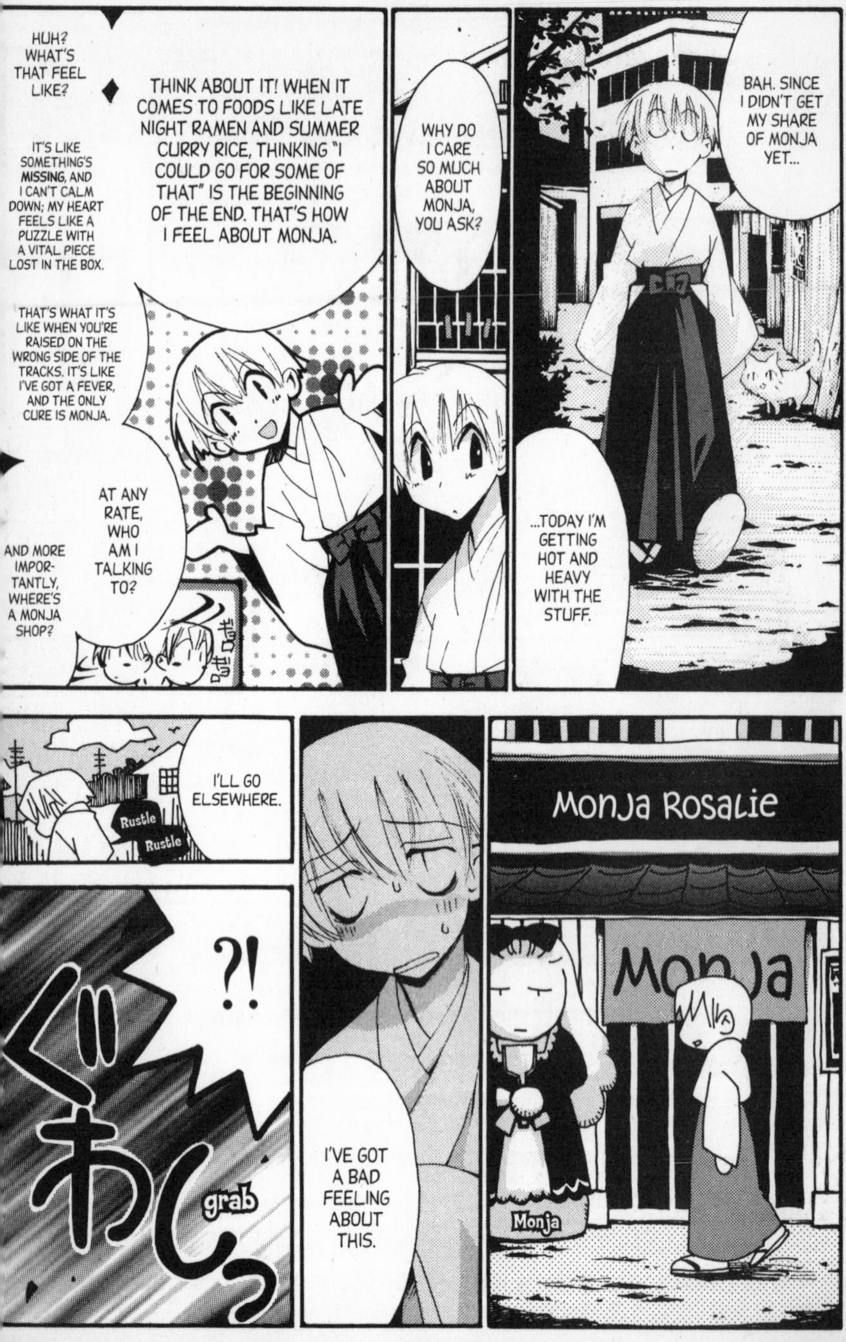
BAH. SINCE I DIDN'T GET MY SHARE OF MONJA YET...
...TODAY I'M GETTING HOT AND HEAVY WITH THE STUFF.
WHY DO I CARE SO MUCH ABOUT MONJA, YOU ASK?
THINK ABOUT IT! WHEN IT COMES TO FOODS LIKE LATE NIGHT RAMEN AND SUMMER CURRY RICE, THINKING "I COULD GO FOR SOME OF THAT" IS THE BEGINNING OF THE END. THAT'S HOW I FEEL ABOUT MONJA.
HUH? WHAT'S THAT FEEL LIKE?
IT'S LIKE SOMETHING'S **MISSING**, AND I CAN'T CALM DOWN; MY HEART FEELS LIKE A PUZZLE WITH A VITAL PIECE LOST IN THE BOX.
THAT'S WHAT IT'S LIKE WHEN YOU'RE RAISED ON THE WRONG SIDE OF THE TRACKS. IT'S LIKE I'VE GOT A FEVER, AND THE ONLY CURE IS MONJA.
AT ANY RATE, WHO AM I TALKING TO?
AND MORE IMPOR-TANTLY, WHERE'S A MONJA SHOP?
Monja Rosalie
MONJA
Monja
I'VE GOT A BAD FEELING ABOUT THIS.
Rustle
Rustle
I'LL GO ELSEWHERE.
?!
ぐわしっ
grab

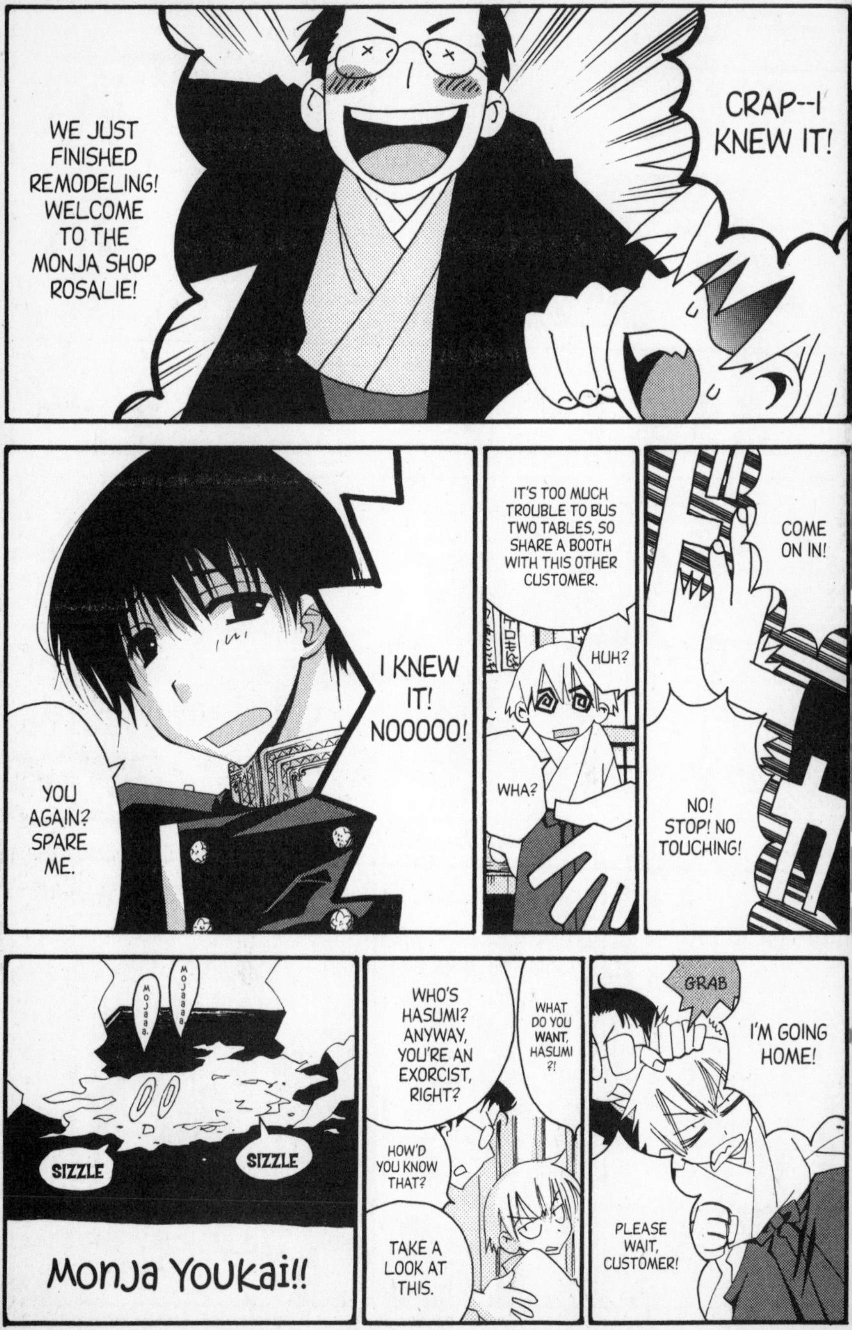
CRAP--I KNEW IT!
WE JUST FINISHED REMODELING! WELCOME TO THE MONJA SHOP ROSALIE!
COME ON IN!
NO! STOP! NO TOUCHING!
IT'S TOO MUCH TROUBLE TO BUS TWO TABLES, SO SHARE A BOOTH WITH THIS OTHER CUSTOMER.
HUH?
WHA?
I KNEW IT! NOOOOO!
YOU AGAIN? SPARE ME.
GRAB
I'M GOING HOME!
PLEASE WAIT, CUSTOMER!
WHAT DO YOU WANT, HASUMI?!
WHO'S HASUMI? ANYWAY, YOU'RE AN EXORCIST, RIGHT?
HOW'D YOU KNOW THAT?
TAKE A LOOK AT THIS.
MOJaaaa
MOJaaa.
SIZZLE
SIZZLE
Monja Youkai!!

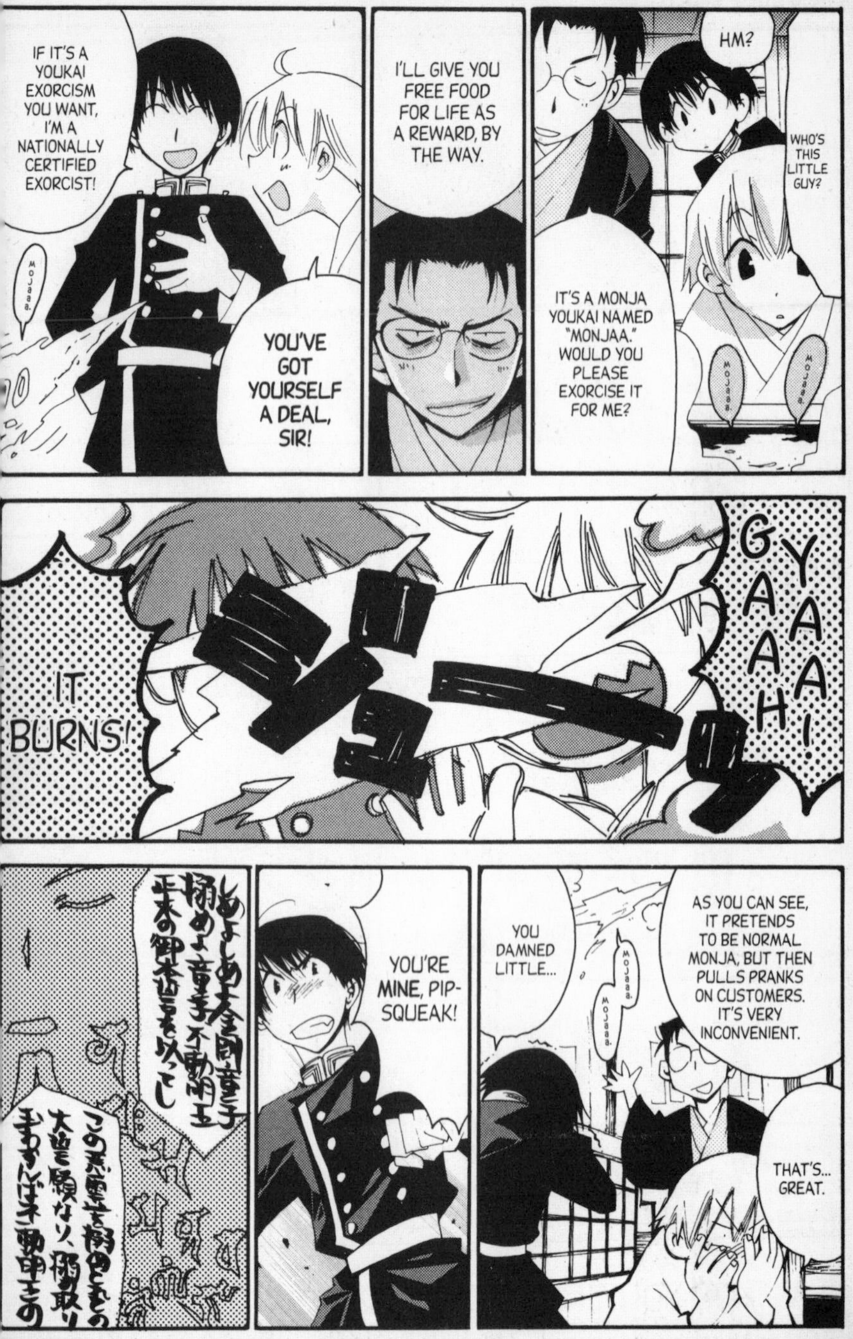
HM?
WHO'S THIS LITTLE GUY?
IT'S A MONJA YOUKAI NAMED "MONJAA." WOULD YOU PLEASE EXORCISE IT FOR ME?
MOJaaa.
MOJaaa.
I'LL GIVE YOU FREE FOOD FOR LIFE AS A REWARD, BY THE WAY.
IF IT'S A YOUKAI EXORCISM YOU WANT, I'M A NATIONALLY CERTIFIED EXORCIST!
MOJaaa.
YOU'VE GOT YOURSELF A DEAL, SIR!
GYAAAAH!
IT BURNS!
AS YOU CAN SEE, IT PRETENDS TO BE NORMAL MONJA, BUT THEN PULLS PRANKS ON CUSTOMERS. IT'S VERY INCONVENIENT.
THAT'S... GREAT.
YOU DAMNED LITTLE...
MOJaaa.
MOJaaa.
YOU'RE MINE, PIP-SQUEAK!
しめよしめよ金剛童子 搦めよ童子不動明王 正末の御本誓を以ってし
この悪霊を搦めとれとの 大誓願なり、搦め取り まわずんば不動明王の

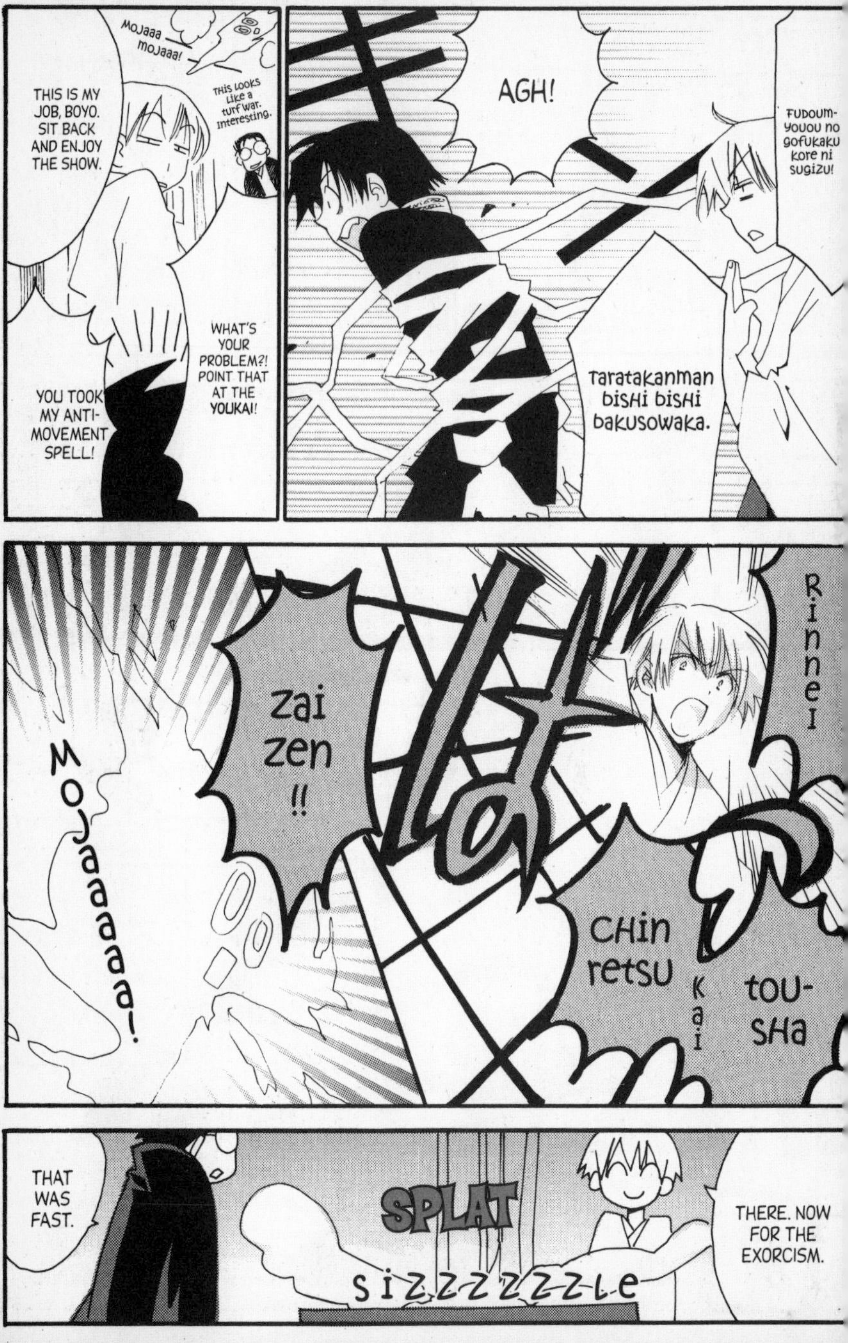
Fudoum-youou no gofukaku kore ni sugizu!
AGH!
Taratakanman bishi bishi bakusowaka.
Mojaaa mojaaa!
This looks like a turf war. Interesting.
THIS IS MY JOB, BOYO. SIT BACK AND ENJOY THE SHOW.
WHAT'S YOUR PROBLEM?! POINT THAT AT THE YOUKAI!
YOU TOOK MY ANTI-MOVEMENT SPELL!
Rinnei
tou-sha
kai
Chin retsu
Zai zen !!
Mojaaaaaaa!
THERE. NOW FOR THE EXORCISM.
SPLAT
sizzzzzzzle
THAT WAS FAST.

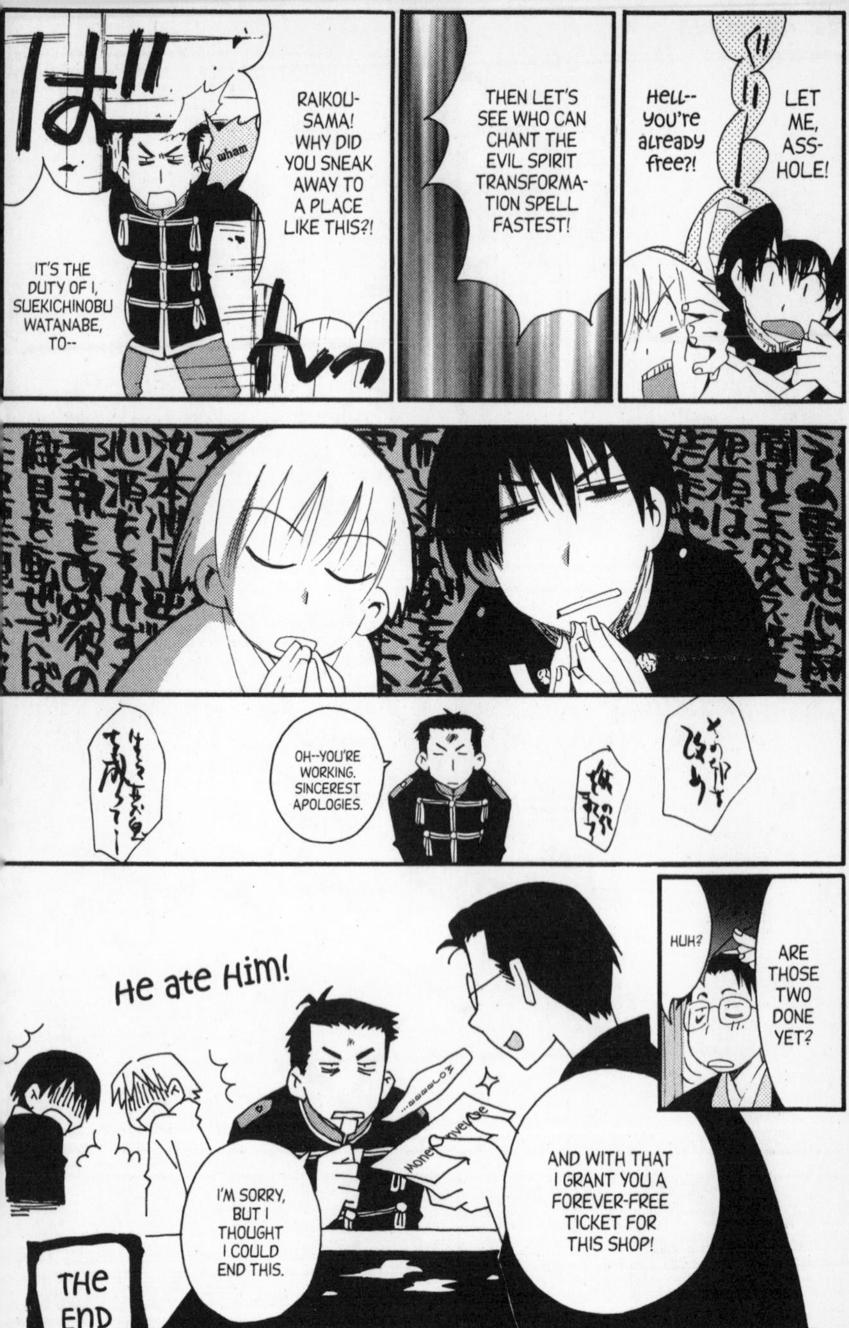
LET ME, ASS-HOLE!
Hell-- you're already free?!
THEN LET'S SEE WHO CAN CHANT THE EVIL SPIRIT TRANSFORMATION SPELL FASTEST!
RAIKOU-SAMA! WHY DID YOU SNEAK AWAY TO A PLACE LIKE THIS?!
wham
IT'S THE DUTY OF I, SUEKICHINOBU WATANABE, TO--
OH--YOU'RE WORKING. SINCEREST APOLOGIES.
ARE THOSE TWO DONE YET?
HUH?
AND WITH THAT I GRANT YOU A FOREVER-FREE TICKET FOR THIS SHOP!
I'M SORRY, BUT I THOUGHT I COULD END THIS.
He ate Him!
THE END

Sorry it was all the guys. Hope to see you in Volume 6!

IN THE NEXT VOLUME OF

tactics

Haruka is ready to finish his fight with Father Edwards after helping Kantaro, when Minamoto shows up takes the man away from the fight! In turn, Haruka goes to the Minamoto estate to try to pry some answers out of the man, however, he ends up with more questions when he runs into someone unexpected...

Language and Culture Notes on Tactics!

Kiyohime Stage:

~The suffix "tan": a cute version of "-chan" which already denotes endearment and preciousness.

~ Gidayuu: a form of ballad drama that started as the narration and song from the puppet theatre, accompanied by shamisen. When these dramatic recitations are performed by young girls, it's called musume gidayuu.

~Doujouji Genzai Uroko: a bunraku play that premiered in 1742. The story is covered quite extensively in this chapter of the manga.

~Miranai: "To learn through observation." A young maiko will train by watching her geisha mentor. This is also how classical Japanese theatre or music is also taught.

~Hydra: the word used in the original volume was "nue," which is a Japanese chimera.

~"Badgers of the same hole": this idiom is equivalent to the English "villains of the same stripe." In Japan, a badger is called a mujina (or anaguma), and isn't to be confused with a tanuki.

~Nekomata: a fantastic feline with a forked tail.

~Jami: the name of a serpentine youkai.

~Shirouneri: a youkai that transforms from inorganic materials like the moisture that ferments on dishtowels in the kitchen.

~Kappa and cucumbers: According to Japanese lore, Kappa love cucumbers. That's why cucumber rolls are called "Kappa Maki"!

Kanbarinyuudou Stage:

~Kokkuri-san: the Japanese equivalent of the Ouji Board.

~Kanbarinyuudou: a Japanese "god of the privy (bathroom)" in charge of making the toilet a safe place.

~Kimon: the northeastern direction. It is often considered unlucky.

~Dry Tenmon: tenmon means "heavenly gate."

~Animals on the map: represent signs of the Chinese zodiac. Each sign also has a corresponding time of day and a month.

~Waka: 31-syllable poems.

~Haniyasu: a female god of earth. Mizuhanome is a male god of water

~Mikkyou: Esoteric Buddhist teachings. Ususamamyouou is a deity of Mikkyou and Zen sects who is enshrined in impure places (like the privy) and has the power to burn up and exhaust impurities.

~"On bishibishi karakara shibari sowaka": a binding spell

~Shugendou: a Japanese mountain asceticism-shamanism incorporating Shinto and Buddhist concepts.

Kyoto trip:

~Koubou Daishi: named "Kuukai" posthumously. He was the founder of esoteric Shingon Buddhism in Japan during the Heian period.

~Mimizuka: a monument in Kyoto dedicated to the Seven-Year War fought against Korea from 1592-1598. The name translates to Ear Mound, and the monument enshrines the ears and noses of approximately 38,000 Koreans killed during that time.

~When praying at a shrine: ring bell, clap twice, bow and pray silently, then clap twice to close prayer.

~Tsuchigumo: Earth Spider, a creature of legend. Also refers to a historical tribe of Early Japan.

~Seimei Shrine: a shrine in Kyoto dedicated to the Heian-era yin-yang master, Abe no Seimei. He is the protagonist of the "Onmyouji" film series, and a common figure in popular culture.

~Monja is like okonomiyaki, where you can make the pizza-like batter-veggie-meat dish together on the grill provided at your table.

Fruits Basket
By Natsuki Takaya
Volume 20

Can Tohru deal with the truth?

After running away from his feelings and everyone he knows, Kyo is back with the truth about his role in the death of Tohru's mother. But how will he react when Tohru says that she still loves him?

Winner of the American Anime Award for Best Manga!

The #1 selling shojo manga in America!

FOR MORE INFORMATION VISIT: WWW.TOKYOPOP.COM

STOP!

This is the back of the book.
You wouldn't want to spoil a great ending!

This book is printed "manga-style," in the authentic Japanese right-to-left format. Since none of the artwork has been flipped or altered, readers get to experience the story just as the creator intended. You've been asking for it, so TOKYOPOP® delivered: authentic, hot-off-the-press, and far more fun!

DIRECTIONS

If this is your first time reading manga-style, here's a quick guide to help you understand how it works.

It's easy... just start in the top right panel and follow the numbers. Have fun, and look for more 100% authentic manga from TOKYOPOP®!

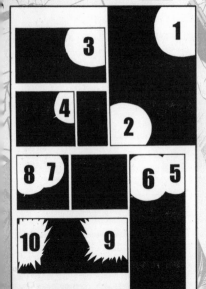